D0402926

Also by Jonathan Coleman

Exit the Rainmaker (1989)

At Mother's Request (1985)

LONG
WAY

Atlantic Monthly Press
New York

TO GO

BLACK AND WHITE
IN AMERICA

JONATHAN
COLEMAN

Published simultaneously in Canada
Printed in the United States of America

FIRST EDITION

Epigraph on pg. 24 is from Black Rage, *copyright © 1968 by William H. Grier and*
Price M. Cobbs. Reprinted by permission of Basic Books, a division of HarperCollins Publishers, Inc.

Library of Congress Cataloging-in-Publication Data

Coleman, Jonathan.
    Long way to go : Black and white in America / Jonathan Coleman.
      p. cm.
    Includes bibliographical references and index.
    ISBN 0-87113-692-9
    1. United States—Race relations.   2. Racism—United States.
  I. Title.
  E185.615.C643   1997
  305.8'00973—dc21   97-25823

DESIGN BY LAURA HAMMOND HOUGH

The Atlantic Monthly Press
841 Broadway
New York, NY 10003

10 9 8 7 6 5 4 3 2 1

For Logan Coleman,
light of my life,

in the name of all those
whose lights and lives have been extinguished

PROLOGUE

If you stand before a towering oak tree and look closely, you will see the roiling story of race in America woven deep into the bark and branches of the tree itself; a long, twisting, looping story made up of many strands—all disparate, all finally, crucially, connected. Race is a subject about which there are points of agreement, and about which there is no agreement; a subject that is either spoken of reluctantly, or not spoken of at all. Race is used, by all of us, in the most manipulative ways, is often force-fit and reduced to something it isn't, to something that gives us a sense of comfort, a false one. Many of us thought—needed to feel—the whole business was "settled." But it's not, never has been. Laws have only taken us so far.

Much as we might try, from under the powerful and permissive umbrella of democracy, to deny it, run from it, not think about it, act cynical about it, and even try to wish it away, there race remains, this "malignancy," this "great Achilles' heel of our nation's future," cornering us, dividing us, and exhausting us; there it remains—visible and invisible, mainly separate and unequal—patiently waiting for "the better angels of our nature," as Lincoln once said, to take permanent root and work toward common ground and common good.

Race, as I've learned without enthusiasm, is incorrigible, defies a writer's natural, cozy desire to order things, to have a tidy beginning, middle, and end. However grudgingly, I accepted that fact long ago. I accepted it because as long as race—and all the tentacles that attach to it—continues to be America's greatest burden and greatest dilemma; as long as we continue to argue over what truths we truly hold to be self-evident; as long as roughly three-fifths of whites continue to think of blacks as both intellectually inferior and lazy; as long as our ghettos continue to deteriorate and vast numbers of people are not connected to work of any kind; as long as eleven-year-old girls like Jessica Bradford, living not far, and yet so far, from the White House, are busily planning their own funerals (as she was in 1993) instead of their next birthday parties, there can be no satisfying conclusion, none at all.

As we move unsteadily toward a new century, the dialogue on race relations in America—one that is honest, that punches through easy rhetoric and political expediency, and that leads to solutions which just might last—must continue. It must continue because so much, so much about the way we live, is at stake.

. . . in our sleep, pain, which cannot
forget, falls drop by drop upon
the heart until, in our own despair,
against our will, comes wisdom
through the awful grace of God.
　　　　—Aeschylus
　　　　　(as quoted by Robert F. Kennedy)

Black and white people have to stick
together, because we're all going to
the same place: down in the clay.
　　　　—James (Son) Thomas

PART ONE

ONE

So this was how it began, this journey through a labyrinth. It was a Sunday, the first Sunday of November in 1989, and I was in Montgomery, Alabama, studying faces, the reassuring sounds of "amen" and "yes" punctuating the Indian summer air. It was a day devoted to remembering, remembering those who had given their lives in the hard battle for civil rights. Some of the faces were familiar to me and some were not. Rosa Parks had come home to Montgomery from Michigan, a small figure who, by refusing in 1955 to give up her seat on a bus, had, it turned out, taken a large step and launched a movement. Mamie Till, mother of Emmett, was still recognizable from the photographs all those years before in *Jet* magazine, especially the one of her teenage son in an open casket, the photograph she was determined the world should see and not forget. Myrlie Evers, widow of Medgar, had come from Los Angeles, never dreaming that four years later she would have her measure of justice. Chris McNair had come from Birmingham, recalling a different Sunday, the Sunday his daughter Denise, eleven years old, and three other little girls were blown to bits at the Sixteenth Street Baptist Church.

> *... Until justice rolls down like waters*
> *and righteousness like a mighty stream.*

Those words, spoken by Martin Luther King Jr. and taken from the Bible, were inscribed on the black granite wall that was part of the Civil Rights Memorial, the dedication of which was the reason that five thousand people had come.

But there was something wrong with this picture, this picture of harmony, of black and white together. It should have been a satisfying picture—it represented, after all, much of what King had pushed for—and, in many respects, it was. Along with the historic legislation of the 1960s, the black middle class continued to grow in number (there were four times as many black families with incomes above fifty thousand dollars than in

1964), continued to symbolize the group who had benefited the most from the movement and the social programs of that era, the group who was exerting its influence in all aspects of American life. And yet in 1989, despite its various accomplishments, the black middle class was nearly as isolated (either by choice or circumstance) as those who continued to live in the inner cities, where conditions were getting worse, not better. And it was impossible to escape the fact that too much unsavory stuff was still going on. Howard Beach and Bensonhurst had become the new places of reference. Nearly every college campus, it seemed, had an incident to report or to hide.

Speaker after speaker remarked on how important it was to have this memorial, how important it was that people not forget, how important it was that one's children and grandchildren learn about the struggle for the first time. But speaker after speaker also remarked on how the decade that was coming to a close had threatened to undo so much of what so many had worked so hard to achieve. "Turning back the clock" was a phrase one heard often to describe the Reagan Administration's stance on civil rights. And when the Great Communicator himself spoke of welfare queens, well, then, that made it okay, acceptable even, to actively voice all the racism and prejudice and anger that hadn't been put to rest anyway.

As the words to "We Shall Overcome" reverberated up and down Washington Avenue, to the White House of the Confederacy where the ghost of Jefferson Davis was still in residence, to the state capitol where the march from Selma ended and the Confederate flag was still defiantly aloft, and around the corner to the Baptist church on Dexter Avenue, the church where King had been pastor, the song had not lost one ounce of its power to stir deeply, to make all things seem possible.

Oh, oh, oh, deep in my heart,
I do believe
We shall overcome some day. . . .

Everybody was singing, swaying from side to side, joining hands, locking arms. Seeing Martin Luther King III standing near Ethel Kennedy took me back to 1968, to the assassinations of Dr. King and Robert Kennedy two months apart, to the profound sense of loss.

And yet it also took me back to something else, something that occurred one month before King was cut down in Memphis: the stark warning from the Kerner Commission that America was "moving toward two societies, one black, one white—separate and unequal." The prime culprit, a summary of the commission's report concluded, was "white racism"—for not only creating the ghettos, but perpetuating their existence. I had come to Montgomery to remember those who had died and to honor the struggle, a struggle that had a rhythm and a rightness to it that was all its own. But I left Montgomery with a different purpose, with a focus on the present, on trying to determine how far the country had come since the days of the civil rights movement . . . and how far we had—or wanted—to go.

In order to do that, I eventually realized, in order to explore race in America today through the looking-glass of one place, I couldn't choose a place like Birmingham or Selma or Montgomery. I couldn't choose them because they were places forever frozen in our memory, the very mention of their names bringing forth images of children being flattened by hoses, of marchers being driven back and beaten down on the Edmund Pettus Bridge, of Freedom Riders being ambushed and viciously struck as they descended from buses. The South was permanently tied to the history of the movement. There was no getting around that. Both for that reason and because the Kerner Commission had come about as a result of the 1967 riots in a number of Northern cities, I would have to find the story elsewhere.

T W O

S ay Milwaukee to most people and they will conjure up images of beer, bratwurst, and bowling, of *Laverne & Shirley,* of the Braves and Hank Aaron, of the year Kareem Abdul-Jabbar brought the Bucks a championship. They will not necessarily know that it is situated on a lake, or that it can be steaming hot in the summer; that Anthony Trollope wandered through during the Civil War, or that it had a Socialist government for many years; that it has been referred to as "the heartland of the Heartland" (perhaps explaining why Procter & Gamble test-markets so many of its products there); or that it is one of the most segregated metropolitan areas in the country—so much so that it has been labeled "hypersegregated."

They will also not necessarily know that it has one of the nation's highest rates of black-to-white unemployment, one of the highest rates of black teenage pregnancy, one of the highest turndown rates for minority loan applications, one of the lowest percentages of black owner-occupied housing, and one of the highest percentages of blacks living below the poverty line.

If any of that was unknown about America's seventeenth–largest city, this was not: as of March 1990, Milwaukee (pop. 628,088) was living under a threat—a threat, made by one Michael McGee, head of the Black Panther Militia and an alderman with an office in City Hall, that if millions of dollars for economic development, health care, and an emergency employment program were not directed to the inner city by the end of 1995, there would be violence in the streets—sniper attacks, the cutting of electrical wires, burning tires being rolled down the freeways—all-out guerrilla warfare in an age of political correctness no less.

So who was Michael McGee and why was he saying these things? I found myself wondering, as news of this threat reached me one morning in the tranquil town of Charlottesville, Virginia, hallowed land of Thomas Jefferson. As I looked at Monticello from my kitchen window, I couldn't help also wondering what Jefferson would make of America's state of affairs at the beginning of the last decade of the twentieth century. Would he think that the words he had written in the Declaration of Independence had been ineffective—accepted in theory but not in practice? Would he be flattered yet appalled that all these years later the document would be subject to endless analysis and deconstruction? And how would he react to his life—both public and private—being put forth as a symbol of contradiction on the question of race: his belief in individual liberty and the equality of all men at odds with his belief in the inferiority of black people and his ownership of slaves; his opposition to racial mixing and intermarriage countered by his possibly having fathered children by a mulatto woman?

The only book he ever wrote, *Notes on the State of Virginia*, stands, more than two hundred years later, as an unsettling echo of many attributes, both good and bad, that are ascribed to blacks today. Phrases like "unfortunate difference of colour," "disposition to theft," "disagreeable odour," and "more ardent after their female" stick in the mind longer than "as brave, and more adventuresome" and "more generally gifted than whites [in music]." That he publicly deplored slavery but didn't manage to abolish it in his lifetime looms larger than his unusual determination as a slave-owner not to break up families. Despite all his contradictions over race, he is practically viewed as a saint in the town in which I live. I prefer to think of him as imperfect and human.

As it happened, I wasn't the only one thinking about Jefferson. So was Michael McGee. In announcing the formation of the Black Panther Militia on February 28, 1990, the manifesto McGee laid out not only contained, word for word, the beginning of Jefferson's Declaration (as did the original platform of the Black Panther Party, of which McGee was a member), but McGee, in speaking of poor black people, gave it a contemporary spin. "We are destined for incarceration, death, and complete and absolute sadness, instead of the life, liberty, and pursuit of happiness promised by the Declaration of Independence."

Citizens of Milwaukee might not have liked the apocalyptic tone of the message; they might have been angered and repelled by the threat of violence; but it was hard to argue with the essence of what McGee was saying. If the Bush Administration had a domestic policy, no one had been able to find it.

So I left the land of Jefferson behind and headed out, knowing that I couldn't resolve Jefferson's conflict for him and not knowing exactly what

lay ahead. As a white person, I could never fully understand what it meant
to be black in America. I couldn't say, as Walt Whitman had in a different context, "I am the man . . . I suffered . . . I was there." In deciding to
go to Milwaukee and stay for a while, I was going to a city that had, like
so many cities, seen its economy shift from manufacturing to service; a
city that had recovered from the recession of the early 1980s and found
new ways to prosper—except that this prosperity was not generally
shared by its black citizens. By crossing back and forth over the fault line
of race, I would not only confront the complexity of the issue head-on—
all the prejudice, anger, fear, and stereotypes, including my own—but
would, I hoped, gain a deeper, fuller understanding of why we are still
divided after all these years.

"THE KIND OF FIGHT I'm talking about bringing to Milwaukee is the kind
that once it starts here, it's gonna spread throughout the country. It's the
white establishment's worst nightmare. You can't cope with an internal
enemy, underground, tied up into the fabric of society. So that means
that any black anywhere could be a sympathizer or a member—and I've
got white members."

It was early April of 1991. The voice—Michael McGee's—was softer
than I expected. I had been in Milwaukee for five days and he had been
dodging me. Actually, I'd been prepared for that. Since he had been on *60
Minutes* and *Donahue,* been written about in the *New York Times,* the *Washington Post,* and *The Economist,* and was giving speeches all around the country, it was probably difficult to see how talking to an author could help his
cause in the short term.

Anyway, he finally agreed to meet at the offices of WNOV, a black
radio station owned by Jerrel Jones, one of McGee's patrons, so to speak,
though Jones made it very clear that he was a black Republican millionaire, a man who knew Richard Nixon personally and considered him to
be one of America's greatest presidents. The whole situation was designed
to test my patience (perhaps even confuse me). I was told to come at one,
which I did, and was then told that Mr. Jones and Mr. McGee were in a
meeting, a meeting that might last another half hour, and then, when a half
hour had passed, that they were not there at all, that they were out at lunch,
but would almost certainly bring me something to eat.

At about two-thirty I was finally summoned and up the stairs I went. I had thought I might find McGee in his militia uniform, ready for battle, but he wasn't. He sat reading a book when I came in, and didn't bother to look at me. He had a dark shirt on and a black hat and a full beard and he actually had two books with him—Zora Neale Hurston's *Their Eyes Were Watching God* (the one he was reading) and Hermann Hesse's *Siddhartha*, which he picked up after he presumably finished a chapter in the other. I wouldn't have put those two authors together myself, but the combination seemed to suit McGee.

He listened to me talk with Jones for a while, then said, "How do we know that you're not a chump?"

I was used to being challenged by people I wanted to interview, but the challenge was usually along the lines of why they should expend valuable time and energy for that purpose. This was a new one. I offered my credentials and then said that, as far as I could tell, I was no chump. In truth, I didn't mind the question It served as an opening for the two of us to drop protocol and begin to talk.

The *Milwaukee Journal* had begun a series on race the day before ("Race: The Rawest Nerve") and I wanted to know what McGee had thought of it. "Too little, too late," he said dismissively. "All they're doing is verifying what everybody in the country already know about. I wouldn't even read it."

McGee was referring to the national exposure Milwaukee's "race problem" had received—exposure that had intensified since he formed the militia. Among the many things the series touched on was the question of whether McGee's threat of violence in 1995 was serious. A majority of both blacks and whites surveyed seemed to think it was.

If McGee were simply a fringe figure, perhaps it would have been possible to dismiss him as a crackpot. But he had been an alderman since 1984 and had worked in community development organizations before that. He served in Vietnam, won a Bronze Star, and was proud of pointing out that the only time he had ever committed violence was over there, in America's name. Considering that he had nine children and a wife he had been married to for more than twenty years, it was not readily apparent why he was so willing to risk so much.

Because nothing else had worked, he said. The many studies and task forces he had been a part of had not met with the kind of response he believed was essential. He was frustrated, he was angry, and he saw this as the best way to get people's attention. What it all boiled down to was a question of mind over matter. "They don't mind because we don't matter."

They don't mind because we don't matter. It made my blood boil to hear him say that, and yet it wasn't until later that I was able to go beyond my initial reaction and figure out why. I knew that *I* didn't feel that way and I resented his sweeping generalization; that kind of demagoguery and polarization wasn't going to solve anything, and could easily make things worse. But I also knew that not everyone shared my opinion, that there were white people (as well as middle-class blacks) just as angry and frustrated as McGee was but for a different reason: in their view, blacks had been given every opportunity to succeed, to lift themselves out of poverty, and they had no one to blame but themselves if nearly a third in the country had not. If they insisted on dealing drugs and killing each other in record numbers, then they would have to face the consequences. That point of view was just as onerous as McGee's. The solutions to the problem were far more complex. If they were to be found at all, it would be in the gray areas.

As for my blood boiling, I didn't care. McGee knew how to provoke a reaction, put you on edge, and keep you there. I have always respected that ability in a person. Even if the line of thinking isn't always rational, even if the personality grates, it forces you to respond. McGee was heavily invested in pushing buttons. When Jimmy Carter came to Milwaukee to build houses for Habitat for Humanity, McGee and some of his entourage showed up and began blowing whistles and carrying signs that read "Missionaries Out of Milwaukee" and "Jobs, Not Charity"—all for the benefit of *Good Morning America.* When the Common Council posed for its official 1988 portrait, McGee wore a paper bag over his head—his own Ku Klux Klan–type protest over the company he was forced (by election) to keep. On two occasions, once in 1987 and again in 1990, he threatened to disrupt an event that is near and dear to the heart of most Milwaukeeans— the Great Circus Parade. In the first instance he was going to throw eggs; in the second, he was going to try to shut it down altogether, a threat that was answered with a legal injunction. But these antics were mild compared with his claim, made in the summer of 1990, that the sausages at Usinger's had mysteriously been poisoned. It was one thing to blow a whistle, quite another to set off immediate panic. The mayor, John Norquist (whom

McGee had begun calling "Norqwurst"), decided that the only response to a "demented mind" was to fight back and try the sausages himself. The whole incident cost Usinger's money but actually gained Norquist political capital. Somebody had finally stood up to McGee. At least that was the perception.

Beyond these tactics, though, the question still remained: was he serious about this 1995 threat he had cast over the city? "I've been talking to people, some in your district," I told him, "and they agree with the message, but they're apprehensive about violence."

So was he, he said, but there was violence all around them, every day, everywhere they turned. "It comes a point," he said, "that if somebody invaded your home, raped and robbed and beat up everybody in your family, stole everything in your house, what would you be willing to do? That happens five and six times a day in the black communities all across the United States."

Though he was talking about the present, about gangs and black-on-black crime and drive-by shootings so random and so senseless that stray bullets were finding their way into houses and killing children while they slept, he was also talking about the original sin of slavery, about blacks being put on ships and brought to America against their will. Somebody should pay for that, McGee thought, "for all of the turmoil and strain we've went through just being brought over here from Africa . . . and worked like dogs from sunup to sundown. . . ." It was time for reparations, time to get the forty acres and a mule that were supposed to be coming after the Civil War but never really did. McGee had a way of bringing everything full circle, of making it all fit into a philosophy that made sense to him: if reparations were offered to black people for all they had been made to suffer, from the moment they were forced onto slave ships until the present, then "that would solve everything because we would probably be the wealthiest group in the world." And so it goes, of course, that if you are the wealthiest group in the world, then you have power, you are in charge, and you don't have to give a good goddamn what the Man thinks anymore.

As McGee continued talking, going on about how he couldn't just launch into the kind of revolution he had in mind overnight "because people don't understand me yet," how it might take him until 1995 to explain his rationale to "the average mass of person that you might see on the street," how, in the meantime, the militia would do everything it could "to bring dignity, hope, and revitalization" to the people of Milwaukee's inner-city community, and how, in the end, he wasn't afraid to die for a cause he believed in, I was listening intently but putting him into context at the same time—seeing Huey Newton, George Jackson, and Malcolm X, among others, in my mind's eye. I thought about a conversation that Huey Newton, cofounder of the Black Panthers, had had with the author Shiva Naipaul in 1979. Naipaul was writing about Jonestown and the People's Temple and was trying to learn from Newton what support the Panthers had given to the sect. In leading up to that question he asked Newton what, in his opinion, had gone wrong for the Panthers. Newton spoke (as McGee did now) of COINTELPRO, the counterintelligence operation that the FBI had set up to ultimately destroy radical movements. He spoke (as McGee did now) of victims who are like slaves, who decide "to demand some dignity" for themselves by taking up arms "to enforce that demand" because they have been "so demeaned, so humiliated." Newton didn't view that as provocation, and neither did McGee.

Being demeaned and humiliated—not to mention physically hurt or killed—can take many forms, and police brutality is one of them. As it happened, one month earlier the world had witnessed the beating of Rodney King in Los Angeles, and McGee wanted me to know that it was "a cakewalk compared to some of the ass-whoopings I done seen." Among the black man's greatest fears was being stopped, often for no good reason, in a white neighborhood (especially late at night) or being mistaken for someone else. That was what happened to a young man named Ernest Lacy in July of 1981, an incident that resulted in McGee and fellow black activist Howard Fuller successfully mobilizing thousands of people to seek justice for Lacy, who was thought to be a rapist the Milwaukee police were looking for and who died of injuries from a beating he received while being stopped and questioned. The police department at the time was run by the legendary Harold Breier, run in much the same shoot-first-ask-questions-later style of Daryl Gates in Los Angeles. It was a department that had fought hard to keep blacks from being hired; even when they were, Breier simply didn't speak to them. Breier retired in 1984, but the black community's deep distrust of the police remained. For every Rodney King and Ernest Lacy the public became aware of, there were countless others, McGee said, you never heard about, who never got in the paper. McGee had once remarked that the police were merely "the KKK in blue" and he still thought that way. "There are places you can't go in Milwaukee, period. The whole time you feel like you in jail."

He was painting a picture of life that was constrained on all sides, of life lived in a war zone, of being hunted and preyed upon, of constantly being in a state of siege. He had been to Vietnam, but this, in his opinion, was worse. It was hard to listen to, and yet . . .

There were no lights on in Jones's office. That and the freezing rain beating against the window only added to the gloom of what we were discussing: the number of black families on welfare; a system that made it more cost-effective to stay on welfare than to take a job with no benefits at McDonald's; houses that had twenty or so people living in them; the difficulty black businesses and individuals had in getting money from banks. (In 1989, the *Atlanta Journal-Constitution* reported that the Milwaukee metropolitan area ranked first in the nation in turndown rates for residential loans to blacks.)

"When you're in a black business," Jerrel Jones said, "there is a difference between black people and white people, whether the white people want to admit it or not. . . . When it's convenient they'll admit the difference, but when it's time to pay the bills you're an equal-opportunity bill payer. Nobody cares what color you are. But when it comes time to spend money, that's when you become a minority, a Negro, colored, nigger, spook, coon, African-American, Afro-American, Black, black with a small *b*, negro with a small *n*." As far as Jones was concerned, no matter how much money he had, no matter that he lived in an upscale, predominantly white suburb—large house on a hill, big backyard, his own pond, the works— no matter that he sent his children to the finest private school in the area, he would always be viewed, by whites, as a nigger. And if I didn't understand that, he suggested, then I was probably a chump after all.

The force of Jones's declaration took me aback in a way that none of McGee's statements had. Perhaps it was because I could more readily understand the anger and frustration McGee expressed on behalf of his race than that of someone who had grown up comfortably and continued to live like that. But the problem with that way of thinking, I realized later, was that I was viewing it through my lens, not Jones's. It was a mistake I would have to keep in mind as time went on, a mistake that in large part had to do with the unconsciousness of being white, of not appreciating, or being constantly aware of, all the things that intrinsically come to you—

that you don't have to do battle for on a daily basis—because you are white. It's more subtle than *They don't mind because we don't matter*, but far more dangerous.

McGee, for his part, had given me all the time he was prepared to give, and would not promise to see me again. He picked up his two books and told me to be careful. And then he was gone, followed by the two figures who had come with him, whom I had not been introduced to, and who had sat there the whole time, their faces inscrutable, never speaking a word.

"To WHOSE BENEFIT IS it that the problems not be solved?"

That was the question Jerrel Jones wanted me to ponder as I left his office.

"Who benefits from the way things are now? Who benefits from a large black prison population? Who benefited from Desert Storm? I'm in business. I look at the bottom line on things." He suddenly referred to the Chippewas in northern Wisconsin and citizens' complaints about the extent of their spearfishing. "Them Chippewas want to take twenty-five thousand fish out of their own goddamned lake and the tourists take out six hundred and eighty thousand. Now if that ain't wanting it all, you know. You want to just narrow it down to its rawest sense—it's greed. Like the cat says in *Wall Street*, greed is good."

And then Jones unwittingly let slip what he and McGee had been doing while I had been waiting in the reception area: they had been watching *Tarzan*. He looked at me for a moment, then shook his head. "In the jungle, they wouldn't even let the Africans play the Africans. They had the goddamned Africans being played by white people. This is when I was coming up, so you know how fucked up my mind must be."

THREE

Maron and Georgette Alexander were two of the people I had been talking to in McGee's district—an area of 36,816 people packed onto 2.67 square miles. In fact, they lived right around the corner from him, on the top floor of a house that Maron's parents owned, on a street where it had become nearly impossible to tell whether a sudden noise was the ordinary backfire of a car or a fatal shot from a gun.

I had met Maron on my first full day in Milwaukee, over at the Urban League, on the twenty-third anniversary of Martin Luther King's death. A few years earlier the league had published a study that drew on both national and local statistics in outlining the "racial gap" that existed between blacks and whites in Milwaukee. Because McGee had drawn on this study to justify his forming the militia and his 1995 deadline, it seemed a reasonable place to start. On my way there, starting up Martin Luther King Jr. Drive, I drove past a number of buildings that were either boarded up or burned out, past block after block of men, young and old, all of them black, standing on street corners, looking dazed, looking bored, looking angry; past block after ghostly block of vacant land (land that was supposed to have been paved over with a freeway, a glaring reminder of "urban renewal" that had only resulted in "Negro removal," as it was often referred to). And there was something else that happened that morning, a detail I'm only recalling now, a detail I'm not particularly proud of. At the first traffic light I came to, I checked to see if my door was locked.

"WE'RE HERE TO GET needed again."

That's what Bentley Clark was telling a group of eleven men, nine of them black (including Maron), who had gathered together for an electronics class in the Urban League's basement. They were there because the world had changed. Starting in the mid-seventies, heavily industrial cities like Milwaukee, cities whose factories and foundries had had, especially during World War II and afterward, an abundance of well-paid jobs,

jobs that required relatively little skill and that countless numbers of blacks
had migrated north for and supported families on, began to see those jobs
disappear—sixty thousand in Milwaukee between 1979 and 1983 alone.
As the country plunged into a deep recession, workers were still sending
it on down the line but, more and more, they were doing it in Mexico and
for far less money. The employee mind-set of "What's good for GM is good
for me" turned out to be a myth. The increasing inability of American
industry to compete with the likes of Japan forced companies to scramble
for profits and find new ways of doing business. The phrase "global
economy" began to be used more frequently. The less one heard car parts
banging together into a perfect fit, the less one saw workers streaming out
of factories, paychecks in hand after another brutal week, the more one
heard "Hi! Welcome to McDonald's, may I take your order, please?" from
someone whose hourly wage was probably less than the cost of a meal for
two. At the same time, computer companies in spanking new "office parks"
were springing up outside of cities, and if you were displaced from a factory, it wasn't just a question of not having the wherewithal to do the work,
it was also a question of not having the transportation to get there. Everything, and everyone, it seemed, was moving to the suburbs, or trying to, at
an even greater rate than before. (By the 1992 presidential election, the
suburban vote was the majority vote for the first time ever.) "High-tech"
became the new buzzword, and new credentials were needed to enter that
world and speak its language.

And yet, at the same time, Milwaukee was making a stand, brushing
up its downtown—with gleaming new office buildings and a mall and a
new convention center and restaurants, all for the purpose of attracting
business and tourism, of doing all it could to keep residents in the city, to
maintain its tax base, to justify its moniker as "A Great Place on a Great
Lake." Schlitz—makers of The Beer That Made Milwaukee Famous—
may have closed, but the city was determined to stay open and viable. While
all of this activity may have made sense in economic terms, it did not do
so in human ones. From the construction of the buildings (which illustrated
the far-reaching nepotism of "family business" in full swing) to the jobs
themselves, a much greater proportion of whites were absorbed into the
shifting economy than blacks. It may have made city officials bristle with
Midwestern defensiveness when the New York Times ran a front-page story
with the headline "How Milwaukee Boomed But Left Its Blacks Behind,"

but it was hard to dispute the facts. By 1991, only nine thousand of the sixty thousand lost jobs were restored. The unemployment rate for blacks rose from 17 percent in 1980 to 20.1 percent in 1989 (in McGee's district, it was thought to be much higher, perhaps as high as 50 percent for black males, if you counted the people who had given up looking for work altogether), while white unemployment dropped from 5.3 percent to 3.8 percent. As for people on some sort of public assistance, in 1963, a little under one-quarter of all blacks were receiving payments; by 1987, more than two-thirds were.

"I daresay that our black community is not in any worse shape than blacks in Detroit or Cleveland or other cities," Robert H. Milbourne, executive director of the Greater Milwaukee Committee, a powerful group of business leaders, told the *New York Times* in early 1991. "But here the rest of the economy is doing so well, that it sticks out."

Which was not much consolation for someone like Maron Alexander, who invited me to his home the day after I met him and who let me know, early on, that I was in the company of someone who, with his insurance from the Army, was worth more dead than alive. He had four children and a wife he adored, had three years of college, had worked at any number of jobs, was only in his late thirties, and yet here he was, sitting on his porch, doing numbers, and coming to the conclusion that his family might be better off without him around.

It was an unseasonably warm evening, and a thin fog was rolling in. Even so, you could still see the lights of A. O. Smith in the distance, a disconcerting, frustrating symbol for people like Maron, who said, "I can't tell nobody's story but mine, but I'm going to tell you, everybody's story is a little bit like mine." A. O. Smith, maker of car bodies and military tanks, had meant employment—money to buy a house or pay the rent, money for food, money for a car, money to see Hank Aaron out at County Stadium, even some money to stuff in a pillow. But at one time that employment had not been easy to come by. In fact, until 1942, only a small number of blacks had ever worked at A. O. Smith. A series of hearings in Chicago and simple mathematics changed that: workers had gone off to war and more product was demanded. And yet, it was one thing to get the job and another to keep it ("Last hired, first fired" was a rule black workers became quickly familiar with), or be put in a position where you could move up. It wasn't as if an A. O. Smith were thrilled you were there. You were tolerated and kept on the lowest rung. Still, by the late seventies, when one's ability, one's freedom really, to get fed up on a Friday and be at Harley-Davidson, ready for duty, on a Monday was severely diminished, suddenly a place like A. O. Smith was viewed in romantic terms. As I listened to Maron and his wife, Georgette, I continued to stare at A. O. Smith, wondering if it would somehow be easier, for those who had depended on it for so long, if it were not there at all; it was as if the company were an athlete whose best years were well behind him, and whose hanging around was in fact preventing his devotees from storing their memories (however imperfect) in a safe place, from finally coming to terms with the fact that that life, in that form, was pretty much gone forever.

BY HIS OWN ADMISSION, Maron had always had a hard time accepting that kind of truth. He viewed himself as a Peter Pan figure, never wanting to grow up, "because reality is really harsh when you see it. The reality is that there are people living on the street with nothing to eat and this is the United States and people overseas think the streets are paved with gold." Just on his block, he said, you could tell the ones who were trying from the ones who had given up. The ones who were still trying painted their houses and cut their grass; the others did not. Why was it, he asked, that the United States was so quick to feed other countries but not its own? Part of it, he believed, had to do with America's ego, its need to show a benevolent face to the world, but not at home. As a military man, Maron would be asked, particularly by young black men, why he would go and fight for his country when his country wouldn't give him anything, which got him asking himself why he had to "go through hell and high water" to even get a loan. "The United States is not all that it's cracked up to be," he said quietly but firmly. "It's just like an eggshell that's cracked."

"I know it might sound stupid," Georgette broke in, looking right at me, "but can you understand any of this? How was you raised?"

I said that I had grown up in Allentown, Pennsylvania, a town of about a hundred thousand, and that my parents divorced when I was five. That my mother and I moved away for a while, that my father owned a clothing store that his father had owned, that my mother worked, and that I basically had had a comfortable, middle-class life, a life where we didn't have to worry about the next meal.

"Okay," she said, "me and Maron both work every day and we worry about that kind of thing."

Maron was working at Walgreen's, repairing machines in the photo lab, making six dollars an hour, working from six until two in the morning. Georgette was a cook at Marquette University, making five fifty, and didn't get paid during school vacations or in the summer. They had neither medical benefits (which they couldn't afford) nor the benefit of seeing each other that much. In their refrigerator at that moment were lettuce, carrots, and ice. And it was the refrigerator, not anything Maron and Georgette would say directly, that would always cue the kids to what their situation was.

"I might have eggs, I might have milk," she said, "but they don't have their favorite cereal. They know, well, we didn't make that much money this time. They know the difference between four loaves of bread and one and I say instead of eating until you get full, you all only get one slice of bread this time. They have no choice, you know, and they can't argue with me . . . 'cause it's just like that and it's not either one of us do drugs."

For whatever reason, Georgette felt the need to address that stereotype, to make sure I understood that she and Maron weren't blowing what little money they had on themselves in that way, that they were *responsible* parents. Perhaps she thought I had come to their home that evening with some sort of judgment already formed, that I had already subscribed to whatever it was that people living outside the inner city thought of people inside.

Georgette had grown up much less privileged than Maron (who had attended one of the city's top parochial schools) and always knew what was coming down. "You know," she said, "there's *always* been gangs," but they used to exist to protect the neighborhood, not prey off of it. Children used to see their parents go to work every day, now they saw them get kicked out of jobs and have nothing. But that didn't stop those parents from wanting to give their kids everything; though she understood the impulse, she thought it was all wrong that parents essentially say, "If you want such and such, so what if your grades ain't good, you're my child, I don't want you to look poor," and that those children "grow up feeling they don't have to work to get nothing. . . . Most of them feel they deserve Guess jeans, they deserve Adidas shoes; they don't deserve anything but life and death in actuality, you know."

If one child had a stereo, she said, another's parent would get his child a CD stereo, and another's, just to get to the top of the pecking order, would get his child a dual. "That's crazy shit," Georgette said in her husky voice.

At that moment, a voice came up from the street, a voice that was directed at me.

"Hi! I'm Tennille. I'm fourteen and I'm nice."

Tennille was Georgette and Maron's oldest child, and they had told her I was coming. She in particular was the one they were most concerned about. Since the evening was still warm (an unusual commodity in early April in Milwaukee), she said she'd be up in about ten minutes, and in that time, Georgette told me of how she had warned Tennille about not getting pregnant, about how she had told her that she knew she was of an age where "the chemicals talk to you and everything," but that any boy she met was just a boy and she was going to meet a thousand of them, and "when and if she goes out there and gets pregnant, it will not be my fault. It will not be because she doesn't know the difference. It's because she for that split moment did not want to take care of her own self. It won't be because me and her ain't talked street. I talk to her like they talk to her. 'He's going to come up to you, he's going to touch you in the right way. He knows exactly what to do and if he doesn't, his brother told him what to do before he left the house, and if that's what he wants to talk to you for, there's plenty of girls out here he don't even have to try hard and he gets them. Let him. Let him remember you as the one who said no. Or at least said it's not my time or whatever.' "

It sounded like fairly conventional advice from a mother to a daughter, but Tennille had so many friends who were pregnant that it threw that advice into sharp relief. Georgette and Maron wanted her to go on to college, but Tennille was conflicted about it and fearful too—fearful that if she didn't go, no one would love her and she would wind up with a low-paying job, but fearful also that if she did go and failed no one would love her either.

And suddenly there she was, coming through the screen door onto the porch, fourteen going on forty and four at the same time, telling me how much pressure there was on someone like her in a place like Milwaukee and about those friends who were pregnant, who really didn't want to be pregnant but thought they'd be able to keep their boyfriends that way, and how very few of the fathers were around and her friends all had babies and had to stay in the house all the time, and even if they were on the phone with you, the baby was always crying and they were always having to say hold on and she just didn't see that kind of life for herself no way.

The issue of race hadn't come up very much—or very directly—in the short time I'd been with the Alexanders (other than Maron volunteering that when he died, he wanted his headstone to reflect that he was an American, not a *black* American, that as far as he was concerned way too much was made of race, that it wasn't healthy for people to be singled out and labeled). But it was something Tennille wanted to talk about. "I don't see a person as a color," she said. "If I don't like you, it's not because you're white or black. It's because I don't like you because you did something to me or I don't like your attitude." On the other hand, she felt a certain degree of pressure from her friends not to hang around whites "because of what they used to do to us and all the racism and the slavery. But I feel that if we were the whites and we had blacks as our slaves we would treat them the same way so that's in the past now and we're looking for a better future."

In the more recent past, though, as in five years earlier when she was nine and a member of the Mickey Mouse Fan Club, she wrote a letter to the club, requesting a pen pal. Shortly after that, she received a letter from a David in Houston, along with his picture. "I was like, 'Mom, I'm going to send a picture of me!' and she was like, 'If that's what you think is best.'" No sooner had Tennille sent the picture than she got a note back, a note saying that he couldn't write anymore, that he was moving, changing his address. Undeterred, Tennille wrote a couple more letters. She never got a response, but still had his picture in her drawer.

Georgette watched for my response before speaking. She saw my eyebrows lift slightly, then said, "Once they found out she's a black child or she might have black ideas about fighting and killing . . . it was over with."

(It may have been over with, but to Tennille's credit, it seemed to make her more determined to rise above the prejudice on both sides. As it happened, Maron's brother's wife was white and she loved her auntie and she thought it was stupid that a lot of her friends viewed the child of an interracial marriage as "taking a poodle and a German shepherd and making a mutt.")

A fourteen-year-old, any fourteen-year-old, is not going to hang around adults for very long, especially on a Friday night, so it didn't surprise me when Tennille departed as suddenly as she had arrived. She had phone calls to make. That, at the moment, was her reality. But her brief presence had served to focus Maron and Georgette even more closely on race, on how it didn't make much sense to bus black kids to schools in white neighborhoods where they weren't wanted anyway, while at the same time it was plain unfair that an inner-city school should have only a few computers for everybody and a suburban school have an abundance of them.

"Why can't our kids have a computer for each one of them who are ready?" Georgette wanted to know.

"Or at least have the same chance?" Maron said.

"Why say because they're in the inner city they're going to tear them up or they don't deserve them or they're not going to use them?" Georgette added.

The questions they were asking were the right ones. Busing might have started as a good social idea, but it had turned out to be a frustratingly complicated educational one. The prevailing feeling was that it hadn't worked, that blacks had suffered the burden of it far more than whites had, that it broke up neighborhoods, made it more difficult for parents to be involved with their child's school because the school was so far away, and that, in the end, kids were tracked and the schools were even more segregated now than before: a goodly number of whites had simply closed up shop and fled—either to private schools or the suburbs. (The Milwaukee public schools were 21 percent white in 1995; twenty years earlier, the percentage was nearly three times as high.) The inequity of resources was a terrible problem. To all those who said money was not the issue, that all the money in the world was not going to motivate a kid in the inner city to learn, to even come to school, the rejoinder was essentially the same question the Alexanders were asking: was it fair for a suburban district to spend ten thousand dollars per child when an urban district might have only five? Was that a level playing field?

They were not angry or bitter in asking these questions. They were simply resigned—resigned to the inequity, to the way they were perceived, to the way things were. Which brought Maron back to his own situation. He was always baffled that whenever a white person lost a job, blacks were the cause. "'They're getting uppity. That ain't their place. They're taking your job away from you.' Hey, how am I taking your job? It's just as right for me to have a job as it is for you to have it. . . . Hell, I worked in jobs, guys get paid more than me, and they come and ask me what to do."

But like Georgette, he also thought that black families did not do enough to instill a work ethic in their children. He got tired of hearing people in his neighborhood complain about the Iranians or the Koreans or whoever owned the corner store. He got tired of it because some of those stores had been owned by black families, but often a family's children had no interest in carrying on. So the stores would get sold, and it wouldn't be long before someone was throwing a brick through one of the windows, angry as hell that what money they had was being given to a foreigner, to someone they believed had an easier go of things than they did. It all got jumbled up, and the anger often got misdirected, and there was no easy way to untangle it, and drug dealing often presented itself as the way to go—to get the jeans and running shoes and starter jackets that Georgette said nobody had any automatic entitlement to anyway, but which, more and more, people would literally kill for.

And it was these people, Maron and Georgette worried, for whom Michael McGee's threat of violence might have the greatest resonance. "He's got the potential to change things," Georgette said, "but we don't want the junkies behind him. . . . I want the people in his army to be somebody who wants something for their families, because there's not very many families left. There's too many one-parent households. . . . It's just getting stupid. Nobody wants to stay as a group anymore."

"That's why we work so hard at trying to stay together," Maron said, "'cause it seems everybody's trying to pull us apart, not only just people, but society and everything else."

IT WAS PAST TEN and I hadn't eaten, and I knew that even if they had it hadn't been much. Georgette suggested that we go inside and have a cup of tea. I suggested that we have Domino's deliver a pizza.

Maron laughed. "They won't deliver here. The only place that will deliver here makes you come down to the street for it. They won't come to the door."

It was yet one more thing I had taken for granted. As we ate the pizza we had gone down to the street to get, three adults and four children sitting around on a Friday evening, I could better understand how giving up the role of Peter Pan was difficult, yet necessary to do.

FOUR

We submit that it is necessary for a black man in America to develop a profound distrust of his white fellow citizens and of the nation. He must be on guard to protect himself against physical hurt. He must cushion himself against cheating, slander, humiliation, and outright mistreatment by the official representatives of society. If he does not so protect himself, he will live a life of such pain and shock as to find life itself unbearable. For his own survival, then, he must develop a cultural paranoia in which every white man is a potential enemy unless proved otherwise and every social system is set against him unless he personally finds out differently.

The passage came courtesy of *Black Rage,* and I hated it. I hated it for its unremitting bleakness and I hated it because I couldn't just dismiss it out of hand. I had spent a long afternoon the previous summer with a colleague of mine at the University of Virginia, an esteemed black scholar, a person who by every measure had "made it," and she was reminding me that the civil rights movement had occupied such a brief period of time in the whole scope of history—the whole scope of what had gone on with black people in this country—that I shouldn't be that surprised we were still grappling with the issue of race in the 1990s, that black men in particular continued to be viewed not only as dangerous, but, with more of them in prison than in college, as an "endangered species" as well. I thought of her as I left the Alexanders that evening, because she lived in a neighborhood where Domino's wouldn't think of not delivering, and yet no sooner had she moved into her house than helpful neighbors had come by, spurred on perhaps by their own form of calculating, with "suggestions" on how she should best landscape her property, and deliverymen (black as well as white) had come to her door, asking if "the lady of the house" was at home. "You see, Jonathan," she said, "we are all scripted in ways we don't even think about. Our thoughts are not just our own. We inherit them despite our best intentions. *What will happen to the neighborhood if black people move in?* It's that kind of residue. Who lives where and who does what? We haven't completed that work. We think we have—but we haven't. . . .

"Racism is a slippery, resilient chameleon," she said. "It's always there. It's hard to see sometimes. You don't always see it in the form of men hosing down marching children and letting police dogs out—or graffiti on a crosswalk. We have to look for it in other forms and we have to know it takes other forms. It isn't this static thing."

Though she might have been wrong about the motives of her neighbors, the fact remained: stereotypes abound, permeating everything, tainting, poisoning, and eating away at the fabric of our lives, and no one, it seemed, fell under them as perniciously as blacks did. If everybody—Jews, Italians, Irish, Asians, Hispanics, Poles, Germans, what have you—has been fair game at one time or another over hundreds of years, blacks have been singled out the most—marked, labeled, boxed, tracked, steered, gerrymandered, redlined, avoided, tolerated, feared, neglected, hired but not accepted. Is it so surprising then that blacks wonder if things will ever really change, if there ever might be a time when they can let their guard down and just be accepted on their terms, not ours—as Americans who happen to be black?

It might not have seemed so at the time, but it didn't require a great display of character strength to be in favor of what the civil rights movement was struggling for. I'm not thinking of the people who put their lives on the line—the James Farmers and the Jim Pecks, the Fannie Lou Hamers and the Viola Liuzzos. I'm thinking of the people on the sidelines, the people who didn't march, or ride the buses, or sit at lunch counters, or try to get into courthouse doors. It didn't take a great deal of courage, let's face it, to say you thought it was wrong for blacks to have to drink from a separate water fountain or to use a separate restroom or to place their hand on a separate Bible. Even children understood that. Michael McGee was five years old when he asked his mother why white folks had a large waiting room at the doctor's office in the small town in Mississippi where he grew up and they were sitting in a closet.

The questions the Alexanders were asking, the questions Jerrel Jones was asking, the irony of my colleague's situation, and the very existence of McGee's militia only underlined how complicated the problems—and how treacherous the roads toward solutions—had become. In 1944 Gunnar Myrdal called his landmark book on race *An American Dilemma,* but it was always broader than that: it was a human dilemma, fraught with human foibles and insecurities, with all the intangibles that make up an individual or bond a group together and that can't be legislated by law. Either people didn't care or didn't think about race or didn't see how it affected their lives on a daily basis; or they cared but were immensely frustrated that nothing, in their opinion, had really seemed to work in any lasting way (even though there was evidence that some of the Great Society programs were not given enough of a chance).

"I THINK OF WHERE we were in 1965, '66, '67, how hopeful I was. . . . I never would have believed we'd still be asking these same damn questions, that it would still be this hard and we'd still be this divided as a society."

To make his point, Tom Donegan got up from behind his desk at City Hall and looked out the window, at the city that had been his home since he was six. He was forty-six now, had come out of the Great Society, a white alderman (and legal services attorney) whose office was right down the hall from McGee's and who represented the district of Sherman Park, an area of Milwaukee that was more integrated than any other, that was often put forward as an example of how residential integration could work (even though blacks lived mainly in the eastern part of the district, whites in the western).

"We have such a heavy concentration of black, poor people who see failure all around them that the presence of a white, middle-class guy in a suit is really odd now," he said of his visits to a neighborhood. "There is a certain tension that I didn't feel ten years ago. And I think Mike McGee doesn't cause it, I think he is a spokesperson for the angriest and he lends a credibility to hatred, credibility to eye-for-an-eye."

What did he mean by credibility?

"Well, he's a leader, he's an adult, he's a job with a title, and he's saying it. So it's not just me and my friend saying it, that guy in the corner who's never done anything with his life who says, 'Fuck those people if they don't give us what we want.' He's an *alderman* saying it, so I guess," Donegan said sarcastically, "it's okay to say it, I guess it's all right to be public about it and show it. . . .

"We have black males growing up in the cities with no pride in themselves, no sense they could be anybody other than to be tougher than the next guy, no realization based on their life experience living in some of those neighborhoods that to be able to get a job selling something you have to learn the main dialect, not just the street dialect. There are people who can't speak it or write it . . . and they're not getting that at home. . . . They don't have role models doing it and you stick them in the great ideal dream of the integrated school and they feel inferior, they feel isolated, they feel confused, and they're doing worse in those senses than before we did this experiment."

The "experiment" of integration was giving way to a different kind of experiment in the schools, an experiment that was to begin that fall in one elementary school and one middle school. That black males in general were doing so poorly in school had led to the conviction among some educators that one of the main reasons was the curriculum itself —that it was unfairly weighted toward European-Americans, centered around all *their* contributions to society, and that a black person essentially couldn't see himself reflected in the history books that were used as texts. And if you couldn't see yourself in what was being taught, if you had no clear and full sense of the many things African-Americans had contributed not only to American society but to civilization, then this was yet another example of the kind of control and power—through selection of what went into these books in the first place—that white society had over black people.

The severe result of this, some argued, was the feeling of inferiority, isolation, and confusion that Donegan was talking about, an almost complete loss of self-esteem or, more accurately, a virtual absence of it. While in truth it wasn't that different from the feeling of invisibility that Ralph Ellison had written so achingly of in *Invisible Man,* the root of his hero's demand to be acknowledged as someone "of substance, of flesh and bone, fiber and liquids—and I might even be said to possess a mind," the critics of an Afrocentric curriculum were insisting that not only was the history of dubious veracity, but that a curriculum designed to make black males feel good about themselves was not necessarily going to help them perform better, or come more often, or drop out less. Furthermore, Arthur Schlesinger Jr. insisted, there was an even larger issue at stake: the issue of multiculturalism and whether the bedrock credo of *e pluribus unum* was just going to be consigned to the trash heap. As far as he was concerned, if we moved more toward *pluribus* than *unum,* we were doing nothing less than "disuniting America," which of course raised the question of how united America was anyway—and of what being united actually meant.

Given just this one issue, it wasn't that hard to see why a Tom Donegan, who had almost become a priest, found himself nostalgic for the sixties—for the moral simplicity of right and wrong—and totally frustrated and perplexed by the eighties and nineties. If the hope he had had in the sixties hadn't been fully realized, he at least wanted to be hopeful again, and what made him so dejected and cynical was that he wasn't. The more I sat there, the more it was clear I was with someone who distinctly fell into the category of someone who cared, who had acted on that caring, but who couldn't accept that things hadn't worked out, that the results hadn't matched the ideals, someone who was angry that it was in vogue to poke fun at such sixties' liberals as himself, and who, as a result, felt that much of his efforts to make other people's lives better had been in vain.

Nonetheless, he was all in favor of the African-American Immersion Program (as it was known), even if that support was by default, was a painful admission that school integration hadn't worked (or had worked only for some), and he remained committed to cities—to working in them and living in them. During the eighties, under Reagan, "the federal government decided to just write off cities," Donegan said, lamenting the loss of money that had previously gone to social programs and education, and the increasing reliance on property taxes to make up for that loss. "We're unable to influence the agenda as much as we used to and yet we're the greatest need." Tom Donegan might have been in a different position from a Maron Alexander, but they still looked at things in a similar way: without jobs—jobs that Donegan thought should be created by the government—all the training programs in the world wouldn't mean anything and the poverty, as well as the crime that seemed to be inseparable from it, would only get worse. One by one he had witnessed his siblings leave Milwaukee for the suburbs, and that, like so much else, had pained him, had been a kind of personal betrayal. He had argued with them "about why we must contribute to the city's vitality and how much it hurt cities when people like us keep moving out," but his argument didn't work.

It didn't work because they too were calculating. "I think they add it all up," Donegan said sadly. "'I'm losing value on my house, taxes are a little high, little more crime creeping this way and I don't want to expose my kids to it' and mainly, 'We have kids and we know if we put them in school in Wauwatosa they'll be okay and get a decent education and we don't know that for sure in Milwaukee.'"

If Donegan couldn't make collective decisions for them, he could at least continue to make ones for himself. "It's important what I do with my life," he said without a trace of self-righteousness. "To not just keep running away from other people and interaction and trying to find a place to hide. What makes sense is making the quality of life for others richer and better. And I look at Sherman Park and I can find houses all around me where people used to live who were real activists and they gave up and they've been replaced by renters who are just there because they can afford it. . . .

"Part of my thing is I want my kids to understand the whole of life. I think it would be bad for them to live in a suburb and think that is all there is to life. I want them to see the mix. But I will have done that pretty well for them by living where I live and working where I work and schooling them where I school them. The other side of it is once they hit thirteen or fourteen I want to make sure they're in an environment where they're going to learn the skills they need to survive."

What Donegan was saying, of course, was that, as a parent, you had (like any good activist) to be involved. That while it might be harder to get what you educationally need for your children in Milwaukee than in Wauwatosa, it was a mistake to think you couldn't. Both his children were in magnet schools, and his son was going to be able to study Japanese the following year if he so desired. The difference between Donegan and the Alexanders, though, was that Donegan could send his children to private or parochial school if he decided that was the best option and the Alexanders couldn't—or at least not as easily.

And yet it was curious that he had used the word "survive" instead of "succeed." Was that an unconscious acknowledgment of his own lowered hopes and expectations for the city he loved and for the country? I didn't ask him that as I got ready to leave—but I did ask him about something on his windowsill that caught my eye as I was putting on my coat: a photograph of two beaming black children, kids who might very well have yelled, as Tennille had, "Hi, we're so-and-so, we're nine and eleven, and we're nice."

"Who are they?" I said.

"They're my kids. We adopted them."

FIVE

She had been nervous about my coming all day, and it showed. As soon as I came up the steps of her brick colonial on North Lake Drive, a serene street on Milwaukee's East Side where deliveries of all kinds are made with dispatch, Blair Moreland peppered me with questions. Was I sure I needed to talk with her? Could I send her a copy of the tape of our interview? At thirty-seven, she was at a pivotal juncture. Increasingly discontent with the homogeneity—the whiteness—of her life, she said, she had just had "the most transforming experience," coming to realize "the privileges I have as a white person."

She was, I feared, going to take me into the world of encounter-group-speak and it made me anxious—as anxious as she was that I was sitting on her front porch and asking her to talk about things and thoughts she had always kept private and was in the early stages of sorting out. Nonetheless, she was right to identify me as a catalyst, and, as it turned out, I was glad I stayed.

For more than three months she had participated in a workshop called Beyond Racism, and among the many privileges she now realized she had that she had never been conscious of before was the ability, subtle as it might seem, to drive up to an intersection and "*not* have to worry about somebody putting the locks down on their cars."

I smiled (tightly) when she said that, but didn't say why. I let her go on.

"Blacks see that all the time," she said. "Even middle-class blacks in neighborhoods like this will notice or hear the locks go down."

Her awareness of these "privileges" had come from an essay called "White Privilege: Unpacking the Invisible Knapsack" by Peggy McIntosh. It was used in an exercise in the workshop, an exercise in which whites formed an inner circle, their backs to an outer circle of (mainly) blacks and other minorities, and then proceeded to learn about "an invisible weight-less knapsack of special provisions, maps, passports, codebooks, visas, clothes, tools, and blank checks" that they could "count on cashing in each day." Among the forty-four "unearned assets" McIntosh claims whites possess and blacks for the most part do not are the ability to go shopping alone most of the time, "pretty well assured that I will not be followed or harassed"; use checks, credit cards, or cash without skin color working "against the appearance of financial reliability"; feel certain that "my children will be given curricular materials that testify to the existence of their race"; "swear, or dress in secondhand clothes, or not answer letters, without having people attribute these choices to the bad morals, the poverty, or the illiteracy of my race"; "do well in a challenging situation without being called a credit to my race"; "easily buy posters, postcards, picture books, greeting cards, dolls, toys, and children's magazines featuring people of my race"; "choose public accommodation without fearing that people of my race cannot get in or will be mistreated in the places I have chosen."

"If these things are true," McIntosh wrote, "this is not such a free country; one's life is not what one makes it; many doors open for certain people through no virtues of their own. . . .

"My schooling gave me no training in seeing myself as an oppressor, as an unfairly advantaged person, or as a participant in a damaged culture. I was taught to see myself as an individual whose moral state depended on her individual moral will. My schooling followed the pattern my colleague Elizabeth Minnich has pointed out: whites are taught to think of their lives as morally neutral, normative, and average, and also ideal, so that when we work to benefit others, this is seen as work which will allow 'them' to be more like 'us.'"

It was in part this kind of thinking that propelled many, many whites to participate in the civil rights movement. And yet it was, and is, also this kind of thinking—along with these kinds of unearned "privileges"—that has justifiably called the whole process (the successes as well as the failures) of integration, of assimilation into the mainstream, into question. We, as whites, can talk all we want about how the civil rights movement opened doors for blacks and made it possible for a significant middle class to emerge, but it is a disingenuous argument, hollow at its core. It is disingenuous because, for all the arguments we make about reverse discrimination, we haven't really yielded all that much. (Nearly 80 percent of white Americans said in 1995 they were opposed to affirmative action, but only 7 percent could honestly say they had been the victims of it.) We're still in charge, we still call the shots, things do come our way, are granted to us, because we are white. We can't pretend whiteness isn't an identity, that we are somehow invisible, that only blacks stand out—or are not seen, depending on how you choose to focus your lens. So when you get down to it, Catch-22 still applies: you can do anything you want to do in this country—but just check with us.

A good portion of "white guilt" comes from knowing we have this power and privilege, or knowing but denying we have it, or convincing ourselves that even if we have it, we have never *knowingly* abused it. For Blair Moreland in particular that guilt centered around a black woman named Alice Lester, a woman who had worked for her family in Chicago for many years, a woman who had had a large role in raising her, in looking after her, in making sure that her needs were met, and who she thought had been treated poorly—overworked, underpaid, and mostly taken for granted. It was Alice, her "second mother," and the feeling that she had let her down—that she had made promises to her, in terms of seeing she got paid more, and had not made good on them—which, more than anything else, had motivated Blair to join the workshop.

A few weeks before my visit, Blair had been back in Chicago, visiting her parents, when her father suddenly announced, "You forgave us for killing Alice."

Blair was stunned. All she could recall was that when Alice had died five years earlier, "I think maybe at some point I accused them of working her to death." If she in fact did that, she said, she had repressed it, mainly because she had never wanted to risk losing her father's love, and yet she felt they must have known "how deeply her death affected me and how much I blamed them for her death."

Whenever Blair or her siblings were in trouble, Alice sided with them. "I didn't know it at the time, but whichever kid was in trouble with my parents they had an ally to the end. Only later did I come to understand that it was her own identification as an underdog in our culture."

Which brought her back to one of the things she had learned in the workshop—"that until there's full equality, everybody's black" (echoing a prevailing sentiment of the civil rights struggle that *None of us is free until all of us are free,* a code she was now trying to live by).

Another thing she lived by was a belief in fate, and in that vein, she was convinced that growing up with Alice, coming to live in "the most segregated city in the country," and finding her way to the Beyond Racism project had all happened for a reason.

Her belief in fate aside, the important thing was that she now felt strong enough to confront racism whenever and wherever it occurred, as she did the previous Thanksgiving when a relative made some comment about blacks at the dinner table, saying, "That's how they are." Blair challenged her, said that she shouldn't generalize that way, that it personally hurt her to hear that kind of remark. Needless to say, this didn't endear her to her relative, or to anyone else at the table for that matter, but she had made her point.

Of all her memories of Alice, her most powerful ones were of the last week of Alice's life and of her funeral. Alice had just come back from the hospital, to her one-room apartment on Chicago's South Side, happy that she was getting better, or seemed to be. As she always did when Blair came to visit, Alice stuck her head out the window and waved, wanting to make sure that Blair got to her car safely when it was time to leave. "And that was my last memory of her, that beautiful, beautiful hand, that loving face watching me out, and then she died a week later, alone. Just convulsed and died."

At the funeral, a funeral Blair's parents organized, "we saw for the first time so many people who loved Alice. We knew of her friends, of course, because she talked about them and they sometimes came to our house, but we didn't know how loved she was."

Blair gave the eulogy and then they all made the long drive to the cemetery, her fury with her father peaking as they got there, to a place that was "horrible" and "desolate," unlike the cemeteries where her grandparents were buried, which were "beautiful and close by." Her father had paid for the cheapest possible funeral and she did confront him about it. Of that, she had no doubt. "To see her go in the ground in that area" was so excruciating for Blair that "what I've had to do is rebury her in a sense and realize that that doesn't matter at all. That her body went down there but her spirit lifted up and her spirit was certainly with me and with all of us."

And so, as it happened, was her voice. Not long after the funeral, Blair came upon a journal that Alice had been keeping, a journal that contained the thoughts and emotions that Alice had not been able to express directly to the Moreland family.

I wonder what white people think of color people, or I should say what they think of me. I know but I would like to know from the ones I'm working for. One thing I know is that they do not think that you need money. Just a little will do you they think. As long as you work for them they seem to think that thats a big thing. They feels that you really doesn't know what to do with it anyway. Yet they spend money for things that they could do without and really they would rather spend it foolish than give you a few dollars more.

They will always say you are nice or good to the children and that should be just fine. Well it isn't. So you see its not fun working for nothing when you have bills to. Some time they have to learn the hard way. . . .

The real truth is that they should say we should give her more money but instead they will say Oh: If it hadn't been for Alice we couldn't have did this or that. I can't spend that.

In this whole world there is only one Alice and you better beleave it to. Mrs. Moreland could not get another person like me. . . . People that have us working for them just dont give a dam, as long as they get what they want and their work done.

I do just can make it. You cant save either. Its hard to work when you can't save a dime.

. . . what can you do? Stop working for them and let them feel the mistake of not giving you more money which they will never feel. At least they wont admit it anyway.

. . . they say color people are the nasty people there is but they should look at themselves. They are the ones. If they are not why would they have a color person working for them? I will tell you why because they aren't clean and they need somebody to clean up their nastyness that why.

You can never sit and talk about little things with them, because they are to busy and what you have to say anyway is not important to them because you are dum and you don't know what you are talking about in the first place. But if they want to talk to you, you listen.

White folks really dislike color people and yet where they are today some where or some one Black was the Cause of it all.

S I X

Wherever I turned, it seemed, I was surrounded by the question of race, by the endless number of roles it appeared to play, as if it were some character actor whom directors loved to use time and again. Race and how it would affect the 1992 presidential election; race and how, in the person of Willie Horton, it *did* affect the 1988 election; race in education; race in the workplace; race in where people live; race in how people socialize; race, race, race. Not only was the *Milwaukee Journal* running its aforementioned series, but the *Atlantic* had a cover story, *Newsweek* had one, *U.S. News & World Report* had one, *Business Week* had one. The Bush Administration was fighting hard against passage of a new civil rights bill, designed to regain some rights that had been lost during the 1980s when "the Supreme Court misinterpreted and undermined long-standing civil rights law," according to the *New York Times*. The *Times* also wrote, on page one, about the difficulties blacks continued to have in obtaining loans, and then, a few weeks later, about the difficulties blacks, with exactly the same qualifications as their white counterparts, had in obtaining entry-level jobs. There was yet another piece about the treatment blacks received in stores—the suspicion they aroused when they walked in, and the diffidence with which they were waited on by white saleshelp. An "integrated" school in Illinois was going to have separate proms; another, in Georgia, separate valedictorians.

The cumulative effect in reading all this was one of bleakness. While I could understand why people with even the best of intentions might think that nothing they individually could do would make one scintilla of difference, that racism was so deeply and insidiously woven into the way institutions operated that no one human being would have any chance whatsoever to alter that fact, I couldn't accept it. To accept it was tantamount to saying that white America had gone as far as it possibly could, that the civil rights movement and affirmative action had resulted in a burgeoning black middle class, that there was a large number of blacks elected to political office, that more blacks were in college than ever before—but that the problems of drugs, crime, joblessness, gangs, welfare dependency, teenage pregnancy, infant mortality rates, and poor housing were insurmountable, that the problems were so confounding and pervasive that one not only became easily fatigued just thinking about them, but that white America, as one person told *Newsweek,* was "tired of being called guilty," tired of feeling permanently responsible for every social and economic ill that beset the inner cities.

Ironically, the person responsible for the term "race fatigue" was a black essayist and academic named Shelby Steele. But he was not referring to white America. He was primarily referring to the black middle class and to his contention that since "race does not determine our fates as powerfully as it once did," this group feels "a deep weariness with things racial." He didn't stop there, though. He extended his argument, suggesting that *all* blacks needed to stop holding on to race, to stop using it as a crutch, as an excuse for their own individual lack of progress. The opportunity was there, Steele insisted, to make it in mainstream America, and all that "integration shock" was was "essentially the shock of being suddenly accountable on strictly personal terms," of refusing to see oneself as a victim any longer. While there was truth to what Steele was saying, and while he also acknowledged (almost grudgingly, it seemed) that "blacks still suffer from racism, so we must be concerned," he was nonetheless writing the words to a song of absolution that many white listeners wanted to hear, a song that Booker T. Washington had sung a century earlier, a song whose notes offered a simple answer when something deeper and more far-reaching was called for.

IN MILWAUKEE, WHOSE NATIVE American name means "gathering place by the rivers," there are a number of bridges that go over three rivers, but none is probably as significant, or as infamous, as the James E. Groppi. Extending over the Menomonee River, it is a bridge that a lot of Milwaukeeans (especially those who live on the south side of the river) still wish was officially known as the Sixteenth Street Viaduct, as it still is stubbornly called. Even now, the name James Groppi raises the ire of many a South Sider because the white priest had the audacity to lead hundreds of marchers, beginning in August 1967, hard on the heels of Milwaukee's riot that summer, across that bridge—The Bridge that Separates Poland from

Africa, as it has also been known, or the "longest bridge in the world"—in an effort to gain fair and open housing for blacks. For more than two hundred days, the marchers weathered spit, rocks, and every imaginable invective in an effort to achieve on a local level what became federal law the following year. Father Groppi and his marchers ultimately triumphed, but it was a Pyrrhic victory. If landlords wanted to get around a law, there were all sorts of ways to do it, and they did. Or if real estate agents wanted to exploit that law, all they had to do was "steer" black people to a white neighborhood, knowing that it would be a forceful catalyst for white homeowners to move. After all, the more houses you had to sell, the more commissions could be made. American capitalism, it seemed, was as alive and transcendent as ever, attuned to the nation's sea changes and ready to pounce.

Father Groppi had been an inspiration to people like Tom Donegan—but the question of integration, of what was gained and what was lost, was complex and troubling, as Donegan continued to realize. What little hope Donegan still had, though, for realizing racial harmony and equity in Milwaukee was partly bound up in the person of another sixties activist, Howard Fuller, the head of the Department of Health and Human Services, who was hoping to become the next superintendent of the Milwaukee Public Schools. Fuller was the person who had, along with Michael McGee, organized the campaign that resulted in justice for the family of Ernest Lacy and who was generally considered the most respected black leader in Milwaukee, even though (unlike McGee) he did not have nearly as high a profile outside it.

Fuller was fifty, nine years older than McGee; despite their alliance on Lacy and some other issues, they were not close friends and, more important, did not view the world in the same way—another damaging stereotype about black people (*All black people think alike*) that the existence and contrasting philosophies of Malcolm X and Martin Luther King, of Booker T. Washington and W.E.B. Du Bois, had somehow failed to eradicate from the minds of most white Americans. In fact, the path Fuller had chosen—to essentially work within the mainstream—had elicited comments of "lackey" and "hypocrite" from McGee, and when a Molotov cocktail was thrown at his house in February of 1990, the same month McGee announced the formation of his militia, McGee, or someone associated with him, was suspected of doing it. The notion that any black, not just Howard

Fuller, who decides to work within the mainstream is a mere puppet of the white establishment is precisely the kind of polarized thinking that conspicuously stands in the way of racial harmony. In fact, an objective comparison of the careers of Fuller and McGee would reveal that Fuller's, ironically, was consistently more radical and revolutionary by far—which made his current situation all the more surprising and interesting.

Fuller's name had come up in every conversation I had had since coming to Milwaukee. An only child, he was born in Shreveport, Louisiana, in 1941 and came to Milwaukee at the age of six. Even as a small child, his mother recalled, he was always a giving person, making certain that each child who came over to visit had enough food to eat, beginning a pattern of looking out for others that would vary little as time went on. In Milwaukee, he and his mother were among the first residents of Hillside, a public housing project, and though they didn't have much money, they never thought of themselves as poor, and it never occurred to Fuller that he wouldn't make it, that he wouldn't be able to achieve *anything* he set out to achieve—even though he couldn't have known how thorny the process of "making it" would turn out to be.

The black community as a whole was small and tight-knit back in the late forties and fifties, and saw its responsibility as a collective one, especially to each other's children. If a Howard Fuller was somewhere he shouldn't be, doing something he shouldn't be doing, he could be sure that his mama would hear about it by nightfall, if not before. More significantly, though, it was a community in which people went off to work, all sorts of people—from the factory workers who punched in at A. O. Smith and American Motors to teachers and clergymen to doctors and lawyers in fine suits with snappy briefcases. If there were any pluses to segregation, this was perhaps the biggest one—because everybody, regardless of income, more or less lived within close proximity of everybody else, there was a sense of unity, of being part of a larger family, a feeling that if a doctor lived next door to you, what was to prevent you from becoming a doctor too?

The civil rights movement unwittingly changed that. In its noble effort to do what had to be done—break down the legal barriers of segregation and open up equal opportunity in every conceivable phase of life—the movement hadn't counted on the gap that would be created within the black community as those same doctors and lawyers, with newfound freedom of choice, moved out of the neighborhood, removing not only themselves but taking the role-model symbol of their success with them. The triumph of the civil rights movement was not unequivocal; its majestic rising tide did not lift all boats.

"For every gain there is a loss," my colleague at Virginia reminded me; within the context of any grand movement of social change, progress has its price. As much as she nostalgically recalled the neighborhood in the Alabama city of Bessemer where she grew up, as much as it made her bristle when she moved into her current one in Charlottesville and people made assumptions or veiled their true concerns through "helpful advice," she wouldn't ever want to revert to the days of segregation. Even though integration, in her view, has resulted in blacks both fearing the loss of their identity and "being saddled with 'white problems'"; even though it has "muddied in ways that are good and ill the codes of black-white interaction" ("*before*, you knew how people felt; now, everybody *speaks* the language of harmony . . . there is a lot of politeness, a lot of skirting around, and a lot of real conversations that never take place"—a state of affairs in which "I'm not comfortable" becomes an easy out); to go back to a time in which "people's freedoms were being abridged" would be like "going back to colonialism."

Not everyone would agree with her, and in some respects, oddly enough, Howard Fuller would be one of them. As recently as 1987, he was actively engaged in trying to have a separate school district for blacks in Milwaukee, an effort that actually won Assembly approval in the state legislature. And eight years before that, he fought, successfully, to keep his beloved alma mater, North Division High School, from becoming a magnet school in the name of integration—which meant that a large number of whites would bus in, a large number of blacks would be displaced and have to bus out, and North would no longer be a neighborhood school. It was Fuller's way of saying, of forcing others to acknowledge (as Tom Donegan did), that busing was a bad idea, that while it might be important for a variety of reasons to retain as many white students as possible within the public schools (the main one being a desire to keep their parents' tax dollars within the city of Milwaukee), that that effort should not come at the risk of further fracturing the black community.

And now, four years later, here he was—the first black male to attend nearly all-white Carroll College on a scholarship *and* the founder of Malcolm X Liberation University, an individual who at one time was known as Owùsu Sadaukai and at another served as Secretary of Employment Relations in the administration of Wisconsin governor Tony Earl. Here he was, right on the verge perhaps of becoming the superintendent for all of Milwaukee's children in public school and a man about whom, not surprisingly, everybody seemed to have an opinion— or a suspicion.

Back in February of 1988 he had returned the Martin Luther King Jr. Humanitarian Award to the city of Milwaukee, an award he had been given just two weeks earlier. He had returned it because "I did not see the leadership of this city, private or public, taking seriously the continued deterioration of the quality of life and life chances of the poor in the African-American community. I saw no real effort being made to alter the powerlessness" of the community. The other main reason for returning it, he said, was that he wanted to distance himself from the man who had been mayor of the city since 1960 and who was now stepping down, Henry Maier. Maier was being honored at the same Martin Luther King Day ceremonies as Fuller, and Fuller believed "that his legacy was one that stood in direct contradiction" to King's. "There may very well be good reasons for Henry Maier to be acknowledged and honored," Fuller said in a statement at the time, "but being a positive force for empowerment of black people is clearly not one of them."

Two years later, though, he decided to give the keynote speech at the King Day celebration—not because he thought that conditions had improved in the black community (some, he said, were actually worse), but because he felt that the new mayor, the new county executive, and the new superintendent of schools were three individuals "who understand and are committed to changing this community" (not just the black community, but all of Milwaukee). But, he cautioned, Milwaukee was still "a long distance away from being the place that we can all feel good about. I believe, however, there is a different level of sensitivity, that indeed there is a 'consciousness' about these issues. I choose to work with those who are willing to tackle these problems."

It was this spirit of cooperation in the longtime firebrand that so irked Michael McGee and others in the black community, that led McGee to call him a hypocrite and a lackey, and that had *Milwaukee Magazine* asking its readers, "Who Is Howard Fuller and What Does He Want?"

As much as it might have hurt Fuller's feelings to have his motives questioned, to be viewed as a chameleon, as someone who had fought the power structure for so long (there are still whites in Durham, North Carolina, who rue the day Fuller came to, and changed, the "Jewel of the New South") and who seemed now, in the view of some, to be doing its bidding, it perplexed and angered him even more. In truth, he was a man who knew who he was and knew what he stood for. He had protested, he had marched, he had organized superbly and successfully, he had deliberately gone to a white college and had started a black one, he had risked his life, and he had learned that Frederick Douglass was right—that "power concedes nothing without a demand"; and he had come to the conclusion that the way he could be most effective on behalf of the black community was by placing himself firmly in the mainstream and seeking to influence decisions and shape policies—to build bridges—from there.

Unlike Shelby Steele, Fuller was a "race man," someone committed to more than just individual advancement, who saw himself as having a much larger obligation. And even if physical fatigue would fell him from time to time, the concept of race fatigue was not only anathema to him, it was his very concern about it—about other blacks forgetting or choosing to forget or deny their history—that drove him. As far as he was concerned, if you were black and had achieved any measure of success, good for you; live wherever you want to live with whomever you want to live with. But continue to give something back. Howard Fuller no longer lived in Hillside, but hardly a week passed that he didn't return there, to remind himself from where—and how far—he had come. As circumscribed as his world was at the time he was growing up, the world of Hillside—of many, many inner-city neighborhoods—was more limited now. The landscape had changed, from safe haven to war zone, and though he had a hard time coming to grips with that change—with the fact that gangs and the drug trade were the new A. O. Smiths, with the soaring rate of violence and teenage pregnancy and the shockingly low value that was placed on life itself—it didn't stop him from talking to kids, *all* kids (not just the ones who reminded him of himself, determined to make it no matter what), about how crucial it was to get an education, talking to parents, and trying to help, to

"clear the way for others" (the English translation of Owusu). And if
that effort meant little personal time, little sleep, health problems,
and two failed marriages, in his opinion it was the price you paid for being
a race man.

ON MAY 29, 1991, Howard L. Fuller officially became the new superintendent of the Milwaukee Public Schools; the man he was replacing, Robert
Peterkin, had stayed just three years. Of the many lobbying efforts Fuller
made to get the position, one involved a meeting with Michael McGee, at
the Crossroads Supper Club on Teutonia Avenue, directly across the street
from Jerrel Jones's radio station. It was not a meeting designed to patch up
their differences, but an acknowledgment on Fuller's part that he needed
McGee's support, needed McGee not to stand in his path, to at the very
least give him his blessing, however passively. McGee agreed to do that;
as long as Fuller stayed out of politics and focused on education, he felt
they could coexist. (The previous summer, in the *Washington Post,* they had
sniped at each other; when Fuller was told that McGee and Jones basically took the position that there were no laws that the United States had
made that blacks should feel bound to obey because they were "white laws,"
Fuller said, in a choked voice, that that attitude was "a sign of how much
trouble we're in. The definition of whether you're on the side of the people
has somehow become linked to how outrageous you can be in condemning white people. . . . We have to make ethical decisions. Anyone who's
studied Malcolm knows the importance of self-responsibility.")
        If the night of May 29 augured new hope for Milwaukee's school-
children, the reality of what Howard Fuller was inheriting was being played
out that same evening in a town meeting over at Washington High School.
Designed to let the community discuss with public officials (including Tom
Donegan) the issues that concerned them and the solutions that might be
found, it was more a heartrending bulletin from the front than any kind of
polite and reasoned discussion. It's one thing to sit on somebody's front
porch and have them matter-of-factly inform you that the sound you just
heard was probably gunfire and quite another for a mother to hold up her
son's bloodstained T-shirt, a son who was on his way to college when he
found himself in the middle of somebody else's argument and was shot six
times. When, the woman demanded to know, was this going to stop? What

right did the white police officer who questioned her have to just assume that her son was a gang member who carried a gun, as if there were no other explanations, as if this were the first time an innocent person was caught in gang crossfire over the protection of turf? How was it and why was it that gangs had become so powerful that fifteen people had witnessed this happen and not one—*not one*, she shouted—could be found to bring her son's assailants to justice, mainly because some of their houses were shot up and, as a result, the others backed out? If witnesses couldn't be assured of protection, she asked, shaking as she stood there, why should they come forward?

The district attorney told her the unfortunate truth: there was a limit to what could be done to protect witnesses, and all the persuasion in the world couldn't force a reluctant person to testify. The police chief said there was now a hot line to call if you knew of someone who might be in possession of a gun illegally.

A woman named Marlene Royalty told of her son being wrongly detained at the 7th District precinct and how she had never been treated so rudely as she had when she tried to gain information about the incident. "It's demoralizing and degrading to go down there," she said. "I'm an intelligent person. Why is it that people of color don't get a fair shake? I work in customer service, and if I'm rude or abusive there's an internal system that takes care of it. Why don't you all have that?"

Her question seemed to hang there endlessly, but she didn't wait for an answer. "I'm crying wolf now," she said, "before you kill my child."

There was thunderous applause. Her recounting of what happened had been punctuated by the same shouts of "amen" and "yes" I had heard in Montgomery, but these were shouts of anger and despair.

A young man named Mike Connor stood up and wanted to know what was being done to spur economic development in the inner city. It was a simple enough question, a question that had been asked many times before, in many different forums over many, many years, and would doubtless be asked many times again, a question for which there was no one simple answer, or even a particularly satisfactory one. There was no single, driving vision, no true consensus of any kind, in Milwaukee or elsewhere, of what was needed, or of how to collectively address those needs (those nagging, ever-patient "socioeconomic problems," as they are known in the world of public policy and social science). In its place was something scattershot, an alphabet soup of programs with impressive-sounding names, names that spoke of hope and achievement, of respect and self-esteem, of fighting against adversity: the New Hope Project, Project Respect, Stop the Violence, Step-Up, Start Smart. Something here, something there, sometimes working, oftentimes not. And always, despite the determined, feel-good names, there were the stark facts—that the needs far outweighed the number of people who could be helped; that if all the existing job openings in Milwaukee were filled, there would still be roughly forty thousand people (mainly blacks) unable to find work; that a virtual Marshall Plan would have to be in place for the situation to be corrected.

Tom Donegan told Connor that the city was working with the governor's office to develop "enterprise zones" for minority-owned businesses, that job programs for youth had already placed four thousand people for the summer, and that money was already earmarked for neighborhood-based business incubators. Sherry Hill, from the governor's office, said that the state was making loans available to minority businesses, and Mike Morgan, from the mayor's office, talked of the Disadvantaged Business Enterprise Program (which provided for the city to contract with minority firms) and the city's Land Bank Program (vacant land that was specifically geared toward encouraging businesses to locate in the inner city). Just two weeks earlier, Mayor Norquist had told the *Milwaukee Journal* that economics was the key to dealing with racism, that "the trouble with confronting racism is that it means feeling sorry for somebody. But that isn't going to do it. I acknowledge that there's racism in our community and that it affects a lot of things," but the only way to truly combat it, he suggested, was with power and money. It was a blunt statement that was characteristically Norquist, a statement that reflected that whites didn't want to feel guilty anymore about blacks and that empathy, in any case, could only go so far in solving the enormity of the problems.

The ongoing dilemma, though, was this: In terms of the power and money Norquist said were necessary to confront racism, the resources were scant (as Donegan had lamented the month before), and much of the reason they were scant—not just in Milwaukee, but throughout the country—was that the power structure did not place the plight of the inner city very high on its priority list, regardless of any earnest lip service to the contrary. After all, the people who didn't want to feel sorry for somebody were constituents, considerable in number, who cast votes and paid taxes, whose goodwill had been depleted by affirmative action and two recessions in ten years, and that was just as harsh a reality in its own way as the one the people who had come to Washington High that night were talking about.

LOUISE KIDD ACCEPTED THAT reality. She didn't necessarily like it, but she accepted it. And she also accepted the need for the black community to take responsibility. One of the last people to speak at Washington that evening, she was a divorced mother in her mid-thirties who lived in Tom Donegan's district (in an apartment above the Domino's that wouldn't deliver to the Alexanders), a woman of boundless energy who worked in a bank and had a skin-care business on the side and who was adamant that blacks better not be hanging around waiting for something to fall from the sky because they'd be waiting a long time, and who said, straight out, that she wasn't afraid of anybody, that if people were hanging around her doorway when she got home and they weren't there to visit her, they had better move, right now, that if they didn't respect her front door she'd call the police, confident they would come. And the reason for that confidence—which is not universally shared by the black community, not by any means—was that she had organized her block, made her neighbors, both black and white, more vigilant about crime, and in the process had good relations with Officer Fyfe, who patrolled by foot and by car. When children on her part of North Forty-first Street saw her coming, they straightened up. Louise Kidd saw it as her personal mission that no child on her block, from Burleigh to Auer, have idle time on his or her hands; she got them to help her sweep the street (forced would be more accurate) and she played softball with some of them on Saturday afternoons at the park. And that she did all this, she told the audience that night and later reiterated to me, on top of trying to raise her daughter and work two jobs and volunteer over at Hillside, should be proof enough that it could and must be done, that everybody in the black community had a role to play—echoing the collective responsibility the community had always understood to be theirs during the bittersweet days of legal segregation.

She had grown up in Chicago, in the Nation of Islam (her older brother had been a strong follower of Malcolm X), and she believed the rigidity and discipline of her upbringing had instilled in her the right values, especially a love of her culture—precisely what she saw lacking today.

"We don't love our people like we used to," she said one night in her apartment. "If we did, this killing wouldn't be going on. . . . When people say they are tired of this, tired of that, I put the question to them, 'Okay, what are you doing? Besides working your regular job, going to school, and partying or whatever, what else are you doing? When was the last time you helped a little girl up the street do her homework? Or helped an old lady with her bags or took her shopping? When was the last time you reached out to somebody because they needed your help and you felt you could help them?'"

When she was still married, she overheard a conversation her husband and some friends were having about the "race problem" in Milwaukee, about the way "they were doing blacks in the city." She listened and listened until she couldn't listen any longer. "I said, 'What are you guys doing to change it? You just sit here and talk and talk and talk. I don't see you out here trying to train black guys how to do carpentry work, how to get into the system. Somebody helped you, you went through an apprenticeship. . . . When was the last time you worked in a community organization to try to bring about change? But you are going to sit here and say that the system is fucked up. That is a sorry excuse.'"

Part of what propelled Louise Kidd stemmed from something else she had come to accept. Integration hadn't worked. "It started out trying to help—with better opportunities for blacks—but it is not ending up that way." It made her sad when a little girl came up to her daughter in a park near Wauwatosa and asked if she could touch Shawna's braids. "I figured that little white girl had never seen a black girl in braids before because she asked her mommy if she could do her hair like that." At the same time, though, Louise was sad that many of her friends wanted nothing to do with braids or dreadlocks. "I say that is part of our culture. But because we have experienced white people's culture and integrated that into our own lifestyles, we don't know how to accept our own culture anymore." And yet she also resented that a person could be labeled so easily by skin color alone. Because her father was from Barbados and the product of a mixed marriage, Louise considered herself the product of one; she treasured her French and Scottish blood and always checked "Other" on any form that asked about race: "Why should I just limit myself by saying I am black? I am from all the cultures." Her mixed background had resulted in sandy hair and hazel eyes and a fair complexion that often led friends in high school to mock her as white. Since the whole issue of *How black are you?* had been around a lot longer than she had (an issue she considered "a race problem—within our own race"), there was no reason why she would be able to avoid it.

Beyond everything else, though, beyond her fury that the bank she worked for wouldn't give her a loan, beyond her fury at a welfare system that enabled "so many people to make money from people sitting home doing nothing except waiting for a check," beyond her fury at those welfare recipients who sent their kids to day care and didn't try to either better themselves (by going to school) or volunteer at the school their children went to, beyond her fury that "double standards" seemed to be "the American way"—beyond all of that was her determination to keep trying to make things better, to keep reaching out, to keep pressing the system, to put people on notice if they acted out of line, to basically be a thorn in everybody's side, regardless of race. So if, for instance, a middle- or upper-middle-class black declared, "I don't want to live next to them niggers" as a reason for moving out of the inner city, Louise Kidd's attitude was this: "First of all, a nigger to me is anybody that acts foolish or stupid. And secondly, I don't want to live next to a crazy fool either. But if I think that crazy fool can be readied to change their state of mind, I will do it."

As zealous and selfless and too-good-to-be-true as she might sound, she was actually motivated by a selfish desire, selfish (in the best sense), timeless, and understandable: the desire, as a parent, to see her child's life be more fruitful than hers. And that meant education. Louise didn't want Shawna to be handed anything except an opportunity to compete—to compete and *earn* any scholarships that might come her way. And in order to do that, Louise had done everything she could to provide the right environment—a school that required her to wear a uniform (so she wouldn't either be distracted by name brands and who had what, or be killed for possessing them); and a home life in which rules, honesty, respect, and homework came before anything else. But Louise Kidd was realistic enough to know there were limits—even for her—of what she could do.

"It's going to be a long, hot summer," she said, looking blankly out her window, "and there's been a lot of killing already."

SEVEN

"Have a good weekend … and stay off the homicide rate," was the sign-off from Matthew Skelly on WNOV as I came by the station to pick up Jerrel Jones. It was Saturday, June 1, and even though Jones seemed to work all the time—or be engaged in high-powered games of chess—he had offered to drive around the inner city with me, show me the sights as it were, and pick up Michael McGee along the way. We stopped by the headquarters of the Black Panther Militia, at 2636 King Drive, and Jones went up to the door. The building was painted red, black, and green, had a small lawn and flower bed in front, and a sign that read "Fighting evil is obedience to God. The original order." Inside, on the wall, were posters of Marcus Garvey, Malcolm X, and other black leaders.

Jones stood there for a minute or two, then came back to the car. "He's in there," Jones said, "but he probably just doesn't feel like coming to the door."

I was prepared for this from my first go-round and didn't mind in the least. In fact, I had some concern about McGee giving me some sort of orchestrated grand tour of urban decay and misery. (I was already finding that on my own.) On the other hand, Jones's offer hadn't troubled me; it seemed an opportunity to see things through his eyes as well as my own, without feeling hotboxed or blithely nodding agreement or understanding to things that I would doubtless need much more time to reflect on. In any case, McGee had been busy since last I saw him and probably needed his rest. In the middle of May, during a *Good Morning America* broadcast from Milwaukee, he began blowing whistles and was arrested; he had been in Atlanta on *Tony Brown's Journal,* he had been in Detroit, he had been in Dallas, and he was about to do *Geraldo.* Normally, on Saturday mornings, he went fishing early and then played basketball. Today, as it turned out, he had gone to the dentist, was in a certain degree of pain, and just didn't feel like answering the door.

Jones, meanwhile, seemed buoyant; he had a large new tower going up for the station and was of the opinion that his businesses (which also included the *Milwaukee Courier,* a black newspaper, and a lot of real estate) had boomed since McGee formed the militia. "Mike takes the 'bad guy' role off everybody," he had told me the day before. "Now we can act normal because we've got a lunatic running loose. Nobody's so hard about the *Courier* being a far left paper. Mike makes it seem like the Good Book now." There was a white-owned car dealership, for instance, that had never run ads in the city's three black newspapers before but had recently bought some space. Jones saw it as a sign that the white community was taking McGee's threat seriously. As was the middle-class black community, mainly in the form of anonymous donations ("You can't get a check from a black guy with his name on it"). As for the city, Jones felt they had responded too. Buildings that had been shown to the media (especially to *60 Minutes*) as examples of the deterioration and living conditions that McGee was talking about had either been razed or made to look, Jones exaggerated, "as if they came out of *House and Garden.*" Actually, he joked, it was getting pretty difficult to find good footage anymore. The city might want to say (and was saying) that this work had long been planned and had nothing to do with McGee, but the timing of some announced efforts certainly gave the impression that it was more than coincidence, and the Greater Milwaukee Committee formed an Inner City Task Force right after the *60 Minutes* broadcast in December. "I think by 1995," Jones said, "as pessimistic as Mike talks, the city will have answered every one of his demands."

And what if that was not the case, if the "racial parity" he was seeking was not realized?

Then he had to go through with his threat, Jones said. "If he wasn't serious before, I think he has to be serious now. That's the whole problem. Now he's got too many people involved."

ONE OF THOSE PEOPLE was Walter Farrell, a professor at the University of Wisconsin—Milwaukee, who had first met McGee in the mid-eighties. McGee had learned that Farrell was researching the high number of taverns and liquor outlets per square foot in the inner city and wrote him a letter, curious about his conclusions. McGee was shrewd enough to know that he would need someone to lend academic/intellectual credibility to his efforts, and he was right. With his finely tailored suits, his cellular phone (which he never turned off), and, not insignificantly, his own dislike of both Mayor Norquist and Howard Fuller, Farrell was a perfect fit. Shortly after McGee announced the formation of the Black Panther Militia, Farrell wrote in the *Los Angeles Times* about "the devastating social and economic problems confronting African-Americans in Milwaukee" and said that they were "replicated in major cities from Los Angeles to Miami and in all other urban centers in the United States.

"If we do nothing," he warned, "we could find ourselves unwillingly fueling the creation of urban militias across America."

Now, as he sat across from me at the Crossroads Supper Club, eating catfish on a Friday night, he was elaborating on that article, saying that Milwaukee, like most large cities, had been run pretty much like a plantation for a long time, and a good part of the reason was the paternalism of well-intentioned liberals—individuals who were sure they knew what was best for the black community, individuals like Tom Donegan. "It's a fundamental flaw in trying to eradicate poverty that the people who need to be in the room are never in the room," he said. The people who are actually in poverty "never get to participate," and the people who participate on their behalf are "so distant from them in class terms that they really can't meet at the nexus of what it takes." So what happens, and what happened with the War on Poverty, Farrell said, is that "they do a lot of stupid things—programs that didn't work or weren't funded properly, thinking that these things are the answer, and then when they don't work as quickly as they wanted, they become disenchanted.

"The issue is very, very complex and no one wants to deal with the substance of it all and the people here, when Mike raised this issue, the white community took a very specific stance: *That guy's out of his mind, he's a radical* . . . and they became angry that black people didn't get up and condemn him. Most black people knew that he was right, even those who weren't living in poverty." And they were afraid to say anything, Farrell said, because most of them worked for white people.

Farrell had grown up in North Carolina and entered graduate school in the fall of 1969, "the era of the riot scholar," as a direct beneficiary of the civil rights movement ("blacks from the streets created opportunities for blacks in schools"). Not only did he come to Milwaukee, in 1978, as a tenured professor, but he came at the time when the economy was changing from manufacturing to service, from being labor-intensive to being information-intensive. Even if the intent of this shift wasn't racial, Farrell said, the effect was. And even though nobody in Milwaukee was prepared for "the long-term infliction of this severe economic dislocation" (because of the cyclical nature of factory work), Farrell was of the opinion, as a social scientist, that policy makers had to have known this was coming and yet "made no provisions" for it.

Once again, I was struck by the military language. McGee had used it, and now Farrell was. Apparently, this sense of the inner city having become a war zone had so insinuated itself into people's thinking that they spoke this way without being conscious of it, or perhaps it was a view so embedded in people's minds since the urban riots of the sixties and the War on Poverty that nothing had appreciably changed to encourage people to think in a different way. (But there was something else in what Farrell was saying, something more subtle, something that had a certain amount of currency in the black community: the notion of conspiracy, that the white power structure was, through both action and inaction, creating a situation that would make it harder and harder for the black community to survive. It was implicit in McGee's saying "They don't mind because we don't matter," and it was explicit in the suggestion that the rampant drug trade was operated by whites, who in turn directed it toward blacks who needed money and couldn't make that kind of money any other way and who would either kill to protect that money or be killed or who would wind up in prison for a good long while. This belief in genocide, which the original Black Panthers had talked quite a bit about, mainly in terms of the FBI, was part of the reason that black men were referred to as "an endangered species.")

As a result of this tremendous rise in unemployment in the black community, Farrell said, there had been, nationwide, corresponding increases in teen pregnancy, crime, violence (homicide in particular), the drug trade, arrest rates, heart disease, domestic abuse, and child abuse.

One of the difficulties blacks (males in particular) had encountered in trying to find jobs in the service economy, Farrell said, was the perception that they were more threatening, and that was why "you don't see many of them in hotels, as managers, desk clerks, that kind of thing, because those racial factors play in." A black female was suspended from a job as a cashier in a grocery store in Milwaukee because she wore a sweatshirt that said IT'S A BLACK THANG, YOU WOULDN'T UNDERSTAND. (She was eventually reinstated.)

I had seen sweatshirts like that, but I had also seen sweatshirts that said 2+2=4. IT'S A WHITE THING, YOU WOULDN'T UNDERSTAND. I thought both messages were not only flip but that they might serve only to further polarize things, to allow people more justification, however groundless, for respectively feeling that there exist unbridgeable differences between blacks and whites, and that we would all save ourselves a lot of anguish if we just accepted that.

Farrell referred to things like this as "special social nuances" and he had experienced his share of them. On one occasion, he had been doing some pro bono work for a corporation, but someone from the university, clearly skeptical that Farrell would do anything for free and sure that he had pocketed his fee, insisted that he file a form showing how much he had been paid. On another, an untenured white colleague proposed to him that they collaborate on a project, a project that would use only Farrell's research, but proposed it to him in a way that suggested the material belonged to both of them equally. Just took it for granted, the element of white privilege surfacing once more. Nonetheless, Farrell considered himself, as a black professional, to be better off in academia than in corporate America, where "so much of your success depends on your ability to get into networks" and where the game of "work sabotage" (hiding information, misrepresenting what it is you stand for, making it difficult for you to recruit white clients) is in full force.

If all that Farrell was saying was true (and there was enough corroborating evidence to suggest that it was), was it any wonder, then, that there was very little after-hours social interaction between black and white professionals—that, as Farrell said, "some have been so stretched out by the daily workplace, they're anxious to get away from white people during social occasions"?

So how alienated, in general, did the black middle class feel in America? Did one have to give up too much to be in the mainstream?

It varied, Farrell said; it depended. He praised companies like Corning and Xerox as being unique, companies that had made "major strides" to "accommodate" the changing workforce. He praised Miller Brewing and Philip Morris "to some degree." But they were the exceptions, not the rule.

These were painful questions, he said, because many blacks believed that by "sheer competence" they'd be able to overcome the obstacles. That even though they would "go into a corporation and see all these dead black bodies, you know, strewn around, they would say, 'Well, I won't make the mistake. I'll play the game and I'll do a good job,' then ten years later they still find out it's not enough."

Given that, did he think too much had been and was still being made of integration?

How one defined integration was crucial, he said. "Being around white people, that's not what integration means. Integration means just the opportunity to participate and if you elect to live in an all-black neighborhood," that's your choice. "Some of my first-class colleagues say, 'Well, most black people like being around black people.' But that's only after they have been maligned and attacked, harassed, in white neighborhoods."

What pleased him was the assertiveness he saw in the current generation, an assertiveness on college campuses, for instance, reflected in blacks saying, "'I'm not going to act white or get along just to prove that I deserve to be here. I deserve to be here because I'm here and now you'll deal with me, with my culture, with my food preference, my music preferences, all that. You have to deal with that because I'm here and I'm hustling or I borrow or pay this money like everybody else did. I'm not trying to be Jackie Robinson anymore.'"

So instead of lamenting separate proms and separate graduations in the 1990s, Farrell said, we should be trying to understand why this has occurred. It has occurred because this generation has tired of accommodating and has tired of "not simply being respected in their schools." And so the dual and dueling events become symbolic "beachheads," Farrell said. "It's like when you're at war, people say you took the hill, Iwo Jima, a flag is up. We haven't captured the island yet, just taken the hill."

I knew he was right. I knew it from the university where I taught, where black students sat separately from whites in the dining hall and had a variety of separate social activities, and I knew it from the overwhelmingly white composition of the faculty, and I knew it from a black student I had had the previous autumn, a student of enormous talent named Sean Chambers, who started off well enough but fell further and further behind in meeting deadlines. I kept after him, called him repeatedly, asked him to come and see me. He seemed genuinely taken aback, even alarmed, by my persistence. He wasn't used to it, he said, not from a white teacher. He was testing me, to confirm yet again what past experience had shown him to be true: that he was not expected to succeed, and because of that I, as his teacher, would either forget about him or would allow him some sort of special dispensation. To his surprise (exasperation, really), he found out he was wrong. Not only would there be no special dispensation, I told him, but I was going to keep pushing him. "Harder, actually," I said, "because you have the talent to be a really fine writer." My faith in him, my belief in his ability, he said, unhinged him, made him nervous. I wanted to quote Frederick Douglass to him, that line about "If nothing is expected of a man, he finds that expectation hard to contradict," but I didn't. I simply said that he wasn't the first, and he wouldn't be the last, person to have, for his own reasons, a fear of success, and that our time was up and that he'd better go back to work. When he graduated, he sent me a note, thanking me. While the note, on one level, was personally gratifying and reminded me why teaching was worthwhile, it was the experience of having Sean as a student that had given me a clearer understanding of the many obstacles, real or imagined, that black students face. Sean could have gone to Howard, but he chose the University of Virginia. He knew it wasn't going to be easy—that a lot of garbage would come his way—and it wasn't. But he got what he came for, and moved on.

Sean Chambers was a good example of something else Shelby Steele was talking about: black students coming into predominantly white institutions and being given the distinct impression that they didn't belong there, that since affirmative action was their key to the kingdom they would always be perceived as inferior subjects. This was at the root of Steele's argument that affirmative action had not been a good vehicle, that its implied inferiority enabled blacks to hold on to race and not be accountable for their own success or failure, and that it gave whites a powerful tool with which to wield their perpetual argument of *We're doing you a favor by allowing you to be here.* When I mentioned Shelby Steele, who had given a talk in Milwaukee a few months earlier, to Walter Farrell, he said that some of what Steele said made sense, but that he minimized "the impact of institutionalized racial discrimination" and that what he had to say was "comforting to white folks." And even though the white folks he was referring to were conservatives for the most part, he wanted it understood that he much preferred them and knowing where they stood to white liberals who joined the NAACP.

WHITE FOLKS. WHITE FOLKS in all-black neighborhoods and the reason blacks figured they were there. That was one of many things Jerrel Jones wanted to instruct me about as we drove around that day. "When a white person comes into a black person's house, it's either to collect a bill or serve notice." That's why there was trouble with the census, he said, referring to the recent report that the 1990 census had been undercounted, primarily in urban areas, but that nothing was likely to be done about it. While I had gotten used to Jones's exaggerating to make a point, I had not quite adjusted to the very contradiction he seemed to represent: a black millionaire who had not turned his back on the very considerable problems that surrounded him every day he came to work. When I told him about the contents of the Alexanders' refrigerator and that they were living meal to meal, he said they were among the lucky ones, they were at least working, and that the people McGee was talking about were eating "oatmeal in the morning, cornmeal in the afternoon, and a mission meal at night," people who "never work," "grown men who have never held a job, period."

Jones was doing the driving. That was the one string he had attached to his offer of taking me around. Said it would make him feel more comfortable and it would allow me to concentrate better.

"This is the blood bank," he said. We were at the corner of Twenty-second and North; three other blood plasma centers were a minute away. Men were lined up, dozens of them, to give blood in exchange for ten dollars. They were supposed to do it only twice a week, but nobody enforced the rule; consequently, they would go from place to place, becoming more and more dizzy, taking their earnings and often disappearing into stores for beer and other spirits.

"You know what they use the blood for?" Jones asked.

I said that I didn't.

"Cosmetics."

He said that if we pulled up and attempted to talk to any of them, they would act differently than they would if Jones were not with me.

Why was that? I asked.

"Because white people represent authority to black people. You've got to remember that everybody in authority that black people meet is white."

There he was again, generalizing. Since we had been talking about Howard Fuller just the day before, about his getting the superintendent's job and Jones's feeling, disgust really, that whenever the city "needs a nigger for something, they choose Howie," that it would have been better just to leave him in place at Health and Human Services and find somebody else, it was disappointing to see him slip back into sweeping statements. He and Fuller had gone to North Division together and Jones's contempt for Fuller was clear: even then, he had been a Booster Boy, a goody two-shoes who mostly hung out with white girls, and Jones didn't trust him.

Jones kept on, wanting me to understand that a black person's language with a white person would be different from his language to another black. "Take the word 'motherfucker,'" he said. "You have to listen to the expression in his voice. I can pull up to this guy here, right now, and I'll tell him, 'You know, you're a funky motherfucker,' and he'll say, 'Thank you, brother.' But if he said to you, 'You're a motherfucker,' that means you're full of shit. It's very subtle."

But more than shades of language, more than acting differently, more than assumptions about why a white person would show up at a black person's door, Jones wanted to make sure that I was *seeing* who was in front of me, that I wasn't looking past and through these people. Ralph Ellison had taken this notion of blacks as invisible to white eyes and transformed it into an enduring crucible, but as far as Jones was concerned that was a book that came out forty years earlier and the same stuff kept happening anyway.

We drove on, down Walnut Street, into what was once called Bronzeville, in the 1940s, where the sounds of Count Basie and Duke Ellington and Cab Calloway and "Gator Mouth" Moore and Earl "Fatha" Hines could be heard long into the night by both blacks and whites, at places like Art's and the Moon Glow and the Flame and the Cleff Club. We drove past the sixteen-room house where Jones had grown up, where the trees "used to meet in the middle of the street," an area that he found both difficult to describe and difficult to talk about; past the Black Holocaust Museum; past so many places that no longer matched his sweet memories of them. His father had had one of the first black-owned movie theaters in Milwaukee, the Century, and he recalled that they, father and son, had been the first blacks in the projection union ("I showed *The Ten Command-ments* so many times, I could repeat that goddamned thing verbatim"), and that his father also owned a grocery store. And then, as quickly as we seemed to descend into the past we came out of it, back into the present, passing all the makeshift stalls where bartering had become the new economy, where everything seemed loose and fluid and tentative, noth-ing permanent, where the blood bank was still doing a booming business.

"You know," Jones said after we'd bought some food at Speed Queen and brought it back to his office, "the only thing that we're equal about is the amount of time we get in a day. And for a long time, that one equal thing was taken away by white folk, so if we had twenty-four hours in a day, eighteen of mine belonged to you."

He said all this, as he said most things, with panache and without bit-terness. The issue of slavery, of being owned, would always be there, in some form or another, and would always distinguish the relationship between blacks and whites, would always mark it apart from that between whites and Asians, or whites and Hispanics, or between whites and any ethnic group that had emigrated to America and faced adversity. That is not to downplay or minimize the considerable animosity and prejudice those groups encoun-tered, but adversity and being owned are not the same thing.

Jones had told me that we needed to be back by three, but he hadn't told me why. Until now. There was this white woman, an artist, whom Jones and his wife had known for about twenty-five years and who had cancer and was taking morphine and simply couldn't get around. Jones had known her mother and father, and all three of them, when Jones first met them, "couldn't stand black people." But their relationship evolved, and the woman's parents died, and now Jones and his wife represented "the only family she's got left," and they took care of her—taking her to the hospi-tal, shopping for her, cooking for her, basically making sure that all her needs were met. "This woman could never, even in her wildest dreams, ever have thought that one day black people would have to take care of her. . . . She is going to die in the next couple of months. We've got to bury her. She's left everything she has to us, you know, every kind of thing. It's crazy, but it teaches you a very valuable lesson. You never know who it is you're going to have to depend on in the long run. You've got to watch how you treat people and what you say to people. . . . I mean, you might be the person that ends up saving my life."

E I G H T

Sunday was Unity Day in Milwaukee and everyone was being urged to attend, to come out to the Marcus Amphitheatre and UNITE FOR OUR FUTURE, to SHOW YOU BELIEVE IN MILWAUKEE. The idea had come about five months before, in early January. Robert Odom, the head of the Social Development Commission, was sitting in his room at the Astor Hotel, sitting and staring at the faces of nearly all the 165 people who had been murdered in Milwaukee in 1990. "And I thought about how much pain that must represent," Odom was telling the four thousand people in attendance (not the twenty-five thousand he had hoped for), "because I couldn't even look at all the faces before I was overwhelmed with it and I thought about the families who lost someone, but I also thought about the families who had someone commit the crime. . . .

"What I wanted to do is have Milwaukee take a time-out, have Milwaukee pause for a minute and give us a time for reflection, a time for healing, a time for calm, a time for oneness, a time for love, a time for understanding, a time for compassion, a time for caring."

Hearing him say that transported me back to the sixties, to the Byrds singing "Turn, Turn, Turn," and had me wondering if Tom Donegan was in the crowd somewhere, lost in thought. But it wasn't the sixties and Odom said that a lot of people had expressed the concern that it was just going to be "a black event" or "a religious event" or that it was just going to be "a feel-good event," and that he had said, "If all of us here today feel good at the same time, if nothing else was accomplished, it was worth doing."

But that still wasn't a sufficient answer for his skeptics. They wanted to know what the *outcome* would be. "Well, I'll tell you this," he said. "In the past month, more people have been talking about unity than ever before. Whether pro or con, they still have been talking about unity. 'Well,' folks said, 'that's not good enough.' They said, 'Still, what is going to be the outcome?' And I said, 'You know, it reminds me of when I was teaching my daughter how to ride a bike, and we know how that is. You run up and down the block and you're behind the bike and it's flipping from one side and it's flipping from another and you figure they're never going to get it and then within a split second they're out of your hands and off they go riding down the block. Once that happens that child can ride a bike the rest of their life.' Well, today is Unity Day. We are now just learning how to ride a bike. We will know unity tomorrow, the next day, and from then on. So this is what the outcome is going to be."

JERREL JONES HAD TOLD me that going to this event wasn't even worth my time (even though he had given money as a sponsor) and Louise Kidd had scorned it as just a day, an event, and that the real work had to be done *every* day, on blocks and in neighborhoods and businesses all around the city. I could see what they were saying—it was easy to be cynical about things like this and hard to grasp what *exactly* was going to be accomplished—and I could see why a Tom Donegan was in a perpetual state of disbelief, with things like Unity Day representing, on one level, such endless déjà vu. But I had come anyway, and since I had, I wanted to find out why someone else had. So I found myself talking to a young black man named Steve Tipton, who was twenty-two and went to college and worked for Time Insurance and who said, against the pealing sound of "Amazing Grace" in the background, that in his opinion the problem with race relations, both in Milwaukee and in the country, all boiled down to power, about blacks feeling they deserved to be put in positions of authority and whites saying we'll give it to you when we get ready or we'll give you the pieces that we want you to have. That was where things "collide," he said. Even trying to further your education was a struggle, he said. Financial aid and scholarships were hard to come by, he said, and "when a person is frustrated they turn to different means. Some may even turn to violence or taking what they want without working for it."

"Do you have friends in that situation?"

"I know some that are in that situation. Yes, I do." Actually, he knew several. "They're all just frustrated, man. Frustrated because if white folks can get it, you know, either way I can get it, I'm going to get it."

He had never had any trouble with the law, his parents were still together, they were both employed, and, frankly, he had come to Unity Day out of a hope that it would help eliminate the hypocrisy, prejudice, and racism that still existed, that it would bring about change.

What about Michael McGee? Did he think that he was helping to bring about change?

"I feel he's doing a good job in his own way. It seems like that's the only way the white man will listen—by threatening violence."

He was less equivocal about Howard Fuller. "He's been criticized, but unless you are in his shoes you really don't know nothing about it." As far as Steve Tipton was concerned, Fuller deserved to be accorded power and everybody's respect.

"Do you know a lot of people who came here today?"

No, he did not. He was disappointed that more people hadn't come, that "this is just a fraction, not even a fragment of Milwaukee," but he also said that the people who had come were "saying something" by their presence. He liked the fact that a black man (Odom) had engineered this, but he was realistic enough to know that even if a white person had, "most people don't understand the real seriousness of the problem because they've never been poor or broke or deprived of certain things."

LATER THAT DAY, AS I was eating dinner in a friend's backyard near the University of Wisconsin, I heard a sound coming from the garage. My friend and his family acted as if there were nothing unusual about that, and kept right on eating, talking about how they had been sixties liberals but that the experience of living in an integrated neighborhood in Seattle and having been robbed a few times had changed their views somewhat. They weren't happy about it, they said, but there it was.

So what about the clatter in the garage?

Oh, that. Somebody was back there—someone they knew but didn't know—gathering up empty aluminum cans; aluminum brought fifty cents a pound, they informed me. When they first moved in, it was alarming to go out to the garage and find a black stranger there. But a neighbor told them that it had been going on for quite a while, that everyone had gotten used to it more or less, that it was easier just to let them have their way with the cans than to report it, that "these people" were pretty desperate. After all, the neighbor reminded them, "they're not like us, you know. They're not like us."

NINE

Milwaukee is probably no different from any other city when it comes to fierce civic pride and concern about its image, but the city fathers couldn't help feeling that "A Great Place on a Great Lake" was unfairly singled out and besmirched when *Newsweek* (appearing the day after Unity Day) listed it as first among America's new murder capitals—among cities with populations under one million—citing a 126 percent increase in homicides from 1985 through 1990. After all, it had been only six months since the story on *60 Minutes* and three since the front-page piece in the *New York Times* (about Milwaukee booming but leaving its blacks behind), and then of course there were all the appearances Michael McGee continued to make, often with whistle and slingshot in hand, and now this.

The mayor's office told the *Milwaukee Journal* that "we don't deserve this kind of label. And if they used the kind of statistics that the FBI, the Justice Department, and everybody else uses [statistics that compare homicide rates on a per capita basis], we wouldn't even be on that page." Rhetoric and political posturing aside, though, the problem was there, and they were well aware of it (even if they weren't keen that the rest of the country should be). Continuing to rationalize that the city did not have the same magnitude of problems as a Chicago, Los Angeles, or New York was not only disingenuous, it wasn't going to solve anything. Of the 165 murders committed in Milwaukee in 1990, 62 of the accused defendants were children. On the same day that *Newsweek* came out with its story, the Children's Defense Fund released a study showing that in 1989 roughly one of every five American children was living in poverty (2.2 million more than a decade earlier); another study showed that more than two of every five black children were. Overall, 31 percent of blacks in America were living in poverty, while in Milwaukee 42 percent were. In fact, of the one hundred largest metropolitan areas in 1990, Milwaukee was the most segregated by income, rising from ninth in 1970 to fourth in 1980 to first. Given all this, quibbling about how numbers were compiled seemed not only petty but beside the point, dangerously so.

Just as the ongoing quibbling over the proposed 1991 Civil Rights Act threatened to keep in place some rulings of two years earlier—rulings that made it more difficult for victims of job discrimination to sue and collect damages. According to the *New Yorker,* the bill was "only in part about civil rights. It is also about the searing racial tensions that have developed in this country, making race our most divisive and explosive domestic issue."

The phrase "have developed" gave me pause. From what I could tell, the racial tensions had always been there, had never gone away. They might at times have appeared to be dormant, to have gone into remission, but they had never been resolved. Reagan and Bush not only had not helped, they had aggravated the situation; when they weren't assuming a stance of patrician indifference, they were aggressively moving us backward— through changes of law, cutting of programs, and divisive language—further polarizing us as a society. No wonder somebody like Walter Farrell was wary of any white person who boasted of being a member of the NAACP; George Bush never tired of reminding everyone that he contributed to the United Negro College Fund, yet, the *New Yorker* said, he was "not above exploiting racial tensions for his own political advancement." As "shameful" as his performance was on this particular bill, though, he had more surprises in store.

SINCE COMING TO MILWAUKEE, I had been living at a small hotel on the East Side that catered more to permanent residents than to overnight guests. From the moment I took a room there, I was intrigued by the woman who managed the place, a Milwaukee native named Bert Sweet, who had a brash, plainspoken manner and whom you clearly didn't want to get on the wrong side of. The people who lived at the Plaza were an eclectic group: actors with the Milwaukee Repertory Company, cops, confirmed bachelors (who looked to Bert for mothering and advice), young people who saw it as a college dorm, men who (like Howard Fuller at one time) sought refuge as they underwent the process of divorce.

One day, not long after I arrived, Bert agreed to sit down with me in her little apartment on the second floor. She was born in 1938 and had grown up at the corner of Sixth and Juneau, right downtown, had lived there for the first fifteen years of her life. There were a lot of blacks living in her neighborhood and a lot of bars, and her parents had always warned her and her siblings that "if you served blacks liquor, they turned into something else." At the age of eight, she witnessed a black man cutting another black man's throat "from ear to ear," an incident, her parents told her, she was not to discuss with anyone. When the Hillside Terrace housing project was built a few blocks from her home, she recalled that it was "just beautiful" and "spiffy," but in no time at all it was "the pits. There wasn't any grass. What was painted nice and white and spiffy was now gross-looking." She remembered that people's trash never made it to the trash can ("They just pitched it, and where it landed is where it stayed"), and that black children her age "thought the fact their mother was being beat up—whupped—was a way of life." But she also remembered that she had forged a strong friendship with a black girl named Carolyn and that another black girl had given her some canny advice on how to clean windows—wash them with vinegar, warm water, and newspapers—that she used to this day.

To the extent that she was able, she had not succumbed to her parents' prejudice, but it was not easy. By the time she was in eighth grade, they made clear their preference that she not associate with black children, and by high school she and her father had a confrontation. A former Milwaukee policeman, he had begun working for Allis-Chalmers and would constantly come home complaining about how lazy and unproductive the blacks he worked with were, and how they would always "reek up" the bus on the way to work, especially in summer. Given his opinions on this subject—opinions he kept "pounding" into Bert and her siblings—he was not the best person to approach about Lincoln and slavery, which was what Bert did one evening at the kitchen table. As far as he was concerned, Lincoln shouldn't have freed the slaves, but when he did, they should have immediately been sent back to Africa. As far as Bert was concerned, there shouldn't have been slavery in the first place. "I told him that this was wrong; that man could not own other men, women, or children . . . that someday I felt God was going to punish us for having treated the black people the way we've treated them." Bert's father just glared at her, told her she didn't know what she was talking about, and became "so angry he wanted to reach across the table and backhand me."

As time went on, though, Bert's point of view started to change—
not about slavery, but about blacks; not all blacks, but those without education or steady jobs, who, she noticed as the sixties began, became more
and more aggressive, propositioning white women such as herself right out
in broad daylight, and she didn't like it one bit. "It was out of line," she
said, "it was just way out of line"—a mild way of echoing what had always
been understood, especially in the South, to be a boundary not to be
crossed; and when it was, when a black man was found to have been with
a white woman, or even to have said something to her that might be con-
strued as suggestive, it often resulted in a lynching or castration.

In her business, Bert said, "I run into black people all the time—some
good, some horrible, some that have threatened me, and some that milked
me out of lots and lots of money, but again, it's the individual, it's not because of his skin color, and yet when you read in the papers they are thirty
percent of the population [in Milwaukee] and ninety percent of the crime,
what are you going to think? . . . A lot of times when you read the Monday
paper about how many people were killed over the weekend, they were
shot or they were murdered or stabbed or whatever the circumstance is,
you'll hear people say, 'Well, they killed three more,' or, 'They killed five
more,' but they can't kill them off as quick as they produce.

"How come those people don't have morals?" she wanted to know,
becoming visibly upset. "How come they think it's okay to just have sex to
have sex? Why is that okay?" She had been raised a Lutheran, considered
herself a devout Christian, and this apparently was the issue that troubled
her the most. She wanted to know why the Baptist Church wasn't teaching abstinence and celibacy. "There's a time and a place for these things
and being twelve or thirteen or fifteen or seventeen is not the time to be
practicing and having babies."

I could have stopped her and pointed out that while a great deal of
criticism had been leveled by blacks themselves at the church for not doing
more to help parent children, she didn't know for a fact that the Baptist
Church wasn't teaching these things—and that even if it was, that was no
guarantee that teenage pregnancies would cease immediately. I also could
have stopped her and pointed out that the percentage of whites, ages fifteen to nineteen, who had babies was nearly the same as that of blacks. But
I didn't. These were her perceptions, and statistics weren't about to deter
her. Her furor over so many kids being unmarried and having babies

quickly and naturally took her to the subject of welfare (three-fifths of all mothers under thirty on welfare had their first child as a teenager), to her belief that it had become a way of life and that everyone—from the government to the recipients themselves—was to blame for a system that allowed this kind of dependency. Bert Sweet had had a job from the time she was fifteen, and the way she saw it, nothing, *nothing*, could substitute for having one, regardless of what it paid.

Did she think there was a lot of job discrimination against blacks?

No, she really didn't. Her experience had been that "they want top dollar for the least amount of work" and that "if you don't stay there and watch them, you'll find them sitting down." Black housekeepers, she said, will go in a room and sit down and turn on the television; "an hour later, they run the vacuum cleaner and say they've cleaned the room. Well, there's more to cleaning a room than running a vacuum cleaner and making the bed. . . . Sure the pay is only five dollars an hour . . . but if all I could get was a five-dollar-an-hour job, I would give them five dollars' worth of work."

Bert's youngest daughter had taken the civil service exam in order to get a job at the post office. She scored a ninety-eight, but some blacks who had scored in the seventies got hired and she didn't. Eventually she was hired and soon became a supervisor. But she quickly became resentful that blacks would come in and do one-third of the work she did, but earn more money (ninety cents more an hour) because they had been there longer.

Having said all this, she also wanted me to know that there was a black couple from Sherman Park she socialized with. The man was a police officer and the woman a schoolteacher and in fact she was going to their house in a few days for a cookout. "Are they my friends or are they my acquaintances?" she suddenly asked herself with no prompting from me. "I guess I would have to say they're my acquaintances because my friends I would go to if I was in trouble."

At that moment she wasn't in any particular trouble, but she was convinced Milwaukee was. Michael McGee, for instance. "He's going to get his people in a lot of trouble, he's just overstepping his bounds." And when you added to it the "smash and grabs" and the carjackings and the drive-by shootings, what you had was a situation where "there's no respect, no respect for themselves, no respect for other human life.

"What is going on?" she asked, her voice rising. "Where does it all end? One black lady told me, 'You know, one of the things with black people is that they never had anything, so when they get something, they want more of it.' And I said, 'Well, why is it that they never had anything?' You know, my parents were not rich people, they were poor people, and they treasured the material things they had, and they took good care of them, but the black people don't even take care of the things that they've got. They don't take care of one another in their little family groups. She said, 'Well, they're not educated.' I said, 'Why aren't they educated? The opportunities have been here for fifty years,' and I'm saying fifty years because I've been here fifty years and I know they had the same opportunity when they sat across from me in school. . . . They learned about hygiene the way I did, they learned about morals the way I did, they learned all of the component things that make us the people we grow up to be. It didn't absorb into them, why didn't it absorb? Is it because their mother or father didn't care, didn't say, 'Yes, that's the way it's done,' 'Yes, that's how we do it'? . . . Somebody out there has got to care, somebody out there has got to have some compassion, and it's got to start at home, it's got to start in each and every home."

"But do you honestly believe, Bert," I said, "that black parents, whether they're together or whether it's a split family, don't care about their kids?"

"I'm sure that they care about them, but in a different way than we know about caring for ours."

Like those of Jerrel Jones, Bert Sweet's sweeping generalizations didn't hold up to scrutiny—including her own. Some of them had to do with a young black man who was serious about her niece—a relationship that Bert's brother and his wife were distraught about. Her niece had first met him in high school, out in the suburbs where they both lived, and they had been living together the past three years. "Her parents have told her that they want absolutely nothing to do with him, he's not welcome in their home, and the reasons that they give her . . . is that children born of mixed marriages always end up in a dither, not knowing which side of the fence they belong on . . . and that women who marry these men always end up in agony because they're not stable marriages, they're marriages born more out of lust than love, and just a hundred reasons."

Bert didn't necessarily see it that way. For one thing, she was open-minded enough to go out with them together, to form her own opinion. She liked that he had gone to college, that he had a full-time job, that he was in the Air Force reserves, and most important, that he was so attentive and polite, not just to Bert's niece, but to Bert herself. By the end of a long evening of bowling, an evening her brother didn't know about, Bert decided he was a "perfect gentleman" and that the couple loved each other very much.

"I just don't think that any of us are in a position to dispute who loves who," she said. "Am I so good that I can pass judgment on somebody's color? I judge each individual on their merits, not on the color of their skin. I'm not God. I don't even have a whole lot of godly ways. . . . We live our life for our children, but we cannot live our children's lives for them."

TEN

I slowly made my way back to my room, thinking all the while that Bert Sweet was probably no different from a lot of people. She had started off innocently enough, color-blind and open to the world. She had fought off, as best she could, perhaps better than most, the prejudice of her parents, but had gained her own along the way. Her point of view was conflicted. Despite what she said about not having a lot of godly ways, she emphatically considered herself a highly moral person and the framework for that morality was the ethic of hard work—an ethic that the majority of blacks, in her experience, fell far short of. So when she pointed out her exceptions, her niece's boyfriend and the couple from Sherman Park, who possessed both education and jobs, she was talking about class just as much as she was talking about race, two issues that often are wrongly thrown together and must be distinguished: poor people, after all, are not *always* interchangeable with black people. Nonetheless, by her calculation, she had been burned far more than she had been rewarded. While that was both her experience and her perception, she still remained open—open to the possibility, the hope, that her niece and her boyfriend could forge a bridge that her brother would never be able to cross.

That night, I went to see Spike Lee's new movie, *Jungle Fever*, whose subject, coincidentally, was the relationship between a married black man (an architect who had grown up in Harlem) and a single white woman (a temp from an Italian working-class family in Bensonhurst) who were working in the same office. The movie opened with a still photograph of Yusuf Hawkins, the black teenager who had been killed in Bensonhurst in the summer of 1989, a cautionary reminder that the reason Hawkins was killed was not so much that he had ventured into a white neighborhood (though that was certainly of concern), but that he was thought (mistakenly, it turned out) to be there to visit a young woman who had gained a reputation for dating blacks and Hispanics. Unlike his previous movie, *Do the Right Thing*, which dealt almost exclusively with race, this one dealt with race, class, sex, and drugs. Even though there were three times as many interracial married couples in 1990 as there were in 1970, it was still a hot-button issue for many people, including so-called liberals. "People who are not racist and are liberals still draw the line at couples," Renee Brokaw, a white photojournalist married to a former pro basketball player, told *Newsweek.* "Integration for them means that they go to school together, but God forbid your son and daughter" should date a black person.

A few days before the movie opened, an incident occurred on Long Island, an incident in which a young black man, a high school football star, was viciously beaten with a baseball bat by a group of white youths for being with a white girl (who was asked, "Are you with the nigger?" not long before the attack began). Residents expressed shock that such a thing could happen. They insisted that no racial tension existed in their town, and they resented that the Reverend Al Sharpton was organizing a march to protest what occurred, recalling all too well that the reverend's marches through Howard Beach and Bensonhurst (where baseball bats had also been the weapons of choice) had incited ugly confrontations with angry groups of whites.

What distinguished the incident on Long Island from those of Howard Beach and Bensonhurst, though, was not only the outpouring of sympathy, from both whites and blacks, for the victim, but a concerted effort to raise money on his behalf. There was also a strong denunciation of the attackers (though not without the caveat that all except one were from elsewhere—elsewhere being a few miles away and the one being the principal attacker).

A FEW DAYS AFTER I saw *Jungle Fever,* I was sitting in the office of a man who was willing to discuss anything with me—except his own interracial marriage. "I don't need to see the movie," Bill Lawrence, executive director of the Private Industry Council (PIC), told me. "I've lived it." He had gone to college at Central State University, a predominantly black school, then gone on to Ohio State for graduate work. It was there that he wound up "doing a lot of research" on the subject, "looking at this country's reaction" to interracial couples. The whole endeavor consumed hours and hours of his time—too many, he said now. He had made a choice, and whatever had transpired from that time until this—a period of time far longer than the movie's brief interlude—he was determined not to talk about. Naturally, that piqued my interest, but he was so resolute about his silence on the subject that we moved on to other things.

Lawrence was in his early forties and had come to Milwaukee from Boston, where he had been an instrumental figure in the Boston Compact, a job-training program, primarily for at-risk students, that involved the joint efforts of public schools, businesses, universities, foundations, and the Private Industry Council. For the way it successfully coordinated these efforts, the Compact had become a national model, and Lawrence was hoping to replicate its success in Milwaukee.

So far, by most accounts, he had. In only two years he had not only elevated the profile of the PIC within the community and made it autonomous, but he had also waged a successful political battle against Michael McGee (who wanted to control it) in the process. Since the PIC was dealing with a budget of more than ten million dollars (funding came mainly from the federal Job Training Partnership Act), where and how that money was spent was of considerable interest to McGee. In that organizations like the PIC have traditionally distributed this money to community agencies (which have not always made the best, or sometimes even legal, use of the funds), Lawrence was "criticized" in some quarters for not sticking to standard operating procedure, for not adhering to the cardinal rule of politics: Reward your friends with plenty of pork.

As he sat in his office in Schlitz Park (in what used to be the brewery of that name), impeccably dressed and hyperactive, fingering any one of a number of toys and a bottle of aspirin on his desk, a photograph of him shaking Prince Charles's hand in the background, he said that he had known people like Michael McGee all his life, that he understood what drove him. McGee reminded him of Kafka, he said. "So when Michael is going along and thinking about what to do and you can't read it, it is because you have nothing that approaches a frame of reference. You don't see the world the way he sees it. And basically a logical approach—which is what I say, you find jobs for people, you train them—Michael doesn't see that as working. And he basically doesn't believe in the goodness of society to help black people, so our rules and the way that we look at the universe are just skewed for him."

"What would satisfy him?"

"Nothing. It is not an issue of satisfying him."

Contrary to what the city was saying—publicly—about not doing anything to directly respond to McGee's threats, that whatever efforts they were making to improve conditions in the inner city were efforts that were going to be made anyway, Lawrence said that was only partly true. He mentioned the Metcalfe Park project, a plan to target one area of the city in an effort to improve services and reduce crime, as being "a response to Mike." As was the Inner City Task Force, set up by the Greater Milwaukee Committee. "No one wants to say that Mike created those things, but in fact he has. Is he going to say that? No, because in fact it would defeat the purpose. Can you get him back in the fold? No. Will he ever become the Michael of old showing up at meetings? No, because when he did that, he didn't feel things happened. And in that way he is right. Has life in his district changed over the past eight years? Yes, it has gotten worse. And he was inside the system. Now he is outside the system and he has nothing to lose, by his own statement, so he advocates violence. It is in sort of that strange way, like 'I am going to beat you up if you do that one more time, one more time, one more time.'"

The phone rang and Lawrence took the call. It was David Webster, director of youth issues, from the mayor's office. As Lawrence gave him the latest figures on how many young people had been placed in summer employment through Step-Up (the centerpiece of the many things the agency did), I worried that Lawrence was right: that McGee would never be satisfied, that he would not acknowledge the city's efforts because it would "defeat the purpose." In other words, it was one thing for a Jerrel Jones or a Walter Farrell to maintain, as they had, that the city was responding—however small or inadequate they might judge that response to be—but quite another for McGee to say it. If McGee could have his demands satisfied, he couldn't very well continue to go around saying "They don't mind because we don't matter." It was one thing to worry, with reason, that if something could be judged successful—be it tangible responses to McGee's demands or a noticeable increase in test scores at an inner-city school—much less attention would subsequently be paid; it was quite another to realize that success or improvement, however dramatic or incremental it was, was not likely to count very much in the end to the person pushing for whatever it was the person was pushing for. Because when people who genuinely do care about change become convinced that it is more about ego and notoriety than anything else, they are often inclined to get fed up and redirect their energies to other matters, matters with some chance of resolution.

"From my perspective, one of the most damaging things Michael has said," Lawrence continued, "was on the Phil Donahue show. When they asked him what would you tell young black people about going to school and studying and all of that stuff, he said, 'I'd tell them that it didn't matter.' If he could change that message to 'Go to school and study hard and see what happens,' I think that would be important for the city."

Lawrence had been involved in education for many years, both as a teacher and an administrator, and was on the advisory committee for the two African-American immersion schools that were scheduled to open in the fall. Like Howard Fuller, he was committed to the notion that while an education may not guarantee you anything, not having one would make it extremely difficult, especially if you were black, to escape a life of poverty, to become part of the mainstream. The schools had initially been conceived as being just for black males with black male teachers. But it was unconstitutional (the committee learned early on) for a public school to be set up that way. Even if it hadn't been, there was such a shortage of black male teachers that other schools in the system would not want to lose them—"not to the immersion school or to the Tropic of Cancer or to the Bermuda Triangle," Lawrence said. So the school (only the elementary school, Victor Berger, would be launched in September; the middle school would begin the following fall) would be equally divided between males and females. Two-thirds of the teachers would be white; all but one of the students would be black (which was the composition of the school anyway). So what, it seemed fair to ask, was truly going to be "new"—and why wasn't the population at large made aware of these changes from the original concept?

It was partly to save face, Lawrence said, an unwillingness on the part of "the segregationists"—those who were convinced that certain "rites of passage" were unique to black males and could not be administered by white teachers in the presence of white kids—to admit that the original concept had died. That was less important to Lawrence than the requirement that students wear uniforms and the stress on discipline and the possibility of restaffing the building—the chance to start with a clean slate, to rid the school of people (including blacks) who had their own racial attitudes about the ability of black kids to learn, who didn't necessarily "share the mission": a school that would infuse Afrocentrism into the curriculum. But in order to start over, as Lawrence well knew, you had to deal with the teachers union, and dealing with the teachers union was hardly ever easy, a prospect most administrators would go miles out of their way to avoid.

MY TIME WAS UP. He had agreed to forty-five minutes and I'd been there more than an hour. Even though his organization, since Lawrence had taken over, had placed more kids in jobs every year, demand still exceeded supply—at least in the city. The suburbs had lots of positions. But the kids who lived out there didn't seem to want the low wages that came with them—and the kids who would take them, Lawrence's kids, had no easy way of getting there and back. It was yet another barrier, and it prompted him to tell me what he had been telling a group of college kids the day before, how he had never gotten over the evilness of Robert Moses, as portrayed in Robert Caro's *The Power Broker*.

"When he built the Long Island parks, there were crossways for commercial traffic. He realized that blacks and poor people did not get to those places in cars, but in fact came in buses. When he did the overpasses for the Long Island roads, he had them measure the height of a bus and make all the overpasses two inches shorter than the buses could go.

"It is just amazing to me," Lawrence said, shaking his head, "that a man would take the time to do that, to investigate, study, and execute a plan that was designed to keep poor people from experiencing the beaches and parks."

In telling this story of calculated, covert racism, Bill Lawrence displayed just as much anger, in his own cool, low-key way, as Michael McGee possessed and openly vented any chance he got. McGee could deride Bill Lawrence and Howard Fuller all he wanted, insisting that they were "house niggers" and lackeys for the white establishment. But that image of Robert Moses—that insidious fact of our history that wasn't likely to be taught in schools—had cut at Lawrence and affected him more than anything McGee could ever say.

E L E V E N

It was early on a Wednesday morning, and a group of mothers and grandmothers were carefully placing the items into brown paper bags, one for each student graduating that day from Head Start (perhaps the only program from the much-maligned days of the Great Society and the War on Poverty generally agreed to be a success). A toothbrush, a coloring book, a photograph (taken when they enrolled), crayons, all the work they had done throughout the year, including, most recently, a Father's Day card with a poem about the importance of fathers pasted inside—one by one these pieces, along with a progress report, went into each "going away" bag, a passport to the next level. But the conversation among these proud parents and grandparents at Victor Berger that sweltering June day was not about the ceremony soon to begin, or about the Afrocentric curriculum soon to be implemented, or even anything specific about the children themselves. No, the conversation that morning had to do with an incident that had taken place in the neighborhood the night before, the shooting of a fifteen-year-old boy whom most of them knew. George Edward Brown could easily have been their child. The shooting had occurred on North First Street, near Keefe, an area that had been infested by the Vice Lords, a neighborhood that was considered one of the most dangerous in the state of Wisconsin. The only thing I could ascertain was that the youth had been shot by a policeman and that there was some question whether he had a rifle or was unarmed.

Someone began to play the piano, and everybody broke into song. As the words to "I Am Special" reverberated off the classroom walls and out the windows, they commingled, ever so slightly, with a sound in the distance I had first heard on Maron and Georgette Alexander's front porch. I still had no way of knowing if the sound was gunfire or backfire—I had not yet acquired enough expertise in these matters—but perhaps some of these children had, because one or two of them flinched for a second. As each name was called, as each student of the Head Start class of 1991 came forward out of the cloakroom, nervous, excited, and beaming, blue mortarboard on head, to receive a certificate and a hug, I couldn't help wondering how long their innocence would last—or to what degree it had been violated already.

AFTER THE CEREMONY I began talking with Bridget Wilder. One of her four children had graduated, and she herself had been in Head Start back in Mississippi. She went on to graduate from high school, complete one year of college, and was now, at twenty-seven, a single mother who would have been a surprise to Bert Sweet—she was on welfare but didn't want to be ("I had to get on it because I couldn't get the baby-sitting help I needed"), and was currently in a job-training and job-search program that had not yielded the job of manager at a McDonald's that she would most like to have, a position she had already held, and performed well, in Mississippi, with the references to prove it. "Just being on welfare," she said, "is gonna pull you down. The more you think about it, all you are doing is hurting yourself." It made her depressed, but she was determined not to show that depression to her children. As for taking a job and getting off welfare, she wanted to make sure of two things: that any job she took would be, more or less, commensurate with the $912 a month and medical benefits she currently received ($708 from welfare and $204 in food stamps) and that the child care she chose would meet her own high standards.

Like Louise Kidd, she did what she could to protect her children, who ranged in age from two to six, from the violence of the streets. She wouldn't let them play outside by themselves, and even in their apartment, she kept them and their beds away from the windows. There wasn't a lot of furniture in the apartment, but what little there was Bridget kept shifting around, constantly, compulsively, one of her ways to stay a step ahead of an enemy who could strike at any time, without warning.

She had heard about the shooting of the night before. Her apartment was located one block east of where the incident occurred, but since so much shooting was going on, she was not surprised—fearful, but not surprised. It was as if she had become numb to these occurrences, had long ago accepted them as part of her daily life. Since most of the shooting took place at night she didn't tell her children about it.

But surely, I asked, they must know what was going on—either from hearing it themselves or from hearing other kids talking about it?

She couldn't say. She didn't bring it up. When she went to sleep at night she always prayed for God to take care of her family and that when the morning came, the children always said their grace and thanked Him for waking them up. When Kennard, her oldest child and only son, would ask why he couldn't play outside, she would say, "It's bad around here," and he would ask why was it bad and she would just keep saying it was or she would take all of them to the park in a different part of town, which she did often, or she would bake him some cookies or play games with him and tell him how much she loved him and how special he was and that she didn't want him or his sisters to get hurt. She found it difficult to be a single mother and felt that Kennard, especially, needed a male influence in his life. Her brother (who, along with two of her sisters, lived in Milwaukee— one of the main reasons she had come north in the first place) had filled that role for a while, but the hours of his job changed and he wasn't able to come around all that much. That was why she was interested—initially —in Kennard's possibly coming to Berger in the fall. She had heard that the immersion program was going to have males available as mentors for the male students and she was all for that. But when she found out that the school was not likely to be mixed in terms of race, she was not as interested. At his current school, there were six white students and twenty-one black students in his kindergarten class; as best she could tell, he wasn't aware of color, and if she could help it, he never would be.

BRIDGET WILDER POSED A problem for somebody like Ken Holt, who greeted me in his office with the world-weary look of someone who had made his case a thousand times and who, regardless of all the studies he had gathered together showing that in general black males did not do well in conventional school settings, seemed to be resigned to the fact that he would have to make it a thousand more. Holt, a middle school principal, was one of "the segregationists" Bill Lawrence referred to, one of the people convinced that black males needed to be taught about their history by black male teachers. Giving them a stronger sense of self-worth would, the thinking went, in turn give them a better chance of succeeding in the world, a world that was tailored, Holt said, to Anglo-American ways.

"I'm saying that I think, more than in any other time in our history, it is evident that what we're doing to kids in school is not working, specifically African-Americans. I mean, any time you have more of us incarcerated than enrolled and attending higher educational institutions, something is wrong. . . . Whatever these young men are not getting in the schools in terms of being educated properly—the culture and the curriculum and seeing themselves in the curriculum—it's going to be played in the streets. The successes you don't experience in school you get by involving yourself in some very serious antisocial activities, and as an African-American I can't simply sit back and say that we continue in the present direction."

He stood up, paced. He was very concerned that he not be misunderstood, not be viewed as advocating a return to the period before the 1954 *Brown* v. *Board of Education* decision, a return to schools that were separated by race and purportedly equal (even though the enforcement of that decision, as history had shown, was another matter altogether). No, he was saying that "we need to try an approach that may require African-American students to be together in a setting to redirect what has happened to them, to guide them, to reconnect them to their culture. From culture comes tradition, come values, expectations, and gives you some sense of who you are. Right now, we've got young people out here who are raising themselves. . . . No one has sat with them and talked about the changes—the physiological, emotional, psychological changes—that are needed to become a man. They're just out here learning from those that are in the streets who clearly were not properly raised either, in most cases, or had some kind of dysfunctional problem, dysfunctional home. We're trying to reattach these young men to the notion that within the African culture there are principles, there are values, there are contributions that made us what we are, and those contributions ought to be recognized and they ought to understand that they have a responsibility . . . to put back into the society what they're taking out of the society."

Everything he was saying was so earnest, so clearly heartfelt, that it seemed almost inappropriate to ask why this process, which sounded both therapeutic and surgical in nature, could not be undertaken in the presence of black females, let alone whites.

He told me about a school in Florida, in Dade County, where two classes were formed, solely made up of boys, nearly all of them black, who were "the terror of the school." The teachers for these "new" classes were both male—one black, one white. After a relatively short period of time, the academic learning time lost to disruptions and suspensions had decreased dramatically, attendance was almost perfect, and test results were "fifteen to twenty points above those young men who remained in the so-called mainstream with girls." Beyond that, he said, "we know that boys tend not to be very open and talk about personal, intimate kinds of things if there is a girl in the classroom. They wouldn't talk about these things to a female teacher. . . . What can female teachers tell young men about male development?"

Even though the plan for the immersion schools was not proceeding as he had originally envisioned, he seemed reconciled to what had been agreed upon. After all, he rationalized, male mentors would come, it was hoped, on a regular basis; the Urban League's Rites of Passage program would be conducted on Saturdays; and everyone who taught at the school—blacks as well as whites—would have to learn about Africa's history and its contribution to civilization, and about the ways in which blacks, males in particular, were said to learn differently from whites. Ken Holt was especially pleased with this requirement. He saw it as being a first step toward "demystifying all of those false perceptions" whites have of blacks, a first step toward "relieving tension because of the element of the unknown." None of the textbooks currently used in MPS said anything about thousands of blacks fighting in the Civil War or about the many things blacks have invented, he claimed. "The only time you see African-Americans is when we were slaves sitting around on the plantation. . . . Right now we're laying this one Western Europe focus on these kids for the most part. And that's not fair, not rational, to continue doing that in a society where it's rapidly becoming a majority of people of color."

Time and again, whether it was a question about the content of textbooks or the holding of political office or how money was going to be spent or the getting of a job, the answer had to do with power and control, of inclusion and exclusion. Equality in law was not equality in fact. Being legally allowed to live or go to school anywhere was not the same as being embraced. Being hired was not the same as being accepted. *With all deliberate speed* was a phrase, rich in ambiguity, that would continue to haunt (as well as give comfort), that went beyond its application to the *Brown* decision and helped racism maintain its elasticity.

Ken Holt knew all about that. He had come to Milwaukee as a teacher, one of only two black teachers at Edison Middle School when the student body was still predominantly white and before busing in Milwaukee had begun to take hold. A local Nazi group marched in front of the building, as did scores of white parents, determined to either keep black kids from coming to Edison or let them know they were not wanted. But Holt was equally determined. He had grown up poor in Arkansas, one of eight children, but his parents had "pounded into my head" the importance of education and the importance of the civil rights struggle, and had helped instill in him a sense of self that he admitted could be perceived as arrogance. When he went north, having given up his dream of going to the Air Force Academy and becoming a pilot ("Where was I going to get a congressional appointment?"), he wasn't about to let them—or himself—down.

He didn't. When he was next seen in Pine Bluff, he was behind the wheel of a gold Buick Skylark Grand Sport and making plans for his parents to have a carport and a cement driveway. Tears welled in his eyes as he talked about his folks, both now dead, and as he talked about the unwillingness of white America to praise blacks too much, lest white America lose its feeling of superiority. It made Holt furious that so many blacks still felt, as Du Bois suggested years before, that they had to deny who and what they were in order to fit into the mainstream. The result of all this "masking" was responsible in part, he was certain, for the high rates of hypertension and heart disease that afflict African-Americans.

To the extent that he could change any of this, could somehow take black youths who were "out here killing each other" and enable them to eventually gain the same sense of self-worth he had and be part of the workforce, this program was, to his way of thinking, a crucial step.

TWELVE

At Miss Katie's Diner, at lunchtime, right off I-94 at the corner of Nineteenth and Clybourn, over and against the clatter of plates and the buzz about how hot it was and how poorly the Brewers were playing, about how Howard Fuller was going to save the public schools and how he was only one person and didn't stand a chance, ReDonna Rogers was intent on making her points. I had met her two hours earlier, at the office of New Concepts, the community organization where she worked, and we had decided to go on to lunch because there was more she wanted to say.

A few months before, she had gone to see *New Jack City* and could hardly believe what had happened at one point during the movie. A character in the film is shot, a teenager, and all around ReDonna young men start shouting, "Homeboy's gonna get up! C'mon, homeboy, get *up!*" The young man on the screen was clearly dead, but the young men in the audience did not see it that way. "Homeboy's gonna get up!" they continued. "He's gonna live. He's gonna live through *me.*"

Not able to follow that logic, ReDonna suddenly found herself shouting, to the young women she had taken with her and to anyone who would listen, "Y'all hear this. Don't y'all get caught up in this."

Day after day she tried to dissuade young people in the inner city from joining gangs, getting pregnant, dealing drugs, and bearing arms. Day after day she tried to encourage them to stay in school, to see a place for themselves in society. It was an uphill battle. She hated that violence and weapons had come to seem *normal,* routine, that so many youths she encountered since the movie had the mind-set of *I can overcome this bullet wound, I can overcome this stabbing,* instead of thinking, *I can get my degree, I can get this job.* At the same time she hated that people assumed all areas of the inner city were dangerous, that all women on welfare wanted to be, that all black youths were pushing drugs and to be feared. Unfortunately, she said, "it's so *natural* to think that a black woman is a sexual thing or is promiscuous. It's so *natural* to think that people who live in a certain area like to be poor, don't want anything, because that's what you've been taught. That's what you have read. That's what you have seen on TV. And so, without much thought, when you start thinking, those are the things that come out."

It was a fair point, and a nice, understated way to describe an ugly process—the process of allowing particular events in a particular place to balloon into overblown assumptions about everyone and everything associated with the place. That's what so many of us do, that's how we keep the fear away, that's how we keep ourselves falsely elevated. It's so natural, ReDonna said, so natural that we (blacks as well as whites) don't even think twice about it, and the perception sticks, unwilling to be dislodged.

The office of New Concepts is located in Hillside, the public housing project where Howard Fuller grew up and where Louise Kidd volunteered. Many of ReDonna's black middle-class friends would ask her why she would work down there, occasionally until late at night. She was safe, she assured them over and over, her car was safe, people knew her there, knew why she was there. She wasn't naïve enough to think that nothing could happen to her, but she wasn't about to let that prevent her from going on about her business. She had already overcome enough crap from white people.

When she was in college, at a small school in Illinois, somebody's cigarette lighter was lost and she was immediately suspected of stealing it. White students complained that when they were in the bathroom with just their bra and panties on they felt uncomfortable when she walked in. And during her classes, "what came out was whites are so refined, blacks are dirty, blacks are drunks, they *like* to live like that."

If you subscribed to this way of thinking, ReDonna said, a way of thinking that stemmed from denial and ignorance and only in being around people you knew, it "takes responsibility off people to build better low-income houses, or to provide more economic opportunities for people who have been shut out of economic opportunities." But here again, race and class often get easily tangled up, with skin color an easy but often misleading corollary to being poor.

ReDonna wound up staying all four years at the school (she had known other blacks who had went there and gone on to be superb teachers) and doing some positive consciousness-raising along the way. Still, in retrospect, she was not sure she shouldn't have gone to an all-black school, where it would have been less of a struggle, where she would have had more contact with other blacks as ambitious as she was.

But even if she had, it wouldn't have shielded her from the racism she encountered in her professional life. When she tried to cash her very first paycheck (from her job as director of special programs for one of the Boys Clubs in Milwaukee), at the bank that had issued the check, "they wanted all kinds of ID." The teller went and "got somebody" and ReDonna told that person, "I don't know what the problem is, give me my money. I work hard, I don't have time to wait here, you go through whatever you're going through, thinking whatever you're thinking, but give me my money. You have all the proof you need to prove that I'm the person that that check is written out to."

She got her money, but that wasn't the end of her problems with banks. In Dallas, where she worked for a year, a white woman thought ReDonna had gotten in front of her in line. All of a sudden, the woman started saying, loud enough for everyone in the bank to hear, "'You people, *you people* are always like this,'" and then she pushed her. ReDonna retaliated, shoving the woman "so hard up against the wall she thought she was going to break into pieces."

But just as ReDonna was constantly being confronted by white stereotypes of blacks, she discovered that she had her own erroneous stereotypes of whites. For some reason she was always certain that *all* whites earned more than thirty thousand dollars a year. In fact, it was only recently that she discovered otherwise. She had gone to a conference where most of the participants were white. "We got on to talking about income and living in America or whatever and they started griping about money and I'm like, 'They need to shut up,' this is what I'm thinking. 'They got all the money, you know, what are they complaining about, I need to complain.'" So somebody asked everyone who made more than thirty thousand dollars to raise his hand. When a number of whites didn't do so, "that was a real eye-opener for me," she said. Not only did it show her that all white people didn't make that kind of money, it helped her to the larger realization that "white is a generic term"—that just as blacks aren't monolithic in thoughts or actions or whatever, neither are whites.

This notion, if looked at rationally, seems ridiculously obvious. And yet the only thing ridiculous—and tragic—about it is how few whites and blacks apparently subscribe to it.

Almost from the moment I decided to explore race in America and why it continued to be such a painful dilemma for most people, why it continued to be so corrosive and volatile an issue, I had alternated between feelings of deep sadness and soaring hope, neither willing to stay mired in the former nor allowing myself to feel secure about the latter. ReDonna Rogers had every reason to be angry with white America, but she had long ago decided that anger alone wasn't going to take her very far. So she took that anger, drew from it, and molded it into a weapon, a weapon of knowledge she was using to enlighten the black youth of a new generation—a generation that couldn't afford to be lost. Even if violence and guns had come to seem normal and routine to many of these kids, she would not allow those things to become commonplace to her. She was tired of innocent people feeling like hostages in their own homes, tired of hearing about children getting shot by stray bullets while they slept.

Just the night before, a thirteen-year-old boy was brought in to the youth detention center, having been relieved of an Uzi and a grenade: while it would be hard to imagine that sort of detail escaping anyone's notice, no matter how numb or indifferent or callous one might have become to the inner city, it was precisely that sort of detail—that desperate plea for attention, as ReDonna saw it—that reignited her anger afresh. Bert Sweet had asked me, "Where does it all end?" but she had no answers, implicitly challenging me to find some. ReDonna Rogers was convinced that somehow, some way, we—blacks as well as whites—had to get beyond race. It wasn't going to happen if people continued to cling to their perceptions, to paint everyone with the same brush—bad behavior is, after all, bad behavior, regardless of race—and be unwilling to share more of the power that is necessary to shape policy, ensure "cultural perspective," and diminish, if not eliminate, the kind of racism that Robert Moses exhibited, the slippery, chameleonic kind my colleague talked about, the kind you are often unaware of, but which shows itself eventually, and punitively. And it wasn't going to happen, in ReDonna's opinion, if blacks just accepted things as they were, continued to view themselves as victims, and continued to view violence "as a way to achieve status and success." Even when she was small, her parents had advised her that she would have to push herself "because people will think because of the color of your skin or the area you live in that you're not an achiever." And they warned her that if she didn't make it, she would have no excuse. "You can't say the world was whatever," she recalled them saying. "The world is that way and there's going to be some barriers for us, but we still have to find avenues to achieve."

There was a war being fought and it was being waged on all fronts. The last thing ReDonna Rogers wanted to do was give the Bert Sweets any more ammunition. And yet, at the same time, she wanted to see to it that a Bridget Wilder and her children, whom someone in the white suburbs was unlikely to read about or see on the news at night, could live with quiet dignity and not become its latest casualties.

THIRTEEN

On the day after Father's Day, George "Poppy" Bush, still awash in the glow of Gulf War celebrations that seemed never to end and sporting an approval rating of 75 percent for everyone to see, descended into Milwaukee from on high, late in the afternoon, in town to show support for Republican senator Robert Kasten's reelection bid. Bush's limousine went into the back entrance of Bruce Hall, so he wouldn't have seen the group of protesters who had gathered across the street, urging him not to stand in the way of the civil rights bill that had now been passed by the House and that he was still threatening to veto. He wouldn't have heard Rita Tenorio, Wisconsin's Teacher of the Year, say, "We're being told that there is no money for education, and I challenge that. I say that indeed the money is there, but our priorities are not. . . . Americans need public schools and public schools need money." Another protester wanted to know "how sending jobs to Mexico and other countries is going to create jobs for the U.S."

Two days earlier, a number of Democratic presidential hopefuls had come to Milwaukee, and one of them, Governor Bill Clinton of Arkansas, railed against Bush and the Republican Party for not only allowing the country's social problems to deteriorate, but for continuing to employ the sort of divisive tactics that only kept working blacks and whites apart, preventing them from focusing on shared economic problems. "They're trying to make a white person, every time they look a minority person in the eye, think: 'There's somebody who wants my job, who wants my promotion, who wants my neighborhood.' Because as long as you're both looking at each other, he can stop you from looking at him and asking, 'Why have you let all of our incomes go down?'" But Clinton was also quick to say that Democrats couldn't keep recycling the party's same programs and policies, that they needed to view things like welfare in a different way, making work a requirement. As any Little Rock used-car salesman might, he said the party had to ask, "Why haven't people been buying what we're selling?"

Bush had an answer for that, and it ironically echoed an aspect of Clinton's. "I get sick and tired of hearing Democrats crying that there's no domestic agenda," he told the fund-raiser crowd of a thousand. "The problem is, they want *their* domestic agenda, the same old tired ideas of the past." And his problem, he said, pleading for sympathy, was a Democratic-controlled Congress that made it difficult, if not impossible, for his measures on the budget, education reform, transportation, crime, and civil rights to gain passage. In other words, it was not his fault. He could give the American people what they wanted—what they elected him to do—but those damn Democrats wouldn't let him.

If all that sounded, on some level, like politics as usual, there was politics of a similar sort unfolding within the NAACP, the nation's largest civil rights organization. More and more, the organization was coming under attack for being stodgy and hopelessly stuck on its traditional agenda of integration and looking to the courts to fight discrimination. Instead of worrying about the current civil rights bill, which primarily affected the black middle class, members themselves were saying the organization should be focused more on the problems of the inner city (drugs, poverty, crime, and teenage pregnancy), should realize that what worked in the fifties and sixties wouldn't work now. For the most part, the group's leaders were defensive about this criticism, saying that programs were in place to fight drugs and inspire kids to stay in school and that they were doing what they could, given the meagerness of their resources. "One thing we won't do is abandon the fight against racism," Benjamin L. Hooks Jr., the executive director who was nearing retirement, told the *New York Times*. "I don't know if our critics understand; our charter is to fight discrimination. If they're telling me there's no longer a problem with police brutality, no more job and housing discrimination, and most people are not worried about it, they're wrong. We're not struggling to find a mandate; we've got one. They don't seem to realize the connection. It's because of discrimination in jobs and housing that people are stuck in the underclass and the ghetto and receiving inferior education. I can't say we know how to stop little girls from having babies, or prevent drug abuse and crime, but we're working on them."

Nevertheless, the organization was willing to concede that it had gotten "a little complacent," according to Dr. William Gibson, the chairman of its board. And complacent was the last thing it could afford to be—

especially if it hoped to attract new members, to keep or regain its vitality, and to help fight a corresponding air of languor that seemed to prevail
in the country with regard to racial problems, which were more daunting
and more intractable than they had been thirty years earlier. When whites
and blacks in the *Milwaukee Journal*'s series on race were asked if the issue
of race was important to America's future, 74 percent said it was; but when
whites were asked if it was important in their daily lives, only one in four
could honestly say yes, and less than half (45 percent) thought they had
any power to improve things.

TWO DAYS AFTER BUSH'S visit, Juneteenth was celebrated in Milwaukee,
the day in 1865 (June 19th) when word of the Emancipation Proclamation finally reached slaves in Texas, Oklahoma, and Louisiana, inform-
ing them they were free. Milwaukee was the first Northern city to have
a Juneteenth celebration, in 1971, and this year marked the twentieth
anniversary.

My first knowledge of Juneteenth had occurred ten years earlier. I
was in Texas, working on a documentary for CBS News, when I learned
of a disturbing incident that had occurred east of Waco, in a speck of a
town named Mexia. Festivities were taking place on one side of Lake Mexia
and were being monitored by the police. Apparently, the police felt the
festivities had become too festive, and three youths were arrested and put
into an aluminum fishing boat; along with the three officers, their combined weight was far more than the boat could support. Two of the three
boys were said to be excellent swimmers and yet all three drowned, while
the officers swam safely to shore. Witnesses said the boys had been hand-
cuffed; the officers said the handcuffs were removed before they were put
into the boat. In any case, none of them had been given life jackets, in direct
violation of Texas law. Less than a year later, the officers were acquitted
of negligent homicide before an all-white jury in Dallas. The whole incident became a national story, briefly, but I could never put it out of my
mind. While I was frustrated that it might be impossible to ever determine
exactly what happened and why, my frustration was beside the point. What
mattered was that what had occurred was wrong and senseless, and the
means didn't justify the end—the loss of three young lives. Oddly enough,
Ernest Lacy's death at the hands of Milwaukee police occurred three weeks

after the drownings in Mexia, and as I now walked around King Drive on this Juneteenth, I wondered if the true origin of this book hadn't been back then.

The theme for this year's celebration—Rebirth, Reconstruction, and Resurgence—was geared to the same purpose of coming together as Unity Day had been two weeks earlier. "With all the violence and lack of jobs in the Milwaukee community," said McArthur Weddle, the festival's organizer, "we need all these things"—the three R's of the theme—"to happen." (The initial celebration in 1971 had come about for economic reasons; many businesses, primarily white-owned, had begun leaving the North Third Street [now King Drive] area as a result of the riot in the summer of 1967, and new development was needed.)

On the surface, it seemed like a huge street festival, with a parade, music, and the usual mélange of vendors, selling everything from food and jewelry to dashikis and baseball caps with a prominent X on the front. But interspersed among them were people dispensing information about job training, various careers to consider, and the newest form of community participation—community-oriented policing, the much-ballyhooed notion that if crime was to be combated effectively, the police had to know the community better and citizens had to work more closely with them. (Frankly, the notion didn't sound very new—it actually sounded old-fashioned and obvious, a reinvention of the wheel—but since it had the modern term "proactive" attached to it, it was being promoted as such.)

I saw so few white faces that the appearance of Mayor Norquist, towering above the milling crowd at six feet seven inches, took me by surprise, with some people calling out, "Hey, Norquist, what you doing here?" as if the event were a private party.

While the mayor was giving a talk a few minutes later as part of the official program and then joined everyone in the singing of "Lift Every Voice and Sing" (the black national anthem), I spotted Greg Stanford, a columnist for the *Milwaukee Journal*. Greg was one of the first people I had met in Milwaukee, and he had been helpful in suggesting others he thought I should speak with. For a while, I had been carrying around a column he had written, a column that suggested City Hall needed help improving life in the inner city—the problems were simply too monumental for the city alone to solve and were ones, like "massive black unemployment," that "by and large" the city hadn't created in the first place; in any case, he wrote, the mayor's initiatives needed to be given time to work. At first, I read the column as an apologia of sorts from a black journalist on behalf of the white establishment, and to some extent it was. But when I read the column's ending—his sentiment that were the unemployment situation reversed, that were the white jobless rate "hovering around 20%" as opposed to the black, there would be some sort of major public works program in place— I revised that opinion.

"Hey, man, what are you doing here?" he joked when I came over to him. "How's it going?"

I said something to the effect that I couldn't exactly miss Juneteenth, but dodged the second question. I wasn't trying to be coy. I would have to be around a lot longer before I could even begin to know how it was going.

Out of the corner of my eye I could see Michael McGee, in full uniform, holding court outside the Black Panther Militia headquarters, surrounded by other militia members. One of them, James Cameron, was the founder of the Black Holocaust Museum, which Jerrel Jones had encouraged me to visit.

A week or so earlier, I had. And from the moment I walked into the storefront building at the corner of King Drive and West Wright, I was transported uneasily back in time, with the seventy-seven-year-old Cameron, a nonstop talker, as my prodding teacher and guide. He had been inspired to create this museum after a visit to Yad Vashem in Jerusalem, a memorial to the six million Jews who had died in the Holocaust; during their tour, he turned to his wife and said, "I know what I'm going to do. I'm going to build a museum to depict all the things that have happened to us black folks and freedom-loving whites." So in 1985, beginning with a donation of five dollars from a Reverend Love in Chicago, he had done just that. He had created a place that, to my mind, was a testament of how anger and obsession could be transformed into a labor of love and a font of information. He had a copy of the Constitution prominently displayed and he challenged me to read that document, which he was reasonably sure very few people ever had, and find in it anywhere the word "white" or "black." "There is nothing declaring the Negro should *not* be a citizen of the United States and nothing declaring a white man should be." Besides, he said, "one of the most well-kept secrets in American history" was this: Free blacks as well as whites voted to send delegates to the Continental Congress, where the Articles of Confederation were drafted and eventually became the Constitution. (These blacks, who lived in six of the original thirteen colonies and were recognized as citizens, were slaveholders—of both blacks and whites—and property owners themselves.) Not only that, he said, but a black man, Crispus Attucks, shed the first blood in the cause of American independence (in Boston, in 1770) and there were five thousand blacks in George Washington's army. If things like this were taught in school, if people were made to realize that "Anglo-Saxon man is not the only totem on the pole," Cameron said, inching toward me with a smile, "we wouldn't have all this racial friction."

He called the Emancipation Proclamation "a half-assed measure" because it didn't free all the slaves, and he praised the Thirteenth Amendment as the instrument that did. In fact, he felt so strongly about its ultimate ratification on December 18, 1865, that he was urging his congressman to support a measure that would make that day a national holiday. As for the period of Reconstruction, he considered the first eleven years especially, from 1865 until 1876, as "the best of times." The Fourteenth and Fifteenth Amendments were also passed, stipulating that everyone should have equal rights and the right to vote; there were two blacks in the Senate (both from Mississippi, though not at the same time) and twenty blacks in the House of Representatives. All of this was fine and good, Cameron said, but the Southern states were not going to allow this "progress" to last; they didn't want to recognize the Thirteenth Amendment or anything else that would view their rights as subservient to the country's laws. "The only thing they would recognize," Cameron said, "would be a certificate of manumission showing where the master had set the slaves free. They wouldn't let us in the houses, they wouldn't sell us any houses, they wouldn't rent us any land, they wouldn't sell us any land." They would allow blacks to become sharecroppers—even if the war had been lost, there was still cotton to be picked—but it was an arrangement that often turned out badly; at "the settle," there was usually a debt to be paid—a debt that had frequently come about because they had been cheated by the landowner. The forty acres and a mule that Thaddeus Stevens, the congressman from Pennsylvania, had talked about blacks having would remain just talk, and demand for reparations, not just from Michael McGee, continues to this day.

In no time at all, it seemed, the segregated era of Jim Crow had been established and the window of freedom, however illusory in many ways it had been, was closed.

In talking about all this, in fingering the documents and photographs he had gathered together over twenty-five years, he was edgy and intense, determined that I *understand;* yet at the same time, he seemed remarkably free of bitterness: he was intent on seeing America become a "single and sacred nationality." During the time I spent with him, James Cameron asked me a lot of questions (probably as many as I asked him); of all of them this one stood out: If the Berlin Wall could come down, why couldn't the walls in this country? Part of his hope for that happening had to do with a group of farmers, black and white, who had recently formed a co-op in Mississippi. He had seen a white farmer tell Bill Moyers, "'Since we formed a co-op with these black farmers down here we've been making more money than we ever thought was in the world. If somebody had told me a year ago I'd have been working with black folks and on a partnership basis, I would have knocked him down.

"'All they want,'" the farmer realized, "'is just the same thing we want—a nice place to stay and something to eat and to send their kids to school to grow up to be good people.'"

It sounded simple enough, sounded within reach. But in truth there would have to be hundreds upon thousands of experiences like this—and the epiphanies that came out of them would have to sustain themselves and endure—for something larger to take hold.

IN THE COURSE OF the afternoon Cameron stressed again and again how extremely racist a city like Milwaukee was. Even in places like Sherman Park that were somewhat integrated, "housing toleration" would be a more accurate description, he said. If you called the police to report a disturbance, you would be asked the race of the people causing it ("If you report a black man beating on a white woman, the police will come. If it's black on black, they may"). He had gone to an FBI seminar, a huge picture of Captain America looming in the background, and asked, point-blank, where all the dope was coming from. "They go around and put everything at our disposal," he said. "Some of us are stupid enough to go ahead and indulge in their program to make the prophecy come true of what certain white people think about us."

It was a vicious circle, with the specter of white conspiracy limning its edges, and it had to be broken. "The black family structure is shattered," he said. "I hope it isn't shattered beyond repair."

Which had brought him to Michael McGee and Howard Fuller. Both of them, he said, were crucial to the future of not only the black community, but Milwaukee. "Black people pick out leaders like Michael McGee, and the power structure don't want anything to do with leaders like Michael McGee or Malcolm X or somebody like that. . . . The time for acquiescence is past. We can't be silent anymore. We've got to let people know just what's on our mind. For so many years, the white power structure, calling themselves helping us, have been doing things *for* us, instead of doing things *with* us. . . . McGee is my man. I'll go to hell for that guy. 'Cause I know he's honest, dedicated, determined, and he's not a white folks nigger, you might say. We need black people like him to speak up . . . to keep just sticking the needles into the power structure . . . because he's voicing the opinion of all the black people, even these so-called doctors and lawyers who don't want to have anything to do with McGee. He's still voicing their opinions. Because deep down in their hearts, they believe in McGee."

So what about Howard Fuller, I said, what about how some people, including McGee, who had been the most vocal, said that he was precisely what McGee was not—a "white folks nigger"? Didn't that contradict what he had said about what the black community needed?

Howard Fuller was good for *all* of Milwaukee, Cameron said, bristling a little. "The thing of it is, the white people put him in thinking he's going to be a yes-man, and they're going to get the surprise of their life when they find out that he's not a yes-man, that they can't control him. . . . He's not just there as a tokenism for black people. I want that understood. . . . He is somebody that Milwaukee should be proud of. And they should work with him to help make this city better than it is. And the only way we're going to do it is through education."

As I CONTINUED WATCHING McGee and his entourage, a group of teenage girls I had met the day before came by in the Juneteenth parade. They were part of a New Concepts program called Sisters Against Self-Destruction and they had been preparing for the parade when I stopped by to talk to them. Most of them lived right in Hillside, and they wanted to be elsewhere, anywhere but there. The program was about "getting you off the streets and into your culture," one girl said. Their biggest concerns about living in Milwaukee were "the killings, the violence," they had all said in unison; each of them knew someone who had been shot or murdered. As for racism in Milwaukee, they said there was a lot of it; they even had fresh evidence to offer, an incident from the weekend before, when they went to the Festival of Arts, where they felt stared at, out of place, in the mostly white crowd. They had tried not to let it bother them, but it was hard: when they wanted to sign up for the craft exhibit, they were told that it was booked. Yet when Yvonne Wunderlich, who was light skinned and worked for New Concepts, approached the woman in charge of the exhibit a few minutes later, she was told it was free and she should go right in.

"Do you feel that comes up a lot?" I asked Yvonne, whose father was white and mother was black. "That if your skin is lighter people act differently toward you?"

Yes, as a matter of fact, she did. And so did one of the girls in the program, who was a mix of black and Puerto Rican, who said that a lot of racism didn't "come toward me" because of that. The old expression, "If you're black, stand back; if you're brown, stick around; if you're white, you're all right," still seemed to have a lot of staying power. Louise Kidd had called it "a race problem—within our race," but it appeared larger than that; it placed the light-skinned black in racial limbo, less threatening to whites but not authentic enough to blacks. And yet there were enough exceptions to this—Malcolm X perhaps the largest one—that it seemed to be an issue that needed to be placed in its proper context, neither made too much of nor too easily dismissed. As long as whites continued, on some level, to view light-skinned blacks as "acceptable" because they looked more like them and continued to view the majority of dark-skinned blacks as stereotypically menacing because they did not, this was yet one more strand in the weave of racism that needed to be untangled.

But even that strand extended further, extended beyond skin color and extended beyond class. The reality, Yvonne said, was that no matter how light or dark skinned you were, no matter how rich or poor you were, no matter if you were a product of an interracial marriage, "you are always black first. That is just the way you are, that is the way you are seen." Not accepting that, she said, had caused a great deal of anguish for blacks—especially those who had gained the most from the civil rights movement but had turned their backs on the black community, those who "think they are white, or want to be white." They may listen to Helen Reddy, and, driving to work in a BMW, observe another black listening to rap and think it disgusting, she said, but a white person (or the black person listening to rap) might look over at them and think, "'A nigger with a BMW. He must be a dope dealer,' even though he might be a doctor."

Jerrel Jones had said much the same thing, with considerably more bombast. And three days after I talked with Yvonne Wunderlich, a young black entrepreneur named Chester Hopper provided his own echo, saying, in another variation on the theme, that blacks suffered from a "crab mentality," that everybody was "pulling each other down in an effort to get to the top." This happened, Hopper said, because there was another kind of mentality underlying that one—a "doomsday mentality"—which suggested that no matter how much education a black accumulated, it ultimately didn't matter because "there's no way to use it properly." There weren't a lot of black businesses, and there weren't a lot of jobs. If you wanted to "create your own areas," he said, you're often "blocked by economics." A seemingly hopeless job situation, Hopper insisted, had led to an increase in crime and a decrease in self-esteem.

In hearing all this, I thought once again of Sean Chambers, the black student I had had, and realized that I had overlooked something in my dealings with him. I had overlooked the degree to which blacks who succeeded in school were ridiculed and called "uppity" and "Incognegroes" and "Afropeans" by other blacks, and how Chambers could have concluded that it was easier to fail than to feel guilt about any success he might achieve. I had begun this exploration of race assuming, I realized now, that the majority of blacks I spoke with would blame whites for whatever grievances they felt. Without being conscious of it, I was guilty too, guilty of thinking of blacks as monolithic. I had done enough reading to have known better—to have recalled, for instance, how often Martin Luther King was sarcastically referred to as "De Lawd" by other blacks, or how at odds two figures like Booker T. Washington and W.E.B. Du Bois had been—but somehow my absorption of that knowledge had been incomplete. I had still begun this journey with assumptions, assumptions that were wrong, assumptions I needed to continue freeing myself from if I was going to move closer to a fuller understanding.

FOURTEEN

"We fought for you guys. We opened doors for you guys. Don't have them close by being a fool."

It was Friday, June 21, and James Bevel, one of Martin Luther King's closest aides, had come to Milwaukee, to the Silver Spring Neighborhood Center, with things on his mind. He arrived as a piece of living history, as someone who had been in Birmingham, had been in Selma, had been in Mississippi, had marched to Montgomery, had been with King in Memphis when he died, and he had come to tell young African-American men that if they didn't rid themselves of their contempt, disdain, and enmity for three things—knowledge, intelligence, and truth—"you will be eliminated as a species and rightly so."

These three things, he insisted, were the foundation for every system in the universe that man operated ("Governments are built on that, education is built on that, economics is built on that, manufacturing is built on that"), and he said that he didn't have the answer, didn't have the data, couldn't figure out for the life of him why black men so blatantly rejected something that was available to them. In case they didn't know it, he shouted, they were *free,* free to gain these things and free to do anything they wanted to that made sense *under the law.* Dealing crack, shooting each other, and going to jail didn't make sense. Men weren't in these jails, he said. Animals were. So why, he wanted to know, would they choose to be an animal when they had the option of being a man? Was it a spiritual problem, or a genetic one, or something else? He didn't know, but he meant to find out. Actually, he said, he wasn't sure that they knew what it was to be a man in the first place. Ever since the death of Martin Luther King, he had been searching high and low for *one* African-American man and, he claimed, he had not been able to find anyone who fit that description.

Unlike most preachers, whose sermons build in intensity, the Reverend Dr. James Bevel was shouting from the start. It was apparent what he was trying to do, but far less clear if it was, or was going to be, effective. If anything, his self-righteousness was likely to work against him. The young black men who were there identified themselves far more with a sharp homeboy like Malcolm X than with a soft preacher's son like Dr. King. That was not to take away from King; but it was still true. And quite apart from their not knowing enough about King, not knowing that he stood for more than nonviolence and an integrated society, it was also true that they didn't know all the aspects of Malcolm's odyssey either, didn't know anything about what he did—or how his outlook changed—after his break with the Nation of Islam. After all, anybody can don a cap with an X on it and delude himself into thinking he knows what he's identifying with. That lack of knowledge was Bevel's point, but his method was all wrong. It was sixties rhetoric, thirty years removed, and he wasn't preaching to the converted.

The moment that Adrian Blevins became convinced that Bevel was yelling at him, dissing him in a way, he got irritated and stopped listening, turned his mind elsewhere, to what he was going to do that evening, which was see *New Jack City* for the fourth time. The more Bevel talked about "when I came along" blacks couldn't vote or sit in the front of the bus, you could see, among the teenagers, the simultaneous rolling of eyes throughout the room, but not in the revival way that Bevel would have liked.

I sympathized with Bevel. His intentions were good, they were noble. He had been on the front lines, he had risked his life, and he had succeeded in knocking Jim Crow down, but he was frustrated because things hadn't progressed in the way he and Dr. King had hoped they would. I had heard so often by now that if Martin Luther King were alive today, he would be pleased by the gains blacks had made politically (especially in the South) and by the way the black middle class, of which he had always been a part, had burgeoned, but that his pleasure would be far surpassed by his utter despair that not only had so little changed in the inner cities and backwoods all across America, but that things had backslid, that the dream he had so eloquently given voice to was so far from being realized. And so here was Bevel, one of his disciples, trying to carry on the good fight, talking about how "education is a scientific process through which you acquire knowledge to become institutionally sovereign and economically independent," telling them that the Italians knew that, the Swedes knew that, the Germans knew that, and asking *why* it was that black folks didn't know that, cautioning them that in America it was *unlawful* not to educate yourself, warning them that without knowledge, intelligence, and truth, "God will get out of your way, God won't fool with you," and urging them to accept that they couldn't go on blaming white people for their oppression, that their oppression was a result, an outgrowth, of their rejection of these three things.

He was done. There was applause, but it came mostly from his generation, from those who had lived through the struggle and remembered. Bevel seemed exhausted, eager to leave. I went up to him and asked how his week had gone (he had arrived in Milwaukee four days earlier, the same day President Bush had), what he felt he had accomplished. He looked wearily at me, then shrugged his shoulders. He didn't know, he couldn't say. He had dropped by to see Mike McGee on Juneteenth, but McGee did not seem very interested in his ideas. Given Bevel's continuing belief in the importance of nonviolence, he shouldn't have been too surprised. All Bevel could do, he was saying now, was speak his mind and hope that enough young people would listen. He was an embattled figure who deserved more respect than he had been given on this afternoon. As he stood there now, away from his pulpit, he seemed more a lonely traveling salesman, packing his wares and hoping for a better reception in the next town, than the proud civil rights activist he had been for so long.

At Silver Spring that afternoon and three days later, I talked with youths who were either working at the center for the summer or had come to play basketball and just hang. Nearly all of them lived in Westlawn, the housing complex that encircled the center (in the same way that Hillside did New Concepts), and they were brimming with attitude.

One young man, Jermaine Zollicofer, known to nearly everyone as Pooker, said that he had nothing against any race but told me, straight up, that he had a lot of friends down at Hillside who wouldn't allow him to stand there talking to me, would be furious to know that he was. I asked him about gangs and he said that he knew a lot of people in gangs, that a lot of his family were members; somewhat reluctantly, he admitted that he was too. He had almost gotten arrested that morning, he said, but was unwilling to provide details.

I told another group why I was there and one of them said, "Racism is a lot of bullshit because slavery happened way back then. It's different now. You gotta live, you gotta live by the day. Anybody's trying to fuck you, black, white, no matter what color they is, you still fucked up. For real."

Another youth tried to amplify that, saying that a lot of whites probably feel that blacks are shit, that they "ain't worth nothing," and that blacks must believe that because they call each other names and kill each other off.

Was that why there was so much black-on-black crime?

No, it was more than that, another said. They go ahead and "jack the nigga" in order to be able to tell somebody about it and "get higher up."

He made it sound like just another chilling day in corporate America, office politics as usual, the seamy rules of the game. By whatever means this message had been conveyed to him it had, it appeared, become Darwin's rules of the street. If you're not going to become president of IBM, you might as well become head of the Vice Lords or the Black Gangster Disciples, or, if you're less ambitious, head of a smaller gang like the 33rd Lynch Mob, but the problem there is, you still got people on top of you, higher up still, watching your movements. You might get killed in trying to attain your goal, in trying to get and control some turf, but hey, life is a risk, there are no guarantees, you could get cut down just crossing the road.

If black-on-black crime (94 percent of all blacks killed are killed by other blacks) was somehow viewed as an accomplishment, that becoming a person of consequence, no matter how that stature was attained, was far preferable to not standing out and not being feared, so was the making of babies. There were fourteen-year-olds in the group who had already fathered babies or given birth, others who had babies "on the way," and still others who only claimed they had; some who insisted they were going to take care of the baby and others who were pleased that the baby's grandmother would and that they could go by whenever they wished to see the child, this object of their success.

Standing there, talking to them, made me sad, though I disguised it. It also made me furious, but I didn't know where to direct my anger, not with any certainty. I tried to keep in mind that I had already talked to many black people who had spoken of gangs and dealing drugs and black-on-black crime as abhorrent—as destroying both the black family and the black community, which had always prided itself on its strength—as giving kids a false sense of family and a guarantee of a short life; tried to keep in mind another fourteen-year-old, Tennille Alexander, who had seen what had

happened when her friends had babies and who didn't want that for herself no way, just as there were white teenagers who had children out of
wedlock; tried to keep in mind that gangs (as well as peer pressure) had
been around forever—that white kids in the suburbs had rebelled and
joined them and continued to worship James Dean (or at least what he
represented), that the Irish and the Italians and the Chinese had formed
gangs as a way to combat the persecution they experienced upon arriving
on these shores; that white kids dealt drugs; that proving your toughness,
so to speak—even if, in the event of a drive-by shooting, it was also a way
of confirming your cowardice, even if the method of doing so had changed
from fists and knives to all manner of weapon, the more stylish and high-
powered the better—was not the exclusive province of black kids in the
inner city.

I tried to keep all this in mind and find the precise root of my anger,
but I wasn't having much luck. Right at the moment I was angry at these
kids for the blithe, uncaring, no-big-deal way they talked, but then I realized, or hoped, that they were probably disguising their true feelings as
well, that they were just as frightened of the violence that surrounded them
as the Sisters Against Self-Destruction or Louise Kidd or ReDonna Rogers,
that they probably wanted to chart a different course for themselves but
weren't convinced they could, weren't convinced that the opportunities
that existed for other people existed for them.

So who was to blame, and what was to be done?

Back in 1965, in his infamous report ("The Negro Family: The Case
for National Action") to President Johnson, Daniel Patrick Moynihan was
accused of blaming the victim. Five years later, as a member of the Nixon
Administration, he had suggested that a stance of "benign neglect" (and a
guaranteed income) might be the best (that is, most astutely political) approach to race. Liberals, ever sensitive to the perceived failure of the War
on Poverty, blamed Reagan and Bush for giving up on the cities altogether,
masterminding ways to upend some of the gains made by the civil rights
movement, and setting a tone that enabled people to feel comfortable, in
the name of free speech, to vent their anger and hatred and disgust toward
blacks and the "special privileges" they now had, privileges they insisted
had come at their expense, amounted to reverse discrimination in their
view. Shelby Steele was saying blacks had to get beyond race in order to
get ahead, that race was holding them back. Cornel West was saying that

the proliferation of material goods, the symbol of success that the possession of those goods represented, and a general lack or decline of morality
were to blame. Blacks and whites alike blamed gangsta rap for giving kids
the wrong message—about whites, about women, about virtually everything the lyrics were about. The black church was blamed for not doing
more; the black middle class was blamed for not doing more; whites were
blamed for putting drugs on the streets; the overall lack of jobs (or the
difficulty in getting transportation to the ones that existed in the suburbs)
was cited, over and over, as the reason that crime had shot up.

    With all these theories about what was wrong, it didn't seem unrea-
sonable to expect that a corresponding set of solutions or "prescriptions"
was at the ready. After all, this is a big country, spilling over with smart
people, black and white. And yet finding a consensus is, as it has always
been, nearly impossible, and reason often has little to do with it.

FIFTEEN

The first thing I noticed about Howard Fuller when we finally had the chance to sit down together, on the last Thursday of June, was the disarmingly casual way he welcomed me into his office, the "Hey, how ya doing?" and the easy smile that would have convinced any observer that we had known each other forever. He had been on the job about a month and he already looked tired, a condition I would come to realize was normal for him, workaholic that he was.

The school board had met until three-thirty in the morning and now, six hours later, he was sipping tea and eating graham crackers and willing, or so it seemed, to talk about anything. He was tall and lean and slightly stooped, the result of a bad back that never stopped bothering him, that prevented him from playing basketball anymore. Even though he was fifty, even though he had a mustache that gave him the appearance of a wise old owl, even though he was sitting there with a pressed blue shirt on and red suspenders, he seemed more a schoolboy—standing on the corner of Eleventh and Vine, as he had so often, talking about anything and everything with guys like Donald Jackson and Kenny Tatum—than the superintendent of the Milwaukee Public Schools. Perhaps it was the top button undone or the tie lowered slightly or the sleeves rolled up that gave me that impression; or maybe it was his gaze—a gaze that was both intense and friendly at the same time; whatever it was, Fuller struck me as the sort of person you could engage with, who didn't put on airs, who didn't come across as intolerably arrogant or *important*, but who, because he was passionate about the things he was involved with, *whatever* they were, and there were many, was not one to sit there and participate in any sort of small talk. Even when he hung at Eleventh and Vine, he and his friends talked about weighty matters (basketball being one of them); and even when I would later see him in more informal settings than this one, when he would be dressed in jeans and a baseball cap and a North Division High School sweatshirt, his manner would still be casual, but there was always an urgency in his voice about whatever was being discussed. Howard Fuller did his own form of calculating and his calculations had to do with time, with a belief that it was precious, that it mustn't be squandered. "Real reform takes time," he told the *Milwaukee Journal* about education. "Unfortunately we don't have any time." The time to lose another generation of kids.

In coming to this job, the former director of Health and Human Services ("the manager of misery," as his successor called it) was moving to the front end from the back end, as he saw it, moving to a position where if you could help put a child on solid footing in terms of caring about school and attending regularly, of believing in the value of an education, the child had a much better chance of avoiding drugs or gangs or detention homes or welfare—some of the many things that Fuller had had to deal with the past three years. This way of thinking was not unique to Fuller; many policy makers and social scientists (those with more of a liberal bent than a conservative one) shared it, the idea, bluntly put, that if you invested in education now, you wouldn't have to pay more, much more, in terms of welfare and prison, later. "Clearly there is a relationship between what is happening to people on the back end and their kids and their ability to perform in schools," he said. "In other words, kids that have been abused and neglected by their families, that is going to make it very difficult for them to learn. So there has got to be a relationship between HHS and MPS in terms of how do we work together to make sure that the school system changes so that it can teach kids and that those kids are coming in with some chance of being able to learn."

I asked him about the Afrocentric curriculum that was going to be implemented at Victor Berger Elementary and he said that it was the right thing to do but warned that there were limits to what could be done in public schools—that if you really wanted to target black males, the community had to play a role, much in the way Jewish people sent their kids to Hebrew school. Only four years earlier Fuller had called for a separate school system for blacks—a proposal that gained him the enmity of many blacks because he was, in effect, telling white conservatives exactly what they wanted to hear: that black self-determination was the best (if not the most realistic) way to achieve equality, that whites shouldn't bear the primary responsibility for the socioeconomic conditions of the inner city. Since he was now the superintendent for all of Milwaukee's children in public schools, he could no longer be the partisan community activist, at least not in any obvious way.

As a product of the sixties, I told him, I was troubled by the immersion program's element of separatism. Knowing what I did about his own background, I was well aware that I was provoking an answer.

"But there were two sixties," he said. "There was the civil rights sixties and then there was the black power sixties. What we have to do is go back and understand what the links are between those two things and the links between all of those movements. Then we have to look at no matter what was happening then, what is the reality that we face now?" The answer, he said, was a generation of black kids "with absolutely no connection to their history and culture." And without that, he said, a kid had no ability to see himself in the world. A "multicultural curriculum" had to be pushed, he said, but at the same time, "the child will still have to be able to read, write, compute, analyze, and think critically."

Since the King-Malcolm dichotomy was much on my mind, I raised it with Fuller.

There was a class he taught on Saturday mornings, he said. It was over at the Commando Project on North Avenue and those in attendance were mostly Muslim students from Milwaukee Area Technical College. When the class first began, Fuller had had them study Marcus Garvey, W.E.B. Du Bois, Booker T. Washington, Martin Luther King, and Malcolm X. "My purpose for doing that was to get people to understand the trends in the development of African-American history in this country. And these trends"—a separatist (or black nationalist) trend, an accommodationist trend, a go-back-to-Africa trend, an integrationist trend—"have always been with us." What he tried to do was make young people understand that, understand why it was important that both King and Malcolm X be given their due, understand that the Malcolm of the Nation of Islam period did not entirely define him, just as King's "I Have a Dream" speech did not sufficiently categorize him. "You don't have to raise Malcolm by condemning King," Fuller cautioned.

It sounded reasonable enough—were it not for the fact that polarization was easier and less threatening for people, regardless of color and regardless of fairness. Even though polarization sometimes made sense (as in the case of the civil rights movement's rightful attempt to break down what was clearly wrong—the legal barriers of segregation), generally the kind of Reaganesque *We're up, you're down, he's good, he's not* thinking kept one safely away from the gray areas, the very areas in which complexity

lies and from which illumination and understanding has the potential to
spring forth.

So what about him and Michael McGee, where did he see them fitting into all this? Could someone praise McGee without having to criti-
cize Fuller?

The look on Fuller's face told me this was a tender subject, one he
would rather not discuss. He claimed they had been close friends at one
time, and that their relationship had begun with the Ernest Lacy case. "We
are different personalities, but I feel as strongly about my people as anyone. I have taken a particular route and Mike has taken another one. There
is really not much more to it than that."

Obviously there was, but since I hoped to spend a good deal of time
with Fuller I decided not to press the subject, decided not to bring up
McGee's comments about his being a lackey and a hypocrite, or the
Molotov cocktail that McGee, or someone close to him, was suspected of
throwing at Fuller's house the year before. Once I got to know him better,
I would come back to it.

He was much more comfortable talking about the Milwaukee he grew
up in, the "tremendous support base" the black community always provided, the fact that he was still in touch with every player on the 1958 North
Division basketball team that won the city championship and came within
a game of winning the state. He had led the student body of every school
he had ever attended. He had succeeded in a segregated world and he had
succeeded in an integrated one, and along the way he had immersed himself in and explored all the different trends of which he had spoken: he had
gone to an all-white college and he had founded an all-black one; as a
member of the Congress of Racial Equality (CORE) he participated in the
demonstration in Cleveland that resulted in the death of Bruce Klunder
(whose name is on the Civil Rights Memorial); he fought for fair and open
housing in Durham, North Carolina, was arrested and had his life threatened in the process, but he won; he gained the enmity of many whites and
returned that enmity with remarks like "We live in a country that has only
two priorities—property and profit—and whites only value these. Don't
waste your love on them." He gained a spot on the CIA's list of people to
watch and was subjected to congressional investigation. He carried his role
in the black power movement over to Africa, in 1971, where he not only
met with black leaders, but wound up traveling for a month with a group

of freedom fighters in Mozambique, a month in which the group was bombed, strafed, and walked about four hundred miles in the bush. He took on an African name, Owusu Sadaukai, but felt himself to be an outsider. While he could admire Marcus Garvey and Stokely Carmichael, both of whom moved there from America, Africa was not where he wanted to stay. He wanted to continue to work on behalf of Africa's liberation, but he wanted to do it in America. In May of 1972 Fuller organized African Liberation Day, an occasion that was celebrated in a number of American cities. Fifty thousand dollars was raised for the African Liberation Movement and Fuller was publicly acknowledged for the event's success by a sea of clenched fists as he rose to speak in Washington.

But Fuller learned something in Africa that had not been entirely apparent to him before. He learned that the oppression of blacks could not be solely placed at the feet of whites; he saw enough instances of blacks being controlled and oppressed by other blacks to know that economic status had to be considered as well. Intellectually, of course, he had always known this, but in Africa he was seeing it firsthand. Trying to determine whether factors affecting the black community turned on race or class or, as they often do, on both, became a lifelong obsession of Fuller's; his sad realization that many blacks who gained tangibly from the civil rights movement had the attitude of "I want to get as far away from you niggers as I possibly can" only reinforced what he saw in Africa.

Once back in America, despite the success of African Liberation Day, he also witnessed how the very trends he spoke of could clash—a clash, between the Pan-Africanists and the black nationalists, that led to the dissolution of Malcolm X Liberation University. Fuller had explored both of them, had ultimately chosen what made most sense for him, but lost his college. Perhaps this was the harsh, invaluable lesson he needed, the age-old political one that says you can't appease everybody, that you have to take a stand. Fuller stayed on in North Carolina, organizing hospital workers at Duke, winning reforms on their behalf, but losing his marriage in the process. Even before Fuller married, his mother warned Viola (as she would Claudetta, his second wife) that if she was expecting him to be the sort of husband who would come home at five in the afternoon and be fully focused on her, she would be well advised to look elsewhere; Howard had things he wanted to accomplish and was not likely to allow much to deter him.

Being an activist and a revolutionary, constantly trying to give more and more to other people than to himself or his family, not only took a toll on his marriage but brought him to the edge of a breakdown. During the summer of 1976 he took a group of people with him to a retreat that the Revolutionary Workers League was holding in New Jersey. Even though Fuller was viewed as an important figure in the organization, he did not anticipate the scenario that would unfold, a scenario that had echoes of the Holocaust. For two grueling days, the group was subjected to humiliation, mental torture, and physical abuse, all for the alleged purpose of making them pure. Fuller was devastated. He had risked too much, gone too far, and blamed no one but himself. When he returned to North Carolina, he was a different person. "All of a sudden," his good friend Barbara Aaron told *Milwaukee Magazine,* "it was there: I'm sitting and talking with a man that can't complete a sentence. He looked like he aged overnight. He was bent over, couldn't walk and couldn't talk. . . . We were shocked that someone could be brought down so far. . . . He tried to do too many things at one time; I think it crushed him."

Fuller came home to Milwaukee, unsure of what to do next. Since he had three children to support (all of whom remained with their mother in North Carolina), he took a job selling insurance. Within a short time, though, he was back on the front lines, leading the battle to save North Division from becoming a magnet (in other words, predominantly white) school and forcing black kids out of the neighborhood, and leading, along with McGee, the coalition that was seeking justice for the wrongful death of Ernest Lacy. To Fuller, the landmark *Brown* decision of 1954 was important and imperative, but was based on a notion—that blacks would have to achieve equality within a white system that was assumed to be fair and just—he was highly skeptical of. Even though he had chosen to go to Carroll College, he resented the idea that black schools, given the proper resources, couldn't be just as successful as white ones. It was this belief that had led to the founding of Malcolm X Liberation University, had propelled him in the successful fight for North Division (which represented the largest organized protest in Milwaukee since Father Groppi's housing marches a decade earlier) and in his call for an independent black school district in 1987.

But separatism was only one of Howard Fuller's many components. He had learned early on from one of his mentors, a man named John

Wheeler, a black chief executive officer of a large financial institution in North Carolina, that "you can go into the halls of 'power' and still maintain your sense of rage, but you can do it in such a way that you stand some chance of coming out with what you went in there to get." Though Fuller hadn't always followed Wheeler's way of thinking, he had never forgotten it. Mentors like Wheeler and figures like Frederick Douglass (his remark about power conceding nothing without a demand was prominently featured on one of Fuller's office walls) were never far from his thoughts, were part of the reason, in fact, he had lobbied so hard to be sitting where he was at that particular moment. He wanted to continue the work he had been doing all his life, but if he was going to have any chance of making a large impact, of effecting change, he had to do that work from a position of power.

"Children today face a different world from what I faced when I was growing up," he was now reiterating. "It is much more violent. The social problems are in some ways much more intractable. The drug thing—when I was growing up people might every now and then drink some wine, or you might hear this weird story about weed or something—but the kinds of things that these kids are facing today is way out and above anything that I faced." And yet when he went out and talked to these kids, as he did constantly, he saw himself. And because he did, he wasn't giving up on them.

Fuller was inheriting a public school system that, in his own words, was failing; a system of high dropout rates and low attendance and a mean grade point average that hovered between a C and a D. He faced all sorts of obstacles—a powerful teachers union that seemed resistant to reform, a budget that relied (in the opinion of many) far too much on personal property taxes for its funding and did not receive enough from the state, an unwieldy centralized bureaucracy that did not allow for enough of that budget to reach the student in the classroom. The violence that kids were facing was not only being faced in the streets, but in the schools themselves. Weapons were constantly being confiscated and elementary school kids were being recruited into gangs with the same intensity that Uncle Sam used to enlist high school graduates into the military. There was nothing wrong with thinking that schools should be islands of safety, should somehow be immune from all this, but it simply wasn't the case. When the shooting of a fifteen-year-old boy dominates the conversation of three mothers preparing for their children's graduation from Head Start, something is askew. Everything touched on, was tied to, and permeated everything else. For every Howard Fuller who was determined to make it, no matter what, there were far more who frankly didn't see the point, didn't see how the odds would ever be in their favor, didn't see how, as one person put it, they would ever get more of the gravy and less of the jerky.

As far as Howard Fuller was concerned, he would do, on one level, what he had always done—expect a lot, both from the students and from himself. To him, no challenge was too great, and he had never backed away from one. If he saw something that needed to be fixed, he moved, without hesitation, in that direction. Every time he heard that "black kids can't learn" he always had an answer: "If they can learn the lyrics to Queen Latifah and Ice-T, can know every last word by heart, how can anybody say they can't learn?"

It might be clichéd to say it, but Howard Fuller saw the glass as half-full, refused to see it any differently. When he was down in North Carolina, there were black people who said that "Howard is our Jesus." In ascending to this position as superintendent of the Milwaukee Public Schools, he was once again being looked to as a savior, an expectation that he did little to dispel.

SIXTEEN

On my way back from Fuller's office, I was listening to the car radio when I heard the news that Thurgood Marshall had resigned after twenty-four years as a justice of the United States Supreme Court. As the chief attorney for the NAACP (and head of its Legal Defense Fund), he had been the legal architect for many significant pieces of civil rights legislation, appearing in thirty-two cases before the very Court he would eventually grace with his presence, winning twenty-nine of them, none more dramatic than the 1954 *Brown* decision. But as a justice he had increasingly become a lone but eloquent dissenting voice on many of the decisions the Court handed down during the seventies and eighties, some of which the embattled 1991 Civil Rights Act was trying to redress. In 1974, in *Milliken v. Bradley,* a case in which the Court narrowly voted 5–4 against ordering school desegregation across school district lines in Detroit and its suburbs, Justice Marshall wrote, from personal experience, that "desegregation is not and was not ever expected to be an easy task. Racial attitudes ingrained in our nation's childhood and adolescence are not quickly thrown aside in its middle years. But just as the inconvenience of some cannot be allowed to stand in the way of the rights of others, so public opposition, no matter how strident, cannot be permitted to divert this Court from the enforcement of the constitutional principles in this case."

The Court's decision, he feared, "is more a reflection of a perceived public mood that we have gone far enough in enforcing the Constitution's guarantee of equal justice than it is the product of neutral principles of law. In the short run, it may seem to be the easier course to allow our great metropolitan areas to be divided up each into two cities—one white, the other black—but it is a course, I predict, our people will ultimately regret."

How difficult it must have been for Marshall to sit on a Court that arrived at decisions that flew in the face of what he had worked so hard to achieve. How painful it must have been for him to live through government cuts in education, to witness the various ploys and maneuverings that

were constantly being concocted and set in motion in an effort to circum-
vent *Brown,* or the violence that seemed to attend each effort to implement
it. Great-grandson of a slave, son of a father who had insisted that if anyone ever called him a nigger, "you not only got my permission to fight him,
you got my orders to fight him," Thurgood Marshall wasn't just a hero for
black people; he was a hero for all of us. Even if his hope of integrated
schools and an integrated society was not, then or now, shared by "our
people" to the degree he would have liked, his accomplishments will stand.

ON THE SAME DAY that Justice Marshall resigned (to be effective, he jaun-
tily wrote President Bush, "when my successor is qualified"), word also
came out of Washington, specifically from Wisconsin senator Herbert F.
Kohl's office, that the Bureau of Alcohol, Tobacco and Firearms wanted
to send a task force to Milwaukee to help combat a growing gang and drug
problem. For so long the Cream City had lived in Chicago's shadow, content to go on about its business, merrily existing in a state of denial. (When
the 1967 "disturbances," as so many Milwaukeeans gingerly recall the riots,
began on a hot July night, James Cameron first heard about it on a Chicago radio station.) But this was becoming harder to do.

"Milwaukee has been identified by ATF as one of the priority cities
experiencing the most serious of gang violence and drug trafficking activities," Kohl wrote in a fund-seeking letter to the Appropriations Committee. The letter referred to the "vast arsenals of weapons" these gangs
possessed, weapons ranging from pistol-grip and sawed-off shotguns to
assault rifles and Uzis, and it was equally specific about some of the groups
that possessed them: the Black Gangster Disciples, the Vice Lords, the
Crips, and the Bloods.

The Vice Lords were the gang that had infiltrated the area of First
and Keefe, the area where George Edward Brown was shot on the night of
June 11, where Bridget Wilder would not let her children outside to play.
On the last Saturday of the month, some of these same Vice Lords came
to the Friary of St. Elizabeth's Church to meet with longtime neighborhood residents, people who were determined not to be run off their land.
The gathering had been arranged by Harambee, the community organization that had grass-roots responsibility for the neighborhood. I had met
the director of Harambee and two of his organizers the day before and they

said it would be fine for me to come, provided that I be willing to identify myself and my purpose when, as is customary at such events, I was called upon.

As I approached the church shortly before two that Saturday, the local news media was set up outside, as if they were awaiting a celebrity. And celebrities, in a bizarrely American fashion, were what these gang members had become; sought out for interviews, deemed good copy. Even glimpses of them were making it onto the nightly news.

As it happened, they had come in the back door, accompanied by some members of the Nation of Islam, of the branch that was headed by Louis Farrakhan. In their pressed white shirts, dark suits, and ubiquitous bow ties, the Fruit of Islam had been asked, by Tommie Williams of Harambee, to do what they had always done: provide security, make sure things didn't get out of hand.

But things quickly did. To begin with, the small room wasn't air-conditioned and so the temperature inside was considerably higher than the temperature outside, which was brushing a hundred, none of which helped when a man named Arthur Gordon stood up, a man somewhere in his fifties or early sixties, furiously waving a brown paper bag at the youths who were seated at the front table. He was a coiled spring just waiting to be unleashed, a ball of rage, a man who said that he had lived in the neighborhood for twenty-five years, *for twenty-five years,* he kept repeating, had worked for American Motors, had raised a family. "And as far as I'm concerned," he shouted, "y'all are nothing but rats trapped in a paper bag. Feeding off each other. Killing each other. And I'll be goddamned if you're going to chase me out of my house. Twenty-five years I've been living here, *twenty-five years.*"

A young man in a yellow T-shirt stood up to respond, to say, calmly at first, that the members of the organization were merely doing what they had to do to survive, that that's the way the world was, that was the situation they found themselves in, and that he realized that Mr. Gordon, "an older brother," would have a hard time in understanding that.

"But you've segregated yourself in your own community," Gordon said, still standing.

"That's your fault," the young man said, "not ours." His generation's fault that they felt so confined, that more opportunities didn't exist, that there weren't any places to go for indoor or outdoor recreation, that the older brothers had got theirs and didn't worry about those who would come after. "We don't break into your houses or steal your cars. All we're trying to do is survive."

Suddenly a striking woman in her late thirties shot up and strode to the front of the room. Staring straight into the eyes of Arthur Gordon, she said that he ought to be ashamed of himself, that he shouldn't forget that the American Motors plant he worked for—that had made it possible for him to support his family—was closed, that the freedom he had had to leave one manufacturing job for another was not there for this young man, that the last thing, *the last thing,* blacks needed was to be turning on each other. Maybe there would be less black-on-black crime if they tried to help each other instead, she said, maybe he should realize that what this young man needed was his support, not his wrath. Belinda Pittman went on to say that she herself had grown up a few blocks from this very church, that she had come from very little but was now a successful businesswoman, and that part of the reason for her success was, in her opinion, because people had believed in her, which in turn helped her believe in herself. Her anger, it became clear, was not just with Mr. Gordon; he was merely the convenient target for it. Her anger, she was now saying, her eyes sweeping the room, was with any and all blacks who had made it but felt no responsibility to give anything back. They, she said, her voice rising, they were just as racist as any white.

THIS PLEA FOR COLLECTIVE responsibility, for not just waiting around for whites to do something for blacks, was recurring nearly everywhere I went. It took different forms, but it was the same message, and it carried with it the same burden of guilt. And even though I had heard it many times before coming to St. Elizabeth's that afternoon, and even though Howard Fuller had told me two days earlier that black self-reliance and social changes had to take place at the same time ("in order for the quality of life for the least powerful in our community to become different"), hearing Belinda Pittman speak directly to Arthur Gordon had a greater impact for me. It helped me better understand that Howard Fuller's constant state of exhaustion reflected more than just a penchant for working at the pace he did, better understand his feeling organically connected to Frederick Douglass and Malcolm X (whom Fuller credited with making him "face up to my blackness in a way that nobody else did"). At the same time it helped me better understand why a Shelby Steele would boldly argue— and be attacked for doing so—that being accountable for one's own actions was, selfish as it might seem, paramount to constantly feeling the burden for the well-being of other, if not all, black people; that it was in fact the best way to get beyond race, to prevent it from being a crutch, from being synonymous with a perpetual state of victimhood.

Forty-eight hours later, Steele's argument would begin to be played out, agonizingly and divisively, on a national stage.

SEVENTEEN

I t had been hinted at, but now it was a fact: Clarence Thomas was President Bush's choice to succeed Thurgood Marshall on the Supreme Court. He was black, he was conservative, and he was against affirmative action, three things that made him a good candidate to sing the song of absolution that Shelby Steele had helped write and that many whites were happy to dance to. Marshall had said he would step down "when my successor is qualified," and the president was now saying that Thomas was the most qualified person he could find—a claim that bore no more relation to the truth than some of the things the young man was saying at St. Elizabeth's two days before.

Marshall had also said this: While he knew race would play a role in the selection of his successor, it shouldn't be employed as "an excuse for doing wrong—picking the wrong Negro and saying, 'I'm picking him because he's a Negro.'" President Bush, for his part, denied he was doing that, denied that he was filling a quota (the very issue, ironically, he claimed he was fighting against in the 1991 civil rights bill). That aside, what he was doing was presenting liberals with a tricky problem: how to reject a minority candidate—especially one who had risen from abject poverty—to replace Marshall, even though he held views that were diametrically opposed to what Marshall stood for. It was a shrewd move on Bush's part, an attempt to throw his critics a bone and yet have someone on the Court whose views closely aligned with his own. After all, the ability to fill vacancies on the Supreme Court was (usually) a president's best, and least obstructed, opportunity to shape a Court in his image, a Court that would continue to reflect his philosophy long after he left office. It all depended on timing, of course, and in that respect Richard Nixon, Ronald Reagan, and George Bush had been lucky and Jimmy Carter had not: during his one-term presidency he didn't have any opportunities to appoint a justice.

"I emphasize black self-help," Thomas wrote to the *Wall Street Journal* in a letter to the editor in 1987, "as opposed to racial quotas and other race-conscious legal devices that only further and deepen the original problem."

In an opinion piece in the *Los Angeles Times* a year or so before that, a piece that rightly argued blacks didn't all think alike and that it was racist to assume they did, he was essentially setting himself apart in a way that seemed defensive and edgy, even arrogant: "The real issue," he wrote, was not who represented black America. "The real issue is why, unlike other individuals in this country, black individuals are not entitled to have and express points of view that differ from the collective hodgepodge of ideas that we supposedly share because we are members of the same race. . . .

"Anyone who . . . has a viewpoint that disagrees with the 'black viewpoint' is immediately cast as attacking the black leadership or as some kind of anti-black renegade. . . . Many of us accept the ostracism and public mockery in order to have our own ideas which are not intended to coincide with anyone else's, although they may well do just that. . . .

"We certainly cannot claim to have progressed much in this country as long as it is insisted that our intellects are controlled entirely by our pigmentation, with its countless variations, even though our individual experiences are entirely different."

Thomas's own experiences included living in a rural Georgia house without a toilet until he was seven; being told by his grandfather, a former sharecropper who became a fuel and ice dealer, that the more he prepared himself the less dependent he would be on the white man; going into the seminary but deciding against becoming a priest when he heard a fellow seminarian remark, on the day Martin Luther King was assassinated, "That's what they should do to all the niggers."

In college, at Holy Cross, he became a student of the writings of Malcolm X, was involved in any number of black student protests, and used to conclude his letters with the oft heard cry "Power to the People." This Clarence Thomas, said people who had known him a long time, was hard to reconcile with the Clarence Thomas who, in jobs as an assistant attorney general of Missouri and legislative assistant to Missouri senator John Danforth, had deliberately veered away from becoming involved with civil rights issues and who, as chairman of the Equal Employment Opportunity Commission, was viewed as fairly passive in terms of enforcing bias laws to protect the elderly and minorities, who labeled affirmative action policies "social engineering," and who complained to the *Washington Post* that all the country's traditional civil rights leaders did was bitch, moan, and whine. For someone like Lani Guinier, who had known Thomas for twenty years and had also worked for the NAACP Legal Defense Fund, his nomination was cause for concern; she wanted to know "if the person I knew ... is still there lodged somewhere deep inside of him, and if the public person he's become over the past fifteen years is more than a veneer."

At the time he was nominated by President Bush to sit on the United States Court of Appeals, in 1989, those same civil rights leaders reiterated their concerns about his stewardship at EEOC and now that he had been nominated to the highest Court they were repeating them again, urging the Senate to move carefully and study his record closely.

Barring some unforeseen problem, though, Clarence Thomas (so intent on being viewed as an individual that he had a Confederate flag on his office wall in Missouri) was expected to win confirmation and take Thurgood Marshall's seat on the Court that fall.

ON THE SAME DAY that Thomas was nominated and the dilemma his nomination created began making its way around the country, the Vice Lords were helping residents clean up the neighborhood and Alderwoman Marlene Johnson was pushing for a children's playground to be constructed on some vacant land right by Bridget Wilder's apartment. It wasn't that *no* indoor and outdoor recreation was available (contrary to what the young man at the church had said); it was just that there wasn't enough of it, and, unfortunately, what there was afforded little or no protection. It wasn't easy, after all, to play basketball or jump rope when you might have to hit the ground at any second or give up your sneakers or else. And it wasn't true that gangbangers didn't break into houses or steal cars. But it was true that something needed to be done, and the meeting at St. Elizabeth's had at least brought people together, and it encouraged Harambee to try to arrange for something larger—a meeting on July 15 that would include the Vice Lords and a variety of city officials.

Underlying all this was a dilemma of a different kind: the question of why the city should reward groups of individuals who terrorized the community, who kept residents in a state of fear and in the same state of confinement that the gangs complained they themselves were in. The short answer was that if the city didn't continue to channel money and programs to the inner city, it was the equivalent of giving up and giving in; of acknowledging, inadvertently or not, that the gangs had won; of saying that the idea of hardworking people ever being able to have a decent life again was folly, that the youths who wanted an education and to make something of themselves weren't entitled to do so.

As I write this, I realize that my anger, which had been hiding behind my disbelief, had deepened further. These gangs, in an effort to protect their turf, were oppressing the residents (and rightful holders) of that turf, oppressing them in the same way that whites had oppressed blacks for so long. As for me, I didn't feel safe using a pay phone on the street and I resented it, just as I resented the possibility of not being able to use the phone at all. They were public pay phones, and yet drug dealers often claimed ownership of them—one of the reasons that more and more of them were being blocked from receiving incoming calls.

At the same time, I kept reminding myself, the gangs were made up of kids, kids who had been recruited into them and who had joined them for a hundred different reasons and who, it seemed fair to conclude, might not have joined them if the approval, acceptance, and sense of support they were seeking had come from their own families, if more fathers were present, if more mothers weren't addicted to drugs or alcohol, or if these kids were strong enough to somehow rise above all of it and not be vulnerable to the next bad idea, to know the importance of a good education. Gangs, as Georgette Alexander said, have always been among us, but the innocent high jinks of Spanky and his motley crew were quite different from the high-powered, often deadly dealings of the Vice Lords and the Black Gangster Disciples, or from the all-male Spur Posse of suburban California, which viewed teenage girls (and younger) as chattel. But I also kept reminding myself that it was more complex than that, that some of these kids came from loving, supportive families, single parent or otherwise, and still they found the lure and what appeared to be the glamour and easy money of the streets too hard to pass up, the status and power an Uzi accorded you far more impressive (and easier to obtain) than any degree.

When I visited with Reverend LeHavre Buck, the executive director of Harambee, the day before the gathering at St. Elizabeth's, we talked about this and other matters. The reverend received me at his office (which was just up the block from James Cameron's museum) in a white suit and a red-and-white-striped shirt and began calling me Coleman right away. While that put me at ease, I hadn't forgotten what Jerrel Jones had said, about black people talking to white people in a different way than they would to other blacks. But in this case, I couldn't have cared less. The reverend was a writer's dream, this figure who did and did not seem like a man of the cloth, given that he was loquacious and running this agency and yet had been the principal owner of a wholesale purveyor business at one time. Anyway, just a few days before, his fourteen-year-old son had been hit over the head and robbed of his tennis shoes by three kids on dirt bikes who had put a gun to his face. When he took his son down to the 7th District precinct to report all this, the same precinct that Marlene Royalty had complained about during that town meeting at Washington High School, "they treated me like I wasn't even there, they never even turned around. I mean, Coleman, I have *no* record whatsoever, so why would someone with a record want to have anything to do with the police?"

He had brought this up because we had been talking about the shooting of George Edward Brown and the ongoing mystery as to whether the boy had actually had a rifle when he was shot or, as some people who had witnessed the shooting were claiming, the rifle had been "planted" by his side after the fact. Tension between the police and the black community was nothing new, of course, but this shooting had come on top of two others, one ruled accidental, the other justified, and it came just before the Fire and Police Commission released a report showing that out of 219 complaints filed with the commission, only two officers were ever disciplined. In the hope of correcting that situation, the reverend had decided that Harambee was going to be a place where citizens could come to file their complaints—a decision that the city was not all that pleased with, just as it wasn't thrilled that the agency had begun dealing with the Vice Lords.

Buck's position was this: Harambee wasn't there to condone drugs or violence or anything of the kind. And even though he was placing his agency in a situation "where nobody else has treaded that we're aware of," a situation that could affect the amount of block-grant money they received, he felt it was worth it, worth trying to persuade them to come in, perhaps once a month, to talk about education and sexuality and spirituality and things of that kind. "If you don't have any direction," he said, "if you are

stuck with nowhere to go, seeing nowhere to go, people can take you anywhere. Now if you take a person who has no future and does know nothing of his past, you have a person that is in the middle of doing whatever
he has to do, because what does he have to lose? 'I'm not going anywhere.
I'm not becoming anything. I don't have a goal. I don't have skills to obtain decent employment. What do I do? I deal drugs and become part of a
gang.'"

Being unemployed was no excuse for going out and "knocking folks
on the head," Buck said, but he could understand it. Blacks encountered
racism practically wherever they turned: in their jobs, shopping in stores,
trying to get loans, driving in white neighborhoods (in some cases, neighborhoods they lived in) and being pulled over for no reason, guilty until
proven innocent.

"You go to school, you're intelligent, you're highly motivated, you
come on a job, you work every day, but yet people dog you out," he said,
"they don't treat you the same." His daughter's boyfriend graduated from
Northwestern and took a job as an underwriter for an insurance company
in Cincinnati, the only black in the firm. In a short period of time, however, he wound up leaving the job, feeling so mistreated that he had serious thoughts of killing his boss.

If you wanted a job in the construction business, Buck said, affirmative action could help you—provided it was a job tied to a federal government contract—but it couldn't help you gain acceptance. His brother was
an apprentice electrician who found out from the first day that he was not
wanted on the job, found out through racial jokes, epithets being directed
at him, and wet concrete being dropped on him, "little things like that."

"See," Buck said, leaning forward in his chair, "that's what you live
through. You live through *that*. You live through folks questioning whether
you can pay for something."

He had a friend, a partner in a law firm, a man who made two hundred thousand dollars a year, but who decided that what he really wanted
was to be in business for himself. But when he went to the bank, the bank
where he had all his money, and explained his desire to a loan officer, the
officer wondered why he didn't just continue doing what he was doing,
pointing out (as if the attorney didn't know this) that going into business
for yourself was a risk. The reverend encountered similar problems when
he owned Angel's Distributors (delivering tobacco, candy, potato chips,

and beauty aids to inner-city stores), having to "constantly convince the banker that I could do what I could do, even though I had stats and papers and P&Ls that said we could." He and a cousin bought the business for twenty-two thousand dollars and by the time he sold his share to his cousin in 1980, when he became a minister full-time, the business was grossing $4.4 million a year.

Although his cousin eventually ran into tax difficulties and the business was lost as a result, there was a bigger problem. Arab wholesalers from Dearborn, Michigan, were beginning to come in and make it possible for Arab-owned stores to buy on credit, something that black-owned stores had not been permitted to do. Consequently, those stores found it increasingly difficult to compete.

Buck was not blaming the dearth of small black-owned businesses entirely on the Arabs, or on the banks, or even on the lack of education of how to run an operation. But talking about buying merchandise reminded him of the fact that unlike Asians, Hispanics, and Jews, among others, who had come to America intact ("Culture, religion, everything. They came to America as a people"), "African-American people came to America as a product. Stock. Like horses, cows, pigs. We were treated that way. So none of which we knew from our forefathers is with us; we're just now retaining some of that. . . . We were so busy working on becoming like the melting pot that we've melted a lot of our culture right away."

E I G H T E E N

When John Norquist goes to bed at night in his modest Victorian house on the South Side, a house in which the television rarely works or, when it does, is rarely on, he might pick up Aristotle for some light reading before drifting off to sleep, a sleep that is often filled, on good nights, with soft, dreamy images of trains and streetcars and, on bad ones, with the harsh specter of automobiles racing along freeways, racing away from the city on cheap gas, toward places like Elm Grove and River Hills, affluent, cloistered, squeaky-clean places that, to his way of thinking, would be purgatory if he were forced to live there. Even though John Norquist's official job description was "Mayor of the City of Milwaukee," his real occupation—his obsession, would be more like it—was that of "foamer," one of those people who spend a good portion of their lives waiting for the sound of a train in the distance, whose whole countenance and demeanor can change, in an instant, when they see or hear one approach. Whether they themselves are actually supposed to board the train is of no consequence. There are very few things, it would seem, that can make John Norquist swoon, go weak in the knees. His Nordic background, one might conclude, would make such display of emotion unlikely. And yet there it was, direct and unabashed, this deep affection and longing. In looking back at the history of the city he had presided over since 1988, he found that his mind zoomed instantly and disdainfully back to 1952, to the cataclysmic year that the Milwaukee Interurban ground to a halt.

"The assholes back then tore it up," he said in the characteristically blunt manner he was both admired and disliked for. "Excuse me, the leadership of the community tore it out."

"How extensive was it?" I said.

"It was a hundred-and-ninety-eight-mile system and that was just the interurban," he explained, warming to the question. "The streetcar system was even bigger than that. It was a rapid transit line that went west from downtown and it was an elevated line. Once you got past about where

County Stadium is, about One Hundredth Street, then it went down to-ward Hales Corners. . . . It was magnificent. If you look at pictures from the time, the land-use patterns and beautiful public spaces that developed around the system, it would be wonderful today if we had them. It was a system as good as you could have. Couldn't have a better system than that. It was like Vienna, where you can go out to the Vienna Woods in a street-car. You could take the interurban all the way out to Pewaukee Lake. Some-body who lived in the middle of Milwaukee could hop on that streetcar and go to the beach way out in Waukesha. Hike around. Go in a catama-ran. It was fast, too. Seventy miles an hour when it was on a long run."

If it was as glorious as he said it was, what happened? Well, it was privately owned and operated, but in order to keep afloat it needed the support of the government and the government, particularly the state government, felt that the only things they should own were highways and airports, Norquist said. "It's peculiar to America that there's this sort of public policy bias against public transportation, a bias heavily against cit-ies. So what happened in a lot of cities happened here."

If the system were still in place, he went on, "the middle of the metro area would be more important economically. There'd be more jobs, more opportunity. We'd still have a lot of the American city symptoms of drugs and drug-related crime; cities that have good transit systems aren't auto-matically without social problems or social injustice."

After 1952 and the end of the interurban, the next significant date in Norquist's mind was four years later, the year that President Eisenhower signed the Interstate Highway Act, a piece of legislation that, according to Lewis Mumford, caused as much damage to American cities as "the bombs that devastated the City of London in the Blitz." An "iron ring" of suburbs had begun to encircle Milwaukee nearly ten years before the act's passage, but now "the federal government was coming in and helping to completely dismantle something that the economy had built around and replace it with something that would have this new economy far away from the city. And they left behind people that didn't have the resources to deal with the new situation. They even tore down whole neighborhoods."

His mind wandered to St. Louis and a trip he had made there with his family in the fifties, when he was about seven. They had gone to see a movie in Forest Park, an area he recalled as beautifully old. There were streetcar tracks, but no streetcars; five or so years later, when he went back, there was nothing. "All of it was gone. All leveled. Because it was old, it wasn't modern. They replaced it with shit like Pruitt-Igoe" (a high-rise public housing project). "A lot of these problems are a lot worse because of the federal government doing that. Like they dropped a bomb on every city. Now, the ones that were lucky enough to have political movements to resist are now doing pretty well. In Boston, Jane Jacobs and her buddies fought for the North End not to be ripped down. As a result, the North End is a very chi-chi neighborhood today. . . ."

So his main source of upset was "the promise" of urban renewal?

"Well, it made the problems that we face today much more severe than they would have been. I'm not saying that we wouldn't have had racial conflict. I'm not saying we wouldn't have had drug-related crime," he reiterated. "All of those things are also afflicting European cities now. Amsterdam, Paris, Berlin, wherever. But those cities aren't going to be physically damaged by it. Those cities will not lose their economic value because of those problems."

I had known that Norquist (his Democratic affiliation aside) was no fan of the federal government, that he viewed any money that came from Washington and ultimately made its way into the city's coffers as a gift, a gift that was terribly unreliable and often misused. What I hadn't known was how strongly he felt about these matters. Cities had to look after themselves, he believed, had to be viable without depending on help from elsewhere, couldn't be run on pity.

If one could categorize Norquist in any way, it would be as a social liberal and a fiscal conservative. But unlike Tom Donegan, he saw the Great Society and the War on Poverty as an exercise in futility. It was scattershot, it was "shooting into the abyss," and, with the possible exception of Head Start, it didn't get at the fundamental problems. What frustrated Norquist about unswerving liberals, particularly those in elective office, was their tendency to "make every city issue a social services issue," while at the same time voting for "all these highway appropriations that undermine a city's economy. . . .

"Concentration of poverty happened mostly because of this transportation/land-use thing, *not* because of something else. Because of *that.* I just want that understood, that's fundamental. You can look at every stat and they all have impacts and factors, and yet if the land-use stuff doesn't get fixed," he said, clearly exasperated, then began again. "There's stuff you can do to minimize it: reform education, improve the lot of minorities that have been discriminated against, change the way the city government operates, motivate the business community. You can do all those things to mitigate the problem . . . but the most important negative impact we get in cities is America's uniquely harmful, destructive urban policies."

It's not that he begrudged people cars—he had one himself (and it worked)—he just wanted them to have more choices. Why public transit (buses) should primarily be "a social services agency for the nonmembers of society—the poor and the injured"—was something he was hoping to remedy with his proposal for a light rail system in Milwaukee. If he could emulate in Milwaukee what Neil Goldschmidt had achieved with mass transit in Portland (after many tries), it would be the capstone of his time in office.

But how, I wanted to know, would even the most ideal transit system attack the problem of residential segregation?

It wouldn't, he said, not in any direct way. What it would do, he emphasized once more, is tackle the problem of economic segregation, make the middle—and the people who live there—more important. And that was much more crucial, in his view, than trying to achieve something that was impractical, counterproductive (if it was too intrusive on individual freedom), and, finally, insulting to blacks, this notion that blacks would somehow be better off if they lived alongside or in close proximity to white people. He had recently gone to a meeting of the Fair Housing Council, a group that, among other things, tried to pinpoint race discrimination through the use of testers. As a state legislator, he had been supportive of the organization; but as mayor he wanted no part of their new plan to persuade "well-off minorities" to live in places like Fox Point and River Hills. "I'm not interested in encouraging people of means to move out of the city, whether they're white or black. I'm not interested in having a black upper middle class move to the suburbs. If they want to, I'll defend their right to do it, but I don't want to encourage it." That Milwaukee's suburbs were overwhelmingly white was something he viewed as their problem.

It was only natural that Norquist would do his own form of calculating, would, as mayor, want to keep the city's tax base solid and secure. Encouraging people to integrate, away from Milwaukee, was only going to make it more difficult for the city to be economically viable. He found it amusing that certain public policy experts thought the magic solution for the survival of cities lay in the notion of consolidation, of merging city and suburbs into one big entity and calling it a metropolis, all assets and expenditures coming from the same pot. It wasn't as if this were some brand-new idea, some sudden news flash. Back in 1934, a commission was appointed in Milwaukee to explore that very possibility, but the idea was quickly rejected by the state legislature. Twenty years later, with Republicans controlling the governorship and both houses, Milwaukee's boundaries were essentially frozen, "making it real easy for all the townships around Milwaukee's borders to incorporate into cities and deny us the ability to take them. If that hadn't been passed and we had had our annexation plan, Milwaukee would have 1.2 million people," he said, a number roughly twice as many as the city had in the 1990 census. "We would have had a rich tax base, wouldn't need state aid."

But the "iron ring" didn't want it and wouldn't allow it—bluntly put, that's why people moved out there in the first place, to flee "urban problems" and create their own idea of Shangri-la—just as they had no interest in allowing scatter-site housing to litter the landscape and cut into their precious tax base. Since Republican administrations were quite comfortable with that and didn't want to alienate their constituents, the Department of Housing and Urban Development was, for all intents and purposes, only paying lip service to enforcing it in the suburbs, while being more stringent about it with regard to cities. To effect scatter-site housing meant taking a certain number of houses off the tax rolls, and, frankly, Norquist was thinking of getting out of "the scatter-site business" altogether, of just not accepting the HUD money. "We're going to solve racial segregation, fifty houses a year, scatter-site housing?" he asked rhetorically. "It's kind of a sad joke. . . . Fifty a year for twenty years, that's a thousand houses becoming government-owned houses. Doesn't sound like a winner to me. It's public housing for the poor and everybody else has a free-market system in the suburbs." He would much rather put his efforts into the continuous improvement of housing conditions overall, be it the opening up of Hillside so that it wasn't so claustrophobically isolated, so that it could seem more a part of the city, or the building of Johnson Square, with its own Head Start program right on the premises. While he never tried to deny that Milwaukee was segregated, both economically and residentially, he simply wanted to point out that the segregation was much more dramatic in terms of city and suburb than within the city itself.

"What should be done about racial segregation?" he asked. "I think you attack it through economic segregation. If somebody black wants to buy a house around somebody who's white, they have the resources to do it. If they want to buy a house around blacks, they can do that too. Leave it up to them. Don't tell them where to live. The other thing won't work. It pisses people off."

This seemed as good a time as any to bring up Michael McGee. To what degree had he pissed the mayor off, made his job all the more difficult?

Unlike Howard Fuller, Norquist wasn't at all reluctant to discuss him. He stressed that he hadn't courted McGee's support in 1988, only that he had met with "the Group of Ten"—a group that included McGee, Jerrel Jones, and Walter Farrell—at the Crossroads Supper Club in order to answer the various questions they had for him and Martin Schreiber, the other candidate. In his opinion, McGee's support for him came by default (he sensed that the group was hedging its bets, that it had already been determined that half the group would support Schreiber, half would support him) and he was immediately suspicious of it, especially since shortly after the meeting "there was material going out on the far South Side reminding people down there that I had just been endorsed by McGee."

Whatever McGee's reasons for the endorsement, the endorsement was given, but something must have happened to alter the alliance, however tenuous and unholy it might have been.

It was a combination of things, Norquist said, and they all fell into the category of political pork, of what are you *now* going to do for me? Jerrel Jones wanted a radio tower moved; there was no way the city could legally help him with that, yet Jones got mad at him anyway. The Opportunities Industrialization Center (OIC) didn't get the money it wanted, so its director, Carl Gee (McGee's closest friend), got mad at him. McGee wanted the city to gain control of the Private Industry Council so that he would have influence over the way its money was spent, but Bill Lawrence prevailed in keeping the group fairly autonomous.

"I would try to play straight with these people," Norquist explained, staring coldly, "and when I didn't do what they wanted, they got mad at me. . . . If somebody messes with me, if they want to fight, sometimes you have to fight back. . . . It's not all seashells and balloons, you know."

Backtracking a little, I wanted to know if he thought there were any positives, any at all, to what McGee was doing, or any contributions that he had made to the city.

Actually, Norquist said, before McGee began trying to incite people to violence, he admired him for being unafraid to stand up for what he believed in, felt that he was an effective alderman. He was for school choice (finally instituted in 1990, it allowed public money to follow a limited number of students to private school) at a time when "if you were black, you were supposed to be against it. Government bureaucracy was automatically considered the friend of the black community. I think McGee understood that wasn't true, sooner than others."

"To hear him tell it, he had this growing frustration from his seat on the council," I said.

"Life is tough. If he has this expectation that somehow the city is going to magically solve all its problems, he is naïve."

But, I suggested, playing devil's advocate, McGee wouldn't suddenly have turned on him because of OIC not getting money (OIC had a history of money problems) and the city not managing to have the Private Industry Council under its wing.

Look, he said, starting to bristle, OIC wanted even more money. And they didn't like audits (which Norquist had initiated because there was a lot of money that had gone unaccounted for). OIC had pretty much gotten what it wanted from Governor Thompson and they didn't like Norquist poking around in their business. In fact, Norquist thought the money that OIC received was being so badly misused—that it was going everywhere but where it was supposed to be going, out into the black community— that he came to think of Gee himself as "a poverty pimp." It was the classic case of continuing to throw good money after bad, Norquist said, and somebody had to stop it, somebody had to say no.

"There's a whole collection of people that were living off OIC and not delivering services, and McGee was part of that group. One of his closest friends, Doris Green, got on the payroll. Half of the militia was on the payroll. Are they delivering good services? I don't think so.

"I just looked at it on the basis of public policy," Norquist said, "and I couldn't do what he wanted. Then he couched it in betrayal and all that. If you don't do what he wants, you don't care about the problem, you're not doing anything."

"And then the next thing you knew he announced he was forming the militia?"

No, not quite. There was the thing with the Private Industry Council. Norquist said he tried to work out a deal with Milwaukee County (to whom the PIC had always been solely accountable) that would give the city half the membership of the organization's board. The county executive agreed to that, but would not agree to allowing the city to pick the executive director. "We didn't get our initial demand," he said. "We agreed to a compromise and he said it was betrayal.... I think he wanted the money out of the PIC to go into OIC.... I didn't cry about it. You want to call it betrayal, fine, give me your best shot. He's a victim, right, that's what he was trying to say, everybody betrayed him, everybody in the world is all screwed up except him. I don't think so. I think it's more the other way around."

"But once the militia was formed, how did you react to it?"

"I didn't," he said. "I underreacted a while just to see how it played out. I didn't want to get all upset about it. Little political theater, great. I think when I sensed that there would be appreciation even in the black community for confronting him on it, then I did. I mean, there were black employees at Usinger's whose jobs were jeopardized by his phony claim that the sausage had been tainted.... He thought he could pick on Usinger's because it's owned by a white family. I don't think it played out the way he wanted it to."

"Then there was the Circus Parade."

"Ridiculous. We got a restraining order so that if he did anything he would do jail time."

"That's a big event here."

"He hurt it a little, attendance was probably down slightly. But it went on, nothing happened. I mean, I'm glad nothing happened. I'm not challenging him to do crazy things."

Did he make any attempts to talk to McGee during this time, I wondered, try to defuse the situation in any way?

"Before he started threatening to kill people, yeah, sure, I talked to him a lot. But he was kind of absolutist."

So the answer was no, he didn't?

"I guess, I mean, I don't quite remember," he said, thrown off-guard slightly. "I don't think he was looking for advice from me."

The Greater Milwaukee Committee, on the other hand, was prepared to meet with him (apart from its forming the Inner City Task Force) and the mayor had been unhappy about it. He told them that if they met with McGee they would simply be responding to criminal behavior. He wasn't saying that there weren't "enormous problems that you have to deal with," but to do so "in response to his threat of violence" would be irresponsible. The meeting never took place.

But that still left the indirect ways in which the city was responding to McGee. What about those?

Contrary to what Bill Lawrence and others had said, Norquist insisted there were none, that whatever efforts the city was making to improve conditions in the inner city had nothing whatsoever to do with McGee's threat, were things that the city had been doing (or had planned to do) anyway. Targeting Metcalfe Park as an area in which to increase jobs, reduce crime, and provide better health services. The Fair Lending Action Committee (which was formed in response to the report that Milwaukee had the highest mortgage rejection rates for minorities in the country). The Drug Abatement Program (aimed at closing down drug houses). The Milwaukee Guarantee (an effort to ensure that students who attend school 90 percent of the time, maintain a 2.5 average, and graduate from high school are guaranteed either job training or higher education at certain state colleges). The Community Service Corps (loosely modeled on the Civilian Conservation Corps of the 1930s, it employed a rolling number of eighteen- to twenty-three-year-olds in a variety of jobs—landscaping, painting, and renovating—designed to enhance the community while at the same time offering them actual classroom learning). He was particularly proud of the fact that his administration had hired more African-Americans by far than the preceding one and had hired them because they were qualified. He was no fan of affirmative action (considered himself right in step with Shelby Steele on that subject) and had no hesitation in getting rid of someone, regardless of race, if he or she was not performing. Once you got into race-based outcomes, Norquist said, you were in the wilderness. And those who wound up most lost in this wilderness were blacks, "because every time something good happens, the white guys did it for you. . . . Well, what if you're a really talented black person and you got a job because you're the best one? How would you feel when everybody thinks you got it because of affirmative action?" That didn't mean that Norquist thought nothing should be done. It meant that "you take advantage of opportunities to create empowerment."

Empowerment. One of the "new" buzzwords everyone was using but wasn't new at all; black leaders had been using it for years. "It's in the interest of everybody in Milwaukee, black or white, for the black community to be more self-sufficient, wealthier, have more value in it. But that isn't going to happen because of some alphabet soup of government programs. I'm sorry, it's not going to happen. And if every time I'm against one of these things it means that it puts me in a position where I'm supposedly against the black community, if people want to think that, so be it."

For all his disdain of scattershot government programs, though, the fact was that he didn't turn the money away and he fought for Milwaukee's share. But when it came to dispensing this money to various community organizations, organizations like Harambee, he faulted himself for not getting more involved, for perhaps allowing his private bias to influence the way he did his job, ordered his priorities. "It's kind of a waste of resources if all you do is just throw little grants all over the place and somebody screws up and you don't do anything about it." (That, of course, wasn't true. As his dealings with OIC attest, Norquist, like any politician, wasn't above rewarding his friends and punishing his enemies.) People in his administration faulted him for not articulating his overall vision for the city more effectively, for not ensuring that the various departments were on the same page, were not working at cross-purposes to each other. The absence of consensus often results in disarray, in duplication of effort, in feverish, often vicious preservation of territory and attempts to expand on that territory. In point of fact, that is true in many organizations, but when the organization exists to serve people, as city government does, that lack of consensus can have a particularly damaging effect.

John Norquist was—is—cool and careful. He had never entered a political contest that he didn't win. He wanted to run for mayor in 1984 but decided that the time wasn't right, that Mr. Mayor, as Henry Maier was known, couldn't be toppled. Four years later, Maier chose to step down and Norquist prevailed. Balanced the city budget every year he'd been in office. Lowered the tax levy each year too. Ran his administration like a business. He might concede that he wasn't involved enough with the community-based organizations, but his involvement (as with his hiring of African-Americans) was a great improvement over Maier's:

Maier basically didn't leave City Hall to deal with these groups at all, acted more like the iconoclastic owner of a plantation than the mayor for all the people.

Control and careerism and the preservation of turf does not fit well, it would seem, with consensus, with collective political will, with the possibility for real change, the prospect of making conditions in the inner cities a priority. Even though there is finally a limit to what a mayor can do—without the cooperation of the state and federal government, the private sector, and other entities—the basic structure of a city's administration is not that different, on some level, from that of the Vice Lords. A hierarchy exists, but so do factions, their eyes peeled for the main chance. Disputes occur; sometimes they get resolved, sometimes not. People come and people go, on to better things, fired or erased. Personal aggrandizement is often in conflict with a greater good. Money factors in. Favors factor in. Who will take your call factors in. Both are organizations, each with its own aims and own way of measuring success, each with its own share of very sharp minds and very dull ones, each with its own ability to affect the lives of people who come into contact with them.

NINETEEN

In retrospect it seemed they had been there for only an instant. But it was long enough to display their defiance, their disgust with having to remove their caps, with a setup that would allow each person only four minutes to speak. Those were the rules that Judge Stanley Miller had instituted for the evening of July 15 at Harambee Community School, an evening that saw the chief of police, some members of his department, and various other city officials sit on a panel and listen to some of the Vice Lords come to the podium. Perhaps their walkout was planned, perhaps it came about impulsively (after all, Judge Miller's rules weren't ones they would necessarily feel obliged to abide by). They had heard Chief Philip Arreola say that the police were not going to allow *any* organization to take any part of the community over, and they had heard Reverend Buck say how the police were desperately in need of "cultural sensitivity training," and they had heard a black funeral director say how sick he was of burying children, that the bodies seemed never to stop coming, most recently two-year-old Felicia Watson, who took a bullet the day before while she was sleeping peacefully on a love seat at 2162 North Thirty-fifth Street.

The Vice Lords in turn had tried to reiterate what they said two weeks earlier at St. Elizabeth's, that they felt cornered, limited by what they could do and where they could go. The young man who wore a yellow T-shirt at the church, who now identified himself as Baba-Il (but whose real name was Anthony Adams), told the chief that he should drop the charges against George Edward Brown (the young man who had been shot on the night of June 11 and whom the district attorney's office was thinking of charging with intent to kill a police officer), that he knew damn well that the police who "patrolled" the area were part of Blondie's bunch—Blondie being Mike Lewandowski, a feared vice squad detective—and that the community should know, straight up, that all the police department truly wanted was "for us to kill ourselves like savages," oddly echoing what Arthur Gordon had insisted they were doing when he held up his brown paper bag.

It was at this point that Baba-Il was told he had exceeded the time limit, but he kept talking anyway, becoming more and more agitated. When he finally walked away from the microphone, he headed for the door, followed by the thirty or so Vice Lords, their caps back on and pointed in the same direction, who had been sitting together.

Once they left, a woman stood up and said her heart was heavy because they were walking time bombs and a man criticized the judge for sticking so rigidly to the rules and another woman, a woman named Lora Gooden who worked for the city, an outspoken figure who was a friend of Louise Kidd's, got up and reminded everyone that "we're talking about our children and *we* better decide what is to be done about them" and not be looking to the police and the district attorney to solve our problems. "When we look at each other now," she said, "we don't see each other. We see a prison, or we see a gang, or we see somebody that might break into our house, or hit us over the head, and that concerns me. We're no longer talking to each other. We're no longer looking at each other in ways in which we can help one another. We're no longer taking the time we need to do the things that we have to do in order to get past it."

Over and over again, the theme of self-reliance and the responsibility parents had to teach their children respect reverberated throughout the evening. The people who had come—who one person said were, unfortunately, not the people who needed to be there—were clearly ambivalent about the police. They said they needed the police to be on patrol and yet they needed to do a better job themselves. They complained that when they phoned the police they were frequently put on hold, and that when the police finally came to the neighborhood they often treated people rudely. Tommie Williams of Harambee, a former police officer, said the Fire and Police Commission should be made up of elected citizens. Another person said that the black churches were a bunch of hypocrites, that they needed to get off their duffs and play a stronger role. And one woman simply said she was tired, tired of rearranging her furniture every time there was a shooting.

The basement took on the feel of a bunker with a strategy session in progress. And yet there was no one general who would or could make the final decision on how to proceed, and there was no agreement on who the enemy was: the police were the enemy and yet the community needed them; the gangs were the enemy and yet they were also children who needed to be guided; the school system was the enemy because it had given up on black kids and yet there was a new superintendent who most emphatically had not; the black churches were the enemy because they didn't do enough and yet they were still what they had always been, a place where people could come together, to sing and to pray and to seek redemption; the drug dealers were the enemy, but the crack and the dope were put there by white people.

The walls of the labyrinth appeared to be narrowing.

A FEW DAYS AFTER the meeting I had lunch with Tommie Williams, the organizer from Harambee who had been instrumental in bringing it all about. Williams was forty-two, had grown up in Hillside, played basketball (with Fred "Downtown" Brown) on the 1967 Lincoln High team that won the state championship, and had lived in Milwaukee his entire life. Because he had had his share of trouble as a youth and now had three sons and one daughter of his own, he believed that he was in a reasonably good position to deal with the Vice Lords. He had come to Harambee only the year before, having spent twelve years in the fire department and six before that as a police officer. When the Harambee Ombudsman Project first started in 1974, its focus for the longest time was on community organizing, but under new directors, the focus shifted to economic development, with the organizing element suffering as a result. That was the reason that Reverend Buck, who had known Williams for years, called on him. Williams had begun his career in organizing in the late sixties, at Northcott Neighborhood House, and had come to feel that grass-roots work was where he could most help his community. All that aside, though, he was nervous about getting involved with the Vice Lords, and he was nervous about the area around First and Keefe, despite having remained loyal to his barber there for many years.

Not long before the shooting of George Edward Brown, Harambee had submitted a proposal to the city that would allow them to set up a crisis center of sorts—not just for the families of victims, but for whole neighborhoods. That way, anytime something occurred—shootings, fires, gang activity, assaults—Harambee could determine what was needed or desired: psychological assistance, referrals to social service agencies, blocks wanting to get together and organize block clubs, or people just wanting to talk about the incident and how it could be prevented in the future. "See, too often with all of this violence that's going on in the central city," Williams said, "these people are beginning to accept this as a way of life. 'It happens, big deal, that's the way it is.'"

I had already begun to witness the state of numbness that Williams was talking about, had already begun to see that it wasn't just whites in the suburbs thinking of an inner-city homicide as a number and not a person, regardless of whether that victim was an innocent party, like Felicia Watson, or a member of a gang. And Williams himself, despite having proposed the idea, wasn't convinced that he was cut out to be so intimately involved with that degree of pain and agony. After so many years of policing and firefighting, he wasn't sure that he wanted to put himself in that kind of position again.

But on the same day that Harambee submitted the proposal, something happened that erased those doubts.

Williams lived in Sherman Park, not far from Louise Kidd, and he came home one night in late May, right around the time of that town meeting at Washington High School, and found seven people standing in his doorway. They were there because of Michelle, a young woman of twenty-three who lived across the street and whom Tommie had known since she was thirteen. Michelle had been stabbed to death that morning, but Tommie hadn't heard. He immediately went over and asked Michelle's mother if there was anything he could do. Yes, there was. She wanted to go to the crime scene and she wanted Tommie to accompany her.

The chalk marks were still on the street, and half a block away, the blood was still on the pay phone, the phone Michelle had apparently used to request help. "People were at the phone booth literally in shock, wondering how could something so vicious happen," he recalled. When he took the mother home, he found Michelle's brothers loading up guns, "getting ready to get Michelle's ex-boyfriend." Though he was able to persuade them to let the police handle it, it made him wonder "how many extra homicides occur because people want to retaliate" and reminded him yet again how important a crisis unit could be.

A FEW DAYS AFTER the proposal was submitted, Harambee held a community meeting at a church on North Sixth Street. Even though the meeting was intended for the people in the immediate vicinity of the church, a few people from the First and Keefe area attended, telling Williams that they were having trouble with youth crime, not having much luck in getting the police's help, and "gravely needed our assistance" in getting their block organized. When the police did come, the residents said, they would often verbally abuse the youths, make racial slurs, say things about their mothers, and, as a result, there had been talk that the Vice Lords might be planning to kill a police officer (Blondie being the person they had in mind). "These people knew that something was getting ready to erupt," Williams said, and before Harambee could even have its block club meeting, the shooting of George Edward Brown took place.

Blondie, as it happened, was not there when Brown was shot, but his partner was. The morning after the shooting, Chief Arreola himself contacted Tommie Williams and asked for Harambee's help in bringing peace back to the neighborhood. Since Williams had been using the department as a sounding board for his crisis unit idea (which they supported), it wasn't surprising they would turn to him and to Harambee; after all, it fit with the community-oriented policing approach that the department and Mayor Norquist (who, many felt, was the de facto police chief anyway) were trying to bring about.

What the department didn't count on—nor did Williams, for that matter—was that the residents would offer accounts that were in conflict with what the police were saying, a situation that put Harambee in a quandary. If they appeared to be resolutely on the side of the police, they would have a hard time in gaining the neighborhood's trust; if they sided unblinkingly with the neighborhood, that choice could have repercussions with the city and future funding. Trying to sort out the truth of what happened on the night of June 11—to determine whether Brown had a rifle or one was planted by his body—was likely to be a futile search, Williams knew; neighbors, fearing retaliation from the gang members, were not necessarily the most reliable eyewitnesses. Given all that, he decided to examine the shooting scene for himself. He was not satisfied with the police account of what happened; it was imperative that the incident not just quietly fall away, and that residents have an opportunity to talk face-to-face with members of the department. Chief Arreola attempted to convince Williams not to go ahead with the meeting at the school and even went so far as to remind Williams of a recent award that Blondie had received. But

Williams and Harambee were determined that the meeting go forward—
the ultimate goal, he stressed over and over to the police, was to find solutions for a better relationship between the community and the police—and
Arreola eventually decided to be on the panel.

When the Vice Lords walked out of the meeting that night, Tommie
Williams's reaction was mixed: on the one hand he felt he had made a
mistake asking Judge Miller to be the moderator instead of serving himself; on the other, he felt that a number of useful things got discussed that
might not have been aired with the Vice Lords there. Either way, he wanted
to underscore what Reverend Buck had told me: the agency would try to
continue reaching them and working with them, but regardless of what
anybody thought—the mayor, the chief of police, whoever—they were not
treating them with kid gloves, not trying to curry favor with them in any
way. They were trying to acquire their confidence, that was true, but they
were not romanticizing them. Williams knew from talking to them that
they were unafraid to kill—especially since they might get out of jail in
five or six years. "That's no big time to them," he said with a mixture of
both sadness and disgust. In fact, if it was up to him, there would be a lot
less plea bargaining going on. "Something has to be done in Milwaukee to
make these young people aware that if they commit crimes they're going
to have to pay time for it."

Five days earlier I had seen *Boyz N the Hood,* a powerful look at life in
South-Central Los Angeles, and I was thinking, as Williams continued
talking, of how much he reminded me of the father in the film, the father
who tried everything he could to keep his son out of trouble and alive.
Williams had a sleepy-eyed look that was deceptive, that belied his intensity. When he met with the Vice Lords the day after they walked out of
the meeting, he took the position beforehand that he had to make them
realize that what they did was wrong and that it was "not up to me to go
crawling back to them asking for their forgiveness." They were under the
impression, they told Williams, that the Vice Lords were to be the focal
point of the evening and he reminded them that the problem was bigger
than just figuring out how to deal—or not deal—with the Vice Lords, that
it was a community problem, a problem everyone had responsibility for
solving. "Basically I told them that if you want to change your community, if you want to improve your community, that's what we're here for.
If you don't trust us, I suggest that you sit back, watch us, and see how we

operate." He told them they shouldn't ask him to set up any more meetings in the future—their walking out had embarrassed Harambee somewhat—but recommended they help in the planning of a block club party to be held in early August.

THE FOLLOWING NIGHT, MICHAEL MCGEE held a press conference in front of militia headquarters on King Drive. In the previous few weeks, he had restated his 1987 proposal that the black community secede from the city of Milwaukee and set up a separate enclave called King's Paradise. Separate police force, separate fire department, separate school system, separate everything. That he would want to call it that was ironic, given that he had begun saying that King's dream had never been more than just that, a dream.

The purpose of the press conference on that sweltering July evening was, on one level, to update people on what the militia was planning to do, to recruit more members—and to ask for money so that they could fund their activities. Street patrols. Escorts for the elderly. A mediation program to help settle domestic disputes. These were only some of the things McGee said they were "working on," things he had given me the impression were already in place. But the real reason for the press conference was to let everyone know that his deadline of 1995 might have to be moved up "because the situation has reached what I call an emergency state.... Sunday morning a two-and-a-half-year-old girl [Felicia Watson] was killed in our neighborhood as Milwaukee prepared to celebrate another fun day, the Great Circus Parade, and here we are sitting in our neighborhoods in a virtual state of siege.... I hear more gunshots in our neighborhood than I did on some nights in Vietnam and we were in a state of war." He was so distressed by what was going on he was even contemplating putting sandbags around his windows.

"You had a hundred soldiers die in Desert Storm. I have more people than that die in my district and we're supposedly not at a state of war.... Some of this violence is gonna have to be spread outside our neighborhoods and then maybe someone will be concerned about it...."

He reminded them that he had received "a lotta ridicule" a few weeks earlier when he reiterated his plans for King's Paradise. If suburbs like Glendale and West Allis could have their own police and fire departments, their own mayor, control of all the institutions that affect their life, why, he wanted to know, couldn't blacks in Milwaukee? Part of the problem, he said, was blacks themselves, always wondering, "What we gonna do without white people? We can't live without them taking care of us." That, he said, was such "a fallacy" that he didn't see how blacks could do "any worse than's being done now if we took control of our own life."

The city received about twenty-two million dollars a year from the federal government for community-development block grants, he said. Since the bulk of that money was earmarked for poor people, he was asking them to imagine what they could do with those resources, reinforcing his argument by insisting that in the days of segregation "we were all much better off."

"Tell it," one person said.

"All right," said another.

"Amen," said a third.

With each pronouncement, each plea/demand for separatism that he blended with the attractive selling points of independence and control, I reluctantly began coming to terms with the fact that King's dream of an integrated society was not only shared by fewer and fewer people, it was viewed as a trap, a way of luring people to something that was conceived with good intentions but, in reality, had become, on some level, another form of slavery, of having to play by the white man's rules. Just as many people did not seem cognizant of the change that Malcolm X underwent after he was forced out of the Nation of Islam and journeyed to Mecca, a trip that resulted in his viewing the possibilities of blacks and whites coexisting, in his backing off from his claim that whites were nothing more than blue-eyed devils, so too were few people aware that King did not simply stand for integration at all costs, did not view it as the proverbial magic bullet that would solve the problems of racism and poverty. Michael McGee was no doubt aware of this, of King's Poor People's Campaign and his discussions with Elijah Muhammad, but found it easier to do what Howard Fuller said shouldn't be done—put down King's dream in order to elevate and push his own vision of what needed to come about.

"If the city of Milwaukee was concerned about us, we could have a Common Council meeting tomorrow, allocate twenty million dollars to start an emergency jobs program, and by the end of the day the mayor could sign it into law." He had seen it done before, for the Bradley Center, "twenty-five million in one day. Milwaukee has a surplus—and I mean a surplus—of three hundred million that's just sitting downtown. Drawing interest while we're sitting here being eaten alive. Look around the neighborhoods. How many people see all these boarded-up houses? We got all these young men that are out of work and we're telling them not to belong to gangs and to Hang Tough"—referring to the name of a program designed to discourage youth from taking drugs. "The city know we hanging, now they want us to hang tough." If the black community didn't literally take matters into its own hands, McGee warned, all that the "powers that be" were going to do "is continue what's called genocide."

There it was again, this notion, promulgated by everyone from Marcus Garvey to Louis Farrakhan, that there was a conspiracy, a plan, akin to what happened to the Jews in the Holocaust, to systematically eliminate black people in America, males in particular. Was it a conscious plan? No one could say. No one had any proof of its existence. At the very least it was subliminal, a number of blacks told me. It was implicit in McGee's saying "They don't mind because we don't matter," and it was explicit in the suggestion that the rampant drug trade was operated by whites, who in turn directed it toward blacks who needed money and couldn't make that kind of money any other way. The conspiracy could be seen, people said, in the density of liquor outlets and tobacco billboard advertising in the inner city. It could be seen in the dearth of jobs, which led men to abandon their families, which led to so many single-parent households, so many people enslaved by welfare, a system that, some argued, should be abolished altogether. It could be seen in education, in the textbooks with a scant amount of material reflecting the accomplishments of African-Americans. It could be seen in the criminal justice system. Because whites had such a negative opinion of blacks, people said, many blacks in turn held that same opinion of themselves, an opinion that was deeply internalized and displayed itself, with greater and greater frequency, in black-on-black crime, in all forms of abuse and neglect. Even for the blacks who, by any measure, were succeeding, who had the money and the houses and all the accoutrements to prove it, there were still the indignities—be it the cab that wouldn't stop, or the policeman who would, wondering what you were doing in your own neighborhood; the sinking sense that no matter who you were or what you did or what you stood for, you were still going to be painted with the same brush. Jerrel Jones, Walter Farrell, Maron and

Georgette Alexander, Blair Moreland (in regard to her parents' treatment of Alice), and Alice herself—each in his or her own way had spoken of it or touched on it, just as Huey Newton and Angela Davis and James Baldwin had.

McGee reminded people of the things he had tried to achieve since taking office, but which had gone nowhere: putting blacks to work fixing housing units, training them in home maintenance and repair; having youths become part of a neighborhood security patrol; taking the twenty-five thousand dollars each year that it cost to send a youth to reform school and putting four of those youths in a supervised group home, a home they would have to renovate and maintain. "In other words, every idea that we come up with, that *we* think is a good idea, is never implemented because *they* don't think it's a good idea. But let me tell you some of the ideas that they come up with." He pointed to the church next door where people came to get their meals, what he derisively called "the great food roundup." Why was it, he asked, that people couldn't go to the store and buy their own meals, that "we've got to have some white people come down here and get their conscience off and feed us meals? . . . I heard one TV station bragging about 'This is the fifteenth year of our great food roundup.' I mean, how can you brag about that? They're not doing nothing to get us jobs, all they wanna do is feed us."

He talked, as he had to me in April, of reparations for the crime of slavery; about blacks, with the exception of people like Michael Jordan and Bill Cosby, having none of the life, liberty, and pursuit of happiness the Declaration of Independence promised. "The only pursuit of happiness I guess they meant for us is you get to drink a forty-ounce in the alley when you get up. You get to go sell aluminum cans to make your money. You get to go down to the welfare department and have them give you less than you need to live. I mean, where our pursuit of happiness at?"

As usual, McGee was generalizing and exaggerating, but he was also distorting. The people in the audience surely knew that more blacks were prospering than ever before. That fact, it seemed to me, deserved to be trumpeted just as much as the grim condition of the black underclass, a group that also was larger than it had ever been. Perhaps it was too much to expect of a politician bent on making his points, but Michael McGee, as he stood there, was not speaking for all of black Milwaukee or for all of black America. For him to suggest he was was just as wrong and just as injurious as it was for a white person to blindly and blithely assume that all blacks were united in thought about all issues. By ignoring the achievements of many, many blacks, blacks whose achievements might seem more realistic and more within reach than those of a Bill Cosby or a Michael Jordan (both of whom, predictably, endured their own share of criticism from other blacks), he was just as guilty of robbing blacks of their individuality as whites often were. Not everybody falls into the same category. The "black community" is not so easily defined, and has never been. To continue to talk the talk of sixties black nationalism was certainly his prerogative, and I understood why he was doing it. But sweeping everybody into the same box was taking away from black people the very dignity he claimed to be so intent on preserving. And frankly, it made me want to wring his neck. Knowing that he could see me in the crowd, I just rolled my eyes instead.

Suddenly a woman began shouting and gesturing. "You can't stop no crimes," she said to McGee. "You can't stop nothing going on around here."

"And what are you gonna do for us?" McGee wanted to know.

"He ain't doing nothing but making a damn speech."

McGee repeated his question, as did people in the crowd: What was she going to do?

"All that I do is be one human being thinking for my own rights. . . ."

"Drink that bourbon," somebody shouted.

"Don't be too critical of this sister," McGee said, "because that's the condition they want us all in." The crowd shouted "amen." "Now, sister, you've had your word now, why don't you move on. Just mosey on down the road. Just go slow now."

As she departed, three sheets to the wind and continuing to mutter, "he can't stop nothing, he can't stop nothing," McGee was telling the crowd how she would be the star of the local news that evening "because she told that McGee a thing or two." The audience laughed. "She really did. She told me a lot. She told me that we got a long way to go."

"Short time to get there," one man bellowed.

"Hey, very short time to get there and the majority of us understand that and we understand her. That's why there's no hostility. I don't want anyone to feel hostile toward her because she don't know any better, but that's the condition we're in. And that's the frustrated state they want all

of us to be in where we just say, 'Well, ain't nothing we can do, ain't nobody gonna do nothing, ain't nothing can help you.'"

He had been all around the country, he said, was receiving mail from
all around the country, and the fact was that "people are looking at Milwaukee. Milwaukee is at the crossroads in terms of the whole United
States. . . . What we do here is gonna have an impact on what happens
all around the United States."

AS THE CROWD SLOWLY dispersed and McGee made his way back inside, I
decided not to go home, at least not right away. I went instead to a small
basement room about ten minutes from there, a room in which a woman
named L. G. Shanklin-Flowers was conducting a racism workshop under
soft lights, a room whose atmosphere couldn't have been more different
from McGee's overheated theater. The question she was asking the blacks
who were there, posed in a direct, unblinking way, was this: What was the
one thing, more than any other, they would like to say to white people, to
say candidly, without fear of any kind?

"Don't keep pretending that you are invisible," a young man named
Steve Haimes said, "that blacks are the only ones who are conspicuous
when you pass them on the street."

The request was offered quietly, but it rose above anything I had
heard from Michael McGee earlier, turning the theme of *Invisible Man* on
its head, so to speak.

During the hour or so I was there, L. G. talked of racism as an equal
combination of prejudice and power; she spoke of "internalized oppression," the feeling blacks have that "maybe there *is* something inherently
wrong with us." And she said that even though most people thought it was
the other way around, the job of ending racism ultimately fell to whites; it
fell to whites because they had gotten "the most benefits" out of racism
and, therefore, were in a better position to end it.

We were all seated in a circle, listening to Emma Felder say that she
couldn't ride a bus anymore because of the painful memory of having to sit
in the back all those years when she was growing up in Arkansas, and listening to John Fitzgerald (who was white) talk about how he would hear racist
comments and jokes made in his presence and not say anything, that he had

come in part that evening in order to find the strength or courage or what-ever the right word was to confront people when they made such remarks.

An evening that, for me, had begun with the repeated threat of vio-lence ended in catharsis, with people who seemed relieved, unburdened really, by what they had revealed, and open to what they were being asked to think about. In the larger scheme of things, a Michael McGee might ask, how much did that matter, how could a more honest dialogue between blacks and whites translate into the hard currency of family-supporting jobs and decent housing that his community so desperately needed? Group therapy, however much it helped the people who participated in it, how-ever much it might result in incremental steps forward, was unlikely to stop him from putting sandbags around his windows, or from calling off his deadline.

PART TWO

TWENTY

"So what brings you to Milwaukee?" Philip Arreola asked me when I introduced myself to him at the Boys and Girls Club in Sherman Park on July 22. The chief of police was all smiles on this Monday morning, sipping coffee, glad-handing, and apparently excited about a program to reduce school truancy that the city and county were hoping to implement, a program that had had a fair measure of success (including a reduction in both daytime crime and teen pregnancies) in San Jose and Oklahoma City.

The moment I answered his question, though, his expression changed. Yet had this brief encounter taken place just twenty-four hours later he wouldn't have asked it at all. He would have assumed, wrongly, that I had come to Milwaukee because of Jeffrey Dahmer and the human cooking school it was discovered he had been operating from his apartment on the West Side.

The news of Dahmer's arrest came to me the next morning, as I was sitting in the office of Scully Stikes, a dean at Milwaukee Area Technical College. In fact, Stikes was right in the midst of describing the deteriorating conditions in his apartment building and neighborhood (which was not far from Dahmer's) when a colleague came in and offered sketchy details of Dahmer's arrest—an arrest, it turned out, that should have taken place at least seven weeks before.

On that particular evening in late May, two teenage girls, both black, phoned the police to say that a teenage boy was out on the street, half-naked, bleeding from his buttocks, and running from a white man. Three officers eventually arrived and were persuaded by Dahmer that there was nothing to be alarmed about, that it was nothing more than a lovers' quarrel, and that the boy (who was fourteen) was not a boy at all, but a consenting adult. The girls were told to go home, to mind their own business, and then the officers went back to Dahmer's apartment, which was strewn with all sorts of graphic material and suffused with a strange smell. With the boy safely back in Dahmer's quarry, the police left, on to their next call. Meanwhile, one of the girls' mothers, Glenda Cleveland, was phoning the police to complain but found herself put on hold, transferred around, and finally not listened to—presumably at the same time that Konerak Sinthasomphone was losing his life to a cannibal, as, it would be gruesomely learned, had sixteen other young men before and after that night.

Only one month earlier, the city had complained about *Newsweek*'s dubbing Milwaukee one of America's new crime capitals. Now they were on the defensive again, saying that someone like Jeffrey Dahmer could have been living anywhere and still done what he had done. No one was denying that. But the fact remained: this had happened in Milwaukee, and there were many elements to it, one of them being race. With each passing day, as it was revealed that the majority of Dahmer's victims were black, as the details of what happened with the two black girls and Glenda Cleveland unfolded, tensions built, everything became magnified, and everyone became involved. So much so that when Dahmer first appeared in court, *not* in the county jail's customary orange regs but in civilian clothes, Howard Fuller irately phoned the mayor's office and essentially said that *no* black man would be allowed that "privilege," and that if they didn't think race was involved in this case, then they were seriously deluding themselves. And when I saw Michael McGee, he not only had something he wanted to ask me, but something he wanted to show me. "A lot of people have been saying that Dahmer doesn't *look* like a mass murderer," he said. "I mean, what is a mass murderer supposed to look like? A black man?" Then he pulled out a letter he had received, a letter that spoke of concern over the killings and what it might mean to the well-being of the black community, but which also suggested that he might "want to come over and have drinks" to discuss the matter more fully. The letter was signed (though probably not from) Jeffrey Dahmer.

Ten years had passed since the Ernest Lacy case, but the coalition that McGee and Howard Fuller had formed then was unlikely, one black conservative told me, to help relieve the suffering of the community now. "If some of the black leaders think one of the ways they can respond to the Dahmer incident is with sit-ins and other civil rights tactics of the sixties, they are dead wrong. It's not gonna work. It's about money and power, pure and simple."

Perhaps he was right, but he was also wrong. None of it, alas, was pure and simple. And though it had taken a while a decade earlier, Howard Fuller and Michael McGee's "civil rights tactics" had resulted in a large amount of money for Ernest Lacy's family and the eventual resignation of Harold Breier. The Dahmer case was different, but like Lacy's, it seemed certain to galvanize the city for an indeterminate period of time.

JOHN NORQUIST FOUND THE whole thing so incomprehensible he didn't know how to respond. It's not as if a person is exactly prepared for something like this. As a minister's son he knew all about good and evil, but this was beyond imagining. A town meeting had previously been scheduled for Wednesday evening, July 24, at the Holton Youth Center, and he kept his commitment to be there. By the time he took his place on the dais, the three white police officers who had failed to arrest Dahmer on the night of May 27 were about to be suspended by Chief Arreola, pending further investigation. In a situation this incendiary, with the potential for "disturbances" reasonably high, any move either way was bound to be divisive. The rank and file of the department still comprised mainly officers who had worked under Breier, and the suspension of the three men was viewed by many as grossly unfair, amounting to a conviction before they were even tried.

But at Holton that evening, little was said about the Dahmer case; it was almost as if the whole city, like its mayor, were so numbed by what had happened that near denial seemed the only appropriate, or possible, response, that to even address the grotesqueness of it would somehow remove it from that realm and put it into the category of fact, of something that had to be grappled with.

So it was business as usual—or at least that was the image that the members of the panel were trying to project as the discussion continued to center around gangs and the area of First and Keefe. "We'll do whatever we have to do to make life miserable for drug dealers," the mayor insisted. "Gangs are not welcome here. We have no interest in hearing what they have to say. We're not interested in a dialogue with organized criminals." Three-quarters of the block-grant money the city received each year went to community-based organizations, he reminded everyone, and not, as had been suggested, to further bolster downtown interests. Until the city targeted the Metcalfe Park area as a place to coordinate efforts in an attempt to reduce crime and provide better health services and more job opportunities, Norquist boasted, there wasn't any neighborhood organization there to speak of.

Tommie Williams, who was in the audience, resented the tone of the mayor's comments, especially since he and Reverend Buck had heard that the city was seriously considering cutting Harambee's funding because of their involvement with the Vice Lords. "Since we became involved with the youth from the First and Keefe area we've been getting quite a bit of negative feedback," Williams said, reminding everyone, somewhat defensively, that Harambee did not condone "any kind of illicit and illegal activities," and cautioning the mayor not to lump all youths into the same category; many of them would jump at the chance to do something else, he said, but not enough opportunities existed. "It's gonna take all of us," he said, "to eliminate the breadth of problems we have."

A young man stood up at that point and said that he was someone who didn't receive a grant from any government agency, he didn't receive food stamps, he wasn't part of a gang, and that the problems people were referring to were here long before he arrived on this earth. Nevertheless, he said, he was poor and he was black and he was not employed and he had had hair pulled out from his dreadlocks by the police for no good reason. "Look, I'm twenty-five years old. I might not live to twenty-six. You all need to think about this instead of sitting up there talking chump."

He was asked for his name and address and telephone number.

"What if I'm homeless?" he said. "I live on the streets of Milwaukee."

But there must be some address where he spent some time, where he could be reached, the city official persisted. "We are beginning to start the process where we will be employing unemployed people in some of our public works. Construction and road-building projects."

Either it seemed like an empty gesture to this young man, or he was in such a state, a state that appeared to be both beyond anger and beyond hope, that he didn't see the point. His answer was the same: there was no way to contact him.

Once he sat down, Reverend Buck came to the microphone, to reinforce what Tommie Williams had said, to say that "these children that hang on those corners are some of these people's sons and daughters. And if you get rid of them you gotta get rid of these folks."

He stopped for a minute to collect himself, then looked straight at the mayor. "We can't work as an organization and get pressure from outside forces that say to us we can't talk to particular people, we can't work with particular groups because downtown they recognize them as gangs. We recognize them as black youths.... They're our kids.... So please don't put us in a confrontation position because that's not where we wanna be."

EARLIER THAT DAY, I had attended a meeting that Bill Lawrence had held for some of the heads of private industry, a meeting that also centered around youth and the job opportunities they needed. Howard Fuller was at the meeting, and Lawrence referred to remarks that Fuller had made two days before, about the challenge for everyone who cared about kids, specifically poor black kids, was to reaffirm the belief that they could succeed in society, regardless of whether that society ever became truly integrated.

"We have to get private industry to be offering the lion's share of these jobs," Lawrence said, "because the government is not going to provide them." At one time, four of every five jobs that the Private Industry Council placed kids in, through the Step-Up program, were public-sector positions. Now it was about half and half. Since the criterion for getting into the program was a 2.0 average and 90 percent attendance, there was an incentive factor at work that was crucial: the better kids performed in school, the better their chance at obtaining scholarships or full-time jobs after graduation.

This was the sticky part. It was one thing for a company to fund a program or have a Step-Up kid work for a few months in the summer and quite another to commit to him or her full-time. A black woman from Firstar said the biggest problem with minority employees was attendance, and the head of the Wisconsin Health Organization said that he had lots of jobs but few people who could, or were willing to, do what was required to get and keep them: read and write, punch numbers into a computer all day, not be disruptive, come to work on a daily basis.

Lawrence was intent on seeing the Step-Up program extended, on upping the ante. But he didn't want to get into a situation where somebody could say the PIC was discouraging kids from going to college, that kids were being "tracked" to entry-level jobs. On the other hand, there needed to be something—something that included training—for the 30 percent of Milwaukee's high school graduates who didn't plan on furthering their education.

"I thought you were asking for hiring *preference*," Robert Milbourne, head of the Greater Milwaukee Committee, said. "Now you're asking for slots."

"No," Lawrence said emphatically. "We're asking for preference."

Preference vs. Guaranteed Job. Race-based Opportunity vs. Race-based Outcome. It is interesting how just the very mention of these terms sets people on edge—and yet it makes it easier to grasp why affirmative action is so flammable an issue, how it is hard to disentangle from fear and anger, especially when the country was in a recession, how quickly one resorts to one's most primal instincts for survival and for seeing someone else as unworthy of "special attention." Time and again, it comes back to yielding, to trying to determine how much is enough without alienating people—the very people who often wind up turning what they see as the crutch of affirmative action into a weapon against blacks, making their lives miserable on the job, the job "they" shouldn't have gotten anyway. Or so blacks are led to think. The human capacity to make another person miserable appears to be boundless.

As for the extension of Step-Up that Lawrence was proposing—for which he suggested the more-octane-in-your-tank name of Step-Up Plus—he said, "I don't want to create a public furor and promise something we can't deliver on. Howard has to be able to go back and say something's there, an opportunity. I mean, there are companies that have *never* hired a MPS graduate in the last five years for entry-level jobs."

"Well," the head of the Wisconsin Health Organization reiterated, "it's a big switch from a summer job to a full-time job."

"And we've got to make sure we can coordinate this," Fuller said, in terms of retraining and money and advice. Since he was still new to the job of superintendent, he said, he didn't know precisely how many guidance counselors he had, but he was fairly certain there weren't hundreds of them. But beyond that, he had an even larger concern, a concern that was borne out of his many years in Milwaukee, a concern that Michael McGee had expressed when he formed the Black Panther Militia. "Our penchant for proliferating new committees in Milwaukee is amazing,"

Fuller said, heads nodding all around. "And the same people always sit on them. Is there any existing committee to deal with this right now?"

"I agree," Lawrence said. "We study stuff in this town until we drop dead." Without directly answering Fuller's question, but trusting that people knew he was someone who acted on his ideas, who did what he could to bring them to fruition, Lawrence said that the next three meetings would occur within six weeks.

Robert Milbourne brightened when he heard that. "I think we're waiting for this program in the business community," he said, then paused, in the equivocal, cautious way of people in business who need to know that nearly every base will be covered and that what they're embarking on will ultimately benefit them. "We're waiting for it if it's PIC-run, has MPS support, carries no guarantees of hiring, can be expected to grow, and that that growth can be measured over time."

Hearing that, Bill Lawrence flashed a smile. "I'm about to become either the most important person in the city," he announced, "or the most endangered."

TWENTY-ONE

From the moment Lora Gooden had begun talking the week earlier at the Harambee Community School, about how when blacks in the community looked at each other now they saw a prison or a gang or somebody who might break into their house, I couldn't get her out of my mind. Beyond the fact that Louise Kidd and Tommie Williams had said she was somebody I should sit down and spend time with, there was something about her calm, unruffled presence that made me curious about her.

So she came to Miss Katie's Diner from her job at the Housing Authority one afternoon, wearing the most striking yellow hat you could imagine, and she said that the reason she had stood up to talk was that she was scared when the Vice Lords had stalked out and because she was not naïve. She was thirty-seven, had two children of her own, nine and eleven, and she hated that "if my black son reaches the age where he decides to meet up with three other black friends and they happen to be standing on the corner, there is inevitably somebody that will drive along and say, 'Look at that gang.' That scares me because I'm hearing more and more of that."

She had grown up in Milwaukee, in the inner city, had gone off to California, where she studied fashion design and married and eventually became a police officer in Berkeley. She had returned to Milwaukee in early 1989, after her divorce, to be closer to her family and now lived in a predominantly white neighborhood. And yet since coming back, there was something else she was hearing: people coming right up to her or driving past her and calling her a nigger. One time, she and a white male co-worker were walking back to the office "when this white guy on a bicycle, late twenties maybe, starts yelling, 'You stupid nigger, you leave these white men alone.' He ranted and raved for a good two to three minutes, which can be a long time when someone's cursing you out and calling you names and things." Another time she was running a small community meeting, was the only black in attendance, when suddenly a businessman, upset about crime in the neighborhood and how it was affecting his store, "came right up and called me a nigger and said if it wasn't for all of these drugs then we wouldn't have these problems. If *you people* weren't doing this."

How did she react to things like that?

She just looked at them, she said, and didn't let herself get outraged "because I've been there before." From seventh grade to graduation she was the only black person in her class, bused to schools far from her neighborhood. In 1966, she was on the front page of the *Milwaukee Journal,* her hand raised to answer a question. "Lora Fits in Anywhere," the patronizing headline read. "And I took it literally," she was now saying, gleam in her eye. She threw herself into every conceivable activity, becoming "the first black cheerleader," "the first black band member," "the first black drummer for the drill team." The reason she was considered "acceptable," she speculated now, was "because some people possibly didn't see me as being black."

That may have been true, but when it came to advising her on what plans she might make for the future, the only things her guidance counselor directed her toward were teaching and social work. She was smart enough to realize that the counselor hadn't taken the headline about her as literally as she had, and smart enough to look for models of inspiration elsewhere, in her parents and in the civil rights activists of the day, especially Martin Luther King. She remembered bricks coming through the window of her house, she remembered the marches, and she remembered not only where she was when she heard Dr. King had been killed, but also what she thought: that all hell was going to break loose all over the country and right there in Milwaukee. "It brought this huge pain inside that a part of our hope was gone."

She could live with the ignorance of people who would come up to her and call her a nigger—she knew who she was and they couldn't take that away from her—but she couldn't abide anything being directed at her children. No sooner had they returned to Milwaukee than her kids were out riding their bikes and white kids in the neighborhood demanded to know where they had stolen them from. When she was exploring a suitable school for them, she called one parochial school and was told there were openings and what the cost would be to nonparishioners and she should call back around one-thirty and speak to the principal. She did that. Within a few minutes, though, "the very classes her secretary told me were vacant were no longer vacant."

And why was that?

She couldn't say for sure, but she felt the principal didn't want any more black children coming into her school.

A couple of days before that, she had gone to visit another private school. "The principal was very cordial, we sat down, I told her what grades I was interested in, and she proceeded to tell me that they didn't have any special counseling available for children with learning disabilities. And I said, 'Excuse me.' And she repeated herself. I said, 'Excuse me.' I went on to hand her a copy of my children's Iowa scores. And when she saw it her mouth dropped open and she said, 'Oh, I'm sorry. Which grades did you say you were interested in?' I said, 'Thank you, I'm not interested in any of them,' and I got up and left."

She wound up putting her son and daughter into their neighborhood school, a school in which the only kids who were being bused in were black. But her children soon came home with reports that whenever a black child raised his hand, the teacher wouldn't call on him. She had never told her kids about the front-page *Journal* story, but she did then. And even though Lora's kids weren't bused, it didn't matter, the mathematical equation still held: "they were black children and therefore they had to be bused." After one semester there, Lora pulled them out and put them into a school that she and they were happy with—St. Rose, the same one Louise Kidd's daughter attended—a school in which they were afforded the same respect and belief in their abilities as any white child.

WHEN I LEFT MISS KATIE'S about three-thirty that afternoon, I made my way to the area of First and Keefe. I had been there before, to visit Bridget Wilder and her children, who lived a block over, and now I was going to see Diane Howard, a longtime homeowner, one of the women who was trying to rid the neighborhood of the Vice Lords.

Even though I had arrived early, I rang the doorbell anyway, but there was no answer. The house where the Vice Lords stayed was across and up the street; the one where George Edward Brown had been shot was now boarded up. The block had a late-afternoon quiet to it that was unsettling.

At that moment I noticed a man at the Howards' front window, stealing a quick, almost furtive glance outside. Had he been inside the whole time and didn't want to answer the door, I wondered as I came up the steps of the house again. When I rang the bell this time, the door opened slightly, just enough for me to squeeze inside.

"Hold it!" Marvin Howard commanded, then he began to frisk me. "For all I know you're another Dahmer." I saw the *Milwaukee Journal* sitting on the coffee table, photos of some of the black victims staring up at me.

"I guess you can't be too careful," I said, hoping to reassure him.

"Marvin, relax," a voice said from the background, two seconds before the voice itself arrived in the small figure of Diane Howard, whom I recognized from that tense meeting at St. Elizabeth's.

She suggested I sit down and then, in a living room where the curtains were always closed and the furniture was strategically placed, she and Marvin began to tell their story.

They had been married to each other for only six years, but Diane had lived in this particular house for twenty-six. She had never wanted to move, never even thought about it, until now. Now she felt she had to. The only problem was this: Who was going to buy the house? Its value had plummeted, and she didn't want to be an absentee landlord, so they were stuck. The rear of the house was pocked with bullet holes and some of the Vice Lords, many of whom she had known since they were babies, had threatened on more than one occasion to burn it down. They had also threatened to kick her daughters' butts if they caught them outside.

It made her furious that the Vice Lords had been seated at the front table at St. Elizabeth's that Saturday, and she had told Tommie Williams that. "Why were they sitting up there," she asked me as she had asked him, "and you got the homeowners who've been here twenty, thirty years sitting in the audience?" And it bothered her when Belinda Pittman stood up and told off Arthur Gordon, the man who had worked for American Motors. Anybody who didn't live in the neighborhood, she said, up and pacing now, had no business telling someone who did, someone who lived there twenty-four hours and was right in the middle of things, what was best for it. "I've seen this neighborhood go down, down, down. I've seen the white flight. I've seen how the children, when their parents would die or retire to Florida, maintain the house and don't care who they rent to. Like this guy where George was shot. This man was afraid to come and get his rent. . . . I've seen a lot of things on this block and that's why I say to them, 'Nobody's going to come here and move me from here. I've invested half of my life in my property. I clean up. You don't put your forty-ouncers out there in front of my house. I can't even have my family come and visit me because I'm afraid you're going to rip their car off. You are going to tell me you have a right to live in this neighborhood, we all have a right to live, but *live*, don't come over here bothering me.'"

In the background a siren wailed, sounding more like an air raid signal than a normal police siren.

"Listen, I hear that all night long. That's the sound they make when the police are in the area. They have lookouts all around . . . little kids looking out. They used to say 'Five-0, Five-0,' but now they just do that *wooooooooo*. . . . I have been afraid for some police officers when they come in to arrest these kids because they get over them like flies on garbage." And she had been afraid for the police because of "the type of machinery" she had seen in the Vice Lords' possession.

Of all the seasons, she hated summertime in particular. Unlike in winter ("when they've got their butts hid somewhere"), in the summer the Vice Lords would be up all night, sleeping in shifts, constantly watching the street. From the beginning of time, no doubt, every block has had a person living on it who keeps a vigil. On the 3400 block of North First Street in Milwaukee, Wisconsin, that person is Diane Howard. If the Vice Lords could be up all night, so could she, lying awake, listening and hoping, listening "to the neighborhood quiet down" and hoping the night would pass without incident.

When I asked the Howards about their own children, their relief was palpable. They spent enough time thinking and worrying about the Vice Lords without having to continue discussing them with me. They both had children from earlier marriages and had adopted two foster children. Diane had sent her two oldest daughters to high school in Whitefish Bay ("White Folks Bay," as it is often called) as part of the Chapter 220 program, and she had been pleased—by the education they had received, not by the indifference with which they were treated, the way they were labeled "220 students, black this, and black that." She didn't send them there out of some crazy notion that they would become smarter by sitting next to white kids. "I sent my children where there was the best education," she said flatly. "I checked it out. They had the best computer system, they had the best musical program for Cathy, that's what she was interested in. They had the best precollege business courses—that's what they both wanted. It could have been a black school, but I looked at all the black schools, they just didn't have that. They just didn't have what Whitefish Bay had to offer. . . . So I just wanted what was best. If North Division could have offered it, I would have been there."

AGAIN AND AGAIN, THE strands of this story intersected at the point of education: the various difficulties one had in obtaining one, the potential consequences—the almost certain lack of opportunity—one faced if one didn't. Marvin Howard, who had attended college for two and a half years, felt fortunate that, despite all the racism he had encountered on his job as a machinist, he had never been out of work. He didn't know what lay ahead for his son J. P. But he did know that even if J. P. managed to avoid being recruited and lured into a gang; even if he secured the education that Marvin and Diane believed it was imperative he get, he was still, as a black male, going to face much greater difficulty than Diane's daughters had. "The black male," Marvin said, "has no job and has to resort to stealing or robbing or selling drugs to have money." But white kids, he said, "through some kind of relative or whatever, can get into nice jobs, making eight, nine bucks an hour right out of high school. . . .

"See, I'm to the point now where I know racism is there and I just expect it to come. That's why I can deal with it a lot better, a lot easier."

"You accept it as part of the condition—," I said.

"As reality, yes," he jumped in. But not without the hope that "perhaps that old stuff will die off. . . . I don't want to see J. P. or any black kids coming up encountering some of the things I've encountered and some of the things my father encountered." And yet, he wanted me to know, he didn't consider all whites bad—just as he didn't consider all blacks good. Still, he said, racism was *learned,* and it would take education (not to mention willingness) to unlearn it.

Just before I left the Howards', they had one last thing they wanted to impress upon me: No matter how bad things were, well, they could always be worse. They had just come back from a week in California, a week in which practically every person they met in South-Central Los Angeles had told them they no longer wore anything blue or red out on the streets; they didn't want to be mistaken for a Crip or a Blood. "This stuff here," Diane said, standing at the front door, gesturing across the street, "is nothing compared to L.A. They would laugh at this mess here."

TWENTY-TWO

The same article that had been Robert Odom's inspiration for Unity Day—the one that contained nearly all the pictures of the (mostly black) homicide victims in Milwaukee for 1990—was something Howard Fuller had also saved, something he now found himself looking at day after day. The anger he had expressed to the mayor's office about the Jeffrey Dahmer incident had not abated by the time we got together again.

"First of all, if this had happened in Shorewood," he said, "there's no way in hell that the cops would have responded in the same way. No way. And there's nothing you can tell me that would convince me. . . . And for anybody to sit up and say, 'That's not true,' is an affront to anybody who's got half a brain in their head about how things work in this society. . . . The mayor, the police chief, everybody has gotta not be defensive about this shit. . . . You gotta fire these three officers. You gotta say, 'This will not take place in Milwaukee. Period.' This is a political issue now. And the politics of it has to do with the general context of black people in the city of Milwaukee."

Fuller had been given a going-away party by the county the night before and wound up standing in the parking lot for nearly an hour afterward, talking about the incident with some of his close friends and coming to the conclusion that, depending on what happened with the officers, the community could become more polarized than it was already, even torn apart.

It was hard for Fuller to keep his former activist persona from conflicting with his current one, especially given the incident in question. He was pained as he sat there discussing this, and was equally so as we switched away from Dahmer and he laid out one of the big dilemmas of his new position so far, a dilemma that had been discussed at the Bill Lawrence meeting a few days earlier and which he wrestled with each day—telling a kid he had to get an education but at the same time telling him there was no guaranteed job waiting for him at the end of it. "'What do you mean?' a kid will say to me. 'Why should I get an education? There are no jobs.' 'Well, it's not true that there's no jobs. But for you to have a shot at the jobs there are, you gotta have an education.'"

He was fighting every day for education, with limited resources, knowing that the only thing he could guarantee the kids who asked why they should bother getting an education was that without one, "they're not even in the fight. They don't even have a chance to fight. So that's my answer. Is that a good answer? It's the only one I know. A kid says, 'Well, I can earn more money selling dope.' I try to lay out to them what their options are." He doesn't tell them they're wrong—they aren't—but he does tell them they better get the dope, sell it, and live quick "'because your ass is going to die. Or you'll be looking over your shoulder for the rest of your life. Or you'll be in jail. All of these things are gonna happen to you. You can go the hard route, get an education, try to get a job. Is that easy? No, it's not easy, but there's nothing in this world that comes easy. You're not gonna get it easy.'"

But at the same time, he said, he couldn't tolerate the way black kids, who *were* succeeding in school, were being called "white" and "wannabes" by other black kids. When he was growing up, he said, he was a square (confirming what Jerrel Jones had already told me about him). He didn't drink, he didn't smoke, was president of this and that, and did well in school. But to "the guys on the playground," it was never a negative.

What he also couldn't tolerate was gangs trying to recruit (or way-lay) some of these same kids on their way to and from school. Partly because of that, he had decided to meet with various gang members—to do what he could to stop them from doing this, and to try to encourage those kids who had dropped out of school to at least consider attending alternative schools. As for the mayor's taking the position that city officials shouldn't be dealing with gang members (in part because, politically speaking, it made him look soft on crime), Fuller didn't agree: "People can say what they want, hard-line this or that, but kids are out there, they're going to have some impact on what does or doesn't help them, and my view of things is, you try to sit down with people who are going to have an impact. I don't have to like them, I don't have to support what they are doing, but I have to understand that they're there and they have to be dealt with."

He stood up and loosened his tie and then began to walk back and forth, his long fingers occasionally touching the desk to emphasize a point.

Just as he always seemed able to distill an issue and articulate all its aspects, he also attempted to put whatever he was talking about into context, into historical perspective. If conservatives, for instance, were so bent on "blaming the victim" for what was going on these days (instead of focusing on how and why the economic conditions in the country had changed), his question was this: What was it they had put forth that had worked so well it could rightly be called "fantastic public policy"? Liberals took a bashing today, he said, because of the "programs of the sixties," but hardly anybody was willing to acknowledge that some of these programs had worked, and a number of them would have worked better had they been capitalized so that they could work. "You can't tell me the Women, Infants and Children program was a bad program," he said. "Hell, it cut infant mortality in this country." Some of the stuff "clearly was BS," he conceded, "but that's the nature of a lot of public policy."

Fuller, of course, had done his own share of liberal bashing in the sixties, railing against their perceived paternal stance of not allowing black people to assume responsibility for themselves, but distance and the Reagan Administration had altered his view somewhat. When I told him that Bill Lawrence (whom he personally liked and thought of as an ally) considered himself a neoconservative, he responded sharply: "I don't know what the hell that means. I don't call myself anything. My view is, people are hungry. We have people every night over at St. Ben's waiting to get a meal. This is not pictures of the Great Depression. This is pictures of right now. We have homeless people in the streets, we have kids not learning in the educational system that is essentially bankrupt. . . . If the same jobs that were there for my stepfather, who didn't have a high school education but could make a fairly decent salary here in Milwaukee shoveling shit in the slaughterhouse, were there for these kids . . ." He stopped, lost in thought, was somewhere else. His stepfather, who was terminated from his job while in the hospital, *one day* before he would have received a pension, was the only father he had really known, the circumstances of his own birth still not entirely clear to him.

The problem he had with people like Shelby Steele, he said, focused once more, was Steele's insistence that what held many blacks back was their clinging to race as the reason they were not getting ahead, their unwillingness to accept their freedom. It's not that Fuller didn't feel there was "a kernel of truth" to the notion; his problem was that Steele was almost completely ignoring the fact of their being "trapped in an economic structure that doesn't allow for the kind of movement" he seemed to take for granted. Even if the eminent sociologist William Julius Wilson appeared to be arguing the same thing in *The Declining Significance of Race*, Fuller said, he was at least acknowledging the economic changes that had occurred. "Wilson makes the point that class issues are much more fundamental to . . . your life chances than race. . . . My belief is that race is still a determining factor in your life chances in America. But if you have money, it is less of one. The danger in the way Steele interprets things is that he in essence says the spread of the underclass is *not* a factor of the economic circumstances or racism, it's a factor of our own anti-self. . . . He's giving a measure of freedom that to me is not real for poor black people in America . . . giving too much credence to the problem being a psychological barrier. Now is that true for an individual—for black kids at Marquette University? Is it true for my daughter? Yeah, it's true. If my daughter is not making it at Marquette University and she is sitting there saying, 'I'm not making it because I'm black,' that's bullshit."

Beyond his own problem with what Shelby Steele was saying was the problem of even getting his students (in the class he held on Saturday mornings) to read Steele at all. They didn't like that he had a white wife (Walter Farrell had said he was never sure whether Steele's ideas were his own or those of "his white psychologist wife"), they thought of him as an Uncle Tom, they didn't like what they understood to be the tenor of his message—that whenever blacks didn't succeed, they invariably pointed to race as the reason. Fuller, in his forceful way, was telling them to get over it, to actually *read* what the man had written, decide if there was any truth to what he was saying, and, if so, to figure out how to attack that problem in the community. It sounded like a good, sound approach, but the visceral reaction of the students so far appeared to be winning out. As for Fuller's own visceral reaction, it came with every mention Steele made of "race fatigue." "To me that's a serious, serious issue, because it moves you away from the whole history of Du Bois and Booker T. and Garvey . . . the whole history of black people who 'had it made' but who were race people." The continuum, the sweep, the role, each person had filled along the way: these were the things so deeply embedded in his thoughts and

actions that he didn't take kindly to anyone—especially a fellow black—
trampling over them.

AT THE CLASS THAT Saturday, Zo and Jerry and Mario (who could have
been a stand-in for Malcolm X) sat around the table listening intently as
Fuller talked, drawing some of Steele's notions together with the Dahmer
incident (specifically the two black girls and Glenda Cleveland being
ignored and Dahmer being brought into court without handcuffs and a jail
uniform), saying that "the way Shelby is laying it on, it's like we keep
holding on to race for abstract reasons, we're holding on to it because it's
comfortable, because it keeps us from having to get out and really face
reality, and to me the larger reason that we hold on to this is because it's
still occurring. You have daily examples of it happening, that continues to
foster it, so it's not just what happened historically."

He was bemused by the emphasis Steele placed on the 1964 Civil
Rights Act, "as if it were a watershed event in the history of Afro-Americans
in that it symbolized this newfound freedom." The bill, he was stressing,
was *not* that big a deal. It prohibited discrimination in public accommo-
dations and in programs receiving federal assistance. It prohibited discrimination by employers and unions and set up the Equal Employment
Opportunity Commission. It enforced the desegregation of schools. These
were all positive things, Fuller said, but they didn't exactly (as Steele would
have it) take one from oppression and land you squarely on the side of
freedom. That was both far too simplistic in his opinion and simply
untrue, untrue in any way you could generalize about. Steele talked as if
blacks were caught in a cultural lag, he said, stuck in a situation where there
had been wonderful, tangible changes in society, changes that blacks were
preventing themselves from taking advantage of because "mentally we still
in the previous era," unwilling to let go of race.

Along with race-holding went victimization, in Steele's view, and the
students began to stir.

"He's saying we look for racism in *everything*," Zo said. "We're sitting
listening to a lecture, we're waiting for the professor to say something that
we could turn into a racial comment."

"My experience," Jerry said, "is that I've excelled in school, I haven't
gone out *looking* for racism."

Maybe so, said Fuller, but Steele was also pointing out how whites thought blacks had "a lot of nerve to be talking about victimization when we let you in here due to some preferential treatment." While there was some validity to this, he said, it also had to be acknowledged that there were numerous incidents of "overt racist acts" occurring on campuses and that individual professors still made comments that were derogatory to black people. Just as it had to be acknowledged that if you're the only black student in the classroom and "something comes up about black people," it's wrong for the professor to ask you to explain it, "as if you are the depository of all knowledge about black people, by virtue of the fact that you're black." But if you turn your shit in late and the professor lowers your grade and you take the attitude that "you're doing this because I'm black," you're out of line. He's lowering your grade because you turned your shit in late. Over and out. Now, if the professor let you turn it in late *because* you are black, that, Fuller said, was just as bad as calling on you to explain something: it still turned on race, but it underlined the preferential treatment that whites are certain you're going to receive anyway. Rules are rules, Fuller said, and if they're broken, there should be consequences, no matter who didn't abide by them. Or, he said, breaking into a wide smile, "if somebody calls you a jerk, you know, it could be that you are a jerk. It don't have nothing to do with that you're black, you're just a jerk."

Zo and Jerry and Mario relaxed when he said that. They knew what he was talking about. Fuller had that way about him, that ability to shift from an intense discussion of a serious issue and leaven it with humor, humor that illuminated certain truths. *If you're a jerk, you're a jerk, and no amount of race-holding or accepting of one's "newfound freedoms" was likely to help you change that.*

But what about situations, Zo asked, where a mass of white individuals might say something derogatory to you that one white person wouldn't say?

"I think you tie race back into it," Fuller said. "The essence of racial oppression is *I have the capacity to oppress you....* White skin privilege gives me power over you as a black. Because no matter how terrible I am, how bad my situation is, I'm better than these niggers.

"Now it's more difficult to actually run that in America today in certain situations, because if you're white and you're looking at TV at Michael Jordan, it's hard for you talk about, realistically, 'I'm better than that nigger,' because this man has got millions of dollars, he's got stuff you couldn't even dream of, so it's real hard to run that."

When was it race, when was it class, when was it a mixture of both, when was it neither—these were the questions Fuller wanted his students to be asking themselves, the threads in society's fabric he wanted them to always be vigilant about identifying. He wanted them to see things as they were, to not be naïve, and yet at the same time to not rush to judgment, to not generalize, to not paint all whites with the same brush stroke that whites often used to portray blacks. And by urging this, of course, he was trying to make them into race people (if they weren't already), to make them see that "race fatigue" was not a viable option.

"Compensatory grandiosity" was another element Steele raised in his book, *The Content of Our Character*, that Fuller wanted them to think about. Along with "victimization," Steele placed this under the heading of "Recomposition"—the ways in which blacks create another reality to mask and deny the real one, the one of racial vulnerability. "There are images of it everywhere in black life," Steele wrote. "The swaggering teenager with his gold chains and suitcase-size ghetto blaster; the 'sister' with an insouciant don't-play-with-me attitude; the black college professor with conspicuously perfect elocution and a Latinate vocabulary; the black dockworker who polishes his fingernails; the inflated grandeur of some black preachers; the above-it-all attitude of 'cool' that makes the pretense of emotional distance a virtue; the magnificent egotism of a Muhammad Ali." All of this, in Steele's view, was "born of the need to assert beauty and grace over degradation, to be beautifully human against the charge of inhumanity. It was compensatory." And yet, he added, it also had "an underside. It can become too much of an escape from diminishment, too much a self-delusion."

"The aspect of what he's saying is right," Fuller told the class, before taking them back into the past, back to 1958, his senior year at North Division, to a time when the Blue Devils were playing basketball out at Country Day, a school for the well-to-do, a place, Fuller said, where "these dudes had cars, they were dressed up in, you know, ties and stuff, there were maybe seven or eight people in the classroom. I can remember as if it were yesterday. We sat in the locker room before we went out to play them, and we said that we were so pissed off about what they had versus what we had, and so the only place that we knew that we could kill them

was on the court. So we actually talked about this, it wasn't a silent unconscious thing, we said we're going to go out here and we're going to destroy these dudes because they have all this other shit that we don't have.
For us it was a racial thing because they were white, but it was, now that I
know more, as much a class thing as it was a race thing." Even if Country
Day had had one black player, he said, they would have felt the same way.
"So we killed them," Fuller recalled, smiling, "but they didn't have nobody that could play."

Ultimately, though, it didn't mean anything, he said, turning serious
again. "It meant something to us because that's all we had as a way to express that power relationship that we felt," but unless you went on to play
professionally, that display of power (other than a temporal charge) didn't
gain you anything, not in any real sense.

"Let me push this even deeper," Fuller said. He had always believed
"in the notion of soul," of black people having a certain style. But the real
issue, he said, was whether having soul was "any better than any other
culture's expression of themselves. What Steele's raising is that we would
ridicule white people who didn't have soul, because if you don't have soul,
you can't dance, and he's trying to raise the point that we make soul take
on much more significance than what it really has in the world but the
reason we were doing that is because we were operating from a level of
powerlessness. So you seek something that raises your level, because you
don't want to sit there and be inferior . . . you search for those things that
would not only bring you to their level, but that would make you more
superior," that would lead you to say, "You don't have soul, soul is this
mystical thing that you can't ever get . . . so we better than you."

But, Fuller wanted to know, how important is it for whoever's in
charge to have soul? Did it even matter? "'Cause if I'm in charge, I don't
have to prove to you that anything I've got is better. . . . You work for me,
I run the government, I do this, I do that. Yet you've got soul, and I can't
dance. Well, I'm leaving this dance now where I can't dance, but you who's
dancing go get my ride. Bring my car around to the front. You're a soulful
dude, but you're my chauffeur, now what?"

If the students were to go back and look at both the civil rights and
black power movements, Fuller suggested, they would be reminded that
blacks couldn't move forward as a people until they came up with "a collective consciousness" that held them together to fight. "The civil rights

movement only took it to one stage. The black power movement tried to pick it up at the next stage and say, 'Look at us, we're powerless because we're black. In order for us to fight we have to come together as a black people.'

"But how are you going to come together if you hate yourselves?" Fuller asked. "There's all kinds of different aspects that combine to make you hate yourself: it's your sense of your beauty; it's the fact that we don't own nothing; the fact that we don't control nothing. You just keep going down the line, right? So if really I'm going to try to ascend to a position of power from where I am, I've got to replace those negative elements with positive elements to give you a positive basis for engaging in a struggle." What bothered Fuller was the way in which Steele zeroed in on "the excesses" of the black power movement without fully exploring why they were necessary.

"Steele says the black power movement was a defense against the shock of vulnerability that comes automatically with greater freedom. What was the greater freedom that he's talking about?" Fuller wondered. If you didn't have money, it didn't matter whether a Holiday Inn would now let you stay there. Freedom for the vast majority of black people was illusionary, he said. But if you had money, you could either try to gain admittance to a white country club (just to prove you had the money to do so, even if you quit a week later) or you could form your own country club because you were simply more comfortable with black folks. What was more apparent to him than ever now was this: Integration, for many black people, continued to represent a strong, basic desire not to be denied *access* to anything far more than it represented some burning desire to be alongside whites.

TWENTY-THREE

Fuller and I left Commando and walked around the corner to a huge mural. It was called "The Patchwork: Piecing Together the History of Black Milwaukee," and Fuller was proud to be prominently portrayed in it. We stared at the wall for what seemed like five minutes and said little to each other. I had been in Milwaukee long enough at that point to have already met some of the other people portrayed there—Booker Ashe and Vel Phillips—and those I hadn't met I had either read of or heard about from Reuben Harpole, one of the city's unofficial historians.

I had met Harpole only a week or so earlier. In fact, he was the person who had come into Scully Stikes's office with the news of Jeffrey Dahmer's arrest. When we finally got together, the first thing he did was press an article from *Fortune* magazine into my hands. "You need to read this," he insisted. It was called "The Ghetto's Hidden Wealth" and it began this way: "Instead of viewing America's inner cities as doomed urban wastelands, think of them as undeveloped countries. . . ."

All right, I said, I'd read it. He had the same bracing yet mildly irritating please-listen-carefully-because-I'm-only-going-to-say-this-once manner of James Cameron, but so be it. He had, like Cameron, lived through much of what he thought it was essential for me to know (even though, unlike Cameron, he had never come close to being lynched, as Cameron had, in 1930, in Marion, Indiana); he was someone whom I could allow to put me on the right track, as it were, knowing, of course, that I would eventually determine for myself where I was going.

The world of Reuben Harpole, I quickly discovered, was a world symbolized by a large rock, a rock that had sat near Eighth and Walnut for as long as anyone could remember. It was called the Penny Rock and it was where children would go to hear, for a penny, stories from their elders. But during urban renewal it was unceremoniously moved, to a spot in front of Lapham Hall at the University of Wisconsin—Milwaukee, and there was no shortage of people trying to have the rock returned to its rightful place. It had to be returned, Harpole strongly implied, because it meant something: the inestimable strength of the community during the days of segregation.

No one I had spoken with talked of urban renewal with as much bitterness as Reuben Harpole. Of the way I-43 had ripped through the heart of the community, leaving razed homes and a housing project (Hillside) that packed hundreds of people onto very little land ("just to prevent the movement north of black people in the city") and didn't even employ blacks to help build, landscape, and maintain it. Of the way one man was able to persuade the city that it was pointless to plant flowers down the middle of Walnut Street because blacks wouldn't appreciate them anyway. (Oddly enough, just that morning, I had seen a woman tending a huge garden on Walnut, hard by that same expressway, a garden that stood in defiance of the decisions and assumptions that had been made years before.)

But he also talked about former governor Warren Knowles and the money he had directed toward the city in 1968, insisting that Knowles was the best governor the state had ever had. And he talked about the unusual care that had been taken to build Parklawn (another housing project) and how it had become a model of the right way to do things. And the efforts he and others had made to integrate suburban schools with students such as Oprah Winfrey (who attended Nicolet High School for two years) and to work within neighborhoods, setting up tutorials at churches and community centers, places where the learning of everything from math and science to sewing and typing could occur. He invoked the names of Lloyd Barbee (an attorney, an intellectual, the community's Dr. King) and Calvin Sherard (who went into R. L. Lathan's church and told people to get up off their knees and start marching) and Isaac Coggs ("Mr. Civil Rights") and Marilyn Morheuser and John Givens, James Dorsey, C. L. Johnson (the "father of the black community," who graduated from Tuskegee in the twenties with a skill in tailoring and came to Milwaukee with the famous Booker T. Washington charge of dropping your buckets where you were), Lincoln Gaines, and Wesley Scott (who was a mentor of Howard Fuller's). Don't forget, Harpole said, stepping further back in time, that Wisconsin was an abolitionist state, a fact he attributed to the large number of German people who had emigrated there, people who "may or may not have liked black people, per se," but who understood what it was to flee an oppressive situation. Don't forget that the Underground Railroad came through and stopped at what was now Wauwatosa. Don't forget the Paris Treaty that Benjamin Franklin signed, the part about the Northwest

Territory (which at that time included Wisconsin) never becoming a slave state. Don't forget Sherman Booth and how he helped a slave named Joshua Glover escape to Canada.

"And don't forget," he said, "to go to the Milwaukee Enterprise Center this afternoon. Governor Thompson will be there, to talk about the Central City Initiative. And then, tomorrow morning, the Community Brainstorming Conference will be holding its monthly breakfast, at St. Matthew's CME Church, and will be discussing this Clarence Thomas nomination. And then, tomorrow night, there will be a reunion of some important folks over at Kern Park, and you should think about dropping by. If you get there before me, just tell them I suggested you come."

I couldn't possibly keep up with Harpole. I didn't see how anybody could. He was such a whirlwind of anger mixed with boosterism that I didn't quite know what to make of him. Except that I was probably bound to disappoint him. And yet when I saw him that afternoon at the governor's press conference, he was firmly in his role as ambassador and greeted me accordingly—as if he had both known me for a long time and didn't know me at all.

"A LITTLE OVER A year ago," Governor Tommy Thompson began, "I was asked to bring some people from the administration to the central city to listen and to take heed of what is needed.... For too long, you know, we've been fighting this war on poverty, but we've been fighting it, I believe, from behind the lines. Today, Wisconsin takes that battle right into the heart of the central city. What we're announcing here today is not a new program, but a new strategy for bringing prosperity, opportunities, and hope to the central city. Our strategy is based not on short-term assistance, but upon giving people assets and help for the long haul. That means jobs, it means homeownership, it means business, it means people with roots in the central city helping other people help themselves...."

The idea being put forward was that there should be one place for people to come, one place where people could find out about job openings, getting a business loan, getting a mortgage, one place where they wouldn't be brushed off and shunted around.

"There's no silver bullet out there," the governor said sternly. "There's no one program that's going to transform the central city into an area of new jobs and new-home ownership. But there's a spirit. And if we can create a spirit and bring all of government together with the central city, you have a way then to improve in incremental steps until we are successful." Until there were more jobs "right down here."

But Governor, one woman said, "we have some 'right down here' jobs—a lot of these fast-food jobs—it's not enough for a person that has to take care of a family. Are these jobs going to be jobs that's going to provide a decent take for a man that has a family to support, a woman that has children to support?"

He was hopeful, he said, that "we can start getting some of the good-paying jobs back in the central city." But in the meantime, if the job was in Waukesha, if it was in Kenosha, if it was in some other part of Milwaukee, the Central City Initiative would provide the transportation for you to get there.

It was a brief exchange, but it encompassed what had to be done, or at least some of what had to be done. It all *sounded* good, but the amount of money earmarked for the effort was minuscule: five hundred thousand dollars, with another five hundred thousand to come.

Thompson was in his second term and enormously popular. His call for the eventual abolition of welfare was part of the reason. His Bridefare and Learnfare programs made it mandatory for teenage mothers to marry and/or continue going to school if they wanted to keep collecting welfare benefits. He wanted states to be able to control their own destiny as much as possible, to not be dependent on the federal government for permission to experiment with different alternatives to welfare. Whenever there was a discussion about jobs, whether it involved a Democrat like John Norquist or a Republican like Tommy Thompson, welfare was implicitly a part of it: a system that nobody particularly liked, but about which no consensus for how to change it—effectively and humanely—had been reached.

If a way could be found to connect more people to work—to train them for a job, help them find one with a living wage, ensure they had the means to get there, ensure they had adequate child care and medical benefits—then perhaps the vicious cycle of dependency could be broken; perhaps the one wire that held the whole bundle of social problems together in a hopeless gnarl could be short-circuited; perhaps all the energy that went into gangbanging and being on lookout for the cops and making the next drug deal, that went into ripping somebody off for their sneakers, that went into watching your back and, literally, hoping you would survive another day—perhaps all of that could somehow be reconfigured into a positive force and channeled elsewhere. Channeled toward gaining the skills required to get the job that had the wage that would make the so-called glamour of the street decidedly less glamorous.

When I asked Howard Fuller what he thought about the Central City Initiative, he said he saw it for what it was—one small effort that was part of a larger effort that had to be made—and was prepared to support anything that had even the remotest chance of having a positive impact. But until that larger effort was made—if ever—he said it would be foolish to see something like this as some exciting breakthrough in the battle to improve the life of those in the inner city.

TWENTY-FOUR

People packed into the basement of St. Matthew's at eight the next morning to discuss Clarence Thomas. People like James Cameron (who was the first to tell me about these monthly Community Brainstorming breakfasts), Annette "Polly" Williams (the controversial state representative who was a member of the Black Panther Militia and the mother of school choice, the plan that allowed public money to follow kids to private school, which the Bush Administration had heartily embraced), and Vel Phillips (Milwaukee's first black alderperson). Reuben Harpole was there, of course, and so were two people from the racism workshop—the young man who had said that whites would do well to stop thinking of themselves as invisible, and the woman who had said she could no longer ride on buses. A representative from Senator Kohl's office had come (the senator was on the Judiciary Committee that would hold the hearings), as had representatives from the NAACP and the Urban League.

It might have been early in the morning, but things heated up quickly.

Webster Harris stood up and said that "Clarence Thomas is a *real* nigger and he'll do things from his heart. One of his idols is Malcolm X. He's a real down-to-earth nigger." Harris reminded everyone that just a few months earlier the black community had been divided over Howard Fuller and whether he should be the next school superintendent, implying how ridiculous it was to have expended that kind of energy.

Polly Williams said there was nothing wrong with both needing help (as exemplified by affirmative action programs) and being a fierce believer in self-help. (Polly was often referred to as a Democrat by party but a Republican in her heart, and I couldn't prevent a small smile from forming on my lips as she spoke.) Williams had just returned from Washington, where she had met Thomas. "When I see Thomas," she said, "I see a reflection of my father, a reflection of my son. Now, if you look at Hugo Black's past, a member of the Klan, he shouldn't have been confirmed. But he turned out to be a good justice. Or look at Benjamin Hooks, who Nixon nominated to the FCC. Let's be *real* about this: Bush has the right to pick who he wants. Black elitists are opposing Thomas, but all the people in my district know is that *a black man* is being nominated for the Supreme Court and they're proud." She understood, she said, why many blacks were having a hard time with the nomination, but she knew, just knew in her heart, that when he got on the Court he would do what was right. He would do what was right because he would be overwhelmed by "chitlin flashbacks."

Now that was pure Polly and everybody knew it and everybody laughed. It broke the tension in the room. Whether her prediction would turn out to be right, of course, was another matter.

Nellie Wilson didn't see it Williams's way at all. She saw a man whose nomination David Duke had come out in support of. A man whose nomination would "lay the groundwork for some more Willie Horton tactics in 1992." A man who symbolized a growing number of conservative African-Americans who had, she said with biting sarcasm, "pulled themselves up by their collective bootstraps." The only reason her sons were professionals today, she said, her body quivering slightly, *the only reason*, was because she was helped by a government program.

"His nomination," Vel Phillips reminded everyone, "will affect blacks for *years and years and years* to come."

"He should be given an opportunity," another woman said. "We're prejudging him."

"His nomination is an *insult* to black people," Wilson said.

Carl Ashley, from the Wisconsin Association of Minority Attorneys, said it was difficult not to prejudge Thomas once you knew the facts. And the facts were that he went to Yale Law School and part of the reason he went to Yale was that he was a minority, which made his position on affirmative action, in Ashley's opinion, deeply troubling. "Let him speak to these issues at the hearing. But he shouldn't be appointed."

The NAACP so far hadn't taken a position. What came out of their recent meeting in Houston, Gerry Hamilton informed the gathering, was this: The organization very much wanted a black on the Court but suspected that President Bush, by nominating Thomas and knowing what a quandary his nomination would place blacks in, would wind up with what he ideally wanted—a conservative white candidate instead. In any case, the NAACP would first meet with Thomas and then decide if they were going to endorse him.

The situation with the Urban League was much the same. They had taken "no position" on Thomas's nomination at their meeting in Atlanta, though John Jacobs, the president, had not forsaken the opportunity to emphasize how ironic the whole situation was: having an affirmative action nominee who was so strongly opposed to affirmative action.

L. G. SHANKLIN-FLOWERS WAS not at the breakfast that morning, but that was hardly an indication of any indifference to the matter. When I saw her a few days later, she told me that Thomas had been much on her mind from the moment he was nominated. In fact, he fit her definition of "internalized oppression" perfectly, far more so, in her opinion, than the seat on the Court he was being put forward to fill. It wasn't that she was opposed to the notion of blacks having different points of view. What offended her, offended her deeply, was this: "He is the consequence of the kind of programs that got initiated in the sixties and seventies to make up for the mistreatment of people of color. This man got into school because of the policies and programs and he has benefited and now he can turn around and say they shouldn't be there? How *dare* he do that? . . . How *dare* this man now sit up there and act like he somehow got to where he was on his own, pulling up his own damn bootstraps? Give me a break. No one ever has. That's a mythology and he certainly hasn't. So I don't argue that he's suddenly going to see the light. He's a lost brother, and I'll pray for him to come home, but I don't expect to see it in my lifetime. I don't think he'll have a change of heart because he has to so prove the other side of the coin. How these people go to sleep at night and live with themselves I can't fathom."

She and Thomas were about the same age. What benefited him had benefited her. And far from having any shame about that, or being unwilling in any way to concede that, she said, quite frankly, that she had been worth the investment, that she had given back a hundredfold. "No one ever gave me anything but some opportunities that I used," she said. "I have worked hard, I have done the things that I was supposed to do, but I don't have very many of the rewards that go along with it."

What specifically did she mean?

"I live in an inner-city community. I drive a raggedy car. I barely make enough to meet my needs. And given the amount of effort and energy that

I have put into getting where I am now, I know that if I had been a white male I'd be running some corporation. There's no question in my mind. I certainly have the intelligence and the capacity, it just hasn't been set up that way. I have consistently, job after job, had enough experiences in my life where people have been brought in that have had less experience, less understanding, less talent, and who end up running things when I was there and I was overlooked. I know it's because of the color of my skin. I am finally, at forty, saying, 'No more.' I'm not going to take that in and say it's because I'm not smart enough, or I didn't try hard enough, or I didn't really want it. Which have been my stories."

She could facilitate workshops on racism and talk about internalized oppression, but it was only recently that she had come to see how she had allowed it to govern her own life and paralyze her in a way, how (as Joan Didion said of all people) she had told herself stories in order to live. In listening to her talk about Clarence Thomas, the way in which each word and sentence dripped with disdain, the assertion that "he could probably flunk the self-hatred test, but he of course would not see that or say that," I already knew the frame of reference from which she spoke, a framework she herself had supplied only moments before our conversation turned to Thomas and which she now seemed unmindful of.

She, like Thomas, was taught by nuns and was married to a white person, from whom (unlike Thomas) she was now separated and with whom she had a daughter, the love of her life. She had met her husband fifteen years earlier, in Washington, where she was working at the time. He was a "golden boy," she said, and what developed was a relationship in which she "always had to look at what aspect of this attraction was due to self-hatred." At some level, she said, she had come to believe "the stereotypes about me and my people," a belief that was formed back in second grade when she was relegated to the role of the Devil in a production of *The Last Temptation of Christ* when she wanted to be the angel instead, and that was reinforced by her own family, and by her Catholic faith, by the whole business of there being darkened spots on the soul.

How many white people, she wanted to know, ever asked themselves, "What does this have to do with myself?" Or black people in relationships with other blacks? "I always had to struggle with 'Am I in this relationship because this man is the right man for me and not because he's the white man for me?'" Her answer, she decided, was that both were true, that David

would not be threatened by her, that she could "do whatever the hell I
wanted to do with my life and his manhood would be intact," that she
wouldn't have to battle that in the way she felt certain she would have had
she married a black man. "He didn't have issues of worthiness because he
had the wrong color of skin. He came into a world that said he was fine
because he was a white male." She wasn't saying, she stressed, that *every*
black woman in a relationship with a black man had this struggle; but she
was saying that black women were angry about being blamed in part for
what was happening to black men, being blamed for not being supportive
enough of them, given "what they're subject to in the world." Black women
want to be there and support their men, she said, even though it often meant
not doing what was right for themselves. As a result of marrying David
Flowers she hadn't had to deal with that.

"Do you feel guilty about that?"

No, she didn't. At the same time, though, she knew there were people
"on the outside looking in" who would judge her (because she married a
white man and because of some of the groups she had aligned herself with)
as having given up. "In my heart of hearts I know that I have never given
up on my people. That has been the major screen upon which I have made
decisions my entire life. Personally, I would like to be a little free from it.
I would like to make a decision just because I want to make a decision, not
because I am trying to figure out if this is going to make our position better. I am tired."

But even if she was experiencing the kind of race fatigue Shelby Steele
talked about, even if she admitted she would think long and hard before
she would ever enter into a relationship outside her race again, her daughter, Davita, was the main result of the choice she had made and for whom,
fatigue aside, she would continue to be vigilant. Unlike her mother, Davita
was fair skinned and, even at three and a half, very aware of color. Only a
few weeks earlier, she and her mother were watching television when an
advertisement appeared for a doll called Kid Sister. Davita immediately
said she wanted it. L. G. reminded her she already had it, that she had gotten
it the previous Christmas. Davita didn't believe her, so they both went to
Davita's room in search of the doll. Upon finding it, though, Davita announced, quite disgustedly, that she didn't want *that* one, she wanted the
white one. For L. G. it was as if nothing had changed since Kenneth and
Mamie Clark's experiments in the 1940s. (And in that regard nothing had.
A recent study showed that black children still preferred white dolls over

black ones, though the reasons were not clear-cut.) Trying not to "just totally panic and be upset that my child is dismissing her African heritage and all that stuff, I said to her, 'Well, this doll looks like your mommy and your danty'—she calls my sister Danty—'don't you want this one?' And so she looked at me, she looked at the doll, and said 'Okay,' and she grabbed her and hugged her and went off to play. And I was trying to think, What was going on with her? Why would she make that distinction? It hit me that the one she sees on television is the white one, she never sees the dark one. So of course that's the one, she has already gotten the message that one is better."

Just the day before, Davita had come to her, the Dahmer incident hanging over everybody's head, wanting to be reassured that the police were "our friends." Given all that was going on, L. G. said, her first instinct was to tell her otherwise. But she didn't. She said, "Yes, the police are our friends, and if you need help and you see a police officer, you need to go to them and tell them you need help." And yet, she said, it was also her responsibility to prepare Davita "to be strong in a world that is not set up in her interest." Because she was fair skinned, L. G. said, "white people will always try to pit her against darker people of color. And black people will react to her because of her fair skin. Part of the internalized oppression will be that people will assume things about her that aren't true, just on the basis of her skin." She wanted Davita to be as proud of her father's heritage as she was of her mother's, wanted to ensure that she never be forced to choose one over the other.

Which brought L. G. back to race fatigue, to the anger underlying the exhaustion, her anger that the color of her darker skin had limited her, had defined, in her opinion, what she could or could not do, had left her with "no real chance to choose" what she would do with her life. She was the embodiment of the internalized oppression she was trying now to relieve others of, "committed to making up for this mistake that I was." She was "a real prime target for not being worthy and therefore having to justify my life through good works to be worthy." It was, all of it, very painful to admit, but she had been determined, from that moment in second grade on, to do whatever she could to ensure she would never again have to be the Devil.

Arthur Ashe said, not long before he died, that race was the greatest burden he had to bear. L. G. was simply echoing that, except that none of it was simple. We are all scripted, I recalled my colleague telling me,

scripted in ways we don't even think about. L. G. Shanklin-Flowers
detested the limitations of the box she felt being black had placed her in.
And yet she detested Clarence Thomas because he wasn't willing to acknowledge the opportunities being in that box had afforded him, wasn't
willing to concede that he had been worth every investment anybody or
any program or any institution had ever made in him. It's only human
nature that the beneficiary of another person's help will ultimately resent
the person offering it; people don't want to feel indebted, regardless of the
helper's motive. Affirmative action came about because it was the just thing
to do; it has attempted to redress the imbalance, and it has even made the
word "egalitarian" respectable again. No one ever said it was going to fit
into place without anger and antagonism (calling it a "preferential program" certainly didn't help); the implementing of laws, any law, doesn't
work that way. Somebody, somewhere, was naturally going to insist that
individual rights had been blatantly ignored, that it undercut the whole
notion of merit, that somebody didn't receive his just deserts.

   In ways that George Bush probably couldn't have fully imagined, the
nomination of Clarence Thomas to the United States Supreme Court was
more than just a political dilemma for many blacks; the man himself was a
mirror each individual either had to look in and see what part of himself
he recognized there, or avoid altogether. After all, it was easier to be proud
that a black man was being nominated than it was to undergo the process
of introspection, a process that often holds its share of unpleasant surprises.

TWENTY-FIVE

Who needs the Negro?

In the course of my discussion with L. G. Shanklin-Flowers she told me of a book she had been reading by that title, a book she thought would further help me understand why blacks—males in particular—were so at risk in our society, why she felt that living in the inner city in the nineties was not that different from being indentured and living on a plantation way back when. The book was published in 1970, its author a man named Sidney Willhelm. Settling into a chair in my room, I began looking at the book, its blunt, unvarnished title provoking in me the same anger and discomfort I had felt when I read that passage from *Black Rage*. Seeing Bert Sweet when I came into the lobby a few minutes earlier reminded me of her father's comment that America would be a lot better off if blacks just packed up and went back to Africa. For the longest time, of course, that wasn't feasible: America was far too dependent on black labor. But automation changed that. The Negro, never welcome to begin with, wasn't required so much. And the antipathy toward him, which had always been there, surfaced more readily. Automation turned out to be a two-edged sword. Initially it had been a godsend, enabling blacks to leave cotton picking and the South behind and seek better-paying jobs in the North, but it wound up trailing them like a bad debt, eventually putting many blacks out of work in what was supposed to be the Promised Land. The American Negro, I. F. Stone wrote, was condemned to live in Egypt, but it was an Egypt that had already built its pyramids and no longer needed slaves. "Mechanization on the farm and automation in industry have at last set him free, but now freedom turns out to be joblessness."

"The truth," Shiva Naipaul wrote in *Journey to Nowhere*, "is starker. Joblessness is a euphemism. It would be more accurate to say that a technologically sophisticated society has no use for these people. They are redundant. They are good for nothing. They do not even evoke fellow feeling. One can think of them as the human equivalent of the radioactive waste produced by nuclear power plants: sterile and potentially lethal. What, the ecologists ask, is one to do with this waste? Bury it miles underground? Shoot it into outer space? Discover some way of breaking it down and rendering it harmless? The junk people, the human waste left behind by American history, are no less negative, no less dangerous a quantity. One sees them on the streets of midtown Manhattan, carrying glittering noisemaking machines, dressed to kill, the ugliness and the hatred of the discarded slave glowing in their eyes. You see them in Harlem, standing drunk or drugged on street corners. What is to be done with them?"

Unfortunately, as I had been discovering the longer I stayed in Milwaukee, nobody seemed to know. For every theory or solution that was put forth, there seemed to be a corresponding reason why it wouldn't work. Scatter-site housing in the suburbs? Forget it. That's why people moved out there in the first place. Find a way to tie welfare to work. Forget it. Abolish welfare altogether, Charles Murray argued in *Losing Ground;* by doing that, you would cut down on teenage pregnancy, the poison root of all the problems. After all, where was it written that anybody was entitled to anything? Besides, as he and Richard Herrnstein would later suggest in their highly controversial book, *The Bell Curve,* there was nothing ultimately to be gained by continuing to wrestle with the race problem. If blacks had, on average, an IQ that was fifteen points lower than whites', then all the money in the world wasn't going to change that hereditary fact. Nobody had to feel guilty anymore, in the supremely humane view of Murray and Herrnstein, nobody had to continue wasting their time trying to solve the unsolvable. The magic answer, grim as it might be, was that there was no answer. Resources, sparse to begin with, not only could but should be directed elsewhere. Genetics rules. Too bad. Case closed.

Just as the abolition of slavery did not eliminate racism, neither, sadly, did the civil rights movement—a dispiriting fact that could especially be confirmed by anyone who had lived through the sixties, the generation that perhaps felt America's failure to solve the race problem most acutely. We can pay eloquent lip service to the idea of democracy and equality and the same starting line, but in those moments when people lay awake in their beds at night, unable to sleep, words like "preferential programs" and "set-asides" are lodged in their throats, unwilling to go down. If a black person gets a job because he's black and not because he's the most qualified, many people lie there thinking, Fuck equality and fuck them. As

Walter Farrell pointed out, he went into graduate school at the right time: the riots of 1967 opened up the doors of academe for guys like him. Try as you might to make someone like him feel inferior, like the token he surely was, his attitude, like L. G.'s, is the same: Fuck you, I'm here, and I'm worth the investment. And you say, well, you're *never* going to be accepted, and we're going to sabotage you every chance we get, and we're never going to invite you to anything, and even if we do, you're going to be ignored, or we're going to be polite to you but you won't for a second have any doubts about what we really think—that you're here because we say you can be here. If you try to move next door to us and be like us, we're either going to move away or act as if you're not here. Day after day, in some way or another, at a moment when you're feeling good and least expect or think that anything could happen to ruin your day or rob you of your dignity, it'll happen, boom, just like that, and it will remind you of what you've known all along: you don't belong.

Fine, you say, but you're wrong about integration. Where do you come off thinking that all we wanted was to get next to white folk? You really are arrogant if you truly thought that's what we cared about. You think we don't know that deep down you're still thinking of us as niggers, you think we don't know that you need someone to look down on, you think we don't know that you thank God every day you're not black. I mean, come on, we know what the real deal is. That's not saying that Dr. King and Malcolm died in vain, but it should help you understand why Malcolm is considered the man now. Every black male in the 'hood identifies with him, wants to speak like him, *be him*. What about the trip to Mecca, you say, when he saw the so-called light and decided black and white working together might be a better thing? Fine, it happened, but that doesn't sell to these brothers, their reality is different, and that's why the Malcolm of the speeches, all that "by any means necessary" stuff, that's what's happening out on the streets, except it's not really being directed against white folk, like white folk think, it's brother killing brother, "jacking the nigga," like that one kid told you. You look at the statistics—you look at the statistics for every other "socioeconomic problem"—so you better look at the statistics, *the facts,* and you'll see that some 80 percent of whites are killed by other whites, that more than 90 percent of blacks being killed are being killed by other blacks. Now that's not saying we don't do our share of robbing, assaulting, and carjacking, but why, you might wonder, if you think about it at all, as you sit out there in the suburbs, safe in your living rooms, watching your TVs, waiting for the "story at ten" or eleven, or pretty much any time of day, why are so many of us getting busted, why do so many of us expect to die yesterday, today, at any moment, why are so many of us dealing drugs or doing time? Do you really think that all our families are fucked up, that nobody cares, that nobody has "family values"? Are you so willing to buy into every stereotype about us—that we're lazy, stupid, don't have a work ethic, just want to feed off the system, and, all in all, are a menace to society? Because if you buy into all that and it makes you feel better in some perverse way about yourselves, then how do you explain people like Maron and Georgette Alexander, or Louise Kidd, or L. G. Shanklin-Flowers, or Marvin and Diane Howard, people living in the inner city, caring for their kids, trying to make sure they get a good education? What would Dan Quayle say about them?

You see where I'm going. On the one hand, people conveniently forget about them because they don't fit all the stereotypes—and yet, on the other, they are trotted out and invoked as examples of people who haven't caved in, who have struggled valiantly, who are "decent" and "hardworking," who won't allow themselves to use victimhood as the reason they're not coping or succeeding or whatever. But what very few people care to acknowledge is that the hurdles of racism—be it personal or institutional—still exist for *all* blacks, and Shelby Steele and Clarence Thomas can talk all they want about putting one's individual advancement over the burdensome needs of their race, about being recognized as an individual instead of a generic black man, but they're seriously deluding themselves, because that is not what's going down. So we'd rather live among our own than keep banging on doors that no one wants to answer.

We're not saying all whites feel this way—but many do. You owned us for the longest time, and in many respects, you act as if you still do. Why not flip Shelby Steele around? Why not stop and wonder what might be gained by letting go of your need to feel so superior—to justify your ownership of us in the first place—letting go of all that and trying to get beyond race instead?

INTERNAL DIALOGUES LIKE THESE were occurring more and more as I stared out the window, or sat downstairs at the café where I ate breakfast, or walked alone along Lake Michigan. For what it was worth, I now saw that my effort to grapple with all this had come from my own deep disappointment and bewilderment, more so than from anyone else's, that we as a country hadn't gotten beyond race, that one step forward had, in some respects, become two steps back. I was Shiva Naipaul's editor for the book I quoted from—a passage so unrelentingly harsh that I practically memorized it when I first encountered it in 1980. Then again, he had a way of putting things that almost branded them into your thoughts whether you wanted them there or not, a way of burrowing so far and deep into the human psyche and not stopping until he reached the point that yielded one's truest, most uncensored position—or at least what he perceived to be such. How valid was Naipaul's paragraph at the time he wrote it, and how prescient? He was writing about what has come to be called the underclass (a term first used by Gunnar Myrdal in 1962), but I. F. Stone's allusion to the Egyptian pyramids seemed more far-reaching, more accurate a description and symbol of American society as a whole. Democracy is a nice civil idea, requiring an equal exchange of ideas in an open, public, inclusive manner, but it is not the way we live. We live in a meritocracy, whether we want to admit it or not, and democracy is foiled at nearly every turn. There's no room for everybody at the top of the pyramid, and those striving to get there like it that way. How, in other words, can you stand out and distinguish yourself if there aren't a considerable number of people below you—people you have either surpassed in ability or in wealth or in perseverance, or people whose place in life was always below your own? In the mid–nineteenth century Lord Acton claimed, after visiting America, that it was a country where there was "no distinction of class," a country in which a child was "not born to the station of its parents, but with an indefinite claim to all the prizes that can be won by thought and labor."

The idealistic picture Lord Acton drew would have been a sight to behold—had it been an accurate rendering. Alexis de Tocqueville, who visited America about twenty years earlier than the good lord, was essentially told the same wonderful story of equality that Acton would absorb, but he was far more cynical about it. In no way that he could discern did the narrative allow for blacks to figure in. Ironically, he said, the end of slavery—if it ever came—would only "increase the repugnance of the white population for the blacks." Whites, in Tocqueville's view, weren't suddenly going to view as equals those whose inferiority was the alleged raison d'être for their indenture in the first place. "You may set the Negro free," he wrote, "but you cannot make him otherwise than an alien to those of European origin." Can one not hear in the Kerner Commission report the strains of Tocqueville, his neutral observation that "the whites and the blacks are placed in the situation of two foreign communities. These two races are fastened to each other without intermingling; and they are unable to separate entirely or to combine." Or, in the Shiva Naipaul passage, Tocqueville's more emotional warning that "the danger of a conflict between the white and black inhabitants perpetually haunts the imagination of the Americans, like a painful dream"?

Nothing, as Tocqueville knew, exists alone, out of context, apart from anything else. And nothing, on a certain level, ever changes. Somehow we find a way to validate (or at least try to validate) nearly everything we do or say. Even when the Puritans insisted they found the institution of slavery abhorrent, they did so for a reason, to falsely claim some higher moral ground. (Abigail Adams, in a letter to her husband, John, wrote: "It always appeared a most iniquitous scheme to me to fight ourselves for what we are daily robbing and plundering from those who have as good a right to freedom as we have.") Rationalization is an exceedingly lethal, hypocritical tool, but that hasn't stopped us—at every level of the pyramid—from using it often, to suit whatever purpose.

TWENTY-SIX

Leaving Tocqueville behind and venturing out onto the streets of Milwaukee, I was stepping back in time to the 1960s. Rallies at churches, "This Little Light of Mine" reverberating throughout the North Side, a Michael McGee–orchestrated sleep-in at City Hall, protests in front of Jeffrey Dahmer's apartment building, a huge, predominantly South Side turnout in support of the police, and now, at Juneau Park, not far from where I was staying, a candlelight vigil on the first Monday night of August, a large crowd having gathered to comfort the families of Dahmer's victims. Speeches were made, including one by Mayor Norquist, who wore a folksy cardigan, his way of saying that Milwaukee was still what it had always been—a good, solid place, its citizens overflowing with gemütlichkeit—his way of underlining that Dahmer was not a reflection on the city or on them, that he could have taken up residence and begun preying on innocent people anywhere. Just before the mayor spoke, Queen Hyler, head of a group called Stop the Violence, reminded everyone that the Dahmer case, horrible as it was, "only brought to the surface many problems that we already knew existed. As my grandmother always said, before you can solve any problems, you first must be willing to admit that there is a problem. We must face the cold white facts that racism is still very much alive in this city. . . .

"Dr. King once said, when asked about love, 'I've decided to stick with love. Hate is too great a burden to bear.' When asked about living together as brothers, Dr. King said that 'we must live together as brothers or perish together as fools.'" She then said, as King often did, that time was running out, that the time to bring an end to racial injustice was now, and, to underline this, she alluded to something that President Kennedy had said in 1963: "If an American, because his skin is dark, cannot enjoy the full and free life that all of us want, then who among you would be content to have the color of your skin changed and stand in his place? Who among you would then be content with the counsel of patience and delay?"

. . .

AS I LISTENED TO Queen Hyler, a woman who had lost family members to violence and couldn't abide Michael McGee's threat of it, listened to her re-ask John F. Kennedy's question, I silently answered, No one, no one who is white would be willing to have the color of his skin changed—at least not without reparations, reparations of a different kind from those that McGee had spoken of (in regard to all the years of slavery).

How about *a million dollars a year? For the rest of your life?*

That was the tidy sum Andrew Hacker's Queens College students said they would require if they woke up one morning and discovered a "mistake" had been made, that they were now black. Emulating the things you liked about black culture was one thing, literally becoming black quite another.

All up and down the pyramid, calculating one's worth showed no signs of letting up.

And yet when it came to victimhood, the way in which nearly everyone appeared to crave a V on his forehead was remarkable and unsettling. Being a victim in America in the nineties had become alluring and sexy. Having an awful personal story to tell could get you on *Oprah,* get you that fifteen minutes of fame Andy Warhol said everybody would have; even if it got you five, you'd be happy. Forget racism, it was easy to imagine someone declaring, that's in the past. Blacks don't have a monopoly on victimhood. Besides, you've heard it all before. So now listen to this, this is *brand-new,* this is a tale of dysfunction you just won't believe. . . .

In this new world of everybody-as-victim, no one seemed to feel it was imperative to be responsible for one's own actions. Everything now had an explanation, however facile, however far-flung. And yet in this new climate, this newly minted "culture of complaint," blacks (who had perhaps the most legitimate claim to being victims, whose hold on America's conscience was arguably still the strongest) were being told, by blacks as well as whites, to stop being victims, to let go of race, and take full responsibility for their own well-being and destiny.

There was, of course, nothing wrong with that advice—except that some odd double standard now seemed to be at work. Discrimination and intolerance, it was true, did not apply only to blacks. But if it could be argued that no group had been more discriminated against over a longer period of time, it didn't seem right, in human terms, that individual and collective goodwill toward blacks should suddenly be allowed to dry up just because the race problem had been so pervasive and just because people had gotten tired of it, had gotten tired of seeking solutions, and were instead rushing to be anointed as victims too.

L. G. Shanklin-Flowers had wondered how many white people ever looked inward in an effort to determine the degree to which self-hatred influenced the decisions they made (or didn't make) or the people they found themselves involved with. Based upon the evidence, more and more and more—provided they had a chance to gain some notoriety or compassion and empathy from total strangers as a result.

As I snapped back to Juneau Park, the speeches ended and people began walking down State Street, singing "We Shall Overcome" and heading toward City Hall. It had been nearly two years since I had heard it sung at a public gathering. The words had moved me that day in Montgomery, but now, here in Milwaukee, the song's clarion call was more plaintive and elusive, the chasm between hope and reality ever more pronounced.

TWENTY-SEVEN

On the day after the vigil at Juneau Park, a far different crowd assembled at the War Memorial Center, a crowd of Rotarians, sober-suited and mostly white, who had come at the noon hour to hear how a former sixties radical was going to chart a new path for Milwaukee's public schools in the 1990s and beyond.

If I needed any proof that Howard Fuller's talk was not going to be a case of "preaching to the converted," the man sitting next to me at my table provided it, wondering aloud what, "given his background as a Marxist," Fuller would have to say.

Against the backdrop of a banner that asked, "Is it the Truth? Is it Fair to All Concerned? Will it Build Goodwill and Better Friendships? Will it Be Beneficial to All Concerned?"—the Rotary's "four-way test of the things we think, say, or do"—Fuller waded right into a sea of skepticism with a sense of humor that disarmed his audience and allowed them to relax. He said that after the last time he had come before them (to speak on behalf of a separate school district for black students) "there's no way in the world that anyone would have considered the fact that I might come back here. But here I am."

There he was, in his tailored dark blue suit and red tie, telling this audience what many of them knew or suspected: he was inheriting a system that was failing, that despite many good teachers, good principals, good individual schools, and good students, "dramatic changes" were needed. He hadn't taken the job to just come in and conduct "business as usual." Anyone who knew him, he said, knew that was not his style.

His very standing there, though, epitomized the irony and precariousness of his situation. The moment the Greater Milwaukee Committee pronounced Fuller to be someone it could work with was the moment many in the black community became suspicious and wary of him. If the powers that be anoint you, the paranoid thinking went, who's to say you're going to represent the best interests of black people? What kind of "compromises" have you made to become someone whites approve of and can work with?

Fuller had said on more than one occasion that he wouldn't allow anyone to question his integrity, and he didn't, at least not without a sharp, indignant response. It was one thing to hold on to race for the right reasons, quite another to allow it to result in hasty judgments about another person's character or motives just because he had chosen a certain path. He was, as he had said many times, concerned about *all* children getting an education. And what made it difficult for that to happen, he said, was that he was inheriting a system in which there were no consequences for failure: everybody was protected, everybody, that is, but the children themselves. He was inheriting a system in which only 40 percent of freshmen graduated from high school, the GPA for high school students was a D+ (higher, though, for those students who attended school more than 90 percent of the time), a system whose standardized test scores were continuing to decline. He was inheriting a system in which twenty-five thousand children (one-fourth of all students) could not even go to a school in their neighborhood, quite apart from whether it was a good school or not. Busing, he said, was not only expensive, but it had failed. Seventy-two percent of Milwaukeeans believed their children could obtain a better education elsewhere.

It was a dismal picture Fuller was painting and a brutally honest one. It was not in his nature to gloss things over. If Milwaukee turned its back on its public schools, he was suggesting, it was, in a way, turning its back on itself. "If there's one thing that is known in America," Fuller said, "it is that we've got all kinds of research about education. About what to do, where to do it, how to do it, why to do it, et cetera. It is not a question of research; it's a question of the political will to do what has to be done and to do it now." And within that question of "political will"—a notion that had come up time and time again—there was the element of race. "There are going to be tensions," Fuller said ominously, "there are going to be racial tensions. We're talking about changing the culture of an organization."

To do that, he said, five essential things would have to take place: higher expectations; improved teacher morale; safe and orderly schools; increased parental involvement; accountability for results. Coming from anybody else, these Rotarians might well have sat there politely, silently counting the moments until the speech was over and their civic duty done for another week or another month, until they could get back in their cars and head out of the city to the suburbs where most of them lived, where they could play eighteen and then fire up their grills in their vast back-yards, the whole amalgam of urban woes gratefully behind them.

But Howard Fuller—this man they could work with, or hoped they could—was different. He had a way of speaking that commanded their attention and their respect, even if they secretly were convinced that nothing was going to change, that one man, no matter how motivated and determined, wasn't going to be able to alter the culture that he spoke of—a culture in which some kids took firearms rather than books to school, if they came at all.

"We have to have people who believe in these children," Fuller was saying. "We cannot continue to say, 'Well, those are just *those* kids. What can you expect from *those* kids?' We have to expect from those kids the highest levels of achievement, and we need to demonstrate through higher standards that we believe our children are capable of learning, that the children in this city are as capable of learning as children who live outside of this city. And we cannot retreat in any way on that belief."

The curriculum would have to change, to reflect more the multi-cultural student body. This would, he said, cause debate and discussion in the community, as it had all over the country, but it had to be faced: "I know that people are gnashing their teeth about this and are concerned, but we can't run from this as a reality."

Teacher morale was inextricably tied to safe and orderly schools. In the previous school year there had been about a hundred thousand disciplinary incidents, nearly two-thirds involving classroom discipline and the refusal to accept instruction. Beyond a question of whose fault it was there was the question "Why should Milwaukee's students and parents and staff tolerate a school climate that would be unacceptable in other communities?" A new disciplinary plan would be forthcoming, as well as a greater role for "alternative schools" (a polite term for a place to send kids who cause trouble). At first, he predicted, there would probably be more suspensions and expulsions than the alternative schools could handle, but it couldn't be helped, it had to be done. A small number of children couldn't be allowed to disrupt the education of the majority of kids.

Parental involvement was the next piece, and Fuller reminded everyone that "for decades we have been forcing children to get on buses, day after day, distributing them all over the city without a positive educational result." Parents needed to be able to choose where their child attended school and more schools had to be built closer to where many of these kids lived. The school system needed to view parents and their students as customers, as people who had a right to satisfaction and who could take their business elsewhere, without cost, if they didn't find it. As things now stood, a parent could send his child to a suburban school (as Diane and Marvin Howard had, as part of the controversial Chapter 220 program) or, thanks to Polly Williams's efforts, a small percentage of students could attend private schools with public money. But true "school choice" did not exist. Without it, he warned, much of what he was talking about had little chance of working.

Fuller had been careful about mentioning race so far. He had only directly raised its specter once ("there are going to be tensions, racial tensions"), but it would have been counterproductive for him to belabor the point: he knew that his audience knew whom he was talking about. When he said that schools had to be built where children lived, that neighborhood schools would "give us the opportunity to link schools to additional human services that we need for our children," the Rotarians knew he was speaking mainly about black children: anybody in that room who had been in Milwaukee a decade or so earlier and had witnessed the fierce battle Fuller waged to keep North Division as a neighborhood school knew how strongly Fuller felt about this issue.

But he wasn't suggesting that buildings be built for their own sake. He was suggesting that any facilities plan he proposed had to be driven by educational goals and requirements: smaller class sizes, availability of kindergarten for every child, programs for "exceptional education."

Which brought him to accountability, to the need to move from being a school system (with centralized decision making) to being a system of schools, a system in which each individual school would be judged on its performance, a system in which more resources would flow to the schools that were succeeding and in which the schools that were not would be shut down and reopened with new staff.

"Few of you would want to be a manager in an organization where you have no control of anything but somebody told you you were accountable. We have to move to give people authority, give them power, and then hold them accountable for the results. . . . We need incentives and rewards that mean something. To produce them we must allow dollars to follow the students."

In talking about MPS as a business and it being high time that it
started operating as one, Fuller was now talking their language. In their
world it was called site-based management and, in Fuller's opinion, "we
have to now quit talking about it and we have to do it.

"I know there are people who are saying to me, 'Howard, this will
never work.' I will say to you, 'It may not, but we'll never know unless we
try.' What we do know is what we have right now is not working. And I
say to you that when we have something that is not working, don't come
to me talking about how something else will not work. . . . I'm telling you
that this is not going to be easy. This speech is infinitely easier than the
task that's going to be before us on this question. . . . There are people in
our system that believe that the system was created for their job. That they
own the jobs. Not that this belongs to the community, but that it belongs
to them. And we're going to have to root all of that out. . . . I know we're
going to have to wrestle with these issues, but I guess I believe deep down
in my heart and my soul that our children are worth the effort."

Fuller sat down to great applause and then stood right back up to
take questions, questions that touched on all the things he had talked about
and asked him to go further, to be more specific. A new student assignment plan would be ready in October, as would specific suggestions on
parental involvement. He was open to the idea of "charter schools" and to
allowing certain schools to be run by private concerns. As to what part
business could play in all this, he said that a number of businesses had
already come forward and were doing "wonderful things" in certain schools,
but he needed time to figure out the most constructive role that business
could play.

"I heard your idea on the African-American male-only school," one
person said, bringing up something that Fuller had not specifically mentioned in his talk. "How will you get the courts, and if need be the Constitution, to distinguish, Dr. Fuller, between externally imposed integration
and internally requested segregation?"

"First off," Fuller said, "there is no African-American male school.
People started out talking about that, but in reality what we now have is
an African immersion school that's open to any student in MPS irrespec-
tive of race or gender."

Clearly, the public at large was still confused as to what type of school
Victor Berger was to be when it opened its doors in a month. Inherent in

the confusion, of course, was concern, concern that was reinforced moments later when I stood outside with Pete Stolz, who was on his way back to Menomonee Falls.

He informed me that four out of every five Rotarians at the lunch were of the opinion that today's high school and college graduates were unprepared to go into the workplace. While he thought Fuller's speech was impressive, he said the fact still remained: the best college graduates who wanted a career in teaching were going to choose to teach in a better system than Milwaukee's.

What, I wanted to know, did he think of the immersion school that Fuller spoke of?

He was for it, he said, stepping toward me and dropping his voice. "As far as blacks in history, there is no question that they've gotten the short end of the stick in terms of their accomplishments."

Having said that, he began moving toward his Chrysler. I looked at his business card, which he had given me a few minutes earlier. It read Peter "Pete" Stolz and it had his (and his wife's) picture on it. He was Midwestern friendly and meant well and was no doubt a doting grandfather; grandfathers used phrases like *the short end of the stick*. As the distance between us widened, he suddenly turned around. "By the way," he said, "do you know that Milwaukee is one of the most segregated cities in the country?"

I said that I did.

"If you can find out why that is, given that so many people have such good intentions, let me know."

TWENTY-EIGHT

"Good intentions" is one of those things that (like racial identity) resists a clear definition, however much one wants to attach one to it. *"The road to hell is paved with good intentions."* That cliché, I admit, was one of the first things that came to mind when Pete Stolz said that. What, after all, have been the social costs of good intentions? To segregationists in the South, Northern whites had no business invading their little corner of the world in the sixties, all full of morality and wanting to set things right. If one listened to conservatives, the costs of the War on Poverty and the Great Society were enormous, the culprits easy to identify: all guilt-racked liberals who, out of some misguided, patronizing belief that they could help make people's lives better, had only made things worse, leaving deep wounds of inferiority in their good-intentioned wake. Affirmative action, welfare, food stamps—all of these things, conservatives argued, had been impediments to Emersonian self-reliance, to knowing that you had overcome obstacles and gotten somewhere on your own speed.

The truth lay, as it often did, somewhere in between.

Two hours after Fuller's speech to the Rotary ended, good intentions mixed with political necessity to produce a Blue Ribbon Commission at City Hall. Its task: to take "a no-holds-barred look" at the relationship between the police and the community and to find ways, in the wake of the Dahmer incident, to improve that relationship. The commission, Mayor Norquist announced, was to be headed by Father Albert DiUlio, the president of Marquette University, and had been asked to complete its work by October 15. As respected as DiUlio was, Norquist's choosing him was not the same as appointing someone like Warren Christopher to investigate the Rodney King beating, and as a result, it was hard to take the commission seriously. (One journalist categorized the members as "really white bread and butter" and wondered why "someone tough" like Polly Williams wasn't on it.) The committee's report coming out and soon collecting dust on a shelf somewhere was a dispiriting yet likely scenario.

. . .

POLLY WILLIAMS WAS MUCH in evidence the following day, though, because the Reverend Jesse Jackson was coming to Milwaukee to bring about healing, and Polly was the one who had arranged the visit. He spent the day talking with Mayor Norquist, talking with residents of the Oxford Apartments (the building Dahmer lived in), talking with Glenda Cleveland (the woman who phoned the police and was not listened to), and then went on to a church full of people at St. Luke's Emmanuel Baptist that evening.

Since it had come by now to seem so commonplace that Jesse Jackson would charge into towns all across America, within hours or days of a crisis, and try to extinguish whatever fires had erupted, it was easy to understand why some people reacted so cynically to him. "Jesse to the Rescue," one might say. I had attended a meeting that morning with Bill Lawrence in Howard Fuller's office, and just before the meeting began, Lawrence asked me whether I was planning to go to St. Luke's that night. I said that I was (even though seven years had passed, Jackson's 1984 speech at the Democratic convention was still with me). Lawrence, on the other hand, was not. "I assume Jesse will be as eloquent as ever," he said, smiling. "And he will be the only one talking, you can be sure." And, he added cynically, "Farrakhan will be back," referring to the visit the Nation of Islam head had made the previous October.

Howard Fuller introduced Jesse, and Jesse was indeed as eloquent as ever. (They had first met when Fuller was working in Chicago during the sixties.) "What's the difference between what happened here and in Los Angeles?" he asked, referring to the Rodney King incident. "In Los Angeles the police committed the sin of commission. Here the police committed the sin of omission." But Chief Arreola, Jackson said, deserved their gratitude. (Moments earlier, Chief Philip Arreola had entered the church and was thunderously cheered. His decision to suspend the three police officers who had failed to prevent Konerak Sinthasomphone from accompanying Jeffrey Dahmer back to his apartment was viewed by this crowd as brave and just. For what seemed like an eternity, people chanted "Don't step down!" in defiance of the no-confidence vote and pressure to resign he had received from the rank and file.)

"More white people should be at the church tonight," Jesse said, his voice beginning to rise, the church organ steady underneath. "To show us that they care. More police should be here as well.... We must try to turn tragedy to triumph. We must look at the underlying agony and make the city safe." But he had, as it turned out, not come just to help relieve the suffering. He had also come (as James Bevel had two months earlier) to demand that the community face what had to be faced: the black unemployment rate, the performance of blacks in school, the high percentage of blacks in jail, the high rate of teenage pregnancy. Every seat in the church was filled, countless numbers of people stood in the back and down the sides, and hundreds more were outside, listening to the loudspeakers. Who else but a Jesse Jackson (or, for that matter, Minister Farrakhan) could bring such a large aggregate of the black community together and then hold them there, captive to whatever subject he wanted to touch on?

But what would happen after Jesse had raised money on behalf of the families of Dahmer's victims and then departed, on to his next fire? What lingering effects, if any, would there be? Would anything significantly change?

To hear Marvin Hannah tell it, the answer was probably no. He didn't take any pleasure in arriving at this conclusion; in fact, his becoming a "black conservative" was as much a surprise to him as it was to anyone, and a disheartening one at that. He was in his fifties and had lived in Milwaukee for more than thirty years. When he was director of Northcott Neighborhood House, it was his idea to celebrate Juneteenth Day in Milwaukee. He had lived at Eleventh and Keefe for twenty-five years, had put more than forty-five thousand dollars into his house there, but it was time for him to get out. His wife had been pushing him to move for quite some time, but he had held firm—until something had occurred four months earlier to change his mind.

"I was coming up the street," he said softly. "It was real hot and everybody was out. The streets and the traffic was just jammed, it was that warm. I looked at the way people were behaving, I looked at the way people lived, I looked at their demeanor, I looked at the clothes and things they were wearing, the hair that was combed and not combed, the shoes they were wearing or not wearing, and I said, I don't belong here any longer. This kind of just spewed out. *I don't belong here any longer.*"

Integration, in Hannah's view, "killed us as a people." When all classes of blacks lived together (in what he called a "vertical mixture") there was a vigor and energy to the community that didn't exist anymore. When the doctors and the lawyers had the means, both financial and legal, to move away, "it siphoned off those who could give back to this vertical place. *We* took it out. *We* began to feel somehow like we had arrived. *We* began to act white."

But could he honestly say that was true for *every* black who had moved away from the inner city?

"Yes," he said. "You show me somebody who hasn't done it. I used to say it is not so much where the black doctor lives, it's that we don't have enough black doctors living. For seven years I worked at the Medical College of Wisconsin and my job was to bring people in, train them, and then send them out to serve the community. But they didn't serve the community. Lots of them didn't serve the community. . . . They moved out and that's where they stayed, that's where their hospital privileges are. We have black physicians in this community now who don't even come to the black community. Same thing for lawyers, accountants, a whole range of professionals. . . .

"Historically, African-Americans, because of racism, worked together and we gave off one to the other. We survived. Our strength came from one another. What you couldn't do another could do and prop you up. What they couldn't do, I could give and we could all prop each other up. But now if you look in the centers of the cities, what is it populated with? Poor folk. People who need the most but are least able to provide for themselves."

But far from feeling pity for them, he realized they made him angry; *they*—not white folks or race relations in general—were the main reason he had become a conservative. "My conservatism is almost entirely centered on what black people ought to do to regain their ability to be a viable people. . . . We have become weak because we have fallen for a lot of junk that's making us weak. We've fallen for drugs, for a kind of permissiveness that my parents and grandparents would never have stood for. . . . My kids still refer to me as sir, no ma'am, yes ma'am to my wife. That level of manners is lost. . . . The last two generations of African-Americans have lost that. It used to be that a black woman standing somewhere used to not be afraid of a black man. They could expect help from him, not harm." These days, though, the "rat packs" were everywhere, dissing women and not going to school. And that's what really got to him, his inability to persuade more kids in his neighborhood to get an education. All around him he saw kids with basketballs and expensive gym shoes around their necks

but no books in their hands. In order to change that, he had taken to brib-
ing them, offering them twenty-five dollars if they would read five books—
books that he had bought for this purpose—and write a report on each one.
There were few takers.

Was he in favor of the Afrocentric curriculum that was about to be
implemented at Victor Berger?

"I would use any kind of centric curriculum to get young people to
go to school, because I know what education's done for me. Education has
made the difference in my life, made the difference in me being in poverty and not being in poverty. It has been the difference in my having an
understanding or having a lack of understanding." But, he added, he did
know—had experienced—the part racism played in all this, how it had
"sapped the will and expectations of many young people so they don't feel
that there's hope for them. But I would really like to tell them that I have
worked for ninety cents an hour when I was married and had two kids so
I could stay in school." He had torn down furnaces in basements and sat in
dirt with cuts all over his hands so that he could keep learning. In Hannah's
view, you have a *responsibility* to do that—to find a way around racism and
prevail, a responsibility not only to yourself but to the black community.
He had had a wool watch cap shoved in his ear in the service, he had been
kicked in the balls by a white policeman ("Patrolman James Rivers, Badge
998"), he had been turned away from the University of Wisconsin—Milwaukee, but he had prevailed. Much as he admired Martin Luther King
for demanding that blacks had a right to do whatever it was that whites
did and be wherever it was that whites were, Hannah felt that not enough
emphasis had been placed on the responsibility that came with those rights:
what, he wondered, was the point in marching for open housing if you
didn't have the education to get the job that would enable you to have the
money to buy the house?

He was glad the Clarence Thomas nomination was stirring people
up because he felt certain that, on some level, blacks would begin saying
to each other, "Wait a minute, some of the things he's saying are true." The
problem he had with an organization like the NAACP was that it positioned black people as clients of the federal government. "This galloping
mentality of entitlement that African-Americans have" was something
Hannah could not abide. "This thundering herd that 'It's mine, give it to
me.' You have your hand out, this expectation. 'The world owes you a liv-

ing, but you have to work hard to collect it,' I tell these young people. A lot of these folks don't want to work for it now. Some of it I understand. But, my God, I just can't understand where a person gets off saying, 'It's mine, I'm entitled to it, give it to me,' without any effort from themselves. I just don't see it. . . .

"I have often said that the worst thing that white folks did for black folks was to let them have television sets"—he laughed—"because then they began to see what the masses of the rest of the world have without really having to try to work to achieve those things."

THE MOTIVATION MARVIN HANNAH had to further his education did not, it turned out, come from his own family or even, frankly, from himself. Even though he had an uncle who had gone to college, what he basically heard from his parents was how much college cost and he had become so discouraged by being tracked in high school that he dropped out. For what might seem the oddest of reasons, he had yearned to be a dentist; his mother cleaned the offices of the one black dentist in Richmond, Indiana, and whenever Marvin went with her he was transfixed by the sight and smell of "all this clean white enamel." So when he went into the service he did well enough on his tests that he didn't automatically "become cannon fodder" and was asked what he wanted to do. He wound up going to dental technician school and then became a medic. It was during this time that he met "some smart Jewish dental officers" who kept pressing him about what he was going to do when he got out. He wasn't sure, he said, probably go back to Milwaukee and work at A. O. Smith. No, they said, that would lead him nowhere. He needed to go to college and have the G.I. Bill pay his way.

"Those two guys told me things that helped me, nurtured me, and pointed me in the way of education. You know what? I found out I wasn't dumb."

The school he wound up attending—Milwaukee Area Technical College—was the place where he was now an associate dean. The University of Wisconsin—Milwaukee had accepted him by letter, but when a Mrs. Irene Bozack (who wrote the letter) cast her gaze upon him in the fall of 1959 and saw that he was black, she said that he would probably be better off at MATC (known at the time as "Bums College," because that was where the plumbers and electricians went). He knew that he had been discriminated against before that time, "but when Mrs. Irene Bozack did that to me, I knew it with a certainty." Twenty-six years later, though, he had his revenge. He was out seeing a friend of his at UWM and the friend suggested he come along to a retirement party—a retirement party for Irene Bozack. "So this little old lady's sitting there," Hannah recalled, huge grin on his face, "getting everyone's congratulations, and I went up to her and grabbed her hand. I said, 'Mrs. Bozack, you don't remember me, but my name is Marvin Hannah. In 1959 I had a letter from you that said I could come to this school and you refused me. I want you to know that very same institution you denied me a place in is going to give me a Ph.D.' She literally jerked her hand. 'Oh, I'm just so pleased for you, young man.' But she didn't remember me. She didn't remember at all. And maybe just as well. That was maybe a cruel thing to do, but I got her."

As HANNAH RECOUNTED ALL this, we were sitting in a Chinese restaurant on the East Side, not far from the same campus where Marvin had exacted his revenge on Mrs. Irene Bozack. Two hours earlier, when I picked him up at his office, I couldn't help noticing the crowds of people staring at the Ambrosia Chocolate factory across the street. Because Jeffrey Dahmer had worked there at one time, perhaps they thought the longer they stared at the building the better chance there was that some answer might emerge to explain the whole hideous business.

Though Hannah held out little hope that the Dahmer incident would prove to be a forceful catalyst for not only improving the relationship between the police and the black community, but attacking the myriad problems of the inner city, he was more positive about *that* possibility than about anything the presence of Michael McGee and his militia had to offer. "I don't know what Mike's program is," he said. "You can't just say we need jobs. How do you get those jobs? I mean, you can't just say these companies ought not move to Mexico. What kind of incentives do you give them to not move to Mexico? . . . I don't think you can just trot out some platitudes like 'We need jobs' or 'It's racist.' What sanctions are you going to bring to those who practice racism in employment? What are you going to do when you look at a map and see that West Allis doesn't have but three black families living in the whole town? . . . What are you going to do to make sure that they open the doors to something like that?"

But wasn't that why Walter Farrell was there—to articulate the specifics of what was needed?

Hannah laughed. He knew Farrell well. And though he had a lot of respect for his intelligence, he saw him as a gadfly and an opportunist, someone who was quick with a sound bite and quick to point out that "everything's needed." On the other hand, he admitted, he was impressed by the way Farrell appeared at the Community Brainstorming breakfast in late March and was able to "statistically outline why certain things were occurring in the city." Still, McGee had not been clear enough in terms of solutions—in terms of what he would specifically do with all the money he was requesting—"so that the minds and the hearts of Milwaukeeans, and Milwaukee black people particularly, have bought into it. Black people just see him as perpetuating violence. That's what they see first. They don't see his program. I don't."

And yet the same criticism he leveled at Walter Farrell could also be leveled at himself. When I asked him what positives, if any, he had observed over the last few years, he was uncharacteristically silent, his big, ebullient face suddenly transformed. "I guess it's hard for me to say what's positive because so much needs to be done," he said quietly, then corrected himself. Actually, he said, "everything needs to be done. Part of the problem is that the white power structure has not allowed it to occur." Even if a specific idea sprang forth from one of Milwaukee's infamous committees, "the implementation is not gonna get done because those who are in charge of implementing don't want to see it happen. There's this whole thought that if you win, I lose, rather than if you win, I can also win. That's the way the mentality is around here in Milwaukee. If I got to give you something, somehow or another I'm losing. . . . Only if the mayor and the other governmental people and the Greater Milwaukee Committee says *this* is what we need to do and *this* is what we're gonna do and *this* is how we're gonna do it and *these* are the mechanisms to ensure that it's gonna get done is it gonna get done. That's the *only* way. . . . Don't say that this is what we're gonna do and leave it up to those who are in power to do it, because they won't do it. They're there to ensure that they exist. And their existence is predicated on the status quo."

But lest it sound as if he were predictably blaming white people for all of the black community's woes, he reiterated that he viewed those members of the black middle class who turned their back on those problems with even more contempt. What he felt most positive about at that moment was the appointment of Howard Fuller as school superintendent. He had known Fuller for more than twenty years and had even "stolen" for him at one time; when Fuller was starting Malcolm X Liberation University in North Carolina, Hannah would load him up with pens, pencils, paper, books, whatever he thought Fuller could use, from the storage cabinet of Northcott Neighborhood House. (But, he said, laughing, "I was not a thief. I wouldn't send him typewriters and Xerox machines.") It angered Hannah, as it had James Cameron and others, that people in the community had questioned Fuller's integrity, questioned what type of deal or compromise he had made with the white power structure in order to obtain the job. What Hannah never doubted was Fuller's commitment to "demonstrate to everyone walking that poor little snotty-nosed bucktoothed black kids are geniuses if given the kind of love and support that we all need." And yet he also knew that Fuller's commitment went further than his own, that Fuller had that commitment for *all* kids, whereas Hannah hadn't reached that point yet. (Nonetheless, one of Hannah's proudest possessions was a note he had received from a white policeman who had taken one of his courses at MATC on black culture, a note that thanked him for changing "my way of thinking," a note that provided bittersweet compensation for the immense frustration Hannah felt in trying to get through to black kids.)

What tempered Hannah's feelings of optimism about Fuller, though, was something Fuller himself had told him a few years earlier, not long after Fuller had become head of Health and Human Services. Hannah had expressed some interest in working for Milwaukee County and Fuller told him that he shouldn't delude himself into thinking that "once you get into these positions, you're gonna be able to change these people, because the bureaucrats won't let you change them. They will fight you, they will sabotage you, they will do anything in the world just to maintain who and what they are." Whether Hannah already held that point of view, or Fuller helped bring him to it, was unclear and relatively unimportant. All that was important was whether Fuller would eventually triumph over this "fact" or fall victim to it.

. . .

AFTER LUNCH, HANNAH ASKED that we drive back downtown by way of Lake Michigan. This was his favorite route, but it was difficult to see why. Even though he claimed he never tired of the precise moment when you came over the top of the hill and saw the rich blue of the lake for the first time, as we approached water level he kept looking out the window and gesturing, saying that blacks were not wanted there—not wanted on the beach, not wanted around the picnic tables, not wanted anywhere in the area.

He was a man for whom Milwaukee, a city that he loved, no longer had a place, not by the lake and not in his neighborhood. He so missed the Walnut Street of the 1950s, "Chocolate Boulevard," he affectionately called it, a world in which anything you wanted or thought you wanted was right there, yours. And even though it was, he came to realize, a vise, being hemmed in on all sides ironically provided a sense of security and belonging he no longer had. Mr. and Mrs. Marvin Hannah, their children grown and gone, were headed for the suburbs. She was happy about it, he was not. Despite his vow to continue devoting his time and considerable energy to the inner city, a more powerful image came into focus, a picture of Hannah, uprooted and marooned in a place like Mequon, barbecuing for his grandchildren, tight smile on his face, going through the motions.

TWENTY-NINE

"If what I'm suggesting is wrong, then throw me out the window."

The window in question overlooked the Milwaukee River and the person making the suggestion—that what Milwaukee desperately needed was no less than a Marshall Plan for the inner city—was Thomas A. Brophy, Howard Fuller's successor as director of Health and Human Services.

"But if what I'm suggesting is by most reasonable persons' expectations right, then it's a matter of will to make it happen, and the will to make it happen can only rest with the people responsible for making it happen, and that is the leaders of our community. No one individual can stand up and make it happen . . . but there's a phenomenal political opportunity out there." In his mind's eye, this is what Brophy could imagine happening: the governor deciding to call "a summit meeting on the crisis in Milwaukee," a meeting in which it would be decided what resources were needed, how they would be directed, and from which a plan of attack would be presented to the president—a plan of attack that would depend both on federal and state money and on all the leaders involved pledging "to fight tooth and nail" to make a reality. "If we can negotiate hostage returns with foreign countries and if we can bring together diverse parties to support a Persian Gulf war, you've got to believe there's a political will to begin to address solving the employment, the housing, and the educational problems of one city in the state of Wisconsin and in this country.

"How do you work your way out of poverty?" Brophy asked. "I don't know what it takes, I've never had the luxury of doing it. Is it naïve to assume we could do something? Probably. Is it naïve to assume we must continue to try? No. The consequences and ramifications of not trying are here."

Had Marvin Hannah been a fly on the wall he would have been roaring, telling me that Tom Brophy, with all due respect for his good liberal intentions, was kidding himself, that what Brophy envisioned would never happen, and that because it wouldn't it was all the more imperative that blacks look to themselves.

I asked Brophy if he had read Nicholas Lemann's *The Promised Land,* published five months earlier, a book that argued, contrary to what had seemed to become unquestioned fact, that certain social programs of the War on Poverty and the Great Society hadn't so much failed as hadn't been given enough of a chance to work, that the reservoir of political will and funding behind them turned out to be thin indeed. It wasn't just that the war in Vietnam had consumed people's attention; Washington had given up. The end of Lemann's book put forward the deeply moral notion that the citizens of a country as great as America simply wouldn't abide the presence of the ghetto forever.

Brophy had heard of Lemann's book and made no apologies for his own wishful scenario, however unlikely it might seem. After all, it was hard on some level for him to see what he had been working toward these past twenty-five years if no appreciable difference could be made. But he was also fully aware how "the magnitude of the issues oftentimes literally boggles the mind." When Brophy would talk to business leaders about all this, he would "see their eyes glass over," as if he were speaking a foreign language. Even those who genuinely wanted to know how they could help—and Brophy was (like Marvin Hannah) of the personal belief that they were few, the exception to the rule—didn't know where to start. "So you've got that constant frustration of knowing you're trying to get your arms around a problem that is constantly slipping out and away from you," he said, echoing for me what my colleague at Virginia had said about racism, about it being a chameleon that was always there in some form.

Beyond frustration, though, were misperceptions and a lack of understanding, Brophy said. If people only knew, for instance, that welfare was "the most degrading, dehumanizing type of survival that you could possibly be exposed to," that it was just another form of slavery, they would find themselves disabused of the idea that it was some sort of utopia. "They just see millions going out to people that they don't think deserve it, and because of their anger over that they want it eliminated"—eliminated without even knowing that Aid to Families with Dependent Children is not funded by property taxes. He was not saying that certain welfare recipients didn't grossly abuse the system (the flood of people arriving at the bus station from Illinois to collect a second check was only one glaring example). Nor was he saying that a different way of doing things shouldn't be undertaken; after all, the welfare system was as much a part of the status quo as anything else. He was merely stating what he believed to be true: the majority of people had neither any idea of the conditions under which many of these people lived nor any idea of the dignity that many of them (like a Bridget Wilder) struggled hard to maintain.

"If I had a magic wand," Brophy said, peering out the window, "I would magically have everybody that is able to work in Milwaukee work and work in decent-paying jobs. I would magically clean up all of the substandard, deplorable, code-violating housing that we have here and allow people with those decent-paying jobs to live in those houses and rent them or own them and raise children in an environment that is more conducive to being motivated to go to school and learn and to try and make something of yourself. When I look at the educational system and I look at the challenges they face, I say to myself, How can they possibly hope to succeed with children who may have a lot of ability and talent, but when they go home at night and when they go into their community at night they're forced to live in a jungle environment where they're looking over their shoulder to see if they're going to get shot or robbed? How can those people possibly be motivated to educationally improve themselves when their main priority may be to stay alive, or to be able to eat dinner that night, or to have something decent to wear, or to have a home environment that isn't filthy and roach-infested and they don't have to worry about moving every three months because they're constantly being evicted or on the run and to have a normal life, if there is such a thing as a 'normal life.'

"We have citizens in our community who live eight to nine miles away from these pockets of poverty who have no understanding or appreciation for the extent of the despair and deprivation that exists. So you've got a group of people over *here* who are isolated and who are angry that this group over *there* is becoming nothing but a burden to the rest of our community. And they see it in terms of drug stories and death and violence. . . .

"What does welfare do to those pockets of poverty? It helps them survive. It doesn't help them live. You *have* to differentiate between living and surviving. Surviving is an almost animalistic instinct where you worry about today and only today and getting through today. Living has connotations of aspirations and hopes and dreams and goals. You're gonna do something with your life. You're gonna have money for your children, a decent home you can clean and take care of and count on, that's living."

Surprising as it might seem, he was sympathetic to Michael McGee—not to his tactics, but to the point of total frustration he had apparently reached when he formed the Black Panther Militia. "I think you have to take him as a person for what he is and where he is," Brophy suggested. "After years of crying in the wilderness, trying to bring the people to focus on the conditions and the growing problems, he feels that 'if I can't get the attention in the normal, polite ways, I'll try to get someone's attention in radical, unusual ways.' Will he be any more ignored and unsuccessful than he was trying to work through the system? Only time will tell. Probably not."

Once again, Brophy reached for his magic wand, waving it this time with the hope that "something positive" would come from the Dahmer incident. Echoing Queen Hyler, he said, "I think the Dahmer tragedy has pulled back some of the camouflage . . . taken stuff that's been buried under this community's conscience and brought it right up to the top." But Brophy's hope was surpassed by fear, fear that "the only thing that comes out of the Dahmer case is a plan to improve police-community relations, or sensitivity training for police officers, or the firing of three, four, five, or six people. Or the replacement of a police chief. It would be a tragedy, from a community perspective, if all that came out of that were those kinds of insignificant developments. Not unimportant, but insignificant. Insignificant when compared to twenty or thirty thousand jobs made available to the people living in poverty."

OF THE 36,732 HOUSEHOLDS in Milwaukee County that received welfare payments, payments worth less now than they were four years earlier because no adjustment had been made for inflation, one of them belonged to Sybil Leach. She was twenty-eight, had one son, and, like Bridget Wilder, was one of those people on the welfare rolls whom Tom Brophy said many residents didn't know about, were convinced didn't exist: a woman who was doing her best to live with dignity. Not only that, but she was using the system in the way she understood it was there to be used—as a temporary bridge to better herself, as a way to not just survive but to live, to come out of college with the ability, as she put it, to "demand my worthiness."

I had first seen her at an all-night sit-in Michael McGee held at the beginning of August in the Common Council chambers at City Hall. She had come, as she had come to a march from the Oxford Apartments (Dahmer's building) to the police station and as she would go to hear Jesse Jackson a week later at St. Luke's, because she was concerned about what was happening in her community, because she was committed. When she was growing up, her parents had tried to shield her, and though she understood the impulse, it hadn't helped her deal with the racial tensions that developed at her high school. "There was a race riot my first year at Madison," she said of the predominantly white school. "I wasn't brought up to be prejudiced. I wasn't taught to hate white people. In high school it was more painful than bitter because I thought it was unnecessary." She graduated with a D+ average, blaming her performance partly on the fact she received little educational encouragement at home or at school and no guidance from her parents—her mother in particular—about young men. But Sybil Leach was not the sort of person to absolve herself of responsibility, for the son she had had out of wedlock or for anything else. Like Louise Kidd and Lora Gooden, she was the sort of person who could recognize when a situation she found herself in was not likely to change, and what she had to do about it.

Sitting in an apartment on the Northwest Side—an apartment whose rent of three hundred eighty-five dollars a month most of her welfare check went to maintain; an apartment that had books wherever you looked, books with titles like *The Black Experience in America* and *Negro Revolt*; an immaculate apartment in which, she made clear, no drugs of any kind could be found—she talked about the seven-dollar-an-hour job she had had at the American Automobile Association, the job *she* decided to leave in order to go on welfare and attend college.

At the AAA, she had to deal with racial epithets both from her coworkers and the public. "One guy that was in my department would come up to me and say, 'You're black but you don't seem like the other black people that come in. You don't talk black.'" After a while of his saying that, she wound up going to her supervisor, who insisted that he apologize to her. He did so, reluctantly, claiming that he had no idea she had taken offense at his remarks. She said she was just as black as the next African-American, and that even though she might not like "the way some of them carry themselves or the way some of them act or the fact that some of them don't let their levels of intelligence come out," he couldn't just totally ignore her color when he said such things.

White customers would come in and refuse to let Sybil take care of them, saying she was "too young" to know what she was doing. She had been doing the job of "travel counselor" for seven years at that point and was the only black at AAA who was "presented" to the public. One time a nun came in and was "real bad with me," Sybil recalled; the nun said she was rude and, upon leaving, that "'God will take care of your kind.'"

We both laughed at that, but when we stopped she wanted this to be understood: she left AAA not only because she felt humiliated by the way she was treated; she left because she had twice been turned down to become a travel agent (even though she had become certified) and at seven dollars an hour with no benefits she knew she would always be among the working poor. She wanted more for herself and her son and discovered that going on welfare, oddly enough, was a step toward achieving it. By going to college and having her child care paid for, by using the system in the right way, by having a goal in mind—that of being a teacher and hoping, eventually, to be in a position to influence the curriculum—she was proud of herself. Her sisters, on the other hand, she had disdain for. One of them had three kids, was on welfare, and, given the fact she was "doing nothing," had a lot of nerve, in Sybil's opinion, to be so turned off by the system. It was people like her sister who represented one of the main reasons the welfare system had such a bad reputation. She took no joy in saying this, but she had always been outspoken and there it was. Another thing that angered her was the assumptions people made that every mother on welfare was black. Right in her neighborhood were a lot of white women on welfare, women who would just hang around doing the same nothing she said her sister was guilty of, but Sybil was realistic enough to know that perceptions were hard to change.

Even so, she said, moving from the subject of welfare to a frank appraisal of black America overall, it still came down to making choices, *moral* choices. As put-upon as African-American males were by white society, that was no excuse, none at all, for them to rob, steal, shoot, or lose themselves in drugs; for them to go out and impregnate their women and not take care of them or their kids. On the other hand, there was no excuse for black women berating their men the way they did. "I know of a situation," she said, "where a girl is divorcing from her husband and her mother was telling her to take everything from that nigger that you can get. The girl took *everything*, even the grilles off the stove. That wasn't necessary."

Still, she said, "I blame the men because they don't try any harder. I blame the men because it seems they would rather get up in the morning and drink a forty-ouncer than get up and go find a job. I blame the men because they think they're too good to work at McDonald's: those are low-paying jobs, they are service jobs, but you do what you've got to do. I blame the men because they don't seem to want to become any more educated than they are, yet they want to be the dominant one, they want to be the controller, the one to have the say-so. I blame the men because they are in and out of black women's lives as is the welfare check. When the welfare check is there, they're there; when the welfare check is all spent up, they're not.

"I blame the women because in their minds they've become so stupid that they allow themselves carelessly to get pregnant. One time is okay because that's the mistake you learn from, but two and three and four? So there's no excuse for that, none at all."

Her desire to set a strong example for her son, to help him become a better man than the men she had known, as well as her larger desire that he grow up in a world that was free of racial hatred, a world in which people could meet on equal levels, a world in which he didn't have to accept less because of his color, a world in which black people were not isolated—these desires ran deep within Sybil Leach. And despite how self-righteous and almost scolding she at times sounded in expressing them, it was impossible to doubt her sincerity, her fierce determination to "make some sort of dent in society," to make sure she wouldn't live and die without someone noticing.

Two days after I left her apartment I received the following poem in the mail.

CRY FREEDOM

Allow me freedom
like that of a nomad
Give to me all of the earth's riches
All that is rightly due me
the land in which we live is free
All of God's creatures exist in the
open wild of the world
I am a free spirit, a creature

of our creator
Give to me my freedom equal
Allow me to roam the earth without
resistance
Allow me to blossom to the fullest
potential
Accept me for who I am
Do not condemn me because I
am of a richer more dominating
color
Do not oppress me because you are
afraid
Do not judge me before you know
me
My intelligence is naturally inbred
My heart & soul are strong
I will beat you, you will not
stop me I will overcome.

Ms. Sybil E. Leach

THIRTY

It was being called Operation Blue Ribbon, but it had nothing to do with the Blue Ribbon Commission Mayor Norquist had formed to explore police-community relations. No, this operation was different; this operation was the idea and creation of the many spouses of police officers who were sick and tired of the way their husbands (mainly) were being vilified in the community in the wake of Dahmer's arrest. What Operation Blue Ribbon asked of you was much simpler than what Mayor Norquist asked of Father DiUlio. It asked that you wear a blue ribbon in support of the police, of the men and women who had chosen a profession in which, said Alderman John Kalwitz, "they are contradicted, corrected, spat upon, second-guessed, lambasted, ridiculed, exposed to danger, interrogated, prejudged, suspended, hated at one moment and loved at the next."

On the Sunday afternoon of August 18, at cavernous Serb Hall on the South Side, the part of town that for years blacks had feared to set foot in, the part of town where, they understood, they would not be welcome, the part of Milwaukee where Father Groppi had led the marches for open housing, more than a thousand people, people with white faces and good solid ethnic names like Eliopul and Szablewski and Kuchenreuther had come out on a sticky, overcast day to shower the police with the love, Kalwitz said, that only occasionally came their way. Many of these same people had held a rally at City Hall two Sundays earlier, but this was different. They were, at this beer hall of a place, on hallowed ground here, ground they saw as *theirs*, the Poland side of the bridge that separated Poland from Africa.

And they had chosen, fittingly enough, Mark Belling (the Rush Limbaugh of Milwaukee) to make sure their message got across, picked up and then broadcast and written about by the media that they never tired of hating. Prior to Belling's coming onstage, though, it seemed only appropriate that the atmosphere match the choice of master of ceremonies. It did. As the music blared Lee Greenwood's "God Bless the USA," a male singer onstage substituted the word "officers" as he sang his heart out:

. . . And I won't forget the officers who died,
Who gave their life to me.
And I proudly stand up, next to you,
And defend her still today.
And there ain't no doubt, I love this land,
God bless the USA.

Belling wasted no time in establishing his bona fides, in telling the crowd what they had come to hear. "Imagine what we've come to in Milwaukee," he said. "A police chief who won't do a thing about the Vice Lords but, oh, is he going to make sure no off-duty cops carry guns . . . The men and women of the Milwaukee Police Department are the most underappreciated, and the most unfairly judged, human beings in this city. They are held to a standard no person could always live up to. They are told to be compassionate by people who refuse to show them any compassion. They are told to be sensitive by people who have demonstrated callous insensitivity towards them. They are called screwups by people whose daily lives are one big mistake. They are overworked, underpaid, and in their time of need are bashed around by a bunch of opportunistic phonies who don't in a year give this community what your average cop gives it in one shift."

Each statement Belling made was greeted by ringing applause, applause that seemed to be a release of pent-up anger and frustration as much as anything else. To label the whole Dahmer incident the "Rodney King–ing of Milwaukee" was horribly unfair, Belling said. How many people knew, he wondered, that one of the three suspended cops had, four years earlier, "arrested a shooting suspect and then raced inside a burning building in Milwaukee's inner city and helped rescue people inside"? Or knew about the officers who had gone undercover to investigate "a vicious street gang that has targeted cops for killing"? Or even thought about the officers who are told they must be "sensitive and compassionate . . . every time they walk into a rat-infested, stench-filled excuse for a home, where some crack addict is keeping her kids"? Given that, Belling said, it was wrong to judge these three officers on the basis of *one incident.*

When Alderwoman Annette Scherbert was introduced she instantly became nostalgic for "the good old days in the city, when the mayor cared about law and order and when the chief of the city's police department

cared about the men and women who enforced it." She was thinking of
fellow South Sider Harold Breier, of course, "a tough, fair man who
demanded excellence but not perfection," a man who was "always *loyal* to
the men he presided over."

The keen smell of betrayal wafted through the air. The chord of
Breier as someone who always knew that he had human beings under
him—people who, like people anywhere, had frailties that he was well
aware of—was struck repeatedly. And frankly, Scherbert said, it wasn't
possible to be perfect anyway, not when you had a mayor ("Police Chief
John Norquist," Belling derisively called him) who trimmed the police
force when he took office in 1988, the same year it was predicted that big
cities were going to be hit with crime waves related to drug activity, she
said. Now that was good timing. Why, just last Saturday, on the tenth, the
backlog of calls to the police department was four hundred. Divide that
by the seven precincts and you had an average of fifty-seven. District Three,
she said, aware that everyone knew that district was on the near North Side,
had eighty-four. "Every one of those four hundred callers thought their
problem was serious," she said. "And many of those four hundred callers
were mad as hell that they had to wait. Just imagine what fun it must be to
be a police officer answering one of those calls four hours later."

Unaware as he probably was of this, Alderman Kalwitz managed to
inject some irony into the festschrift. "In America, our greatness is built
on freedom," he reminded everyone, "wherein we have a deep compassion for the rights of all individuals. And this also includes the men and
women in blue. In this difficult time for Milwaukee, we must ask ourselves
what kind of community we are and what direction we want to move in.
The vast majority of people in Milwaukee want to live together in harmony. They want to improve the quality of life and subscribe to the principal objective of justice and fair play for everyone." But there was a
problem in achieving this, Kalwitz helpfully pointed out. The problem was
"the constant war on the streets of urban America"—a war whose victory
"depends upon the morale of those who are fighting the war and who risk
their lives on the urban battlefields."

Inevitably, it seemed, it would keep coming around to polarization,
to good versus evil, to blaming the people whose lives, Belling said, had
been one big mistake—the people who, as Shiva Naipaul wrote, didn't even
evoke fellow feeling. It was simple and convenient and easy to grasp. It

was what they wanted—needed—to hear. The police department, out-standing to begin with, Belling said, popping up again on the stage like Ed Sullivan, would be even more so if it weren't for the loudmouths (read: McGee) and "Sensitivity Nazis" (Norquist and Arreola) "trying to score their own points by tearing police officers down."

And then, right on cue, came an announcement: Harold Breier was in the audience. People cheered as if it were a presidential campaign stop. Chants of "Bring Back Breier" and "Give 'Em Hell, Harry" ricocheted throughout as the small, trim figure, nearly eighty, made his way to the stage, the embodiment of the good old days, the days everyone claimed to long for, despite the fact that "the good old days"—any good old days, not just those of the Milwaukee Police Department—were never quite what they appeared to be in retrospect.

"You know," he said, moved by the reception, "those are the words I used to close every command officers' meeting on Wednesdays: 'Give 'em hell.' And we did. . . . This is a fine tribute for the men and women in the department who are out on the streets trying to give the *good* citizens the kind of law enforcement they want and deserve. I always said, 'The good citizens buy what we're selling and the hell with the rest.'"

This rally was sorely needed, he said, because even though the mayor and some others were talking about healing the community, "you don't heal the community when you say the officers on May 27th were racist or that the department is racist. That's a hell of a way to promote healing." As for the "silent majority" out there, the ones who supported the police, they were silent for a reason, Breier said. *They* were busy out there quietly making a living, while "the activists," who didn't work, were busy running their mouths off.

Harold Breier's coming on that Sunday afternoon was more than the throng could have hoped for. It was one thing for them to read his com-ments in the paper over the past month, quite another for him to actually show up, seven years after his retirement, defiant as ever.

The blue ribbons were out, the handmade signs were attached to sticks, and the faithful were ready, ready to march out of Serb Hall and down Oklahoma, ready to, as one woman said, "show this community where our love and support is."

THIRTY-ONE

The room was so dimly lit that it seemed more like the setting for a séance than for a three-day conference that billed itself the Intercommunal Call to Arms Summit, a summit that had not only been organized by Michael McGee, but was a celebration of him and his militia, a celebration no less rabid than the one for the police four days earlier. Jerrel Jones had agreed to broadcast the proceedings live over WNOV, and the widow and daughter of Black Panther Fred Hampton had even come up from Chicago to pay homage and represent a symbolic link to the original party.

The séance atmosphere at the Caribbean Inn on West Walnut was further enriched by an Oneida Indian named Herb Cawley, there to provide a benediction of sorts, who burned some South Dakota sage in an effort to purify both the room and the minds of the people who were assembled. Which wasn't going to be easy, he implied, seeing how everyone was sitting around like white men, with tables and chairs. Next year's meeting, he suggested (assuming there was one), should be held outside in the open air.

But Herb Cawley's presence at this meeting, I soon realized, was just as significant as Harold Breier's had been at Serb Hall. He was there because he was someone who knew, knew all too well, what it was (one militia member said) "to have a whole race of people wiped out."

The specter of black genocide was at the core of this particular summit and Walter Farrell entered from stage left to talk about it. The journey to extinction was a long and tortuous one and Farrell cast himself in the role of tour guide, a tour guide with credentials, who came to the unpleasant subject, he emphasized, with the professional objectivity of a social scientist. And like any good social scientist, he displayed charts to make his points. This was why McGee had reached out to Farrell in the first place—to give legitimacy to his enterprise, to make it possible for people to understand what was going on—and Farrell didn't disappoint.

The social and economic factors that, according to the professor, would "lead to the destruction of the black community in Milwaukee" were noted with an arrow leading from one to the next: general black unemployment being six times that of whites; unemployment of black males exceeding 30 percent (and probably much higher); an average GPA for black children of 1.3 in a city in which a 2.0 was required to be eligible for job programs; the city's unenviable status of having the highest proportion of teen pregnancy of any city in the country; black median income being 50 percent less than white median income; a black infant mortality rate of more than eighteen per one hundred thousand population ("which doesn't sound extremely high, but we have countries in the Third World that have lower rates"), placing Milwaukee among the top five cities in that category; a prison population more than 40 percent black in a state whose entire black population was only 4 percent; the highest rate of turndowns for blacks seeking business loans and mortgages; the pervasive practice of insurance "redlining"; the insensitivity of the police department ("I don't accuse the department of being insensitive," he said coyly, "the community has accused them of being insensitive").

"As an academic," Farrell said, suddenly hedging his bet like any person who wanted it both ways, "I'm not prepared to say all of these are collective moves to wipe us out." And genocide, in any case, was too strong a term, he said. "However, I can say that if these patterns persist over the next generation like they have over the generation that has just passed, then the black community is headed in Milwaukee for oblivion."

After a huge round of applause for confirming their worst fears, Farrell, who had been glued to McGee's side the past month, then proceeded to talk about the letters the alderman had received ever since he had formed the militia, letters that had come in from around the country ("from California to New Hampshire") and to which McGee frequently alluded. Of the one hundred and eleven letters that had been received from blacks in Milwaukee, eighty of them supported the use of violence, urged the militia not to wait until 1995, said that the "time to throw down" was now; nineteen of them supported the concept of violence but expressed the hope it wouldn't come to that; two of them suggested a turning to God; seven came from inmates who said they would like to join the militia when they were released; and three stressed the importance of hard work and self-sufficiency.

Of the ninety-two letters received from whites in Milwaukee, forty-three said blacks were entirely to blame for their problems, for the fact so many were unemployed, on drugs, didn't get an education, and produced babies out of wedlock at such a high rate. "And this is a widely held view," Farrell said. That this was so, he went on, was underscored a month earlier when he testified in Washington before the Joint Economic Committee of the Congress. Of the other people who testified, all of whom were white, Lawrence Mead, a professor at New York University, "basically made the point that the reason the unemployment rate is so high among African-Americans and males in particular is because we don't have a strong work ethic." When it was Farrell's turn, he told the committee, "in a nice way," that Mead's premise was "ridiculous, that a sizable portion of unemployment can be explained by racial discrimination and the view that employers have of black workers, particularly of black male workers, who they find on the average too aggressive or too assertive or they don't want to have in their employ."

Of the remaining forty-nine letters from whites in Milwaukee that they had analyzed, eleven said that blacks needed to practice love, not hate; twelve said violence was not the solution, education and work were; twenty said they flat out didn't like McGee; and six said they were supportive of the militia, "the call to violence and all."

Before he sat down, though, he had one other letter whose contents he wanted to reveal. "It was written by a white female who was living with a brother," he said. "A brother who had gone to school, who had his credentials, and she articulated the problems he encountered here in the city of Milwaukee in trying to get work. Saying that he's gone out, he's well spoken, he presents himself well, but that even when he was placed by the temporary services—these were her words, not mine—'he will be sent to the worst job and the most temporary job.' So she's saying, in a sense, we tried to do it by the book and it's not working, and it hasn't worked for some time."

WITH THE APPEARANCE OF Ahmad Muhammad, the head of the Milwaukee branch of the Nation of Islam, the audience was kept within the realm of genocide and extinction but now found themselves awash in history and religion as well, being asked to ponder the full meaning of the Islamic term "jihad." It meant "holy war" and was derived from *jiha*, meaning ability, exertion, or power: the exerting of one's power in repelling the enemy. One either was engaged in a struggle against an enemy that could be seen—or at war with the Devil. "And I'd like to let you all know," he said, his crisp red bow tie practically glowing in the semidarkness, "that the Honorable Elijah Muhammad was not wrong when he called the Caucasians the Devil. Devil is a scientific term, brothers and sisters. It means one who adds to and takes away from the truth. Covers the truth, makes it different going in and coming out."

I had watched enough footage of Malcolm X's speeches in the sixties to know that Ahmad Muhammad was trying to emulate him. Being in this room was like being in a time warp. And yet outside, on the streets and in the nation, the polarization Muhammad was speaking of was not just an illusion, could not be dismissed out of hand. "We're at war, literally, on a daily basis, and right now we're really at war physically because there's a genocidal plot afoot to kill every black woman and man on this planet." He was intent on going further than Walter Farrell could or would. He had no obligation to the prosody and constraints of social science; he served a Higher Being. He could talk of the need to have "a vanguard man willing to make war with the Devil and not back down" (explaining "vanguard" as "one who is willing to stand out front, take a chance with his or her life"). He could partly excuse someone being a "wino, prostitute, or crack fiend," because the essence of God, as he called it, existed in every person, and every person was capable of redemption. The Honorable Elijah Muhammad, he reminded everyone, didn't spread Islam throughout the black community by the sword, he won people over with love. And yet, he said, the Koran speaks of the importance of fighting "against those who would be the aggressor." He grew up in the Hillside projects, he said, a world in which a raised hand over your waist was an indication you were ready to fight. Today in Milwaukee, he insisted, "the Caucasians and the people that are in power" had raised their hands as far as their waists. "What are we going to do?" he wanted to know, but he already had an answer. Burn the damn boats, he advised, follow Michael McGee and burn the damn boats. An act of violence had brought them to these shores, but he wasn't about to go back to Africa. "I want my Nissan," he said, mimicking the popular jingle, "my Mercedes-Benz, my solid gold and Fort Knox that my parents worked for. People say we should leave America. I say no, brothers and sisters. We have a vested interest in this country. We helped build this country."

FROM ONE END OF Milwaukee to another, on both sides of the Groppi Unity Bridge, rhetoric and demagoguery and icons of all kinds continued to fill the air. The end of summer was drawing near, and the school year was about to begin. But even before the first day of classes, Howard Fuller found himself beset with a new problem, one he hadn't counted on. NBC News showed a classroom at North Division at less than optimal conditions: the teacher was calmly reading a book while some students were out of control. The footage had been secretly shot by someone in the class. For Fuller, it was a double blow. This wasn't just any classroom being put forward as an example of all that was wrong in urban education; this was a classroom at Fuller's alma mater, the school he had waged a fierce battle to protect, a decade earlier, from losing its status as a neighborhood school. As he had promised the Rotarians earlier that month, and every other group he had come before during the course of the summer, he acted, and acted swiftly: the teacher was suspended, pending further investigation. The students who were out of control were black. Fuller's reaction to the incident was interesting. He wasn't angry at NBC and he wasn't particularly angry at the student who had supplied them with the footage. He was angry that the scenario existed in the first place. That was what really mattered. And that, he reiterated, was one of the things he was determined to correct.

Fortunately, that piece of national exposure gave way to the nervous excitement over the opening of the African-American immersion school, an opening that had been much anticipated and was likely to be given instant scrutiny, especially since the topic of Afrocentrism had become even more controversial and heated as the summer wore on, highlighted by cover stories in *Time* and *Newsweek* (the latter asking, "Was Cleopatra Black?" with this as a subhead: "Facts or Fantasies—A Debate Rages Over What to Teach Our Kids About Their Roots"). On three separate occasions during the summer, I had sat in on a class that Scully Stikes offered; it was designed not only to show the various ways in which black children learned differently from others, but to convince one that blacks had, in a sense, been cheated of their history and accomplishments, that those accomplishments had been marginalized (if they were mentioned at all), that blacks had indeed, in Pete Stolz's words, been given the short end of the stick.

Unfortunately, though, the extremists (as often happens, no matter the situation) tended to garner most of the attention, and in the case of Afrocentrism, Professor Leonard Jeffries, chairman of African-American studies at City College of New York, had done just that. By pushing the idea of a conspiracy toward blacks at every turn (his most recent remarks, directed at Jews in Hollywood, had been so virulent that they had prompted Senator Daniel Patrick Moynihan of New York to call for his dismissal), by rigidly categorizing people as Ice People and Sun People, he was threatening to overshadow the positive things Afrocentrism was trying to achieve. One thing that struck me about the classes I had sat in on—classes that were fairly equally divided between blacks and whites, males and females— was the degree to which blacks expressed the opinion that whites could not be as effective in teaching black students (particularly black males) as blacks could, even though many of them were also seeking guidance in how to teach more effectively themselves.

In general, Scully Stikes said, blacks were more extroverted and emotive than whites, but schools were more oriented toward students who were introverted and intuitive, students who had an easier time sitting still. Schools were not avenues of expression, he said, they were avenues of control. Whereas whites moved, in their thinking, from the general to the particular, and vice versa, blacks tended to think about the context—and "personal investment"—of things. Blacks had an expressive way of walking, an expressive way of singing, an expressive style—all of which ran counter, he suggested, to the white world, a world in which the prevailing attitude was "If they'd just act like us, they'd be all right." That wasn't possible, he said, either physically or emotionally. But that didn't mean blacks were deviant. It just meant that until society "affirms us, we're going to have problems." Look, he said, his face breaking into a wide smile, "a black party is going to start later than a white party, and we're not going to talk about work. There'll be more food there, it will be more seasoned, and we might party for two days." After all, time in a place like Africa (or southern Italy, Mexico, and Puerto Rico, for that matter) was irrelevant. Time was devoted to social things, he said, not as a means to conform to hours and minutes.

At the beginning of the class, he told everyone, "I'm going to violate a lot of assumptions, a lot of myths about *me.*" Stikes was trying to be provocative, to work people up, and even though there were good, valid reasons for doing so, the emphasis he kept placing on differences was still discomfiting; it was almost as if he were offering an excuse more than an explanation for the reason black males were not doing better in school, and an excuse, it seemed to me, was the last thing they needed. Including more of one's own history and accomplishments into a curriculum in an effort to bolster self-esteem and provide a more tangible reason for coming to school and achieving was one thing, tying one's difficulty in sitting still to one's inability to read, write, and analyze quite another. Perhaps I was overreacting, or perhaps my frustration had to do with hearing too much negative and not enough positive—after all, there *were* blacks who were overcoming all sorts of obstacles and succeeding—and that the positive was happening so incrementally as to pale beside the massive problems.

At one point, Stikes divided everybody (by race and gender) into four groups and asked them to come up with the things that most concerned them in regard to teaching or counseling black children. Black male teachers said they were constantly searching for ways to get and keep black males interested and motivated, wondering what on earth you were going to tell a kid who might be sitting there with five hundred ill-gotten dollars in his pocket. Or how, on the junior high level especially, you could effectively focus in on *realistic* goals and role models and make kids see that very few brothers were going on to play pro basketball. One member of the group said he showed them articles from the newspaper so that they could see how negatively they were often portrayed; another said that kids should be made aware, as early as kindergarten, that there was a conspiracy to destroy them. Above all, though, they needed to see what a "real man" was.

Black female teachers said they were looking for better ways to involve a child's parents, and they often came across parents who simply didn't care to hear about the problems their child was facing or causing. How could they get a child to stop using profanity? How were they to deal with racist literature? How could they persuade kids to come to school, let alone read in their spare time?

White females wanted to know how to deal with accusations of racism and prejudice; how to deal with other teachers who tried to intimidate black males and how to deal with black males who tried to intimidate them.

Finally, white males wanted to know if they could effectively teach black males (Stikes tried to reassure them that they could), how they should go about imposing discipline without seeming racist, and how to deal with parents who felt they were racist.

Taken together, these four sets of concerns not only seemed to underscore the problems, but constituted a strong argument that something else had to be tried (echoing Howard Fuller's point that if what we're doing isn't working, how could anyone feel comfortable arguing that the more inclusive, self-esteem-building approach of Afrocentrism shouldn't be taken?).

Of all the things I heard in the many hours I spent in the Stikes class, one moment in particular stood out. A white physical education teacher named Matthew explained that he had been consumed for quite some time with both anger and guilt—anger that he didn't feel he could take his best friend, a black male, to his parents' home because of his father's prejudice, and guilt whenever he drove home to his own South Side apartment, filled with nice things.

"Matthew," Stikes said, "you have no reason to feel guilty. You *earned* that." And the fact that he had, Stikes implied, was the most valuable lesson he could pass on to the black kids he taught day after day. He couldn't teach them about being black, but he could set a measure of expectations for them, a measure that, in Stikes's opinion, could (or at least should) transcend race.

SCULLY STIKES HAD (along with Ken Holt and Bill Lawrence) been on the original committee that explored the possibility of an all-black-male school. Even though he did think white teachers could teach black males, he, like Holt, would have liked to see the initial idea of black male teachers and students come to fruition, just as he would have liked the principal of the school to be a black male. The school that opened its doors in September of 1991 had a black woman as principal, a student body that was equally divided between black males and females, and a faculty that was two-thirds white. Given that, it was only natural to ask what was going to be so "different" about it to warrant all the local and national attention?

Tom Bell was the person who happened to be asking. He had been teaching at Berger for eight years, and he was worried that the very same expectations everybody was saying it was crucial to have of the students who came before him would be ones that this "new school" could not measure up to; worried that so much was invested in the idea of Afrocentrism that if tangible results couldn't be seen right away, *instantly,* it would be labeled a failure, just one more innovative idea that sounded great in theory but was not in practice, another reminder that perhaps you could fine-tune the wheel but you couldn't reinvent it.

Bell, a relentlessly energetic man of forty-three, was teaching fourth grade, teaching the same group of kids he had had the year before in third, the idea being that one teacher should follow his kids for three years, that continuity could be a good thing, especially for those children who needed a stabilizing influence. For someone like him, teaching had always been more than just a job. That was one of the reasons he taught at Berger. He knew the kids needed more, far more, than what he attempted to teach them in the classroom. In all the time he had been teaching he had been the epitome of continuity, phoning kids up, checking on them, making sure they got to basketball games, taking them out to eat, bringing them over to his house. When he learned that the "new program" called for thirty-six home visits a year, that was no problem, he had been doing that too. One time, a student informed him that his mama didn't care whether he came to school or not, and so Bell (which is how his wife refers to him) showed up at the boy's house, catching him by surprise. His mother was cooking dinner when he arrived and Bell decided not to address the subject right away. In fact, he waited until he was offered and had consumed a few pieces of chicken, saying right then and there that it was the finest chicken he had ever tasted and wondering where she had learned to cook like that. Her demeanor, cool and distant and downright suspicious when Bell first walked through the door, changed in an instant. Her face glowed. Having succeeded in changing her mood, he then told her why he had come, as her son nervously stood there. Her demeanor changed again, into hurt and frustration and fury all balled into one, and Bell found out what he needed to know, that the boy had been wrong, had used his mother as an excuse, that she did care what happened to him, what kind of future he would have, and that he, Bell, was fairly sure he had managed to do something that the boy had never seen or heard anyone do before—say something positive about his mother.

A few days later, the boy came to school with a piece of cake that his mother had baked and gave it to Bell. He immediately bit into it and exclaimed how good it was and, at the same time, playfully chastised the young man for bringing him such a small piece. If people wanted to view what Bell was doing—which couldn't be learned in a history book, Afrocentric or otherwise—as part of a new approach, that was fine with him. He just did what he had always done: he found a way to establish a bond.

He liked that the school was requiring the children to wear uniforms (although it wouldn't be mandatory until the middle of the year), and he was delighted to see more parents at the first PTO meeting than had ever attended before. He enjoyed seeing the walls throughout the building adorned with so many different African artifacts and he had no problem at all with starting off the day by having his students recite "Hey, Black Child":

> *Hey, black child, do you know who you are,*
> *who you really are? Do you know you can be*
> *what you want to be, if you try to be what you can be?*
> *Hey, black child, do you know who you are,*
> *who you really are? Do you know you can learn*
> *what you want to learn, if you try to learn*
> > *what you can learn?*
> *Hey, black child, do you know you are strong, really*
> *strong? Do you know you can be*
> *what you want to be, if you try to be what you can be?*
> *Hey, black child, do what you can do, learn what you*
> *can learn, and tomorrow will be what you want it to be.*

It's hard to describe precisely what I felt when I heard that poem for the first time in Tom Bell's classroom, coming out of the mouths of Brandon and Bobby and Princess and Shukuha and Latorsha and Montreal, children who were nine and ten years old, many of whom had told me, moments before, how fervently they wished night after night that their mothers would win the lottery so that they could move to the "serberbs," convinced it would all be better there, kids who had simply grown tired of hitting the tarmac of the playground every time a gun went off. (Not long after I visited Bell's classroom, Shukuha wrote my stepdaughter a letter asking if she liked where she lived and then stating, "It is bad where I live it is really bad where I live I wish I could move some where else.")

To me, the poem did a better job of poignantly conveying what Afrocentrism was trying to accomplish than much of the literature on the subject I had read. Building self-esteem and gaining knowledge of your culture, of feeling more included, would not, alone, translate into higher achievement, but even the most cynical person would be hard-pressed to argue it wouldn't help. To those who contend that creating "a separate history for and by black people" will result only in "intellectual apartheid," that is an argument that seemed far removed from Bell's classroom on that day. For Tom Bell, a greater concern was whether enough mentors could be found, enough people who were succeeding in the day-to-day world and who would be willing to come to Berger on a regular basis and "give the kids some time." Many people had said they would come by, but so far only a few had. The merits of having a Rites of Passage class for boys and a similar program for girls notwithstanding, they weren't the same as having a one-on-one relationship, having someone who had made a commitment to you, someone you could do things with, someone who would monitor your progress. "Everybody wants change," Bell told me, referring to adults in the community, "but nobody wants to work for it."

That wasn't true, of course, but Tom Bell was the kind of person who had always found talk to be cheap, who had always found a way to do the things that needed to be done without being at all self-righteous about it. So on a Saturday night when he could have been home with his family, when he could have taken his wife out to dinner, he packed me and two of his children into his van and we made five stops to pick up a slew of his students en route to a professional wrestling match at Sacred Heart Hall on the South Side. The reason he chose that form of entertainment above all others was this: One of the participants (Conan the Dark Rider) was trying to win the title that night, but, more important, he was the father of Wilton Jones, one of the kids in Bell's class. It was a raucous evening and an exhausting one. I couldn't say with any accuracy how many runs I made for soda and popcorn, or how many times Bell would lean over and tell me how Antonio and Tavares ate as though they didn't expect to eat again (and how their mother wouldn't allow Tavares to be in the house alone for fear he would eat all the food) or how Antonio's eyes lit up when he saw leaves that needed to be raked, how crucial it was that these kids be given the opportunity to earn money, to develop a work ethic, and what would occur if that didn't happen: you'd only be giving them a negative message and they would wind up stealing from you. "What's a quarter to me?" Bell asked. "I spend more than that in the street." Even though Conan would "lose" on this particular evening, it didn't matter: what mattered was that the kids had been there, they had had fun, and they had been delivered home safely by someone who was, whether they liked it or not (and at times they didn't), committed to being an ongoing presence in their lives, someone who knew that "being consistent" with his students was the best gift he could offer them.

"Every day," Bell was telling the class two days later, "convince yourself about you. Every day, every day say, 'I like me,' because I do more than like me. What do I do to me?"

"Love yourself," the class said together.

"That's right. And when people feel that way, comments about my hair's nappy or I need a shave, that doesn't bother me. . . . When people call me names, I know me. This is very important. This is what we are striving for." He then asked everyone to recite "Our Civil Rights" together.

> I have a right to be happy and to be treated with compassion in this room: this means that no one will laugh at me or hurt my feelings.
> I have a right to be myself in this room: this means that no one will treat me unfairly because I am black or white, fat or thin, tall or short, boy or girl.
> I have a right to be safe in this room: this means that no one will hit me, kick me, push me, pinch me, or hurt me.
> I have a right to hear and be heard in this room: this means that no one will yell, scream, shout, or make loud noises.
> I have a right to learn about myself in this room: this means that I will be free to express my feelings and opinions without being interrupted or punished.

Along with "Hey, Black Child" and "I Am Special" (from the previous June's Head Start graduation), these mantras had become, it seemed, the school's own Pledge of Allegiance, were just the kind of things that contributed to Arthur Schlesinger Jr.'s worrying about the disuniting of America, about the true meaning of *e pluribus unum*.

. . .

Across and down the hall from Tom Bell's classroom was that of Joe Hartlaub. Hartlaub, who was white and looked like a former altar boy, had just arrived in Milwaukee from teaching in Washington, D.C., had come because he liked what he read in an article about what Milwaukee was hoping to do. In his early thirties and originally from the Midwest, from the small town of Aurora, Illinois, he had spent two years in West Africa in the Peace Corps and many of the African artifacts that were hanging on the walls of the building happened to belong to him. Observing the African tradition of giving someone a gift when you went to visit or stay with that person, he did just that on his second day there.

But it also marked his disappointment—that the school hadn't been transformed in its appearance before it opened its doors—a disappointment that first began two weeks earlier when he saw how many white teachers and how few black ones were going to be teaching at the new school. He had expected that the best black teachers from around the city were going to be teaching at Berger, that it was truly going to be a kind of laboratory school, that he was going to feel, comparatively speaking, as though he didn't know a thing about Africa. What he found, to his dismay, was that he was looked to as a quasi expert, that so few of the black teachers (let alone the white ones) knew "enough about African-American roots to really go to the next step, to really infuse those traditions, those beliefs, those morals, from the African-American and African cultures into the present-day curriculum." That, of course, was one of the reasons the faculty were required to take a course like the one Scully Stikes offered, but Hartlaub's point was that everything should have been further along before the new school declared itself open for business.

Like Tom Donegan, Joe Hartlaub was driven by a need to serve others, fueled by his Catholic upbringing. But he was also aware that one's enthusiasm for doing so, and for trying to relate to all people, regardless of race or class, was not universally shared, could even be viewed as strange or received with hostility. Such was the case when he arrived back in Chicago in 1984 after his two years in Africa. Waiting for his luggage at O'Hare, he tried to make conversation with one of the baggage handlers, a black man who "wanted no part of a conversation with me at all." If he hadn't realized—or accepted—that his Peace Corps experience was over, he did then. "You don't go up and talk to any person of color," he knew now, "and have them be impressed that you know their language or that you're even talking to them and that you're interested in what's going on in their lives."

He may have absorbed that message and become less naïve as a result, but it didn't stop him from the course he had charted for himself. In his current position, the only thing he didn't think he could achieve with his black students was being a successful role model—or at least being as successful a role model as a black teacher (or mentor). He had had a black colleague in Washington who had reached some kids who Hartlaub thought would become failures within the system, and it was that individual whom Hartlaub was constantly in mind of.

What did Hartlaub think was the key to the man's success?

"He was organized, he came in with charisma and enthusiasm, he was motivated, and he was excited about teaching," he said, smiling at the thought of this man. "He came in there every day like somebody who wanted to be there and he showed them, as an African-American male, that someone out there can be successful and happy, be pleased with where they are in life, and be able to express that with the people that they meet. I think that that modeling had a direct effect on the feelings of *Can I do it?* that the students were having, *Can I really do it?* . . . If they can see somebody out there who's done it, and who's just like them in the sense of color and having to step over some of the hurdles that they will eventually have, and to reflect back on this individual and say, 'Well, he must have done something right.' If they see more and more of those individuals through a mentor program or whatever, then I think they will be able to transfer seeing the success of someone else do it to *I can do it too.*"

Hearing Joe Hartlaub talk was not that different from watching him deal with his students. As soon as they walked in the door he wanted to know things: Where was their homework? Who was Nefertiti? Excuses and "Gee, I don't know" were of no interest to him. He treated them firmly and democratically, treated them with respect, respect that he expected in return. He had told me how important it was to gain the trust of students and, from what I could tell, he had it. During the course of the morning, in one of the reading groups he broke the students into, the story in question was called "A Trip with Pilgrims."

"We're not going to read this story," he informed them. They weren't going to read it because it wasn't *their* story, it was his, his story as a white American. "What is *your* story?" he wanted to know. When one student said,

"Well, we were brought over from Africa to be slaves," Hartlaub asked them to try to imagine and write down what that trip might have been like, and what the lives of their ancestors might have been like before becoming slaves. What they created would be the stories they would read.

But therein lay an even bigger problem: of the twenty-four students in the class, half were below grade level in reading ability. It was this kind of dilemma that would lead Joe Hartlaub to soon wonder how he, or Tom Bell, or any of the other teachers, could muster enough energy and find enough time to both focus on the basics and infuse the curriculum with Afrocentrism, to do justice to one without sacrificing the other. One month into the school year, CBS News had already done a piece about the school, the *Milwaukee Journal* had had a reporter spend a week there, and the school's principal, Josephine Mosley, had been doing interviews nonstop with radio shows all across the country, interviews whose tone was both sympathetic and hostile, just like that of the callers who phoned in. Afrocentrism was not only a hot-button educational issue, it was also becoming Big Business; T-shirts proclaiming BLACK BY POPULAR DEMAND, countless varieties of African headwear, and buttons that announced THE BLACKER THE COLLEGE, THE SWEETER THE KNOWLEDGE were selling briskly.

Long before it could be determined if Afrocentrism would ultimately benefit the students who were being immersed in it, if the self-esteem it was supposed to build would result in a greater motivation to learn and succeed, long before any of that could be known, money would be made.

THIRTY-TWO

In the middle of September Howard Fuller gave an impassioned speech at Christ the King Baptist Church. There was much he had to say that Sunday, but one thing struck a deeper chord than anything else: his incredulity at how many kids in the inner city were being made to sleep on floors in order to keep out of harm's way, and at how many kids had asked him what the students at Victor Berger already seemed to know—what should they do when somebody started shooting? His voice was breaking as he talked about this and, everyone knew, so was his heart.

"We're talking about a new form of struggle," he said, leaving no one in doubt that the old one was the one he had been so involved with in the sixties. Seeing how he was giving his talk exactly twenty-eight years to the day after another Baptist church, the one on Sixteenth Street in Birmingham, was bombed and four little girls senselessly lost their lives, I found myself thinking of Chris McNair, the father of Denise, who would be eleven years old forever, nearly the same age as the kids in Tom Bell's class, and how he had searched through the rubble to find something, *anything*, that would confirm what he already knew yet couldn't bring himself to believe, and how he had found one of her shoes and kept it all these years. How would Denise McNair's life have evolved had she lived? Or that of two-year-old Felicia Watson, who died in her sleep on a sofa two months earlier, or that of Brenda Adams, who would be killed in her early twenties for her coat on the last Saturday night of October, a coat that nobody ultimately wore?

When you go into a school like Victor Berger (named for a famous Socialist in Milwaukee), a school that is spotless and full of shiny wood, and you learn from a devoted teacher like Tom Bell that some of his students would rather live in the bathroom than go home at the end of the day, that 90 percent of all the kids qualify for a free or reduced-price lunch, it does make you wonder how cosmetics—dressing in uniforms (even if, as one student said, "people don't be trying to take your clothes now, or be waiting for your Nikes"), or seeing a principal dressed like an African queen, or being surrounded by a sea of kente cloth—will do much to change what seems so unchangeable.

You can learn about Frederick Douglass and Benjamin Banneker, about Mary McCleod Bethune and Nefertiti, you can be surrounded by posters that declare WE ARE THE FUTURE and insist that you BE A GOOD FRIEND, but a stray bullet, which is selfish and unconcerned with how much knowledge you have about Africa (or anything else, for that matter) and what hopes and dreams you might harbor, still finds its own insidious way to involve a sleeping child in someone else's deadly business.

It is impossible not to wonder about such things, not to be affected by the cold calculation and gutlessness of the Birmingham bomber (whose name was Robert Chambliss) or, equally, of a member of the Vice Lords. They are of the same ilk because they achieve the same end—the taking of a life—regardless of the reasons why. Hatred of black people and black self-hatred are closely and dangerously aligned, and innocent people, however high their own self-esteem and their own ability to rise above the tangle, are not immune. Nobody is an exception, nobody is excused, and yet responsibility must be taken. (The killer of Brenda Adams would eventually offer post-traumatic stress disorder—the words of Vietnam applied to the nineties—as her defense, her argument that she was just as much a victim as Brenda Adams, that she killed for the coat because this was what living in the urban war zone caused you to do. The strategy failed and she was convicted.)

"Freedom is the ability, the capacity, to make choices, and to accept responsibility for the choices you make," Fuller said that day at the church, paraphrasing Martin Luther King. This was the stuff that Marvin Hannah had zeroed in on, the stuff he felt people lost sight of, the stuff that kids on his block didn't want to hear. Being dissed and what you had to do about it was far less subtle and easier to embrace. "Jacking the nigga" earned you more respect than knowing who Nefertiti was, and it gave you more air time.

WHICH WAS SOMETHING THAT Clarence Thomas and Anita Hill were getting plenty of, offering their respective views to a transfixed audience of millions. Beyond Hill's allegations of sexual harassment and the unfortunate spectacle of a black man and a black woman pitted against each other before an uncomfortable committee of senators, what was interesting was the way Thomas attempted to play the race card. Having initially run from race when he was first nominated, he was now full of indignation, labeling the proceedings "a high-tech lynching" and claiming that he was being destroyed, that the person sitting before the committee and the klieg lights and the country was merely a shell of the man President Bush had nominated, and that everyone—everyone but Clarence Thomas, it seemed—bore some measure of responsibility for it.

The Thomas nomination had taken the kind of bizarre turn that no one who had come to that Community Brainstorming breakfast in late July or had expressed an opinion to me about Thomas could have anticipated, a development that brought an unwelcome unity on this point: everyone—that is, every black who could bear to watch—seemed profoundly embarrassed that a brother and a sister were involved in such a public, demeaning drama, one that only exacerbated the myth of black sexuality (perhaps white America's biggest fear, according to Cornel West), of the black male's being, as Jefferson had written two hundred years earlier, "more ardent after their female." That Thomas's white wife sat conspicuously behind him throughout only served to overheat a scenario that hardly needed fueling.

Even though the element of sex, sex deemed to be illegal, improper, or inappropriate, had surfaced in the lives of public figures (and had often derailed their careers) since the beginning of time, there was no precedent for this, for a nominee to the United States Supreme Court to be asked about such prurient details before so many. Polly Williams's insistence that Clarence Thomas would have "chitlin flashbacks" and "do the right thing" once he got on the Court was a distant memory now that black America itself was unfairly being placed under the microscope, now that new ammunition was being offered to those who had always said "that's the way they are" and to those blacks who continued to believe that black women, by not being supportive enough of their men, were one of the main reasons that so many black men were kept down, and that, in this case, it was even worse: a black woman, it was strongly suggested, had also allowed herself to be used and preyed upon by the white establishment. The very things that Thomas and Shelby Steele had been talking about—the importance of being viewed as an individual and having one's successes and advancement be paramount to any collective responsibility toward one's race—were boomeranging on Thomas in a way he could never have intended: the charges Hill made against him were placing all black men into the same box. It was hideously unfair, but white America—the "they're not like us" segment—was doing it anyway, just as the "white conspiracy" theorists were out in full force.

For the first time since I had come to Milwaukee, I found myself pulling back somewhat, uneasy whenever I questioned anyone about the Hill-Thomas hearings. As the drama became more and more like a nasty car wreck, as the likelihood that the truth of what happened might never be known, I tried to be as delicate as I could. L. G. Shanklin-Flowers, the racism workshop facilitator whom I had first met in July, was still talking about "internalized oppression" when we had lunch together a few days after the hearings, but was now saying that Thomas's narrowly winning his seat on the Court was as good an example as one could find "of the system maintaining itself at whatever cost," the cost being the utter expendability of women and black people (an identity that she didn't consider Thomas to authentically possess). Since she already considered him a lost brother, she didn't find the whole business that surprising or that shocking. As for the good reverend LeHavre Buck, who (like L. G.) hadn't wanted Thomas to begin with, he told me that white folks were very adept at bringing blacks back to reality, the reality being that no matter how much Thomas tried to run from race, no matter how much he "sounded like the establishment," no matter that he had a white wife, he was still "a nigger like all niggers," a fact that Reverend Buck thought Thomas would be wise to come to terms with. He was not only reiterating something Jerrel Jones and others had impressed upon me months before, he was now attaching it to something specific, something that was larger than his or Jerrel Jones's respective experiences, something I had witnessed myself.

And yet part of what I had witnessed was Thomas's attempt to make himself into a victim—his willingness to become what he claimed to deplore. Buck didn't dispute that, but he understood it, understood that when a person, regardless of color, was pushed into a corner, he will grasp at anything. If Clarence Thomas sincerely thought the hearings over Anita Hill had so ruined him, had reduced him to a shell of what he was, then he presumably would have disqualified himself from further consideration—except that doing that would have been the same as admitting wrongdoing (at least that would have been the perception) and would have almost certainly resulted in the nomination of a white conservative, an unwelcome alternative for Reverend Buck and nearly every black I spoke with. Thomas was not only the lesser of two evils, Buck reasoned, but he would, eventually, be forgiven; he would be forgiven because it was in America's nature, for the most part, to do so. If Richard Nixon could be forgiven, so could Clarence Thomas. As for whether those chitlin flashbacks would ever come, no one could truly say.

The Hill-Thomas hearings so dominated the news that it almost escaped everyone's notice that the Blue Ribbon Commission, formed as a result of the Dahmer incident, had done its work and announced its findings one brisk October morning at Marquette University. One month earlier, Chief Arreola had fired two of the three police officers involved in the Konerak Sinthasomphone incident, and the commission basically had five things to recommend: that a detailed community-oriented policing plan (and how to implement it) be submitted by the chief within six months to the Fire and Police Commission; that all training of officers (both prospective and current) "must clearly reflect the philosophy of community-oriented policing, and must include the goal of appreciating diversity"; that the chief "must declare an unambiguous Department policy of valuing diversity among its members and must enforce discipline against violators of this policy"; that the citizen complaint process be streamlined and a mechanism put in place to help complainants obtain legal help; that the Fire and Police Commission expand its review of the police department's practices.

That all sounded great, but the problem was this: About 75 percent of the department had become officers under Harold Breier, and their loyalty, it was widely felt, was still to him, not to mention their view of policing. (In fact, not long after his appearance at Serb Hall that Sunday afternoon, he took the occasion of his eightieth birthday as an opportunity to tell the *Milwaukee Journal* and the greater citizenry that "you can take community policing and stick it in your ear. There's no substitute for strong law enforcement. First, a police officer doesn't have the training to take care of all the social ills of the city. And second, he should be so busy maintaining law and order that he doesn't have time for that crap.... When I was chief we were relating to the good people, and we were relating to the other people too—we were throwing those people in the can.") It was a problem that the report itself acknowledged. In its Catch-22 conclusion, the report said that "community-oriented policing is not possible in a department which does not value diversity," and that all the right training of recruits would mean little "if the attitudes and techniques they learn are not valued and supported by the entire department."

What the commission learned during its investigation was dismayingly similar to what an earlier commission had found ten years before (a commission that was formed *before* the Ernest Lacy incident) and to what I had heard at the town meeting at Washington High School: slow response time, racist attitudes, and general lack of respect toward citizens. What the commission also learned was that a large number of people—"the good people"—felt the department did its work well and protected the common good. Nonetheless, the perception on the part of minorities that they were "singled out routinely for mistreatment and selective enforcement" was more than just perception, Father DiUlio said. "That these perceptions bear some considerable truth in reality seems beyond question." They had to do "with a word we have heard a great deal of lately, harassment."

Mayor Norquist, who conceded that he hadn't yet had a chance to read the report, insisted nonetheless that the time for studying was over, that it was now time to start making the police department more responsive and more effective "for *all* of us . . . of whatever race, whatever sexual preference, whatever ethnic background, whatever language."

But did the report, someone asked the mayor, really tell him anything about the department that he didn't already know?

He reiterated that he hadn't read it yet, hadn't even read any summaries of it. Even so, he said, "I'm sure there are a lot of issues that a lot of people are familiar with." Hearing all this made me wonder, as it had Tom Brophy, how seriously the report would be taken. If it only confirmed what everyone already sensed, if it wasn't dramatically different from the one ten years earlier, if the mayor hadn't had the time to either study it carefully or read a summary of it, it probably didn't bode well for the report's doing much more than landing in mothballs, along with all the other reports and task force studies—all the other examples of how the city contemplated its navel ad nauseam—that people like Michael McGee and Howard Fuller complained about. The very recommendation for sensitivity training that Tom Brophy cynically worried might find its way into the report was in the report. Even though he had said something like that would be insignificant in the context of the community's overwhelming need for jobs, it still seemed positive in and of itself—provided it became a permanent part of the way each individual went about his work.

In my reading of the report, one thing stood out: the affidavit from Lenard Wells, head of the League of Martin, the department's group of minority officers. "The minority community has put its hope into COP," he wrote of community-oriented policing. "The League feels that it will be difficult to effectively implement the philosophy of problem solving in the community by using an all-white-male staff. The League recognizes and so should this panel that the African-American community is tired of being told what is good for them by white males and conservative Thomases. . . .

"The perception that the African-American community is a victim of a double standard and discriminatory practices when it comes to quality of service delivered is reinforced by the fact that members of the League encounter double standards and discriminatory practices within the MPD. . . .

"If a black officer was accused of 'shaking down' members of the community, immediate action would be taken. So we can not tell the community why no resolution is given them regarding who Blondie is" (the aforementioned detective who was feared and hated throughout the black community).

"A white officer is reportedly found intoxicated and passed out in an auto, no reported discipline is taken. So, as President of the League, I can not explain to a Black officer why he was removed from his bed and ordered to give a breath test and disciplinary action is pending.

"A white sergeant is suspended for misconduct for activities involving a white woman while on duty. I could not tell the Black sergeant why he was fired for similar activities.

"Two white officers shoot at a minority citizen, go home, clean their guns without reporting the incident and receive informal discipline. I can not tell the African American officer that discharged his firearm into the air why he was dismissed.

"This panel should entertain the fact," Wells urged, "that those within the MPD who investigate African American officers are often times the same ones that investigate and 'explain away' the complaints of minority citizens."

Elsewhere in the report, under the heading of "Training Findings and Recommendations," was the following: "It has been suggested to us that racist, sexist and homophobic remarks within the MPD are actually joking and teasing to relieve the stress of police work. If this is true, it is evidence that officers need to learn techniques of stress reduction that do not victimize individuals and groups.... The 'code of silence' which says that officers do not report errant fellow officers is unacceptable. First-line supervisors must set an example to those they supervise, and be held accountable for ensuring that unacceptable behavior is corrected and stopped. There must be a clear message from command staff, reinforced by the organizational structure, that misbehavior of this kind will not be tolerated.... That message must be reinforced by correcting and disciplining every infraction."

So THE COMMISSION HAD done its civic duty, had done it thoroughly, and announced its findings on the day the mayor had asked for it. Everyone knew that there was not going to be some miraculous change overnight— not in the Milwaukee Police Department, or in any organization, really, where people found it difficult to check their biases and barely hidden contempt, even hatred, at the door. But if the nature of an organization was to change, as Howard Fuller was saying about the schools, actions had to have consequences, a premise that might sound harsh in its simplicity, but one, it could at least be hoped, that people who chose police work might be more inclined to accept and live by.

THIRTY-THREE

John Fitzgerald's decision to move to the South Side of Milwaukee had been a tortuous one: to move from an integrated block in Sherman Park, where his son had made lots of friends, to lily white Bay View, was as wrenching a dilemma as Marvin Hannah's, a nagging sense on both their parts that they were giving up and giving in. I had first met John Fitzgerald in July, at the racism workshop L. G. Shanklin-Flowers had organized. He was the person I had wound up sitting next to, who had come because he wanted to find the courage to confront racist remarks when they were uttered in his presence. He looked to be about forty, with a sadness in his face, especially in his eyes, that was difficult to miss. I had jotted down his phone number but hadn't gotten around to calling him and then we happened to run into each other in November at a conference on gangs that Tommie Williams from Harambee had arranged.

Like Tom Donegan, Fitzgerald was a product of the sixties, the oldest son in a large Catholic family from Michigan, a young man on whom duty and responsibility were deeply imprinted at an early age. The sadness in his eyes, I came to understand, was only a window into a larger disappointment about the way the world worked, specifically, about the way life in America had unraveled since the death of John F. Kennedy. It would be easy to merely pass John Fitzgerald off as an idealist—to say that idealists were bound to be disappointed by anything and everything because their expectations were unrealistic, to tell him to buck up, face facts, and anchor himself to the ground—but it would be too glib and it would be off the mark. Fitzgerald was more complicated than that.

Between the time I had first met him in July and now, he had decided to participate in the same three-month Beyond Racism program Blair Moreland had been a part of. That decision, he was telling me over lunch one day, had much to do with the work he did and whom he did it with. John was a social worker at a hospital in Brown Deer, just north of the city, a job in which he helped mainly affluent white suburban teenagers cope with emotional disorders as well as alcohol and drug addiction, and that, to a large extent, defined his discontent: he was working with kids who often couldn't see beyond their own problems and who appeared to have little or no interest in the problems of those who were much less well off than themselves. What, one might ask, was either new or so surprising about that? Not very much, perhaps, but for John Fitzgerald it meant that work each day had increasingly become deadening, compounded by the fact that his move to Bay View only made him more uneasy that he had run from the same things that the kids he counseled had never had to turn their backs on in the first place. It's not that he thought kids of privilege weren't entitled to have problems (or to have help with them), and it's not that he had any delusions that having money was any shield against them. In fact, the degree to which general family dysfunction in the suburbs never seemed to attract the same "attention" as it did in the inner cities was something that disturbed Fitzgerald, another "inequality" he felt powerless to combat.

Idealism aside, John Fitzgerald didn't think he would see racism eliminated in his lifetime, but he was hoping that his son would. And so it was really for Johnny, for him to see that his father did more than just sit around and bemoan the unresolved dilemma of race relations in America, that Fitzgerald attended an overnight retreat on the last weekend in September.

As John went through the exercise of sitting in the inner circle with his back to those in the outer circle, as he was told of the invisible knapsack that Peggy McIntosh wrote about and the forty-four items it contained, many things went through his mind, things he would begin to record in a journal later that night, a journal he decided to write from back to front because he saw himself embarked on a process that was "largely an undoing." Of all the privileges that those in the inner circle were asked to read aloud, none struck him with more force than that of white mobility, "of being able to choose and move in an effort to keep Johnny safe from those I've learned to mistrust," he wrote. "For me none of the 44 privileges struck me as a realization. What hit home were those I knew and knew I'd known before I took advantage of them anyway."

Years before, he had traveled to India, and the most acute memory he had of that trip was his acknowledgment that he was in a place where, as a white American, he was not in charge, not in control, and how frightening that was, how isolated and lonely and helpless that made him feel. And yet once he accepted the situation, which was not easy, he actually

experienced a liberation of sorts, a release from all the things that constrained him, a license to be Huckleberry Finn for a while, drifting on the
margin. But his feeling of liberation was only possible, he now realized,
because he could, barring unforeseen circumstances, return to his life in
America, to all the things he knew and took advantage of anyway, whenever he chose.

"I'm not sure how long we spent in our circles," he wrote, but it was
long enough "to hear an African-American say that he felt whites always
have their backs to him and that he feels it is my culture that suffers because
we lack the interaction we deprive ourselves of in society."

Just before turning his bedside light off for the night, he added something in his journal, something that further explained the role his son had
played in his decision to attend: Johnny had urged him to come. "A number of people have commented on my stated reason for coming to this
meeting. I said that in part I feel a responsibility to my son. Like me people
are heartened to hear of John's feelings and wishes—even demands—re:
racism. I'm proud of him and hope somehow my efforts can help him feel
pride in me one day."

EARLY THE NEXT MORNING, a Sunday, John found a small chapel on the
retreat grounds of Cedar Valley and went inside. He was the only one there.
Standing in his "warm dress shoes" before the simple cornice altar made
him think of Lake Superior, where he and his family so often went on
vacation, but not of any specific prayer. It was only afterward, as he
explored the white outer walls of the chapel, that he noticed an inscrip-
tion that had escaped his attention on the way in:

> *Let us not love in word, nor in tongue*
> *but in deed and truth.*

As he walked back to attend the day's workshops, he repeated this
passage (from 1 John 3:18) to himself.

THERE WERE QUESTIONS TO answer, and he tried to supply them.
    What was great about being European-American?

Freedom, power, autonomy, control, belonging, acceptance, care of my physical needs—feeling safe, education, support, community.

What did he dislike about it?

Isolation, loneliness, sadness, separation, guilt, guilt, guilt, powerlessness, lack of acceptance in a larger community, fear.

What was his next step in his commitment against racism?

Continued involvement in this project. Following through on commitments (small ones) made to others here so far.

When a variation of those questions were put to African-Americans, a man named Carvis said "being in tune with nature, being part of a growing population, having the ability to adjust despite limited resources, possessing patience, compassion, and vision"— these were the things that were great about having an African heritage.

What was hard about it, Carvis said, was the lack of recognition of the many contributions his race had made—and how difficult it was to explain "contradictions" to his children.

A woman named Sue said it was hard working in a white company and being ignored when others were introduced. Another woman, Carrie, said it was hard to have to keep proving herself over and over.

As to what they never wanted to see or hear or have done to their group again, Carrie pointed to black children, and how she couldn't bear to see their spirits crushed, their potential limited. Sue said she never again wanted to hear about "what I can do in *their* structure" or hear that "African-American women only have babies" or see "what society is doing to our black men." Another said she never again wanted to be asked, "Haven't we given you enough?" or to hear "people of color" (the suggested term) put each other down. Everybody at the retreat had been strongly urged the day before to find an ally, someone with whom they could continue meeting after the retreat concluded. John Fitzgerald's ally turned out to be Carvis Braxton.

Someone who would listen, who would display compassion, an openness to ideas, to perceptions, someone who would not be defensive or feel alienated from someone like himself: these were the things that Carvis said he would need from an ally.

What John needed was acceptance, respect, and honesty. What he felt he could bring to the alliance was an ability to listen, loyalty, and a desire to change. The four things, though, that he worried could "get in the way" were lack of time and energy, fear, and doubt. In trying to fully understand why each person was being asked to ally with someone else, John recalled something L. G. had said, something about a study that had been done to determine why certain Europeans had defied the Nazis in order to assist Jews during the Holocaust. The one common thread that emerged was this: Each had had positive experiences with Jews during the course of their lives.

IN ORDER TO BELIEVE in the value of encounter groups like this, full of talk that sounded as if everyone there were trying to hook up with someone else, you had to believe (more or less) that if change was to come about, it would come about, however slowly, because white Americans were forced/ encouraged/persuaded to talk about their fears and doubts, to not allow the subject of race relations to be taboo. That it would come about because somebody like John Fitzgerald and Blair Moreland would no longer allow racist remarks to be made in their presence. That it would come about because black Americans could feel not only that somebody was listening, but that those who were listening were going to head back into their communities as agents of change. (For European-Americans, L. G. said, the work consisted of giving up the role of targeters and becoming healers; for people of color, the targeted group, the job was both to educate and to overcome internalized oppression.) The government could only do so much. Laws could only do so much. People's attitudes, outwardly and inwardly, ultimately had to shift, block by block, cul-de-sac by cul-de-sac, village green by village green, business by business, precinct by precinct, local bar by local bar, country club by country club. Given how perpetually busy people seem to be, is it too much to hope for? Perhaps. But the work needs to be done, the burden must be lifted.

"SLAVERY AND SEGREGATION BOTH, to paraphrase Dr. King, have damaged our souls and weakened our personhood," John wrote in his journal. This observation struck John's Achilles' heel—especially when, just before he was about to leave the conference and return home, Carrie informed him that she had tried to get a home in Bay View but was "rejected due to skin color." As a Catholic, the notion of damaged souls and a weakened personhood was no laughing matter for John (just as "darkened souls" had not been for L. G. when she was in elementary school).

When John got home that evening, he phoned his brother Matt, who lived in Bonners Ferry, Idaho, and told him about the weekend. Matt listened politely and told John how good it was that he was "doing that." He also told him about recently being in a bar in town when a member of the band that was performing suddenly stopped performing, stopped in order to acknowledge the presence of the only black man in the bar, to urge everyone to give him a hand. Matt didn't know what to think of the incident, he told John, didn't know what the band member's intent was. What he did know, or so he said, was that he didn't think the black man was harmed by being singled out in this way; besides, Matt added, "fortunately he was drunk."

As John listened on the other end, what came to mind was an old ("but still fresh") memory of some racist comments Matt had made to him in the past (while Matt was drunk), comments that were passed off with a "We've all got it inside us" (meaning racism), which John did not disagree with.

Before hanging up, John suggested Matt seek out the man from the bar (the only black man in Bonners Ferry, apparently) and speak with him directly. Matt was unfailingly polite, but the conversation ended with no illusions on John's part that this would happen.

MONDAY WAS JOHN'S DAY off from his job at the hospital, and as he sat at home that morning, he thought about phoning Carvis. Problem was, he was already beginning to detect some cynicism within himself, wondering how much of the retreat would stick with him. Part of him wanted reassurance from Carvis that they could form this alliance and sustain it, and yet part of him was afraid to provide it.

Throughout the course of the day, various people he spoke with wanted to know what John's involvement in the project was costing him. John found it odd they were so curious about this. When he said "fifty dollars," no one seemed to think that was unreasonable.

At dinner that evening, John talked with his wife, Leslie, and Johnny about the weekend. John asked Johnny, who was eight, what he remembered about living in Sherman Park and Johnny said, "You heard gunshots."

Sensing that Johnny was only telling him what he wanted to hear, "repeating our recent justifications for the move" to Bay View, John said, "No, do you remember the places?"

Yes, he did. He remembered the library, his friends' houses, the cookie shop, his doctor's office, the grocery store, the high school, the cemetery.

John's own memories zeroed in on two things, two things that pinpointed his ambivalence: that he had lived among "neighbors of every race" and that "except for crime it had qualities Bay View never will."

THE FOLLOWING SUNDAY JOHN and Carvis met for a drink. They had spoken on the phone a few times, each bemoaning the fact that there were very few places in Milwaukee "where the races mix comfortably." They finally settled on the Water Street Brewery, located close to City Hall, as a place, in Carvis's words, "to break bread together." Carvis told John of his various experiences as a community organizer, most recently in East St. Louis, Illinois (one of the most poverty-stricken cities in the country), of how supportive his wife was of the work he did (especially the time away from home in the evening), of his five daughters, of the house he lived in and loved on Twenty-seventh and Hadley. John told Carvis of the frustration he had experienced doing community organizing while living in Minneapolis, but said that the retreat had gotten him excited about eventually becoming a "trainer" and working with kids on the same kinds of issues.

They also talked about pain. When John looked across the table at Carvis he could sense "the tears that weren't there." Carvis asked John about the "white privilege" exercise at the retreat and whether he'd been aware of all those things before. John said he thought he had been, much more so than he had been aware of "the price we inflict on ourselves to enjoy them," the price being isolation.

Carvis, who was fifty, said that he felt cheated of having the opportunity for the kind of education he would have chosen, said it in such a way, in John's view, that "implied bitterness without voicing it aloud." He wasn't just referring to attending the college of his choice; he was also talking of not having had—or being convinced he did not have—the freedom to travel, to hitchhike around (as John had), to literally spin a globe (as John and Leslie had) and live wherever he wanted. To do those things comfortably, to do them without fear, to do them and not have to worry about either sticking out—or not being seen at all.

Carvis spoke of books he had read that he hoped John would read: Booker T. Washington's *Up from Slavery,* Connie Porter's *All-Bright Court* (which was about the housing project near Buffalo where Carvis grew up), and Carter G. Woodson's *The Mis-Education of the Negro.* He spoke of his hopes for his grandchildren, and spoke with resentment of those in the black community who had chosen to "mirror" white culture rather than contribute to their own. Given how much raw talent existed in inner-city neighborhoods, Carvis thought it was wrong that that talent wasn't directed toward making those communities better and more prosperous. If his brother wanted to live elsewhere, that was his choice, but it wouldn't be Carvis's. (When Carvis later said to me that he lived "in the heart of the 'hood," he said it with a blend of pride and defiance.)

But there was something that troubled Carvis, something he wanted John to know about before the end of their evening on Water Street, the end of their first night as allies. Carvis was concerned about how their alliance would be viewed by the very same community he was so committed to helping. He anticipated some hostility, even outright rejection, but this was part of the work he needed to do.

OVER THE NEXT SIX weeks, they talked about the Hill-Thomas hearings. Carvis told John that they should have been required viewing for everyone in their group. John asked Carvis if he had supported Thomas before the allegations, and Carvis said he had. In fact, he took the Polly Williams view that Thomas was "his own man" and would probably surprise many people with his opinions once he got onto the Court. At the same time, Carvis said, he couldn't understand why someone of Thomas's age would want a lifetime job that was, in his opinion, insulated and lonely and without much support. They watched a short film entitled *From Racism to Pluralism* and they took a bus tour of the city, a tour that underscored the ethnicity of Milwaukee and how, primarily through the power and location of the churches, these different enclaves of familiarity and sameness had come about; a tour that encouraged them to look closely at the parts of the community where investment was taking place and where it was not. Not long after that, Carvis came to Bay View for a Sunday afternoon walk in the woods near John's house. Once he had been there for a few hours Carvis joked that he was feeling "too comfortable," yet warned John at the same time that he and his family might yet be kicked out of Bay View once neighbors learned how John was spending his free time.

THIRTY-FOUR

No sooner had Michael McGee's Intercommunal Call to Arms Summit concluded than he came up with a new plan to hold the city's feet to the fire—threatening to disrupt Milwaukee's convention business. Not long after that, McGee announced Operation Corporate Storm, a plan for the militia to picket the homes and businesses of those who constituted the white power structure. One person who had the dubious pleasure of such a visit was Milwaukee Brewers president Allan H. (Bud) Selig. (Though Selig couldn't have known it at the time, the visit of the Black Panther Militia to his car leasing company in West Allis was a mild harbinger of the vilification he would endure in trying to sort out the baseball strike three years later.) There was more. McGee announced he would challenge John Norquist for mayor in the 1992 election, then one week later he said his son would.

In the meantime, the fallout over the firing of two of the three police officers involved in the Konerak Sinthasomphone incident continued (one resident offered the opinion, with obvious disgust, that Chief Arreola had to do something "to get the colored people off his back"); a local chapter of the NAA*W*P was born (a group initially started in Louisiana by David Duke); and there were rumors that a White Kill Day was going to take place at Marshall High School, where fights had broken out and the black principal was removed by Howard Fuller.

A few days after the trouble at Marshall, Mayor Norquist gave a talk at Hamilton High, a talk in which, the *Milwaukee Journal* reported, he had hoped to recount some of "the glories of civilization—Rome under the Caesars, Peru under the Incas, Mexico under the Aztecs"—but instead found himself confronted by students with more prosaic matters on their mind: Michael McGee; the firing of the two officers; why there was so much talk about Milwaukee and its problems (especially the high rate of teenage pregnancy); why the public schools weren't receiving all the money they needed.

Norquist not only declared that militant black groups like McGee's were "outmoded and passé," he also warned that the fallout for the city, if

McGee continued on this course, would be "disastrous"; more and more businesses would just pull up stakes and leave town, head off to friendlier climes. In what could be seen as a preview of his message for the 1992 campaign, a message of cracking down on crime and rediscovering traditional family values, he challenged all young males who were present to think twice about the prospect of impregnating some girl and somehow avoiding the consequences: Wisconsin, he said sternly, had the toughest child support law in America. As for all the bad press about Milwaukee? Well, he went beyond McGee and Dahmer and headed right for the source: the press itself was responsible for the negative news.

Norquist, like any savvy politician, knew how to reiterate a popular point, just as he knew what to leave out. What he failed to say at Hamilton was that the media also spotlighted whatever positive efforts the city was making to address its socioeconomic problems (even though that attention was not always presented in context). When he challenged the business community to invest in the inner city and passed out copies of the same *Fortune* article that Reuben Harpole had given to me (the one that shouted Eureka!, there was money to be made in the ghetto), it was reported. When there was even the slightest hiccup to be heard at Steeltech, the minority-owned company that was going up in the heart of the inner city and was going to yield one hundred or so jobs, it was reported. When the city's Goals 2000 report was completed, some of the goals being the reduction of crime and teenage pregnancy and the school dropout rate by *10 percent each year*, it was reported. When the mayor announced his intentions to include five hundred thousand dollars in the 1992 budget so that the Milwaukee Community Service Corps could double its ranks from forty to eighty, it was reported. When the mayor reminded everyone that there were twenty-two hundred vacant lots in the inner city that could be yours for one measly dollar a year, this benevolence was reported. As was the $950,800 that the city's Housing Authority received from the Department of Housing and Urban Development to reduce drug-related crime in public housing. As was the $825,000 that twelve city lending institutions had committed to in the way of financing for "affordable housing." Even the mayor's seeming distress that the term "community-based policing" was not being clearly understood—that it might, in any case, be "too hot to handle politically," that perhaps a return to just plain old "policing" would do—was reported without the slightest trace of irony, which was surprising, really, given the considerable hoo-hah (and cost) that had gone into promoting this as a new approach to old problems.

THE *MILWAUKEE JOURNAL* CONTINUED its focus on race by devoting a week in October to "Race in the Workplace" and a week the following month to "Race in Education." In the first, depressingly familiar observations that "hit-or-miss strategies barely make a dent" and that finding money to train the unemployed appeared to be a permanent problem recurred, circling back to the troublesome question, posed by one editorial, of "Where do the answers lie?" a question being asked not only in Milwaukee, but throughout the country. Back in April, Jerrel Jones had reversed the question, urging me to think long and hard about who benefited if the conditions in the inner cities of America did not improve. My answer, then and now, was that no one benefited—not in any socially responsible sense. While all the acolytes who continued to worship at the Shrine of the Status Quo took dubious pleasure in knowing that very little was likely to change and affect the way they lived, there was a cost to all this. Once again I found myself thinking about the end of Nicholas Lemann's book *The Promised Land,* the part about America being too moral a place to abide the presence of the ghetto forever, remembering how I was so moved when I first read that, but now feeling much less certain that Lemann was right, feeling that what he was saying amounted to wishful thinking, with his heart in the right place but out of sync with the times. There were indeed people, plenty of them, who would push Tom Brophy out his office window, who would resoundingly say he was wrong for suggesting that a grand-scale, everybody-on-the-same-page Marshall Plan was what a city like Milwaukee or a country like America required. The Darwinians were everywhere, they were angry, and they appeared to be closing in.

THIRTY-FIVE

"**Y**ou all are going to be white today."

The new year had hardly begun when two black children, a brother and sister, were sprayed with white paint on their way to school in New York City. Sitting at the Café Knickerbocker in Milwaukee and reading this in the *New York Times*, I wondered if this was an isolated incident—or a sign of what 1992 was going to be like for race relations.

Just a week or so earlier, *Newsweek* had run a summing-up piece about the year gone past, a piece that characterized 1991 as "lean and angry," a year in which "the path to racial comity turned rockier," a year in which "shut-out minorities demanded more" and "many whites felt it was time to say, enough." The piece recalled the riots that broke out in August between blacks and Jews in the Crown Heights section of Brooklyn after Gavin Cato was accidentally struck by a car and a Hasidic man was consequently slain as a result. It recalled the two professors at City College of New York with differing views: Leonard Jeffries, whose caustic comments were threatening to wipe out, almost single-handedly, the positive aspects of Afrocentrism, and Michael Levin, who offered the opinions that blacks should be accorded their own subway car and, in the great tradition of William Shockley and Arthur Jensen (not to mention a preamble to the clamor of *The Bell Curve*), that blacks were, on average, less intelligent than whites. As for what lay ahead, readers were told (or reminded) that David Duke was planning to run for president and that Daryl Gates might not step down as chief of the Los Angeles Police Department after all.

Depending on your point of view, the good/bad news was that George Bush finally but unhappily signed the 1991 Civil Rights Act, preserving affirmative action but affording no retroactive help to those who had filed job-discrimination suits before the bill's signing on November 21.

In Milwaukee, a group of people polled by the *Milwaukee Journal* said they were more pessimistic than optimistic about the city's race relations in the coming year. "Whites don't respect blacks," a black woman named Sharon Stewart said. "Anytime something goes wrong, it's a black person's

fault." Shorewood resident James Robillard recounted how he and his fellow suburban parishioners performed charitable deeds at an inner-city
church, but didn't stick around afterward (himself excluded, of course).
Throwing money over a fence was the way Robillard viewed it. They got
in and got out, their good intentions still intact. It wasn't hard to picture
them, fleeing back to Shorewood, awash in altruism.

THE MOST SEGREGATED TIME of every week in America, it has been said,
is eleven o'clock on Sunday mornings. On the Sunday morning of January 12, Howard Fuller made his way to Mt. Carmel Lutheran, on the
Northwest Side, to talk about what he was trying to accomplish in the
public schools. As an ongoing part of the Crusade to Save Our Children,
Fuller had been doing this pretty much every Sunday, but on this particular
one his cool composure finally cracked. It happened during the question-
and-answer period that followed his talk and it had to do with Chapter
220, the program that allowed students from city schools to attend suburban ones and vice versa. Since its inception in 1976, the program had been,
like so much else that involved the tentacles of race, an intricate flashpoint
of anger, resentment, and opportunity. Many people wanted to see the program abolished altogether. In any case, a woman stood up and identified
herself as a member of the faculty at Shorewood Middle School.

She was concerned, she said, that there wasn't enough money in their
budget so that *"your kids"* could stay around after school to get extra help
and still have a bus to take them home.

"My view," Fuller said, "is that when a kid comes into your school
district, that is *your kid.*"

She didn't respond to that. She simply said it was her understanding
that nothing could be done about the situation.

Fuller didn't agree. "The question is what do *you* think ought to be
done for these children and what do you do for the children in your district? If a Milwaukee kid decides to come to a suburban school, in my
opinion that kid now belongs to that suburban district, just like any other
kid who attends that district. . . . If you all think that these kids should
all have these experiences, they are *your* kids, so you should think about
how you are going to come up with the resources to make sure that your
kids have what they ought to have, because they are your kids. If they

are sent to your school district and they are not your kids, then whose kids are they?"

This was why Fuller took the job, to make sure that children—*all children*—came first, that their interests were served. To know intellectually that a Shorewood or a Wauwatosa was reluctantly opening its hallowed halls but not allowing Milwaukee kids to feel fully welcome was one thing, but to hear a teacher so openly raise the polarizing issue of whom they belonged to was quite another. It was more than Fuller could abide. Children deserved more, much more, than being caught up in an endless spiral of red tape and bureaucracy, than being viewed as outcasts, surrounded by bickering and hairsplitting about who was responsible for them. What galled Fuller about the 220 situation was the overall fact of its inequity: MPS guaranteed that 10 percent of the spots in their magnet schools be reserved for suburban kids, whereas suburban schools only admitted kids from Milwaukee based upon availability (making it far too easy to say there's no room at the inn).

The Catch-22s of race—the multitude of ways in which barriers and hurdles, fine print and caveats, rear their sinister heads and scuttle attempts to level the playing field—would appear to be limitless. In education, in housing, in employment, in obtaining a loan: someone, somewhere, was always at the ready, it seemed, lurking in the background, in possession of some ingenious scheme that enabled institutional racism to continue. Wasn't it bad enough that a child had to be labeled a "220 kid"? But to not have a bus there so that a child could stay later and get extra help—especially when blacks had borne so much of the brunt of busing—seemed yet one more bitter irony. Was it any wonder that Howard Fuller wanted to ultimately get rid of busing altogether? Students were traveling a great distance to a school that didn't especially want them there in the first place, passing through what one person called an "invisible landscape" (a landscape of affluence that might as well not be there for all the reality it bore to their own lives), and not being accorded all the privileges that should be theirs by dint of being students at the school. If North Division could have offered the same things that Whitefish Bay offered, Diane Howard had said, her daughters would have gone there. Was it any wonder that Howard Fuller desperately wanted more neighborhood schools?

One of the things Howard Fuller tried to do that morning at Mt. Carmel was explain himself to the people who had come. Not only explain what he was trying to accomplish as superintendent, but explain who he was, what he stood for, and what role he was trying to play. "When I look at the city that I grew up in and the city that I love," he said, "particularly that part of the city that is mostly part of who I am, my assessment is that the social conditions that are affecting people are getting worse each day." On top of that, he said, those in power were doing what people in power always do when they can't come up with solutions—pointing fingers at others, making it even more difficult "to deal with the gravity of the problems." Unless the city's leaders and residents were on the same page, "figuring out ways to make sure that everyone will have the opportunity to live with dignity and work . . . to make sure that we create economic and social opportunities to advance . . . the gaps between those who have and those of us who have not are going to continue to widen. We will go to all our respective churches on Sunday and reassure ourselves that we are good Christians and that we are in fact our brother's and sister's keepers. At the same time, we try to make sure that what we have we keep. . . . For a lot of us, Sundays at church are like Sundays at football games. It has an interesting level of enjoyment. We leave and then we go and do whatever we do in the rest of the week and then we can come back again on Sunday and reassert ourselves and be fundamentally good people. It doesn't mean that we are not fundamentally good people, but it means that the impact of a lot of good people is going to lead to very destructive possibilities for our community."

In the pews, some of the parishioners stirred uncomfortably. After all, Fuller wasn't downtown speaking at the Rotary Club, nor was he at an inner-city church such as Christ the King. He was in suburban America on a Sunday, challenging the faithful to pay more than lip service to concerns about how people were living in the other America. He was there to remind them how interesting human nature was, remind them that "the older all of us get, the more angelic becomes our youth." Embarrassed smiles appeared on many faces, others nodded their heads. "I have also found that the older we get the more that we forget what it was really like. When we zero in on the points of nostalgia, it makes *everything* then seem like the rosiest possible things." In terms of public education in America, poor and working-class kids have always faced problems, he said. But there was a difference: in those good old days you could drop out and still get an excellent job; these days you couldn't, because the skills that were required now were not required then.

Public schools were developed from an industrial model of bells and whistles that was no longer valid in today's world. It was a system partly based on children being "on time in their seats so they could learn discipline, so they could learn how to become workers, to work on time, and to do their work by orders. That's not all bad," Fuller said, but there was an aspect of it that was not preparing you to run the world, but to be run by it. Fuller had received lots of letters since becoming superintendent, letters whose message was "We should go back to how it was like when I was in school." It wasn't that things couldn't be learned from the past, but "we have to go forward by looking forward. . . .

"I think one of the keys to all this," he said, "is whether or not America really decides that children are truly our most precious resource. I believe what is happening in America is called the Big Lie. The Big Lie is we say that our children are our most precious resource—except when it comes to finding resources to prove that they are. We find money to do everything else that's important. We find money to draw lines in the Gulf. We find money to deal with the mess that was created in the S&L debacle. We find money for hundred-and-fifty-dollar toilet seats in the Pentagon. We find money for weapons of mass destruction. But when it comes time to start talking about money for our children, when it comes time to start addressing the fact that in the inner cities in this country, one in two black children live in poverty—when we start understanding the impact this is going to have on our world, we then begin to talk about 'We are not going to throw money at the problem.'

"I have always found it intriguing in America that when you talk about community problems, it is 'throwing money at it.' When you talk about putting money in some other aspect of our society, it is called 'wise investment in our future.'" Fuller was not saying that more money was the only way to solve the problem, but to do the things that had to be done resources would be needed. A commitment to have smaller classes, for instance, meant there would have to be more buildings. Anyone who didn't think that, he implied, was either deluding himself or didn't care enough to begin with.

In the question-and-answer session, before the woman from Shorewood raised Fuller's ire over the question of whom the 220 students from Milwaukee belonged to, concerns were raised about Fuller's desire to close failing schools, about holding teachers accountable, about the lack of parental involvement. For Fuller, it all came back to expectations. Even if a suburban school didn't have a high level of parental involvement, what that school did have was "the expectation on the part of everyone who works in that building that if we don't educate these kids, we're out of here." The people in that building were "working for people with money and power," as opposed to those who were working for "poor, nonwhite people" in the inner city. People didn't like him to bring up these things, he said, but he had to bring them up because they had an impact on how teachers viewed their job. He wasn't talking about the vast majority of teachers, he said; the vast majority got up every day determined to do the best job they could.

But there were "some people who for a variety of reasons have given up, have decided that these kids cannot learn." Those were the people—the people who took the view that they had a job for life, that they had outlived five principals and would probably outlive three more—whom Fuller wanted to remove from the system, regardless of race. If there were eighty teachers in a particular building and ten of them were of that mindset, Fuller said, "you will not be able to turn that building around." That was why he wanted to have the authority to close a failing school: to get rid of the people who were there and start with fresh blood, to do what he could to derail the self-fulfilling prophecies that cause inestimable harm.

THE DAY BEFORE, I had been at Fuller's class at Commando, and because I had, I better understood why he became so upset during the exchange with the teacher from Shorewood. The book that he and the class were discussing was *Best Intentions,* the true story of Edmund Perry, who lived in Harlem, went off to Phillips Exeter on a scholarship, and was killed in the summer of 1985 by a white policeman, whom Edmund and his brother had apparently assaulted. The story, everyone in the class agreed, was a story about belonging, about being precariously perched and often torn between the two worlds of black and white America, a story about power and control, a story about resources and being resourceful.

Zo offered the opinion that Perry might have been using his anger about racism—the racism he experienced at Exeter—as a means of "taking it out on someone who may not be racist at all."

What did it take, Fuller wanted to know, to keep a young black man from being "a boy from the 'hood," from thinking, "Hey, this is a white dude and we can take him out." Sometimes, he said, "the world boils down to a particular room you're in, a particular location in time. Your *personal* power, at that moment, is exercised in that instance." Fuller had talked about this before, when he recalled going out to play basketball at Country Day, but now he went further. Edmund Perry's story—struggling with the duality of being black in America, of being considered either too black or not black enough—was not unlike Fuller's own, was not unlike the story of countless other blacks who had the moxie to make it no matter what, but who faced all sorts of barriers along the way.

Fuller recalled how his class at North Division was the last one to have a significant number of white students (at the time they entered in the fall of 1954). When he was in ninth grade, the school was 83 percent white. By the time he graduated, the percentage of white students had dropped to 43. But when he went to Carroll College in Waukesha on a scholarship, it was like being dropped on the moon. Waukesha was not that far from Milwaukee, but it might as well have been. "What happens is you get caught between two worlds. In simple terms, you are *out there* and I was out there and people would say, 'Why do you have a mustache?' People could not understand what I was saying or why I was saying it. I was trying to figure out how I was going to survive out there and then you come home and people are doing new dances and you just in between two worlds and not in either one. It was a bittersweet experience in the sense that during your college years, that is a time of social life and stuff like that. I didn't have no social life. It had a direct impact on how I viewed my abilities to function with black women, 'cause when I was in high school I was mostly lying. I was doing nothing. I was *pretending* to get a piece like everybody else. But in that period during seventeen and twenty-one, a number of people were having experiences that I wasn't having."

Zo and Jerry and everyone who was there laughed when Fuller talked about this. He was, in many ways, an intensely private person, so for him to joke around about things like sex (or the lack of it) made them feel as if he were taking them into his confidence.

Aside from being the first black male to graduate from Carroll, Fuller's duality also came from being an athlete, from being the only black on the team. By going to Carroll he had crossed over to the other side, and even though that did not mean he had suddenly become a different person, he did take on "some of the characteristics of the place" in order to survive. "It's just like when you deal with us historically, people say we are an African people. We are an African people, but we are an African-American people because you can't be away from someplace for three hundred and fifty-some-odd years and not take on some of the characteristics of the place that you live in."

But what characteristics did he bring to Carroll, somebody wanted to know, what did he fall back on?

As he had said to them months earlier, when they were talking about Shelby Steele, he had this unerring belief that he was going to make it, that it never even occurred to him that he wouldn't. And the crucible for that belief was formed by his mother and stepfather, by the guys he grew up with—guys who went on to accomplish things, guys he was still friendly with to this day. "I didn't go to Carroll with a strong sense of black history and culture in the classic sense. I went there with 'I grew up in Hillside, I played on a championship basketball team, I had supreme confidence in my ability as a ballplayer, in my ability as a student.' I have been president of every student body of every school that I have been in, including that one."

In order to dispel any notion that he had been unusually blessed, he told them that in his opinion you didn't have to be bright to learn, but you did have to be willing to work hard. "If you would think about yourselves today as compared to where you were a year ago before we started this class, there would be some of you that would say that the things that you are talking about and analyzing now you couldn't do then. It is no magic. It is simply me getting on you to read the books. Once you read them, you can come back and discuss them. It's practice. Any basketball player gets better from practice. If you want to shoot left-handed, you go out and practice left-handed. Then what happens at a certain point in the game is you do it without even thinking about it. It has become you." There were days when he was working on his Ph.D., though, when he would go into the library and sit down and pray that the learning could happen through osmosis, wish "that this information would just come out of these books and penetrate this permeable membrane but just don't make me have to open these books. If people say that learning is fun, well, it is fun, but it is also hard work. There is no way around it. How to put it all together? Somewhere along the line, someone has convinced us that we can't do this."

During the civil rights movement, there was hope, hope that was tangible, hope that was visible, hope that manifested itself in *change*. "Now,"

Fuller said, "you're not seeing those kinds of visible changes." What you saw instead were young people who either believed that they couldn't go to college or that, if they went, they probably wouldn't graduate; young people who didn't have proper mentors to guide them, to help them see themselves as future taxpayers, contributors to the community. What you saw instead was a community "just living for today and not for tomorrow," a community geared toward immediate gratification, to living on the come.

There was a lot of talk about respect at Commando that day, about how if a person had no respect for himself, how could you possibly expect him to respect you, that if a person placed zero value on his life, how could you expect him to value yours?

"How do we produce a whole generation that don't have any respect for themselves or anybody else?" The woman asking the question was Rose Massey. She was in her early fifties and was working closely with Fuller on his educational reforms, was part of the Crusade to Save Our Children. That she was generalizing, that she was guilty of doing the same thing so many whites did in talking about blacks, undercut for me what she was saying, but what she had to say was valuable nonetheless. She talked of families in which both parents were working, of adults not being around to "impart values," of so many single-parent households, of the community as a whole abandoning its collective responsibility to rear children; one of the fallouts of all this was a huge number of teenage pregnancies, of kids raising kids. Another woman said that rap music and MTV and movies like *Boyz N the Hood* didn't help things either. A young male blamed the media for glamorizing everything, for making material things seem so important that everything paled by comparison, for distorting your thinking to such an extent that your pair of sneakers were cool only until someone informed you that they weren't. But having the coolest pair carried a danger—the danger of losing your life.

"I think self-worth has to be taught early in age," Zo said. "I didn't have to throw rocks at cars, I didn't have to steal Johnny's big wheel. There were substitutes. I was proud of what I had."

"But you had two parents, right?" a woman said.

Not the whole time, he said. From nine on.

Jerry had a different story to tell. "I had a community upbringing. Grandfather, grandmother, lady around the corner catch you doing something wrong, they get you. I was told all that, and I did it all anyway. It didn't matter. I wasn't like Edmund Perry as far as my grades were concerned, but I was considered the one who would be the first one to go to college in my family, to do this, to do that. I disappointed a lot of people. I'm not blaming it on nobody but Jerry. I'm saying I don't care how early you start talking to kids, the street is something that unless you've been there, it is hard to understand. Once the street get a hold of you, it's hard to get it out of your system. It's a constant battle every day for these kids to try to deal with what's going on in the street and what's going on at home and then go and deal with what's going on at school."

"That's what I'm talking about," Zo said. "The streets getting a hold of you. I'm not saying I wasn't still in the streets, I just wasn't doing what you were doing."

"I ain't going to lie," Jerry shot back, "I was doing it."

Everybody laughed when Jerry said that. But when the laughing stopped, Fuller reminded them how important it was not "to approach this stuff in an antiseptic, abstract way," but to know precisely what it was these kids were dealing with. "If you're a student at South and bus over there from the North Side, and you're not a member of the Black Gangster Disciples, when you get up in the hallway, there the Latin Kings are. They associate *anybody that's black* with being a Black Gangster Disciple. Whether you are or not, you don't have any business being over here on our territory. Thursday we had to order buses for all of the athletes that live on the North Side because we are afraid if they come out of practice and go to catch a bus to go home, they may get killed. . . . We just had a sawed-off shotgun found at Washington on Friday. Teachers have been threatened, aides have been threatened. We had a kid follow an aide home and rape her at knifepoint two weeks ago. . . . We have a situation up at King, where one of the basketball players has been threatened. Everybody's nervous about having him on the team because with the way that people are functioning today, you could be at a game or practice and somebody may bust up in there to get this dude and shoot anybody else that's around. That level of pressure is on kids each day and every day."

I had been at Rufus King myself two days earlier, spending time with a teacher who had grown up in the suburbs, a young woman of twenty-eight who had gained a lot of respect among students in the short time she'd been there, partly as a result of having "passed" whatever rites of passage had been devised for her, and there had been many. When she first came to King in January of 1991, she was the fifth history teacher her students had had since September. The fact that she finished the year and returned for another one only enhanced her stature in the discerning, untrusting eyes of her students.

It may have enhanced her stature, but it didn't prepare her for the answer she got when she asked one of them how his Christmas vacation had gone.

"I lived," he said without expression, staring through her.

As the conversation continued on about violence in the schools and about what measures Fuller was taking to prevent it (handheld metal detectors, surprise weapons checks, school security guards), about how unrealistic it was to think schools could be islands of safety when the streets surrounding them were not, a different dialogue about violence was taking place in Washington. The Bush Administration had been working hard on something called the Federal Violence Initiative. At its core was the notion that violence—specifically, violence among youth—had to be viewed and ministered to as a public health problem, as something that could be prevented if such youth were identified early enough and given proper therapy. This was a highly flammable area, so much so that the initiative itself soon collapsed as a result of remarks made by one Frederick Goodwin to the National Mental Health Advisory Council. He was talking about monkeys and how sexual they were and how males killed other males, and suddenly he was saying that "maybe it isn't just a careless use of the word when people call certain areas of certain cities jungles." There was mention of "genetic factors" that inclined human beings toward violence and there was the suggestion that one possible way to target such individuals was through "biological markers." With those remarks, especially coming during a presidential election year, the Federal Violence Initiative officially ended and Goodwin was reassigned.

When Tom Brophy talked about the inner city of Milwaukee as an urban jungle, I didn't associate his remarks with racism in any way. Perhaps I should have, but I took them for what I believed they were—a sad commentary on both the amount of senseless violence that occurred nearly every day and the conditions under which many people lived. If Robert Wright (of the *New Yorker*) is correct, though, Frederick Goodwin was an unfortunate victim of "a vestigial feature of the American liberal mind: its undiscerning fear of the words 'genetic' and 'biological,' and its wholesale hostility to Darwinian explanations of behavior." According to Wright, "comparing violent inner-city males to monkeys isn't necessarily racist, or even necessarily right wing." It was, as almost everything to do with race is, more complicated than that; it couldn't be reduced to one single answer. What the dilemma of violence, the "root causes" for it, essentially revolved around was the age-old argument of nature versus nurture, of eugenics versus environment, now being presented with a fresh spin, supplied by the "new" field of evolutionary psychology, the spin being that the answer lay somewhere in between. Frederick Goodwin, Wright wrote, was unfairly crucified for his remarks. "He was right to compare violent inner-city males—or any other violent human males—to nonhuman primates (though he exaggerated the incidence of actual murder among such primates). The bad news is that his Violence Initiative, in failing to pursue that insight, in clinging to the view of violence as pathology, was doomed to miss a large part of the picture; the bulk of inner-city violence will probably never be explained by reference to head injuries, poor nutrition, prenatal exposure to drugs, and bad genes. If violence is a public-health problem, it is so mainly in the sense that getting killed is bad for your health. . . .

"The point to bear in mind is simply that less eerie, more traditionally liberal prescriptions for urban violence continue to make sense after we've looked at black teen-agers as animals—which, after all, is what human beings are. The view from evolutionary psychology suggests that one way to reduce black violence would be to make the inner cities places where young men have nonviolent routes to social status and the means and motivation to follow them. Better-paying jobs, and better public schools, for example, wouldn't hurt. Oddly enough, thinking about genes from a Darwinian standpoint suggests that inner-city teen-agers are victims of their environment."

If Michael McGee was aware of these discussions, he didn't let on as he held a shotgun high above his head at a press conference on Martin Luther King Day and said that if he were defeated in the April election, violence was going to come to Milwaukee sooner than 1995. He, of course, had threatened this before, but he did manage to accomplish something specific this time with his increasingly tiresome antics: his threat helped to escalate racial tensions at Bell Middle School, where, as they had at Marshall three months earlier, rumors of a White Kill Day kept students home in droves.

By the time Michael McGee made the trip west to Mt. Carmel Lutheran the following Sunday (his appearance there, exactly one week after Fuller's, had been scheduled for quite some time) the parishioners, who filled every seat, didn't quite know what to expect. Other than on television, this was the first time most of them had seen the controversial alderman.

He had come with his wife, Penelope, with whom he "put together" twenty-two years before, and two of his sons: his namesake, who was running for mayor, and Alexander, who was doubling as his bodyguard. He clearly wanted this congregation to know he was a family man and that he had a strong belief in the Lord, that he and his mother had come to Milwaukee in 1964 from Mississippi, had come "for the brighter tomorrow and for things to be right. For everybody to be together. She wanted us to be in integrated schools and all of this." That was why he found it strange, he said, that all these years later, Alexander attended an all-black school. Things were so segregated that he sometimes found himself wondering "if people think there are two Gods. A white God and a black God. Does the same God hear the poor people down here beg at night before they go to bed about having another meal and when are we going to get a job, and when is my daddy going to get this and when am I going to be able to do that? People think that God just sits there and hears all this and he don't never answer our prayers. He just answers other people's prayers." What McGee told people, he said, was that the time was coming when God was going to answer theirs too, "'cause there is only one God no matter what people believe."

And no matter what people believed, no matter what talk they might have heard about his hating white people, he, Michael McGee, truly loved all people. It was the situation black people lived in that he hated—a situation that he blamed on blacks just as much as he did on whites, he said, because if you went back and looked at slavery ("the root of the problem") it was blacks who "sold us out in the first place to get us over here . . . there weren't enough Europeans to go into Africa" to round up as many slaves as were eventually shipped. But as far as whom he liked or didn't like, he said there were "a lot more black people that I don't like than white 'cause I don't know a lot of you."

Everyone laughed at that, though it was more a laugh of nervousness than a laugh of ease.

He talked about his time in Vietnam and he talked about his time in the original Black Panther Party. The Panthers did good things, he insisted, serving breakfast for kids, operating free health centers, running free buses to prisons so that families could see their loved ones. (The Panthers also did a lot of bad things, thuglike things, things that were slow in coming to light, but McGee naturally did not speak of those.) And he talked about what he called the hellhole he lived in, a neighborhood in which 90 percent of the people who lived there didn't want to live there but had nowhere else to go. These were the people he had been elected to represent, but now his district had been unfairly redrawn in such a way that it resembled Rubik's cube, he said, had been redrawn so that "I'm really only forty percent of the people that elected me."

McGee had been relatively gentle and solicitous and funny up to this point, but he was now reverting to form, saying how he had helped Norquist get elected and, to show his gratitude, Norquist had double-crossed him; how Tom Donegan "got bought off" and should never have become Common Council president; how they needed to understand that in politics "things are decided before politicians get to those little so-called token meetings that you all go to, that you're talking about I'm never at." He then read to them something that the Reverend Leon Sullivan (longtime member of General Motors' board of directors and founder of the Opportunities Industrialization Centers) had said in 1988 to a group of "suburbeans" not unlike themselves:

> If we do not ease the problems of the inner cities and deal soon with the problems of homelessness, the drug-addicted, the unemployed, and the poorly educated, with the helplessness and hopelessness that grows and festers every day, within three years at least thirty American cities will explode. We must launch a collective effort to steer this nation from the tragedy of urban violence. There must be a collective effort to avert this disaster because the conditions that people face now and the increasing number being affected will make the rise of the sixties look like a picnic three years from now. We are a crisis-motivated

country. We only move by crisis. Society did not feel threatened by the cities until the cities were set on fire. . . . In three years I say we will have that crisis if we do not act now. I assure you, trouble is on the way.

Michael McGee, of course, had been saying the same thing, and Sullivan had been an inspiration to him. But McGee's rhetoric was over-heated and in your face, filled with allusions to Martin Luther King and how when he was alive "nobody cared you-know-what for him" and how his dream was never more than that and that he, Michael McGee, was wide awake and didn't allow himself to dream because dreaming wasn't reality. Reality was that his kids didn't want to come to Mt. Carmel with him that morning "'cause they said you all were going to hang us," but not him, not Michael McGee. He feared no man, he insisted, his courage coming from the Twenty-third Psalm, that part about fearing no evil. If he had to liken himself to anything, he said, if there was one image of himself that he wanted to leave the congregation with, it was that of a rattlesnake. "You hear the rattles," he explained. "The snake is rattling 'cause he's telling you something. The snake don't bite first and rattle after; he rattles and he tries to get everyone's attention and say, 'Hey, don't come too close, 'cause I am a snake and I will bite you.' I'm rattling and I try to communicate, but most people don't have the opportunity to hear me in context."

He thanked the congregation for giving him the opportunity to speak and the pastor thanked him for coming, for giving them "perhaps a little different look at Michael McGee than what we normally see and normally hear," and then he asked McGee, on behalf of the congregation, the question that you would expect him to ask: "Was what happened this week, with the brandishing of the gun, was that just some game playing on your part, or are you serious about this business of violence?"

McGee was equivocal in his reply. No, he couldn't say he was not serious, but he was trying to give people "an opportunity to head it off." As for what happened earlier in the week, "I could have been on the roof shooting that shotgun at someone versus just showing someone a gun." In the world of Michael McGee, everything was relative—or so it seemed. Besides, he pointed out, he wasn't at City Hall when he did this; he was at militia headquarters, using the gun as "a prop," planting the notion in everyone's mind, "before the reality does strike you. . . ."

"So you are saying, if the——," the pastor came back, but McGee broke in.

"If I get pushed into that position, then I have to. I'm not going to be a sissy."

"And you're feeling that would be the way to accomplish the goals that you have for this community and for your people?"

Look what happened in Kuwait, McGee said. What did America do, and what had America done in the past? When politics failed, there was usually war. "There comes a point where all that early gospel of Jesus begins to wane and you get into the Final Days. . . . I swear to God, right here in this church, that if I have to do what I have to do, I'm going to do it. Someone has to take a stand sometime."

But what specific programs did he have that could create the jobs that would put off this threat of violence?

"I knew you were going to ask that," McGee said, aware that few people there, if any, would know that in 1989 he had spearheaded the Black Community Emergency Relief Task Force, a wide-ranging group of people who came up with nearly forty recommendations. One proposal had to do with recycling, with hiring as many as two thousand people to sort through the city's garbage each day and pull out all the items that could be recycled. Another public works proposal had to do with lead and the degree to which lead poisoning was a problem in many inner-city buildings, with the need to "rebuild our infrastructure." A third idea was to create the position of "police aide," unarmed neighborhood security people who could "walk around with walkie-talkies and work with the police and escort seniors." He told them about his idea of having four kids from Ethan Allen (a reform school) be put into a home with an unemployed black man in charge (as "a twenty-four-hour father") and he explained the "savings" of such a plan: instead of spending twenty-five thousand dollars to house each kid at the reform school, you pay the man twenty-five thousand, spend another twenty-five thousand fixing up the house, and have fifty thousand left over. (He neglected to say anything about feeding the kids, other costs, and how precisely they were to be supervised.) There was no rehabilitation going on at places like Ethan Allen or prisons like Waupun. In McGee's opinion, prisoners only came back hardened and angry, ready to rob, rape, and kill again. "What is rehabilitation?" McGee asked rhetorically. "You got to be habilitated first."

The pastor pointed out that all of McGee's talk about recycling sounded great—except for one thing. The only part of recycling that had turned a profit was aluminum cans. "If you're going to create all of these jobs, there's going to be a tremendous amount of money necessary to support it. Where is the money coming from? People out in this area are already paying forty percent of their income in the form of taxes. Federal, state, property taxes, sales taxes. There has got to be a limit—"

"You're right about that," McGee shot back. "And you know where the money would come from? The money would come from the fact that we're already spending your money and it's not being effective. . . . It's a bust now because no one is doing it right." Instead of simply burying a plastic milk carton, he said, think in terms of the energy that went into the making of the carton and how that energy could be used to try to make something out of it, to melt all the plastic down and perhaps produce a plastic chair. He was clearly appealing to their sense of ingenuity, to the ability Americans had always had to "do things that other people couldn't do."

Speaking of doing things, the pastor wondered if it was true that he had basically decided not to work with any of the "really good" community-based agencies in Milwaukee?

"I'm burnt-out on agencies, okay," he said, getting irritated. "I've been out here twenty-one years. I've worked with every agency. . . . We've made charity an institution. . . . TV6 brags about 'We've had this food program for fifteen years.' It breaks my heart. Little kids that never knew something but somebody throwing in a can of peanut butter for them."

"I understand what you are saying about that," the pastor said, "but for example the Next Door Foundation, working with families and young people in the area of Thirtieth and Wisconsin, doing wonderful ministry. What do you think about those kinds of agencies? We're not talking about giving anything, we're talking about education, we're talking about books, we're talking about lots of wonderful things within families and communities."

Agencies like Next Door (whose current building, he said, he had helped them get) had limited resources. What they could accomplish was only "a drop in the bucket." Only the federal government could deal with all that was required. "We need a real tidal wave down there, not what Reagan called the 'trickle-down theory.'"

Naturally, the pastor tried to end on an upbeat note, saying that his sense was "we're not so far off in terms of our basic hopes and dreams for all of our community." He also said that many people had phoned, after the incident with the shotgun, to say the church should cancel his appearance. "But I'm glad we had you here and I hope you will trust us. . . . There are people out here who care ... and I hope that you might ring our bell and that we can work together."

"People have got to remember," McGee said, "that being an American means more than just sitting on your butt, waving a flag. It means being able to understand different opinions, being able to accept people for what they are, and also being able to understand right from wrong, and most people don't understand that. . . . But we aren't that far apart. If I thought we were that far apart, I wouldn't even be here today. I'm willing to work with anyone." And then he paused for a moment, smiled beatifically, and said, "I hope that your church is not firebombed tonight for having me."

THIRTY-SIX

I f Kristie Jorgenson were to pinpoint the source of her anger toward blacks over all the years she had lived in Milwaukee, it would be the three years she had attended Daniel Webster Middle School, right around the time that busing had begun. She was thirty now, had just become a vice president at the company where she worked, and was a graduate of Carroll College. She had been one of the people who had come out to hear Howard Fuller and Michael McGee at Mt. Carmel Lutheran and she had invited me to her home on two different occasions that January.

When she first heard Fuller speak five or six years earlier, out at Carroll, she did not have a favorable impression of him. In fact, she viewed him as being very racist, very biased, your basic troublemaker, a threat to her way of life. That view, she admitted, had much to do with his involvement in the Ernest Lacy case, a case in which the cops, according to her father (who was one), had been given a raw deal. There was a lot of tension in Milwaukee during that time, she recalled, tension she resented, tension she had blamed Fuller for (partly because it tarnished her excitement over Milwaukee's being in the World Series). But what she realized now, she said, was that much of her impression of him, of his apparent stance that white people owed black people, had been "filtered through other sources" and that something essential had been lost in translation. She had not liked that special legislation had to be passed in order for Fuller to become superintendent, but she had been impressed by him since he took the job and was now saying how important it was to encounter someone face-to-face, to hear *all* of what he had to say, and to not rely on news accounts and sound bites. (That she had also heard all of what he said at Carroll was not something she remarked on.) She told him after his talk at Mt. Carmel that she genuinely believed in everything he had said. She even told herself that if her son, Jack, were of school age, she and her husband would send him to MPS. But what she didn't tell Fuller was that there was a big gap in her mind from what he was saying and what she believed to be going on in the classroom, especially since her own experiences had been so negative, and that she would have to be convinced things had changed.

"I like to think that I'm not prejudiced or racist or anything like that," she said as we sat down to dinner, joined by her husband, a transplant from Minnesota, her brother, her best friend Darlene, and their spouses. "I'm sure that some of my opinions and maybe some of my actions are. And if they are, and if anybody ever says that I am, I'll say that I've earned that."

This was a new form of calculation I hadn't heard so far—or at least heard expressed in that manner.

She had earned her racism, she said, because of what she had gone through at Daniel Webster. In 1973, the school was brand-new, situated in an all-white "near suburban neighborhood" not far from where she lived. On the inside, though, life was far from idyllic. She was scared to go to the bathroom and she couldn't understand why people threw food in the lunchroom, why they screamed and yelled, why they beat each other up. By "people" and "they" she meant black kids, and by the time she left Webster, "I ended up hating black people. . . .

"I felt like I got ripped off in my education. In a fifty-minute class period, at least twenty minutes were spent on discipline. Kids just bouncing off the walls." But half of her classes, she revealed, were "SA classes, superior ability classes, which was all white kids. And you'd have these classes and it was fine—you learned and it was okay." What, she wanted to know, was a seventh-, eighth-, or ninth-grader supposed to think when you got an education when surrounded by white kids and you got total chaos when surrounded by blacks? Race was the answer in her opinion. Race.

It clearly bothered her to say this, but she wanted to be honest with me, she said. It bothered her to say this because her father's beat had been the inner city and he had always told her and her brother that 95 percent of the people who lived there were good people, that all of the problems were created by the other five, but being at Webster had made her seriously doubt that. She had seen a beautiful building "literally destroyed by vandalism," had seen a principal display the same amount of fear that she had ("And they knew it, so they got away with everything"), and she had gotten angry that so many kids who were entitled to free lunches were dressed far better than she was and had more money in their pockets. As if that wasn't confusing enough, that some kids had a surplus of free lunch tickets and were audacious enough to *sell* them was more than she could bear. To witness that and to hear her father complain about how many people would roll up to the welfare office with Illinois tags just so they could illegally collect a second welfare check—surely, she implied, appealing to my sense of reason, I could see how she had earned her prejudice and racism.

Her friend Darlene said that she too had earned her racism, but that hers had come about more in high school, at Washington. Darlene had been the head of the drill team and had been told that she had to have five blacks on the squad "whether they could drill or not." And when one of the five refused to drill at all, Darlene had told her that if she wouldn't drill, she had to leave. "It wasn't because she was black," Darlene insisted, "it was because she wasn't doing what she was supposed to do." The girl wound up bringing her mother to school and, in Darlene's opinion, trying to turn the whole incident "into a big race issue, where it wasn't a race issue. It was an attitude issue, like 'I want this on a silver platter.'"

Another time, Darlene was up for a lead part in a play and the teacher was going to decide between her and a black girl. The black girl got the part, which, because the girl was such a great singer, would have been fine with Darlene—were it not for the fact that the teacher, for some reason, took her aside and said that she would have given the part to Darlene but couldn't *because* she was white.

What angered her the most about school integration (and Kristie and her brother agreed) was the coercive nature of it, of being forced to associate with blacks and of blacks being forced to associate with them. That anger didn't really dissipate, she said, until she came into contact with "good black people."

And who were they? What qualities did they possess that fit them into that category?

"One is a fifty-five-year-old black woman who has come out and said to me, 'You know, I'm so sick and tired of these young black people trying to get everything handed to them. I know what happened to us two hundred years ago. I know that we've been oppressed. I know this. But it's about time to quit blaming the whites because it's not the white people's fault anymore. It's their own.'"

The other person she was thinking of was a black man who was in the same singing group that Darlene belonged to. They were having pizza one night after a performance and in the course of the evening he told Darlene that, much as he hated to admit it, "there are not that many good black young men out there right now." She was surprised by his saying this, but he told her not to be, that there were other black men who felt the same as he did.

Darlene wasn't unusual in feeling this way. Blame and guilt are not exactly things that anybody wants to be on the receiving end of for very long. Absolution, no matter when it comes or what form it takes, is always sweet.

But Darlene was also willing to admit that her school experience—what Tom Donegan had called "this experiment"—had, in retrospect, made her less fearful about the world. "Now I look back and I think, I walked out of there, and a friend of mine can't even walk through a group of black people without getting nervous, thinking she'll be jumped. And I don't get that, I just don't get that feeling. I can ride on a city bus and not get afraid, and maybe that's to my disadvantage. I drove down Center Street with another friend of mine and she was scared to death."

She was talking the talk of survival, just as Donegan had done in talking about his kids. She had "survived" Washington High School, earning her degree and her racism, and was pleased to report that, in some ways, she was better equipped to deal with the many things life invariably threw in your path. The way she looked at it, everything was relative. She hadn't allowed herself to get pushed around, whereas her sister had been constantly harassed by a black guy who wanted to turn her out and become her pimp. She accepted her father's racism (he had earned his by being a meter reader in the inner city), but she was honest enough to point out that it wasn't only blacks who abused the welfare system, that she had a cousin who abused it as well.

THE TRIAL OF JEFFREY DAHMER was beginning that month and as we sat around the table, there was one thing that Kristie and Jeff and Darlene and Joel agreed on: they had become "desensitized" to what was happening in the inner city. That when they heard about yet another murder, they were less likely to focus on who the victim was than on the fact that it was the murder—or murders—of the day. For them, it had become generic. In the case of Dahmer's victims, the fact that Jeff or Joel or Darlene's husband couldn't even imagine themselves being in a situation where they could be lured to a stranger's apartment for the purpose of being photographed made the whole incident seem as far removed from their own lives as possible, as if it had unfolded on Pluto. All of them resented that racism was considered an element in the murders, and that Dahmer's attorney was emphasizing it in regard to jury selection. They resented that Milwaukee's good name was being soiled. A city that donated lots of money to the Jerry Lewis Telethon each year deserved better treatment. That was how Jeff saw it.

As far as Kristie was concerned, she was sick and tired of "everything being race." In fact, she had so many of the symptoms of race fatigue she could have been a walking advertisement for Shelby Steele. Not long before, she was trying to fill an entry-level position at the company where she worked. She was looking for someone right out of school, someone hoping to be a graphic artist. She advertised in the newspaper, received over a hundred résumés, and screened out everyone who had lots of experience. Whenever anyone phoned, she didn't even ask their name; she simply said that she was going to make a decision in a week.

"I selected somebody," she recalled, "and it ended up being a white person, somebody who had graduated from UWM a year ago, and had some kind of experience. In about a week, somebody from—and I don't remember the organization, but it was some black movement organization—called and said they were gonna file a suit against my company because I didn't hire an applicant because the person was black.

"I went through everything, and I didn't even know who they were talking about. I found the résumé, I had never interviewed the person or anything. I looked at the résumé, it didn't say that the person was black on the résumé, but they said that this woman had called me during the week, and that I could tell by her voice that she was black. Now, I had not asked any names so it was really anonymous. She had thirteen years' experience in this field and I explained that I passed by this résumé because it was thirteen years' experience and yet they accused me of not hiring her because she was black. . . . It's incidents like that that contribute to the whole attitude of everybody. Of me being more prejudiced and racist and everything else."

Why, she wanted to know, were people "so quick to accuse employers or whoever of racism"?

Actually, without fully realizing it, she wound up answering her own question. Two days earlier, her company finally hired a black person (Kristie did the hiring), the first one ever, and she was telling me how amazed she was that it had taken so long.

Why, I asked, did she think it hadn't happened before?

"Well," she said tentatively, "I was horrified to find out it's because of the attitudes of the people that were in charge."

Given that she considered herself a prejudiced person (albeit one who had earned that status), "horrified" seemed both strong and disingenuous.

Nevertheless, she had broken the ice, so to speak, had ventured into uncharted territory. Why?

Because she believed in hiring the best person for a job, regardless of color.

But, as it turned out, that was not the only reason.

There was a federal contract she was hoping to obtain and, she knew, this would help her. It was, as John Norquist loved to say, a shining example of "enlightened self-interest."

The position in question was a clerical one, entry level. But this time, Kristie did the screening in person. She had gone through Job Service and they had sent her "a lot of good, qualified applicants." She was looking for someone with "a great attitude" and the person she settled on had one.

But what, I asked, was the person going to find once she got there? Was she going to be accepted?

"I think that eighty to ninety percent of the people will accept her," Kristie said. "Partly because she's coming into a job where people are just waiting for somebody to help them. I know there are some people there who are gonna be extremely upset about it, and are not gonna accept her, and will probably go so far as to try and cause undermining types of problems."

What those things were she would not say.

WHEN OUR DISCUSSION TURNED to Michael McGee, she said that as glad as she was to also see and hear him in person, she continued to have "a real problem with somebody who thinks that being a sniper to innocent people on the expressway is gonna solve anything." Her real worry, though (as it had been Maron and Georgette Alexander's), was that his threats would incite others to act. "He does have good ideas and he does want good things for his people," she said, "but I still don't go along with the way that he's going about it. I don't have any solutions or answers for him. But it was good to hear him say that he doesn't want to live in the rathole that he lives in. Most of the people that live in the neighborhood where he lives, they don't want to be there. But they're struggling to get out and trying to make it better. I feel real bad about that. I really do. . . . It's a sad situation, and I don't have any answers, but I just don't think that violence is the right way to do it."

"Did you have a chance," I asked, "to talk with other people who were there?"

"Just a little bit. Most of the people in that crowd have grown up in a white suburban neighborhood and have no idea of what it's like to even walk the streets of the neighborhood that Mike McGee lives in. Of course his plans sound great and wonderful, and how terrible it is that no one helps them, but I don't think that the people in our congregation have an ounce of the experience needed to connect with what he was saying."

Without being aware of it, Kristie Jorgenson had supplied a partial answer to the question Pete Stolz had asked me five months before, the question about why it was that a place like Milwaukee was so segregated when everybody was bursting with good intentions.

THIRTY-SEVEN

The good intentions of Tom Donegan had finally reached their nadir: he had crashed into a proverbial wall, and he was changing course.

In the same office where I had gone to visit him one year earlier, where he had peered out the window and talked about how he had lobbied his siblings not to move from the city but to no avail, where he had talked about wanting his adopted black children to experience *all* of life, he was now telling me that he had had enough.

"The promoters of divisiveness," as he called them, "seem to have gained more credibility among many poor black people and a certain legitimacy in the mainstream press and that scares the hell out of me. Jerrel Jones, the publisher of the *Courier*, Mike McGee, the 'militia commandant,' Walter Farrell, who writes a column for the *Courier*—more and more of them portray themselves as a spokesperson for the black community, and more and more they're empowering themselves by creating a belief that we're inalterably divided, we're inalterably different, that no matter what happens the best interpretation is that whites are always going to fight blacks and we might as well accept that, and the only way to respond to that is to fight back. I thought we put the lie to that with H. Rap Brown and a lot of people who were just less visionary than a Martin Luther King, that it would all kind of sift out and the bigger vision would last and the smaller things would just be bursts of flame and would go away. And now it seems almost the opposite is true: the Howard Fullers are put down, *you know he's not really black because now he's made it, he's not really black because he's listening to whites.* So that really depresses me, and I think the impact of that kind of talk is spurring the kind of David Duke mentality that's around too. It's like they're feeding on one another, empowering one another, each legitimizes itself by the other. It gives coalition builders, integrationists, less of a foothold, less of a place to go.

"The second depressing thing," he said gravely, underscoring something he had said the year before, "is that I see more kids who are poor and black who have no sense of respecting an adult because he is an adult, more a sense that I'm an enemy in the world because I'm white. Just more profanity in language and more ugliness in actions."

He was beginning to feel, he said, like a man named William Stringfellow, who wrote a book in 1964 called *My People Is the Enemy,* an autobiographical account of being trained (like Donegan) as a lawyer, someone who believed, in Donegan's words, that "the only choice is to fight the plague and the plague is racism and we can't just talk about it, we have to face it." Stringfellow was originally from Massachusetts but was living in Harlem at the time of which he wrote. "Eventually people in Harlem found out that he was a lawyer," Donegan said. "He began serving the community and learning from the community . . . but at the end of the book he gave up and left, realizing that 'my people are the enemy who have created this.'"

"I feel like I'm at the point that he was sometimes," Donegan said. "It's now 1992 and I hope there's energy in some people to keep doing the hands-on battle." As for him, he needed to "rest for a while." He had lived in Sherman Park, he had shopped there, he had taken his laundry to a black-owned store—all in an effort, an effort he now saw as futile, "to show that we can bridge these gaps" between black and white.

What form, I asked him, would this resting for a while take?

He might move to a different home "in a quieter area," he might even move out of Sherman Park. More than anything he felt sadness and disappointment that he hadn't been able to make more of a difference. "The poor are rougher, the poor are angrier, the poor see me as an enemy, and it's harder and harder to bridge that. . . . We cannot pretend that we are close enough and trusting enough with one another—and I hate it."

He was not only the victim of race fatigue, he was the victim of his own high expectations, his sixties-bred ideals. In the year since I had seen him, three people had been killed within two blocks of his house. His children were considered oddities in the neighborhood, not so much because they had white parents but because they used "correct English," a no-no on the streets, a sign that you were getting uppity, striving to be white. And it was to his children, he said, that he ultimately felt responsible. If he was determined that they experience all of life, that wouldn't happen if they weren't around to do it. That wasn't difficult for even an idealist to calculate.

But did he really think, I asked, that all his efforts over the past twenty-five years had been in vain?

No, he didn't. There were far more middle-class blacks than ever, "benefiting from changes we started in the sixties." Steeltech (in which the city was investing fourteen million dollars) was hiring minorities because federal contracts were tied to their doing so. More banks were being pressured to invest in black neighborhoods. Institutions like Marquette University and St. Joseph's Hospital finally had minority-recruiting requirements. The Central City Initiative was providing an opportunity for small, "otherwise unfundable" minority businesses to get started. He was saying all this and yet he still looked as if he had just learned he had a terminal illness. He looked that way because he worried that it was just a pittance—that whatever efforts were being made couldn't possibly keep pace "with all these unemployed people wandering around and killing one another," with what Bill Lawrence called "the forces of evil."

"I think there are very few people who realize what a crisis this city is in," he said. "The depression for me is here we are, we came through the sixties and we were challenging the system, and now we're running the system. . . . And even with us here now, in the prime of our lives with a cooperative mayor, with I think a more liberal racial climate than in the fifties, sixties, or seventies, we have not been able to move fast enough, to get people scared enough to change traditionally hidden racism and some blunt racism, so I guess I'm always frustrated by that."

But he was equally frustrated, as he had said earlier, by all the jockeying that went on in the black community, "all this 'I'll define who's black, I want control of the community needs, not you' stuff" that he saw as so detrimental. The civil rights movement may have resulted in a huge increase in the number of elected black officials, but their power was often concentrated, the pie to be fought over infinitely smaller. Given that, I could understand Donegan's frustration, but wondered at his naïveté—especially for someone who had become a politician.

The April election was less than a month away. He was not running (he was almost certain to become a children's court judge) but he had strong opinions about the chances of someone who was. There had been growing speculation that Michael McGee might lose. In what everyone seemed to view as a cynical gesture, he had done an about-face in February. One

month after holding up a shotgun and threatening to move up his deadline for violence in the event that he lost, he told Milwaukee that he was
officially disbanding the Black Panther Militia and would begin attending Common Council meetings again. This occurred just after the primary,
the results of which were closer than he would have liked.

"He has a good chance of being defeated," Donegan said. "I think
George Butler is going to win if he does his work out there." What that
entailed was being able not only to study McGee's record, but to speak
forcefully about its flaws, to "remind people of the difference between
what he says and what he's done." The ability of McGee and Walter
Farrell and what Donegan called "the gang" to create an image that
McGee was *the* spokesperson for the underclass, the *only* one effectively
challenging the power structure, and that if he wasn't in office the city
might not care about poor blacks at all was an ability not to be underes-
timated, Donegan said. An ability that translated into making someone
who was black and wanted to vote against McGee out to be someone who
was weak, lacking in courage, a copout. This was McGee's genius, if
genius was the proper word. "I think there will be some people who would
vote for Mike against Moses."

What Donegan struggled mightily to understand, though, was this:
"Why aren't there more people out there saying, 'None of this means
anything'? He says, 'I'm going to shoot people,' then he says, 'I love everyone.' He says, 'I'm going to form a militia and we're going to do neighborhood patrols,' and he's never done neighborhood patrols. Nobody ever calls
him on anything. That's what shocks me. He said he's disbanding the militia and coming back for Common Council meetings. So why am I going
through all this trouble of doing the zoning and development hearing?
Because Mike McGee resigned from the committee, so I'm serving in his
place. We're all doing his work for him. We did Steeltech for him, did the
minority contracting requirements for the city. Everything we do it's
because he's not here and yet people buy into this lie he's got them
believing—that he's the only one who cares about the central city. Actually,
all he cares about is Mike McGee."

"You seem pretty down," I said casually, stating the obvious.

"Well, when you get onto this theme, yeah. I don't think this country is doing very well. . . . I know how I sometimes come out as 'God, he

must live this totally depressing life with no hope.' It's not true, but when I get down to the bottom line of how we're doing on race relations, I don't see many positive signs, or not enough positive signs."

"Do you think the city is doing as much as it can," I asked, "given the fact that there's hardly any money coming from Washington?"

"Well, that's a good question. We are strapped in terms of direct financial relief. Cities don't have money. We don't have a tax base that we can tax our own people. Studies show that the city's personal income, on average, is fifty percent of the personal income of the eighteen suburbs around us. *Fifty percent*—and yet we support the total network of social service needs. We can't keep taxing people because we'll tax them out, but we could do much more in terms of building hope and building coalitions and bringing private money in here, even if you have to bring them to their knees to come in here. . . . So what do we have? We have Mike McGee on one hand and John Norquist on the other. Neither one inspires me to anything hopeful."

Had Norquist been an improvment over the previous administration, the twenty-eight-year reign of Mr. Mayor, Henry Maier?

"John Norquist has done a lot of things: he's hired well, he has a good sense of what a city should be. He's not anyone who inspires people. We have a few inspiring people in this community. Howard Fuller is one of them. . . . It's not just a matter of money. It's moral leadership and charisma."

A few days earlier, Bill Clinton had won the Illinois primary, and I was curious to know what Donegan thought of him, whether he was at all excited about his possibly becoming president.

No, not at all. He thought Clinton was "a decent man," but not his idea of a president, not a fitting legacy to JFK. If he were to make Jesse Jackson his running mate, Donegan said, he might feel more enthusiastic.

But one of the things that seemed to work for Clinton in Illinois, I pointed out, was his decision to take a biracial stance, to try somehow to attract both blacks and blue-collar whites, to be after unity, not divisiveness.

Maybe, he said, he needed to focus on Clinton more. Coalition building, after all, had always seemed the right way to go—at least to him. But for now, as he said earlier, there seemed less running room for someone like himself, and besides, he had really lost the energy to do much other than try to figure out what had apparently become a pattern in his life, a pattern in which he came to every new job with fresh vigor and ideas, but found that after about eight years or so, he would reach a point where cynicism and bitterness would wear him out. It had happened to him as a legal services lawyer and it had happened to him as an alderman. And even though he hadn't taken the bench yet, he could see that being a children's court judge might just be more of the same.

THIRTY-EIGHT

Somehow it was oddly fitting that two hours after leaving Tom Donegan's office, I was going to see John Fitzgerald and Carvis Braxton. Oddly fitting in that Donegan was about to do what Fitzgerald had already done—flee Sherman Park for the good of his family. That was how each of them rationalized it. Donegan had given, in his opinion, far more than he had received, and his baffled anger of one year earlier had led to race fatigue and bitterness, to a deep loss of hope. The inherent problem with being a white knight—or, in this case, a white liberal—is this: If you don't feel appreciated, you feel resentful. It was a lesson that Tom Donegan hadn't counted on. John Fitzgerald, meanwhile, had learned, from the Beyond Racism project, that if he was going to live in white Bay View, it was incumbent on him to carry the things he had absorbed from the experience of the project and find some way to spread them throughout the neighborhood, to jolt people into looking at race differently. This, he was told, was even more important than anything he gained from his alliance with Carvis Braxton. The main work of ending racism had to be done by whites; this was the project's basic thrust. Since whites had the power, they were in a stronger position to bring about change—change in attitude, change in hiring practices, change in housing practices, change in banking practices—to enlighten each other, to prod others to face up to the fact, whether one cared about it or emphatically didn't, that racism still existed, that the civil rights movement hadn't eliminated it, that it was still, in many ways, as pernicious as ever, and that it was up to whites to do something about it. Andrew Hacker's *Two Nations* had just been published, and he had come to the gloomy conclusion that racism wasn't going to end because white America didn't want it to end. He saw it that starkly—which was just as starkly as Jerrel Jones saw it when he asked me to consider to whose benefit it was that these problems not be solved.

John Fitzgerald and Carvis Braxton couldn't and wouldn't accept this. Perhaps they were being as naïve as Tom Donegan had been for the longest time—or perhaps they hadn't reached the point, which many people seem to eventually arrive at, where you pull back in order to save yourself, not other people and not the world.

Earlier that day, at seven in the morning, Carvis had met me for breakfast at the Café Knickerbocker. Bearing in mind how much thought he and John had invested in trying to figure out a comfortable place for them to meet the previous autumn, I partly expected Carvis to bring that up, but he didn't. Right away, we realized that we had at least two things in common: he had five daughters and I was about to marry a woman with four (when I told him that, he roared, assuring me that I didn't "stand a chance"); and he was born not far from where my fiancée was, in western New York. His father had been only the second black born in the steel town of Lackawanna and had always told Carvis that he didn't know anything about color until he was eighteen years old. Carvis's grandfather worked for Bethlehem Steel, and everybody who worked there in the early part of the century pretty much lived together in company-built housing "like one big happy family."

Whether that was true or whether that was the way that Carvis's father chose to remember that period was unclear. Just as it was unclear to Carvis precisely what happened to his father at eighteen to change that perception.

Carvis's own experiences were different.

"Lackawanna was a big segregated town. We had a railroad track like a valley going right through the middle of the city . . . and when you went across the bridge, you knew what time it was. Whites completely ignored you." Throughout all his years of school, he never had a black teacher, "never had that experience of seeing a black professional." He was a good enough basketball player to get a scholarship to all-black Kentucky State, but that didn't make up for his not winning the Most Valuable Player award at Lackawanna High, an injustice that stuck with him. "I was a good basketball player and everybody knew it," he recalled. "I spent four years trying to excel and, in my way, trying to be accepted by whites. And the only way that I was being accepted—even being looked at as another human being—was because of my athletic prowess. And when it came time for a Most Valuable Player award in my senior year, the whole school knew I was, it was automatic, I was going to get it."

But he didn't. It went to a white kid, a kid who had even been kicked off the team for a while. Carvis quickly learned that nothing happened in Lackawanna unless Mr. Tom Joyce said it could. Joyce was the superintendent of schools and was the one who decided who got awards and who didn't. "Here you try to work the system, be a part of the system, and here's your reward," Carvis said, a pained expression on his face.

Part of trying to work and be part of the system for Carvis had come from shining shoes in nearby Buffalo. A lot of black kids Carvis knew from Albright Court, the public housing project where he grew up, wouldn't shine shoes because whites would mistreat them and make fun of them. Carvis viewed it differently. Not only was it a way to make money, but it was a way to learn about white folks. And what he learned was that if you dressed neatly and smiled, white folks would accept you "within their ground rules." While this might sound like a perfect description of an Uncle Tom, this knowledge gave Carvis "survival skills" that he had never stopped drawing on. Hearing Carvis say this reminded me of Jerrel Jones's telling me that blacks talked differently to whites than they did to each other. And hearing Carvis say this gave me the impression that he had long ago accepted that he would always exist in a white-run world.

On the contrary. He was essentially a separatist at heart. "The only way that we're going to change our community is for blacks to be in decision-making roles, and they have to interpret what needs to be done," he said. "It's always been something that's been inside of me—that if we're allowed to live by ourselves, make our own decisions, we can determine our destiny. Anytime that you have white folks part of that decision making, it's sort of watered down. And by being watered down, it usually comes out mushy."

Was that his way of saying that integration hadn't worked?

Yes, that's what he was saying. It hadn't worked, and it would never work, he said, because "this country has never allowed us to try it."

I knew what he meant. Blacks had made a lot of gains since the civil rights movement, but had not been given a full measure of dignity and respect. If there was one thing he would change more than any other, it would be to persuade every black who had moved away from the inner city to move back, to channel their considerable energies to bringing along the next generation. Like Michael McGee, he was tired of social service agencies that were nominally run by blacks but fueled by government money. He was weary of hearing them say how every summer was going to be longer and hotter than the previous one, all in an effort to get their slice of what Carvis called "guilt money" but often without a sound plan for how to use it. To give a black youth a summer job (in which he essentially didn't have to do anything) just to say you had given a black youth a summer job, as if it were the most monumental development in the world, as if he were learning a skill, or helping in some way to improve his community, struck Carvis as both pointless and dishonest. That was one of the reasons he preferred grass-roots organizing: you were taking a more direct route to the people who needed mobilizing.

He had learned how to organize through the Industrial Areas Foundation, the group that was started by Saul Alinsky, the academic-turned-activist, and his firm belief that blacks could best figure out what to do about their destiny was first instilled in him when he read Lerone Bennett's *Before the Mayflower* in the early sixties. For him, all the vacant land in the inner city, the land where houses once stood but were razed in the name of progress, was more than just vacant land. It was a painful symbol of the forty acres and a mule that was never fully given to the newly freed slaves. There was a passage in Bennett's book, he said, that was more eloquent on this topic than he could be, a passage he had underlined, a passage that talked of how white America should have allowed blacks to plow their own fields, to vote without interference. He wanted me to understand that he had "nothing against white folks," it was just that he had seen too often how whites used their "special privileges" when they were around blacks, and how blacks tended to act docile and sit back whenever a white person stood up to say anything, how they allowed whites to speak for them. "I have this strong desire," he explained, "this whole thing of empowering our folks who have something to say to say it without having it dictated and manipulated and influenced by the thinking of the best of your white American men. . . ."

He said that, and yet the most recent example he was thinking of had to do with a white nun in East St. Louis, Illinois. Carvis had spent a year and a half there, trying to help the black leadership in the city (which was 98.1 percent black) figure out how to improve things, and he was struck by how nearly everyone had come to a particular meeting thinking a certain way and then, as soon as the nun spoke, how everyone then seemed to gravitate toward her, as if whatever she said was The Word. But when the nun departed (in Carvis's view, having taken the classic liberal stance of "doing for them instead of allowing them to do for themselves"), they reverted to what they originally thought before they came into the meeting. It was this kind of sheep mentality that drove Carvis nuts, especially when the local paper quoted the nun and showed a picture of her leading a group of black pastors to City Hall, where they dumped a pile of garbage (the collection of which was one of the things that needed improving).

If this was his position—a position that seemed not to allow for the fact that a white person might just have a good idea and shouldn't be dismissed out of hand—then why on earth had he participated in the Beyond Racism project and entered into an alliance with John Fitzgerald?

There were a couple of reasons. He had a relationship with the Interfaith Conference of Greater Milwaukee, the group that sponsored the project, that went back nearly twenty years, to when he first came to town in 1974. But, more important, he had become "so overwhelmed with this racism thing" that he felt immobilized.

The irony of his comment took me aback, given that he was someone whose driving impetus in life was to mobilize others. And yet it also brought to mind a similar sentiment expressed by L. G. Shanklin-Flowers, as well as a remark that someone had made in Howard Fuller's class, about how racism had so numbed him that he felt like an elephant on a string.

"It's not a hate thing," he explained, "it's just that I got to a point where I'm fifty years old, and I'm just tired of being manipulated or being influenced and dictated to by white folks." Going through the various exercises in the project helped give him a better understanding of racism and how blacks tended to internalize it, to buy into whatever it was "liberals want us to say and do." He liked the fact that time was set aside for blacks to talk among themselves, to realize that the "same frustrations that I had, they had, about how we all had to compromise what we were, how we felt, what our visions are." He was particularly impressed by a black opera singer ("very distinguished, well educated, well mannered, and who had money") and how she felt she had "to water down to be accepted," how she had to act a certain way in the "public arena" and how "demoralizing and degrading" she found that to be.

What Carvis noticed about John was the way in which he genuinely seemed to be struggling with the issues being raised. "It wasn't this phony kind of sincerity," Carvis said. "We agreed that we weren't going to force it, but do it naturally, not be manipulated into something that we *had* to do to satisfy our little egos." His only regret about the walk in the woods he and John took that autumn Sunday near John's house was that his ten-year-old daughter wasn't with him, especially since John's son had come along. With all his kids, he had never tried to shelter them and had always tried to ensure that, wherever they went, they never attempted to be anything but what they were—"free, brown human beings."

When I told him that, at some point the previous summer, I had stopped interviewing people late at night in the inner city, and that I didn't feel altogether safe in using a pay phone, he didn't exactly deride me, but he told me I was wrong, that I shouldn't allow someone else to interpret the environment of the inner city for me, to classify it in such a way. The fact, whether I wanted to accept it or not, was this: White people walked around a lot more freely in black neighborhoods than blacks did. He could, he was saying, more easily accept his brother's not wanting to come visit him than he could me or John. He had been to John's house for that walk, and he had gone with his family there for a Christmas party, but John had not yet been to his home. "I want him to come into my neighborhood, so he can see what I see," Carvis said, namely that he had nothing to fear.

And yet, at the same time, Carvis recalled his own fear simply shopping in a Kohl's grocery store on the East Side. He had been gone from Milwaukee for two years, living in the southeast (predominantly black) part of Washington, D.C., and suddenly, he said, "this fear came over me, like I'm surrounded by white folks again." Rational or not, this sort of thing led to the immobilization that led him to the workshop.

"Racism has immobilized all of us to move beyond what perceptions that we have of a community of people," he said. When he first moved to Milwaukee, he was told (as every black I had spoken with had been) not to go to the South Side, that he would not be welcome there. He had eventually come to the conclusion that "these old racism things are put out there for us to buy into, to prevent us from sitting down and having conversations."

During the period he was in East St. Louis, he persuaded a white banker, someone who claimed he wanted to "get involved" in the black community and see what he could do to improve things, that the best way to do what he said he wanted to do was to actually go there, to "come out of your damn office and just go downtown and start hanging out." Carvis was drawn to this man because they had something in common: both were involved in the Boy Scouts. But that wasn't enough—at least not at first.

So Carvis kept after him, kept pushing him to discover for himself that the people in question were "just regular folks, just like you are."

Carvis made it sound so easy, so natural, that you almost began to wonder why everyone simply didn't throw off their armor of prejudice and fully embrace the essence of what he was suggesting. The reason we don't, according to Carvis, is that "right most of us are looking at race through our ass instead of through our eyes." The Beyond Racism project was, he said, "at least getting us to come together to look at racism as it is," forcing them to come together and confront each other and, it was hoped, reach a point where "we can trust and feel comfortable with one another and be willing to challenge one another when we catch one another coming up with that old racism baggage that we carry with us."

The task before him (as John had recorded earlier in his journal) was to sit down with other blacks, especially black men, those who (like Louise Kidd's ex-husband) "sit around and talk about how bad it is, how much pain they're going through . . . but never get into a real serious conversation about it . . . about how racism has messed us up and prevented us from mobilizing and moving beyond that point. . . . To me, power means one thing—the ability to act. . . . We spend more time throwing darts at it but don't address it." If anything was going to change the face of racism, Carvis was convinced, the first step would be to sit down with another human being and have an open and honest discussion. "You've got to develop relationships with people in your community. You've got to get to know people that surround you. Many times we look at people, we just see them. We don't *know* them, we don't *understand* them, and we don't take the time to do that. But if you force yourself to do that, your whole environment becomes more comfortable."

In Milwaukee, he said, you might see interracial couples out and about, but unless they were together for professional reasons, you never saw blacks and whites together in groups, just kicking back. Why that was, Carvis said, he wasn't entirely sure, but he had a theory, a theory that was linked yet again to fear, the fear, in this case, of other people's disapproval.

HOWARD FULLER'S NAME HAD come up a number of times in our conversation that morning. He and Carvis were the same age and they knew each other. Carvis was worried about him for a number of reasons, but the main one was this: Not only did he seem to be the one black leader in Milwaukee who was "acceptable" to whites (as opposed to Michael McGee, who, quite apart from his threats, was not acceptable, Carvis said, because he spoke the language of the street), but he was not doing what Carvis considered his greatest strength—operating from outside the system, organizing and seeing to it that fifteen or twenty Howard Fullers were waiting in the wings, ready to take their place on the continuum that Fuller so loved to talk about. The notion of Fuller's being the Head Negro in Charge, of one voice speaking for many, struck Carvis as a recipe for disaster. It not only raised the question of what would happen if Fuller were no longer around—either as school superintendent or on earth altogether—but it put Fuller in a position, partly of his own creation, in which the expectations for him—for *any* one person—were too great, a situation in which, Carvis suggested, he would ultimately fail and be pushed off his pedestal. The white establishment (as Fuller himself told Marvin Hannah once) would only allow him to succeed up to a point. Of that, Carvis was convinced.

TWELVE HOURS LATER, CARVIS and John were sitting in my room at the Plaza, eating pizza, drinking beer, and engulfed in what has come to be known to all basketball fans as March Madness. When they weren't watching the game between Princeton and Syracuse, they were engaged in the kind of easy banter that Carvis said he never saw on the streets and in the bars and restaurants of Milwaukee. They were talking about a night the previous month when Carvis was supposed to meet John at Calvary Baptist Church to hear a debate with Mike McGee and the other candidates for his seat, and how Carvis couldn't make it because he had car trouble, and how John was uneasy driving to the church in a part of town he didn't know.

"I was aware that I was uncomfortable," he said to both of us. "I was driving around looking for a pay phone that I could use. Not just a pay phone, but a pay phone I felt I could use," he emphasized, Carvis's comments to me from the morning still fresh in my mind. "A lit gas station, that was finally one I could settle on. I felt, Okay, there's one, I can deal with that. A lot of the others I thought, No, I'm not going to stop at that pay phone, and I just realized, I don't know if it's because of the stuff that's just inside of me, from all those years of growing up and just the stuff that you pick up and prejudices and just fears about different communities. . . .

"But then I also realized that people in this neighborhood have these fears too and I wanted to ask you about that," he said, looking at Carvis. "Is this just because I'm an outsider in this neighborhood that I'm feeling this way or is it that most people around here don't want to be using this pay phone at this time of the night? I felt that must be true, I felt that I wasn't alone in those feelings, and I felt a lot of empathy for those that lived there under those conditions because to me it was a scary situation."

Carvis told him we had talked about that very thing in the morning. He didn't lecture John or make fun of him in any way. He just told him that he had to get beyond his fear, not become paralyzed or overwhelmed by it, and that he wasn't alone in feeling that way, that, yes, many blacks who lived there felt just as he did, even though, he stressed, he didn't. But it was also important to remember, he said, that *all* people had animal instincts, had the ability to sense when another person felt uncomfortable or insecure. For anybody who was "devious," Carvis said, "they're going to take advantage of that. . . . If you happen to be in the right place at the wrong time, it's going to happen anyway." (Just a few days earlier, a former teacher from South Division had underscored what Carvis was saying, that her black male students had told her they knew that people feared them and so they played on that, allowing whites to find confirmation for those fears, making racism into a kind of game, albeit a deadly serious one.)

Hearing Carvis say that was helpful to John, but it would take a while. After all, he had moved out of Sherman Park because of this fear, and he had experienced a similar unease when he had dropped Johnny off once at the friends of friends on Center Street, wondering why he was being so trusting. But there he was in Bay View, apparently secure, near to woods he enjoyed walking in, sure (or so he wanted to think) that he had done the best thing for his family by moving there, and yet he continued to wrestle alternately with the thought that perhaps he didn't really belong there and with the sense that he was there for a reason, to help impart to others what he had learned from the workshop.

His problem, though, was this: He didn't feel he had yet reached the point where he could do that. Five months earlier, one of his son's friends told Johnny that he was going to be a rapper for Halloween, with gold chains and blackface, and John agonized over whether he should delicately suggest to the boy's parents that another outfit might be better. He actually went over and knocked on the door, but no one was home. The next night, much to his relief, the boy appeared in a different getup. Not long after that, he had come out of a movie theater about ten in the evening and there was a black woman, her ten-year-old daughter at her side, begging for help. She had lost her wallet, she was far from her home in Illinois, and she didn't know what to do. Everyone heard her, and yet everyone walked by her. In its own way, it sounded like the plight of Kitty Genovese—except that she had been killed in her own New York neighborhood and no one raised a finger. "Would I have stopped if the woman and child had been white?" John asked himself in his journal. "Why didn't I stop? Why did I doubt this woman? Do I have any right to doubt her? . . . What inside me allows me to continue walking in such circumstances? Would Leslie [his wife]? How could I proceed without so much as inquiring further? How do I pick and choose my tragedies in conscience?"

John Fitzgerald was the epitome of soul-searching. I might as well have been going to confessional with him each week. The questions he was asking reminded me of the night I had been with Maron and Georgette Alexander, the night they asked why children in the inner city couldn't be afforded the same chance as children elsewhere, why everyone was under the impression that if a black child had a computer he would just tear it up. Even though John's questions were self-directed, they were universal, asking each of us to put ourselves in his place. But he didn't stop there. He supplied his rationale. He wrote how, when he had been in India, he had trained himself to resist the steady barrage of requests for money by devising "a system whereby I ignored anyone who appeared able to work and offered some amount to those too injured, ill, or weak to do so." But this woman, he said, seemed not to fall into those categories. Nonetheless, his rationale continued. *Surely it was a scam of some kind. Surely someone was waiting nearby. . . .*

Or maybe, just maybe, he wrote, she was who she said she was—a lady who lost her wallet and needed some cash—and he would have stopped to help her had she been white.

JUST BEFORE JOHN AND Carvis left my room that evening, Carvis pulled out a well-worn copy of *Before the Mayflower* and read aloud the passage he had talked about that morning. All three of us were standing as he read what Frederick Douglass had written more than a century before, read it with passion, passion that barely disguised the pain and anger and betrayal he emphatically felt, indelibly etching a scene that I would not be able to forget, putting his own coda on the day, gaining the sort of control that had long been denied to him and to his race.

> If you see the Negro plowing in the open field, leveling the forest, at work with a spade, a rake, a hoe, a pick-axe, or a bill—let him alone; he has a right to work. If you see him on his way to school, with spelling book, geography and arithmetic in his hands—let him alone. . . . If he has a ballot in his hand, and is on his way to the ballot-box to deposit his vote for the man whom he thinks will most justly and wisely administer the Government which has the power of life and death over him, as well as others—let him *alone*.

THIRTY-NINE

If I hadn't been aware of exactly what day it was, I might have thought no time at all had passed since I last saw Bill Lawrence in his office at the Private Industry Council, that I had never left the premises. He was still fidgeting with the same toys he had fidgeted with the previous summer, and he was still having a hard time with eye contact.

The Step-Up Plus program that he had first talked about at that meeting of business leaders back in July was now a reality, with seventy companies pledging their support. It marked, in his opinion, significant progress toward ensuring a link between school and work. The original Step-Up program had placed more youths in private- and public-sector jobs than ever before, and had done so with less federal money—a trend that Lawrence expected to continue. "The federal government for the last ten years has said that they are not going to be the solution to the problems of urban America, and I believe them," he said bluntly.

But was the very existence of Step-Up Plus, the meritocrat (and devil's advocate) in me asked, something that would dissuade kids from going on to college?

He laughed. The question apparently amused him. The fact was, he said, "we are not preparing young people for college or for work or for any successful occupation right now. . . . Over ninety percent of the kids who graduate from MPS who are minorities don't go to college anyway. So the question is, if they're not going to college anyway and they're not getting employment, what are they getting? Nothing. . . .

"You've got to realize that when you look at the labor market in this country, ninety percent of the people make less than thirty thousand dollars a year. The average wage in Milwaukee, an industrial hub one would argue, is twenty-three thousand five hundred dollars. . . . To find someone a job, making, in five years, twenty-three thousand five hundred dollars is a success story—and if you could do that without a high school diploma, that would be extraordinary."

Lawrence was fond of a statement Ronald Edmonds once made, a statement that essentially said, "We already know all there is that we need to know to teach our children. The question is, how do we feel about the fact that we haven't done it?" He was fond of it because it expressed what he believed to be true—that we haven't done it because we don't care. He was talking about the children who live in the inner cities and the "we" was the government and the private sector. But out in a place like Shorewood, he said, they cared. All you had to do was look at what kids did any weekday afternoon from two until six. Schools were open, activities were going on; they were going on because parents demanded and paid for them to go on. But if you went across the line into Milwaukee, he said, you would find, except in some pockets, kids just standing on street corners.

I told Lawrence about the exchange that Howard Fuller had had with the schoolteacher from Shorewood that Sunday at Mt. Carmel. He wasn't surprised. In Lawrence's opinion, what it all circled back to was this: Was Milwaukee willing to pay for buildings for its children? Fuller had said that new buildings were going to be one of the things he was going to push for and I recalled Lawrence telling him back in August that this would be his first real clash with John Norquist. There hadn't been a referendum on the issue since 1971, and public officials, particularly *elected* officials, didn't want one now. Since a significant amount of the school budget came from property taxes, there was a fear that, if successful, a referendum would drive more people and businesses out of the city.

Which wasn't to suggest that school-building referendums in suburban districts always succeeded. They didn't. Wauwatosa residents voted down two of them. But if you lived in Wauwatosa and weren't happy about that, you could always move. For a large majority of the parents whose children attended MPS, the ability to just pick up and move was simply not there. "If you tell them that you're not going to build schools for their children," Lawrence said, "they're just shit out of luck."

SHIT OUT OF LUCK. There is a harshness and finality to that phrase that sticks in the throat just as firmly as *entitlement* or *preference* or any word or words one might choose to fill in. No matter how you look through the lens, somebody somewhere on some level doesn't want someone else to have an advantage—at least not if it is going to affect them, and quite apart from whether they have advantages or privileges or special dispensations they would rather not dwell on. Who couldn't, after all, be snared in the net of hypocrisy? For all those who rail against affirmative action, who bemoan reverse discrimination, who among them can honestly say he hasn't been helped by some connection at one point or at many points along the way? Nepotism and legacies are things—are they not?—that the beneficiaries hardly ever discuss, at least openly, in the same way, curiously enough, that no one particularly warms to the idea of discussing race. Nepotism and legacies, after all, imply (rightly or wrongly) an element of inferiority, an inability to move up on merit alone—just as affirmative action does.

But being shit out of luck doesn't have a whole lot to do with affirmative action. Affirmative action has to do with the middle class (even though it is a group whose identity seems more and more ambiguous, that seems to grow exponentially and have less buying power all the time), with being in a position to capitalize on the opportunity that is being offered. It has precious little to do with those who are shit out of luck. If you are part of a family that is living at or below the poverty level, there is nothing ambiguous about what that means. It doesn't mean that it is impossible to counter all the things you have to counter and overcome. There are enough Howard Fullers to stand as living proof of that. And yet Howard Fuller readily admits that what he had to face growing up in the segregated fifties was nothing, relatively speaking, compared to what kids and their parents are facing in the segregated nineties. It is far more complicated. The root cause isn't just white racism (as the Kerner Commission suggested). It isn't just a question of class. It isn't just about economics and the drying up of low-skilled, relatively high-wage jobs. It isn't just a simple matter of blacks bent on self-reliance and not on permanent victimhood. It isn't just about the failures of integration—or about the advantages of being separate, or of what was lost from the tight-knit days of segregation. It isn't just a case of the government feeling less and less responsible, morally as well as financially, for the problems of the ghetto. Nor is it just a case of blacks no longer wanting to feel patronized by white liberals consumed with guilt but still, somehow, convinced that their way is the best way, that what helping really means is ultimately being in charge. Nor is it just a case of "the forces of evil" (as Bill Lawrence refers to gangs and violence and drugs and broken homes and horrendous housing and the like) not working on "the same timetable as the rest of us do," seeming always to move faster than the bureaucracy can, sweeping up everyone and everything in its wake—or at least appearing to. . . .

No, it isn't any one thing that you can safely point to and say, with absolute certainty, that it is *this* and if only *this* can be changed, well, then, things can be different. Marvin Hannah is right. For things to be different, a collective shift would have to take place. No one can plead indifference or absence or argue that it has nothing to do with them, that they didn't bring slaves here and therefore it isn't their fault, or argue that they have, to the best of their knowledge, never discriminated, or been racist, or allowed their prejudices to take shape in any way. I am not suggesting that it is possible for a person, any person, to be beyond reproach. Like Jefferson, we are imperfect; it is part of our nature to be so. But that should not be taken as a valid excuse for the business of race relations in America remaining unfinished, a conspicuous mark on all our lives.

PART THREE

FORTY

The Reverend Leon Sullivan was off in his prediction by one year. On the 29th of April in 1992, Los Angeles burst into flames. The four officers who had been accused of beating Rodney King were acquitted by a mostly white jury in the tiny enclave of Simi Valley, and all kinds of hell broke loose in South-Central Los Angeles and throughout the area. More than fifty people were killed, there was a billion dollars in damages, and gun stores struggled to satisfy the frantic demand of whites who feared for their lives. The Bush Administration handled the crisis by helpfully stating that it wasn't their fault: it was the fault of the Democrats and the sixties and all the people who turned the War on Poverty and the Great Society into a fiasco. The country was still paying for that and here was diabolical proof.

Earlier that month, Michael McGee was defeated in his bid for re-election and naturally blamed the setback on redistricting and election fraud. As to what that meant for the city as a whole, in terms of his threat for 1995, he would not say. But no one seemed to think that McGee would just meekly slink into a corner and not be heard from again. If anything, he would probably become even more of a loose cannon. He had campaigned so indifferently and smugly that it was hard to decide whether he was confident he would win or whether he almost desired his defeat as a way to strengthen his identity as both revolutionary and victim.

One week after McGee's defeat, a man named Jesse Anderson claimed that two black men had attacked him and his wife as they were walking to their car one evening at the Northridge Mall. His wife was killed and he suffered a knife wound. For some people in Milwaukee and around the country, it recalled the case of Charles Stuart in Boston two and a half years earlier, the case in which Stuart claimed a black male surprised his pregnant wife and himself as they were about to get into their car. Stuart's wife was killed, he was injured, and the Boston police put out an immediate dragnet and quickly arrested someone who matched Stuart's description of the assailant. It took nearly three months for the police to determine that Stuart himself (along with help from his brother) was responsible for his wife's death.

In the case of Anderson, the Milwaukee police, to their credit, had suspicions about his story. They had apparently learned something from the Stuart case and they had learned something from the Konerak Sinthasomphone incident of the year before. Anderson's story didn't hold up. Continuing to protest his innocence (unlike Charles Stuart, who killed himself by jumping off a bridge), he wound up in the same prison with Jeffrey Dahmer, where both of them were eventually killed by a black inmate in December of 1994.

When things like this happen and they turn out not to have occurred the way the person insisted they did, there is an unintended positive, an upside, that results: we are less and less likely to accept the race card being played, the idea that whenever bad things take place, somehow, somewhere a black male is behind them. It didn't ultimately work for Stuart, it didn't work for Anderson, and it didn't work in the fall of 1994 for Susan Smith, when she maintained for nine straight days that a black man had carjacked her and her two sons in Union, South Carolina. But it worked long enough to stir the always simmering racial stew and create more rips in our social fabric, rips that the truth can only partly mend.

The Rodney King case was different. It was all there for us to see, right from the start. Whatever King did or didn't do preceding the moment the camera was turned on—nobody ever claimed that he was a person of sterling character—it didn't justify what happened to him on that March night.

And it didn't prepare him for the reaction to the verdict. When he plaintively asked, "Can we all get along?" he appeared as dazed as anybody else, incredulous, it seemed, that anyone would care enough to put his own life in jeopardy as a result of what had happened to him. And even though his question became the object of many jokes, it continues to resonate, in its pleading, unaccusing way, more than anything else does, perhaps, from the whole episode.

"I'VE SEEN L.A. BURN before," Howard Fuller said quietly to his class the Saturday morning after the verdict, recalling the destruction of Watts in 1965. "You all have not, but some of us sitting around this table saw this before, and heard a lot of the same stuff. This is what's so painful about this, why some of us can't even talk about it. It is as if you have lived your life in vain."

In the year I had known Fuller I had never seen him look so distressed. It was as if all that he had to deal with in his job, all the things he had to face each day, were bound up and manifest in the conflagration, in the confluence of anger and frustration that would either only wind up hurting the black community even more—or would, one hoped, become a flashpoint for improving the social and economic conditions of inner cities across the country. According to the *New York Times,* students from Beverly Hills to New London, Connecticut, were discussing this and having their racial consciousness raised (at the same time some of their parents were buying guns and installing ever more powerful security systems). The greatest domestic uprising since the Civil War, some called it, an uprising, it turned out, that Daryl Gates, the outgoing Los Angeles police chief, could have done more to prevent before he left office to become a radio talk-show host.

For Howard Fuller it was such agonizing déjà vu that he told his students that if they were to be shown a film of Watts burning then and South-Central now they wouldn't be able to tell the difference.

Actually, someone pointed out, one of the networks did just that, saying that the only difference was that the Watts newsreel was in black and white.

"The issue is the level of hopelessness," Fuller said, "the level of 'we don't have nothing nowhere.' . . . Think how long it's going to be before they get a store back in there."

"What happened in Watts?" a young man asked. It was an innocent enough question and yet it revealed the lack of historical knowledge that had motivated Fuller to devote his time to such a class in the first place.

What happened in Watts, he explained, also stemmed from the arrest of a black motorist, though the beating he received was not nearly as bad as King's. The question each of them needed to ask, Fuller said, was whether history was repeating itself under the same socioeconomic conditions—or had those conditions changed? "If you look at the riots, the response, whatever you want to call it, you have to ask yourself, 'Is there anything that's different about America today?'"

"The hopelessness is still there," one woman said.

"Right," Fuller said. "But I would argue that there's a group of people that are richer than they were then, and some of them are us."

What Howard Fuller was touching on was something that a lot of black political leaders often conveniently forgot: among the most tangible gains of the civil rights movement (as has already been pointed out in these pages) was the expansion of the black middle and upper-middle class. And it was an expansion that was far different from kids wanting to become the next Joe Louis or Michael Jordan; there wasn't room, in a certain sense, for more than one of them. And yet it was that very burgeoning of the middle class that made it convenient for white and black conservatives to argue that if a Howard Fuller could make it, then anybody could—anybody who was equally determined. It was a selective argument, one with its own amnesia, invariably forgetting to take into account all the factors that might work against such progress. If there was any piece of political advice that stood out among all others, it was (for conservatives) probably this: *Hammer away with the tools that make your point and ignore the rest. Complexity and gray areas will only get you into trouble, and they're too hard to grasp anyway. If you feel at all guilty about taking such a simplistic approach, get over it.*

The woman who said the hopelessness was still there in society didn't disagree with Fuller: there were a larger number of black people who had college degrees and who had attained wealth, and because of that, class had become more and more of an issue for the black community. She didn't begrudge them anything they had gained, but felt it was crucial that they not ignore those who had not made it.

Someone mentioned that Shelby Steele had been on CBS the night before, talking about Los Angeles, and that he'd been identified as "one of the leaders of the African-American community."

This did not go down well, the prospect (as Carvis had said) of someone else—in this case, the media—interpreting the community and its leaders for them. "So was he still saying that blacks should pull themselves up out of their own boots?" another asked, articulating the general sigh from much of the rest of the room.

"Basically, his view has not changed."

Neither, it seemed, had their view of him, despite Fuller's earlier efforts to help them go beyond the surface message and find the kernels of truth in what Steele was saying. They appeared to be clinging to their position just as strongly as . . . as any conservative, actually.

But Fuller kept after them, not about Steele specifically, but about the necessity of thinking things through, of coming to issues from different angles so as to better understand them. He had talked about a "collective values shift" in the black community so often he was sure they were tired of hearing about it, but he brought it up again because the reason that older blacks went on and on about their work ethic was that they had had jobs, and now that there weren't those jobs—or at least as many of them—he wanted them to see why it was harder for young black kids to grasp the importance of working if they had never seen anybody in their family get up and go off to a job, why a different set of values got passed along as a result of that fact.

The same woman who had talked about the level of hopelessness spoke up again. Her feeling was that the very existence of welfare created a cushion of sorts that her mother had never been able to count on, and in her opinion, it was a good thing she hadn't. Her mother's strong work ethic had come from earning twenty dollars a month and having to make do and wouldn't have been nearly as strong if she knew she could sit back and wait for a check each month.

Fine, Fuller said, but too often discussion about the issue of welfare began in the wrong place. Instead of dealing with it as it is, why not go back and ask why it existed in the first place? Originally, he reminded them, it was created for widows and orphans, under the Social Security Act of 1935. It expanded to the system it was today during the Kennedy Administration. Radical social scientists, he said, make the argument that it was created in order to stave off revolution. All of that notwithstanding, when he was the director of Health and Human Services, he would remind his employees—the ones who would speak derisively about the welfare recipients—that "you're here by virtue of this system. The distance between you and some of the folks you're treating like dirt ain't but one paycheck."

MY MIND DRIFTED AWAY from the discussion and toward Los Angeles. Fuller was doing his best to keep everyone focused and rational, but the pained expression on his face never lifted that morning. From the moment he talked about feeling as if he had lived his life in vain, it was difficult to think about anything else other than Los Angeles and the fires that continued to burn. The most depressing thing to me about the whole business was the way people in South-Central were destroying their own community. The attack of retribution on Reginald Denny (the white man who was pulled from his truck and beaten) aside, the object of the protesters' anger was the bedrock things the community needed to exist—its stores and shops. The reaction to the verdict was predictable and yet it was also senseless—senseless in the way black-on-black crime was senseless. It only made matters worse. On the other hand, the reaction to the verdict wasn't just about the verdict; the verdict became a catalyst, gave people permission to act irrationally, to openly and viciously express rage, however self-destructive, that had been tamped down for who knew how long, rage that was understandable.

Still, what was going to be done? Aside from blaming it, all of it, on those damn liberals and the War on Poverty and the Great Society, what, if anything, was going to be done? Would the fervent discussions that were purportedly taking place all around the country translate into something more than talk and "cool-it money" for makeshift summer jobs—or would all this concern fade, just waiting to be subsumed by the Next Big Thing to come along?

I HAD GIVEN A speech at the University of Wisconsin—Milwaukee the night before Fuller's class, and only two black people had been there—a woman who had traveled down from Oshkosh and Carvis Braxton, who had come to the talk along with John Fitzgerald. The speech was supposed to be about the kind of work I did, and why I had chosen Milwaukee as a representative place to write about race in America. But I was prepared (if you could call it that) to answer any questions about Los Angeles.

The woman from Oshkosh told the audience that she had read my earlier work and that that was why she had come. I was flattered, but I really thought she had come because she wanted to see what people—white people—would have to say about Los Angeles, if they said anything at all. Without directly alluding to the King verdict, she asked me how I would define racism.

Her question caught me off-guard. It shouldn't have, but it did. Instead of answering it directly and immediately, I said I wanted to give it more thought, that it was the sort of question that demanded it, and asked if I could come back to her in a few minutes. She no doubt thought I was ducking her question, but I wasn't. I simply was unwilling to shoot back some pat response (or at least one that would have seemed pat to me).

As it turned out, she didn't wait for me to get back to her. I am not sure exactly what prompted her to leave, but it was probably a question from an older white man, edgily asking if the book was going to deal with black racism too. No sooner had I said yes, it would, than she stood up to go. John Fitzgerald followed her out, hoping to persuade her to stay, but he reentered the room alone.

Perhaps her leaving early was a way of making a statement, of letting me know that she had expected more of me, that on some level I had let her down. Since I didn't have the chance to have that conversation with her, I don't know. What I do know is that that evening at UWM, coming forty-eight hours after Los Angeles erupted, was yet another sober reminder to me of how interminably charged the subject of race was, and that nothing I wrote was likely to dramatically defuse it.

THE FOLLOWING EVENING I was invited to the home of Leonard Sykes, a reporter for the *Milwaukee Journal*. He had phoned me a few days earlier, to find out what I was going to talk about at UWM, and while we were on the phone, he had CNN on in the background and was the first to tell me about the King verdict. No sooner had dinner begun than Greg Stanford, the columnist whom I had bumped into at the Juneteenth celebration, was talking about the riots and everyone was listening intently. Suddenly, Sykes shot up from his chair and shouted, "Burn the fucker down!"

Burn the fucker down. That, he said, had been his initial reaction when he first heard the news, a reaction that he certainly hadn't shared with me at the time. Since he had always impressed me as fairly low-key and thoughtful but not especially fiery, his action took me by surprise. And while it was, on the surface, different from Howard Fuller's sad, pained expression of that morning, I took them to be the same, the same passageway to a reservoir of anger within blacks that might dissipate from time to time but never went away, the reservoir of anger that enabled a Howard Fuller or a Leonard Sykes or a Michael McGee to get through each day.

FORTY-ONE

The morning after the dinner at the Sykeses', something else from the evening lingered in my mind. I had been talking to Eugene Kane, another journalist who was there, talking about how race often got injected into situations when it shouldn't, where it didn't have a place, but where it got used anyway because it was the most powerful weapon at hand.

He listened as intently as Leonard Sykes had been earlier when he jumped to his feet, and his reaction to what we were talking about, while quieter, was no less chilling.

"In my back pocket," Kane said conspiratorially, slight smile on his face, "I always carry the race card." He paused for a second, then said, "And I play it whenever I have to."

Long before Eugene Kane said this, I was aware that one of the elements that threaded its way consistently through this exploration of race was the element of, and the value placed on, surviving—surviving more than succeeding as an operative principle. Lamentable as that might seem, it too was understandable, as understandable as the rage in Los Angeles or the fury that propelled Leonard Sykes to his feet.

A FEW DAYS LATER, Carvis Braxton and I were having coffee and talking about Los Angeles. Things had been relatively quiet in Milwaukee since the verdict, partly because Chief Arreola had had various community leaders and organizers come to his office for meetings on May 1 and again on May 4, meetings designed to control the steam (as Tom Wolfe once wrote). I was cheered when I heard that, thinking that perhaps the Blue Ribbon Commission's report must have been read by somebody. (The other reason things seemed tranquil, Tommie Williams told me, was that so much outrage and energy had been expended on the Dahmer incident that people in the community were finding it hard to summon it again.)

Carvis's demeanor that morning was surprising. He was consumed by guilt, practically of the white-liberal variety, guilt because not even a week had passed since the verdict, and he found himself settling back into a routine and it worried him. There he was, sitting at home watching and enjoying a Knicks-Bulls playoff game, when it struck him that if he was doing this, sitting there enjoying himself, what the hell was everybody else doing? He wasn't being self-righteous, but it did occur to him that if what was happening in Los Angeles was "really the tip of the iceberg for most urban communities," then he shouldn't have been sitting there watching a game but should have been out meeting with people, organizing, taking the pulse of his neighborhood, deciding how to approach the next day. Not only did he feel stupid and guilty, he was saying now, but he felt power-less. His sense was that America—not just Carvis Braxton—was "back to business as usual," that the Next Big Thing turned out to not be very big at all, a return to the quotidian. "We've isolated ourselves from what took place in L.A.," he said. "Removed ourselves and went back to watch-ing TV . . . as if things never took place." But television, he thought, re-moved people even further, giving you the sense you were watching a movie—a movie about someone else's misfortune, thank God, a movie that didn't involve you.

And yet television had brought both the violence and nonviolence of the civil rights movement to people everywhere; the leaders of the struggle made sure that happened, it was planned that way, it was one of the key reasons that laws were changed. And television had brought the Vietnam War into our living rooms as well (prompting Michael Arlen to call it "the living-room war"). My impression was that the home video of the Rodney King beating had had the same effect, but maybe it hadn't. Perhaps Carvis was right—that whatever outrage one felt was easily sur-passed by numbness and detachment, the same numbness and detachment that Kristie Jorgenson and her brother told me would set in whenever they heard about another homicide in the inner city. Or perhaps the riots were just another form of entertainment to be sampled and then turned away from as one restlessly surfed with the all-powerful remote control (the name itself eerily appropriate given the circumstances), forever in search of a newer, fresher, better escape.

I mentioned to Carvis what Howard Fuller had said at Commando, about the riots making him feel he had lived his life in vain, and Carvis said he understood that all too well. He had always used his children as a barometer, a way of gauging how much progress had been made since their births. The oldest of his five daughters was twenty-six, the youngest ten, and the way he looked at it, all the things he had tried to do as a community organizer was mainly because of them. "If I can't bring about change and be responsible and try to initiate change for their lives, then my life has been sort of wasted," he said, a glazed look in his eyes. "So I always evaluate what has changed, what is better now than when they were first brought into this world." He had been through this in Buffalo during the sixties, he reminded me, and now here he was across the table, doing his calculations, and coming up with a realization that was similar to Howard Fuller's, the realization that "all this time I should have been pursuing the mighty dollar and all the goodies this society has to offer."

His saying that wasn't totally convincing, knowing how strongly committed he was to the inner city, but it was sobering nonetheless. It made me consider if it was said just out of frustration and would pass, or if it would possibly lead him to the point where he pulled back and directed his energies elsewhere. But he was fifty years old, and it wasn't as if there were that many elsewheres to turn. (On top of that, he had recently learned that his wife, Charlotte, had cancer.)

Despite what the newspapers had said about discussions being held in classrooms around the country, those discussions about Los Angeles were not taking place at Wilbur Wright Middle School, the school Carvis's fourteen-year-old attended. She came home and reported that she and two other classmates tried to bring it up in social studies class, but the teacher wouldn't allow them to.

"If we don't talk it through," Carvis said, "it won't get out of your system and you won't move.... The best time to really cause a person to move beyond their hurt and pain is when there's a very traumatic thing that happens in their life. When people are very vulnerable and open." He was, as it happened, not only talking about Los Angeles, he was talking about Charlotte's cancer. He had been advised that the best thing to do was for everybody in the family to talk about it and find a way to build from there. And it wasn't very different, he realized, from what he had learned from the Beyond Racism project and from what he was trying to do with John Fitzgerald. How, he wanted to know, had we arrived at the point where President Bush's response to Los Angeles was to blame the

Democratic Party for something that took place years before instead of figuring out how to "build bridges over the fire"? And the ones who would be doing this figuring, he suggested, had to include not just "the so-called professional intellectuals" (both white and black), but also "the ones that act out, the ones who become the statistics," the ones he could see outside his window each and every day in the heart of the 'hood.

Changing the subject slightly, I asked him what had been going through his mind at UWM the previous Friday evening.

Well, for one thing, he felt like Sidney Poitier in *Guess Who's Coming to Dinner,* but he also thought that John's and his being there lent a realness to some of what I was talking about. (He and John had come late, and the sponsor of the evening identified them when they arrived.) He said that he, like John, was concerned that there was no real response to the black woman from Oshkosh, especially since she had come, in his view, to seek help in dealing with the pain and frustration of racism. He had been impressed and touched by Rodney King's humbleness in asking, "straight from his heart," why we couldn't all get along, and it prompted him to ask me some questions of his own: What was white America going to do? Was white America willing to put in the time to help solve what the King verdict was merely a catalyst for? If all that came out of the turmoil in Los Angeles was "another program," he said (paralleling what Tom Brophy had said in regard to the Dahmer incident), then the answers to his questions were not really answers at all. Human beings, he insisted, simply didn't respond to programs.

PERHAPS NOT, BUT TWO hours later a group of them allowed me to sit around a table on the second floor of the Social Development Commission's West Division building on North Thirty-fifth Street. Participants in a program called MMOR (Minority Male Opportunity and Responsibility), they were all black, all male, and they had refused to allow me to join in their weekly discussion a couple of months earlier. Their decision had been arrived at democratically—they had voted—and was based on their feeling that they hadn't been given enough notice of my interest. But this time they had, and they warily agreed.

Tommie Williams (who had left Harambee five months earlier and become director of this particular center) was the person who had told me about the group, and when we walked in and he introduced me, they were ready to do what Carvis Braxton said needed to be done—talk about the verdict, about all that was going down in South-Central, and, most important, about what should be done.

The discussion was moderated by a woman in her fifties named Pamela Jefferson, a black woman with a tough veneer but a soft heart, and a light-skinned black named Danny Tinnon. Mrs. Jefferson, as the participants called her, suggested that it would have been a huge mistake to allow Rodney King to testify, that if watching the video hadn't brought forth a guilty verdict, having him on the stand certainly wouldn't have; and she complained that even though whites, Hispanics, and Asians were also doing the looting of the stores, the only ones the media "zeroed in on" were the blacks. The media made it seem like a race riot, she said, when in fact there were white people protesting the verdict who "felt just as bad."

Since many of the young men gathered had committed crimes of their own, had "become the statistics" Carvis talked about, it was only natural that this discussion would stir them to recall their own experiences with the criminal justice system.

One man pointed out (ignoring the whole element of proportion) that "the most hideous crimes" were committed 95 percent of the time by white individuals ("If you check our mass murder records as far as serial killers, as far as baby killers and rapists, they are white males"); another that a white guy got caught with "two ounces and seventeen hundred in his pocket" and that all he received was thirty days, work release, and a thousand-dollar fine, while he got a year, a seventeen-hundred-dollar fine, and three years' probation for assaulting a policeman; and another that a white guy got only four months and "a year paper" (probation) for sodomizing a five-year-old boy and a two-year-old girl.

"So what does that say, brothers?" Tommie Williams asked. "Everything you're saying now, what does that say? It says conspiracy."

"We have a double standard," Mrs. Jefferson said.

"Conspiracy against black males in this country," Williams added.

"I got a question for you, man. How do the black officers feel about that?"

"Black officers," said Williams, who had been one for six years in the seventies, "really felt like they were caught up in the middle. You know, here you are, you're supposed to be serving and protecting the people, but you're seeing your people getting battered all the time.... To me, they only gave me praise when you knocked some brother upside the head. 'Yeah, did you see what Tommie did! He knocked this guy up against the head.' But see, they didn't realize, man, that as a black person, you have to live with these people after you go home. To them, man, a lot of the whites that work that job, they kind of look at this as a hunting expedition.... When you are trained, you're taught to kill. You're not taught to maim, you're taught to shoot in the head, shoot in the chest, and ask questions later." That was why he had been working so hard, he said, to see that more sensitivity training was done within the department. It might take four or five more years before "dramatic changes" could be seen, but he was optimistic—especially if a civilian review board could be put in place to oversee the Fire and Police Commission, "to neutralize things."

Fine, somebody said, provided that it wasn't just Ivy League people and Ph.D. people filling those seats. "You need someone that's gonna represent us from out of the community."

"They got an officer out here now," another man said, "he's white, everybody in this room fear that man—"

That man was Blondie, Detective Mike Lewandowski, and the very mention of his name set everyone off. Each person there, it seemed, had had a run-in with him.

"He knocked both of my shoulders out of place and while he was doing it the handcuffs broke," one man recalled. "And they said I was breaking loose and they was beating me with those sticks, man. He didn't find no dope on me, but he insisted that I had some." And then Blondie played a variation of Russian roulette with him, he said, putting one bullet in his gun and demanding to know whose house it was they were standing in and then clicking and clicking until he got to the bullet and then pausing, pausing long enough for the young man to tremble and shake uncontrollably and then hear Blondie inform him of what he already knew: "I could blow your black-ass head off."

(When I spoke with Blondie about this, he laughed. "The myth of Blondie," he said, "is an inner-city myth." During his twenty-nine-year career, he had been accused of many things—"running a drug business, bringing in dope from Colombia, murder, stealing cars, shaking people down for money"—but playing Russian roulette was a new one. Although he denied these allegations, he wasn't surprised; he even seemed flattered.

Official complaints had been filed over the years, but nothing had stuck. "Every major city has a Blondie," he stressed. "If there were a hundred more like me, we'd all be a lot better off.")

Tommie Williams assured them that he was well aware of Blondie and he recalled the shooting of George Edward Brown on First and Keefe the previous June (though he inaccurately told them that Blondie had shot the boy when it was actually his partner who had), but what was important now, he said, was to begin "making some positive moves for ourselves" and stop dwelling on what was. He said that he had had success in dealing with the Vice Lords from First and Keefe, that he worked with some of them to help start a construction cleaning business with five thousand dollars from an anonymous donor (a business that never got off the ground, but it was as much Harambee's fault as any of theirs), that "once they got settled down and found out that there was somebody in their corner that was gonna help them, they decided that they wanted to change their lives, that they wanted something positive."

Tommie was doing his best, but it wasn't working. He was selling, but they weren't buying. One man who lived in the First and Keefe area said, "They're still out there selling dope. It's right around the corner from me, man. Come on."

Reluctantly, Tommie acknowledged that the first group had spun off and somebody else had come in to replace them. There was no sense in his trying to make them think otherwise. They knew, far better than Tommie, what was actually going down. They knew that groups split off and formed their own tribes all the time—or at least tried to. Nearly everybody was an entrepreneur at heart, wanted a stab at running his own show, the freedom to make the moves Tommie talked about, regardless of whether or not they were positive ones. And these little splinter groups, as Tommie called them, they were the ones "acting all crazy and stuff," the ones that the main gangs were having trouble bringing back into line.

"All these community people," someone said, looking straight at Tommie, "that wants to grab hold and help the gang members, they don't grab on and help them right. They should grab hold of some of the leaders, some of the brothers that have strong influence on them, and let them talk to them. . . . They are sending somebody in that's from the suburbs and don't know nothing about what's happening in the inner city and gonna tell us, 'Hey, this is how you gonna do this stuff.'"

. . .

PART OF WHAT HE was saying was true, but part of it wasn't. Former gang members, some of whom had been high up and were no longer in prison, had been recruited by SDC's Youth Diversion Program to do just what this young man was suggesting they do: grab on and help them right. One of them was Anthony Adams, the same Anthony Adams who walked out of that meeting the previous July, trailed by a defiant group of Vice Lords; the same one who had been at St. Elizabeth's and squared off with the man who claimed they were all, every last one of them, rats in a paper bag, trapped but preying on innocent people nonetheless.

Interestingly enough, he didn't disagree with that assessment, especially since it had once applied to him. "The majority of the individuals that live in the community," he said, "suffer from the ones that have made the decision to say, 'Well, I'm going to peddle this white man's dope, I'm going to sell it to my own people, I know it's poison, but I'm going to sell it to them anyway because I need somewhere to live and I need clothing, I need food.' The ones that have made the decision to traffic these drugs for the Europeans and the Colombians and whoever else imports drugs into this country, people such as my grandmother, myself and others are jeopardized because of this. The community becomes infiltrated with rats. That's how they live, like rats, some of them."

He had grown up on the South Side of Chicago. His father was a truck driver and his mother a homemaker, the person whom all the children in the neighborhood gravitated to. Adams spent two years in a junior college studying business administration and then began traveling around the country, doing what to make a living he would not say—at least not at first. He was now in his late twenties, a follower of the Nation of Islam, and had lived long enough, he said, to know that the odds were still stacked against you if you were black, that "they don't want to see anything better happen for black people. They have this crazy assumption that black people don't want anything, that the men are lazy and good for nothing and don't want to take care of their kids, that the women are illiterate and stupid."

Who, specifically, was "they"? I wanted to know.

"They meaning the ones that run the system, the ones that implement all these illicit drugs and so forth in our community, those that constantly build prisons to incarcerate our young brothers, they meaning the politicians with these farfetched ideas like Duke and all the rest of them. They meaning the brothers that climb the ladder of success and get with the upper echelon, the bureaucrats and the diplomats, and forget where they came from; they, the brothers that misrepresent us, they who are supposed to have our best interests at hand and yet they are scared to open their mouth and speak for us. They."

Of the many things he had observed on his travels, the one that was most vivid to him, that stuck with him the longest, was this: The ghetto and the people who lived in it were not only trapped by gangs, they were trapped on all sides by beautiful homes and people with big jobs, almost as if the people on the outside wanted to make sure they could keep an eye on and control the ones on the inside. His biting comments about the black middle class aside, though, he fell squarely into the camp of not only seeing a conspiracy around every corner, but of feeling that reparations had to be made. "I feel that there should not be a black man in this country without a home, without a job, and without a sound family structure. . . . Society has crippled the black man in this country. It's like they don't want him to progress."

Adams had, he said, been a flight attendant for American Airlines, had managed a Burger King, had worked for the Pillsbury Corporation, and he had learned that there was only so far you could go, that, one way or the other, you would be kept down and in your place, would often be talked to as if you were a child, and that, in any case, the way you had to be, the way they wanted you to be, was a way that was phony and unnatural. When traveling in the South, he found, as had many other blacks, that if someone didn't like you, they didn't like you, and you knew it. "But up here in the North, with all this diplomacy and the flashy suits and the pretty cars and elaborate dialect, they'll fuck you, excuse the expression, they will, without any Vaseline, and pat you on the back."

He had first come to Milwaukee in 1984 and had been riding around on the South Side, thinking (wrongly) that there was a correlation to the South Side of Chicago, riding around with his girl in an old Chevy with only one headlight working when "an Oreo" stopped him and told him he could write him up but wouldn't, and then escorted him back across the bridge, back to "where the brothers are supposed to be." Anthony Adams wasn't the type of person to be told where he was supposed to be. With his "boisterous" personality, his propensity for speaking out, and his fear of no one ("I have no fear," he claimed. "I'm not afraid of no man"), he was more inclined to move in than be relegated to a certain part of town. Though he was a private person (if you didn't see him for a week or so, he said, he had probably found himself something good to read), he had a keen interest in the political process and was zealous in his beliefs: that the inner city needed good health facilities that were close by (the county hospital was too far to go), that the number of places that sold alcohol needed to be cut way back (limited to liquor stores only), that the corner grocery stores should be prevented not only from selling liquor, but from staying open as late as they did (which was when a lot of alcohol was sold). He hated that the storeowners "sit up like fat rats, waiting on it," it being the welfare checks that they know people will come in to cash and then walk out with "meat deals" and forty-ouncers.

When I asked him how and why he had become associated with the El Rukns in Chicago, he turned defensive, his eyes narrowed, his granite face tightened.

"That association came about by wanting to know the truth," he said. "Simple as that, wanting to know the truth. I was tired of the lies. I was interested in my heritage and I wanted to know where I came from. I wanted to know. I wanted to know why they labeled us the name African when Afrikaan was a European conqueror." He didn't like the term "African-American." He didn't like it because it was a farce, a lie. "Why is it that you guys continue to dictate and tell us what we are? Who we are. I'm not an African-American. I don't like to be called that. I don't belong to Africa." He was a Moor, he insisted (Moors were a Moslem people of mixed Arab and Berber descent who happened to live in northwest Africa), and as far as he was concerned, Columbus was a fraud, someone who didn't discover anything other than that he was lost.

Adams was interesting. He had a way of presenting things that apparently made sense to him, that he stuck to, more or less. "I believe in self-defense, but I don't condone violence." And: "People have the wrong impression as to what we brothers are really about. They claim us as radical and militant, but that's not so. We're not radical, nor are we militant. There are those that can be reasoned with, and there are those who can't." He credited the Honorable Elijah Muhammad with teaching him the truth about his heritage and what he called the social structure of things. Through Minister Louis Farrakhan, he had learned about "the law of economics" and "the massive strokes of genocide that's been applied to our people." His ability to communicate, he said, came from reading about Marcus Garvey and his many "exploits." What he learned from Martin Luther King was that his philosophy no longer applied to "this day and age." In fact, the notion (as Adams saw it) of turning the other cheek had made it possible for Reagan and Bush to implement so many destructive programs. Adams stood with Malcolm X, with the idea that blacks had to fight—intellectually, verbally, physically—so that their culture, which was depleting at a fast rate, wasn't eliminated altogether. Two weeks earlier, he had been talking to a Korean tourist, had asked him, straight up, what he had been told about blacks in America, whether he had been told "we couldn't read or write." The man started laughing, a young man of about twenty-five, and said, "'Let me tell you. They tell me you all dumb and stupid.'" Adams then told me about a professor at MATC, a Nigerian who had come to America with the expectation that blacks would steal from him or, worse, that he wasn't likely to have any positive encounters with blacks at all. If it weren't for his talking with him, Adams said, the fellow would still be under that impression.

Anthony Adams was clearly not lacking in confidence about his powers of persuasion—or so it seemed. On June 13, 1990, that gift helped him to save a young boy's life—and marked a turning point in his own. He had woken up that morning with "an entirely different frame of mind," different from the gangbanging and, as it turned out, selling of drugs and other men's women that had been his way of life up to that point. This new outlook, he said, had to do with his love of children, his desire to see them "grow up and not be faced with so many of the things that are going on today," his desire to see them build skyscrapers, to see them utilize every resource available to make a better life for themselves. Anyway, on this particular day, not long after he had gotten dressed, he was in the vicinity of Center Street, coming out of a store, when he saw a fourteen-year-old boy walking with his dog, a boy "about to be killed" (as he saw it) by some young gangbangers, "carrying out orders of some coward somewhere," and he found that he couldn't walk past, that he had to say something. One of the young men had cocked his gun and Adams stepped in front of the boy. "Now you got two people to kill, so what are you going to do?" What he did was shoot the dog.

While the story seemed, on a certain level, bizarre, this sort of thing happened, for no good reason, with sickening regularity every day. Hearing him tell it prompted me to ask if his own family had ever encountered violence.

Yes, they had. He had been shot three different times—the first when he was fourteen, the same age of the boy whose life he had saved—and one of his brothers had been murdered. Shot six times in the back. He had been killed "because he didn't want to be part of the Disciple organization and he had no fear. . . . He had his beliefs and he lived by them and these individuals did not like him because he was a rebel to them, they couldn't intimidate him, so they killed him. He was eighteen, just beginning to live."

AT THE TIME ADAMS was telling me all this, in November of 1991, we were walking on Wisconsin Avenue, headed toward the Social Development Commission's offices, where we were to meet Leon Watkins and Tommie Williams. Watkins, head of the Family Helpline in South-Central Los Angeles, had come to Milwaukee to participate in the gangs conference that Williams and Harambee had helped organize. A former gangbanger, Watkins was someone whose work with gangs and families commanded everybody's respect. As we came off the elevator, Watkins was being interviewed by one of the local television stations. As he finished his comments (". . . it gives them a sense of well-being that they cannot find normally in the environment, in their homes, or in their schools"), the reporter turned toward the camera and reported that, during the night, on Twenty-second and Hopkins, which was only a few blocks from where Maron and Georgette Alexander lived, "bullets were fired at a Milwaukee woman's house, just missing her. Police found three suspects outside, one with a recently fired twenty-two-caliber gun. The ages of these suspects: thirteen, twelve, and ten. Juvenile court authorities are now handling this case. . . ."

Where does it all end? That was the question Bert Sweet had asked me months before. The most truthful answer—one that the Los Angeles riots six months later only underscored—was that no one knew; no one—not the sociologists, the policy makers, the evolutionary psychologists, the evolutionary biologists, the economists, the politicians, none of the people who spoke on television from offices with bookshelves radiating authority in the background—no one really knew.

It had been nearly a year since I had walked into Washington High School, since I had come to attend that town meeting in the large auditorium, the first place where I had heard a chorus of voices talking about Milwaukee. I had come now, in May of 1992, to meet with a group of Step-Up students who were willing to talk about Los Angeles and other matters with me. They were fairly equally divided between black and white, and they were outspoken about a number of things, one of them being history and the way it had a tendency to repeat itself. They had watched *Eyes on the Prize* a few weeks before the Rodney King verdict, and Ronald was saying how he had had an uneasy feeling that if the officers in the King case were acquitted, there would be rioting in Los Angeles. And in speaking of history, another young man said that he thought there was a connection between its being taught in school and a racial tension between white and black children that didn't really exist before that point. He wasn't saying that history shouldn't be taught—quite apart from the loaded and quarrelsome question of how truthful or selective the history was—he was simply remarking that race did not seem to matter, to be of particular interest, to children until then.

Much in the same way that Darlene Siebert had talked about how her initial views about blacks had been formed by her parents, these students were united in thinking that their parents were to blame for whatever prejudices they had—at least at first. And they were united in thinking that the violence in Los Angeles was appalling—that it only confirmed what people thought about blacks anyway. What bothered Danielle, who was white and happened to be class valedictorian, was that people were using both the beating of Rodney King and the subsequent verdict as an excuse "to get away with things they normally wouldn't be able to get away with"—like coming up and snatching someone's purse and shouting "Rodney King" at the same time, that they were doing it "for Rodney King." One young man said he was so ashamed that what he was witnessing on television now (people being pulled out of cars and beaten up for no reason) was similar to what had happened to Rodney King that he felt like crying.

"Black kids now," he said, "feel that white society has a grip on them and they—"

"Why should you feel that?" Danielle wanted to know. "That's what's keeping you back. It's your own self that's keeping you back. Look at Martin. He's, like, I can do anything and he does. He does everything." She was referring to Martin Logan, the vice president of student government. "He has no negative feelings. He knows what he can do and he does it. . . . If you feel that you can do it and you go for it, then you can do it no matter what color you are. You don't let anything hold you back."

Danielle, it turned out, was not speaking from the safe confines of privilege. She lived on her own, with a roommate, and was going to Marquette in the fall on a partial scholarship. Her mother was a drug addict and she hadn't seen her father in years, and she was sick and tired of being blamed for slavery and every ill that seemed to befall blacks in society. "I'm seventeen years old," she said. "I've never owned a slave, I've never wanted to, and they"—speakers who come to the school—"make me feel so guilty for nothing I did. I didn't do *anything*. I've never felt that anybody was any different from me. . . . It's almost like it makes us feel people are making the black kids not like us."

Ronald understood what she was saying, but he wanted her to understand that much of the resentment blacks felt toward whites when they talked—just as she was talking now—about slavery having nothing to do with them, was resentment that came from blacks constantly being passed over for jobs and from being told jobs were "taken" when they weren't.

Danielle didn't deny that that happened (though she professed not to understand why it still did), but she wanted everyone there to know that when she was looking into scholarships to apply for, she discovered that the majority of them were for blacks. "That's hard for me," she said, "because I have no money. How was I going to get to school, you know? So you're not the only people being held back." Danielle came from the School of Positive Thinking, a school whose mottoes were "Nobody's going to get the first job that they go for" and "If you are a good enough worker, somebody's gonna see that sooner or later and you're gonna get up there. And once you're in there, you can just show how good you are and you'll keep going up."

I couldn't stop from smiling. It must be so wonderful to be seven-teen and possess such a vision of the world and the way it worked. Frankly, I had clung to this same vision until I was in my early thirties, when a thera-pist informed me, as nicely as he could, that just because someone hired me, it didn't necessarily mean he was going to be thinking of my best in-terests from that point forward until the end of time. The whole notion of merit is fine, but it often has more to do with the increasingly mythic American Dream than with the reality of life today.

Ronald's reality was that people he knew got tired of looking for jobs that they ultimately didn't get and wound up taking jobs they were overly qualified for, jobs that made it "virtually impossible to support a family."

"But that doesn't just happen to black people," Danielle said.

"I ain't saying that it happens just to black people."

"I've seen it happen to white people, black people, Hispanics," some-one else joined in.

"That's what I'm saying," Danielle said. "I don't know why every-body makes everything racial. Because the way I see it, everybody has their problems. Not all white people are perfect, not all black people are per-fect, not all Asians are perfect. Not all Asians go home and study."

"We are equal," said Pin, the one Asian-American in the room.

"We are all the same," Danielle said. "We may have different types of problems, but we all have problems."

If people truly believed that, I said, then why did a group of white students, students not much older than themselves, claim that they would demand one million dollars a year for life if it was somehow determined that a mistake had been made and that they were supposed to have been black all along?

The what-if Andrew Hacker had posed to his students at Queens College was met with bewilderment by these high school students in Mil-waukee—bewilderment and sadness that whites could possibly feel so superior to blacks they would want that level of payback. Perhaps they had gotten so used to hearing blacks talk about reparations that it hadn't oc-curred to them that whites would engage in that sort of thing. Or perhaps they couldn't go beyond their own naïveté and grasp that they lived in a world where self-interest came before anything else, where preserving the pyramid meant a lot more than just getting "up there," where saying "We are all the same" was nice, idealistic, empty rhetoric that no one believed or could abide anyway, not because it didn't speak of how "unique" each of us is, but because it contradicts how we ultimately see ourselves—as doing better than this person, as having more money than that one. We can talk all we want about being equal, but find someone who actually believes we are and I'll find a way to get them the money that Hacker's students would want.

Which brings us back to the question of merit, of whether it can coexist with the notion of equality, or whether they are simply odd bedfellows, unhappily wedded, destined to war with each other for the rest of their lives. In order for the two to coexist, there has to be some general consensus of what equality is, of whether the terrain is level and smooth enough for race and class not to matter, for merit to triumph.

But even if merit wins out, that in no way guarantees that the person who has benefited is a person capable of being "truly integrated" in society. If one subscribes to the idea that all of us possess, to varying degrees, an "emotional intelligence," an ability to be empathic, and that having that ability is crucial to any reasonable definition of what success is, then being the smartest person in the room will only get you so far. It may enable you to have a lot of money, it may enable you to live in a gated community, it may afford you the ability to drive straight into your garage without having to talk with anybody, and then, once you are safely inside (or so you would like to think), to cruise the Internet and contend that that constitutes about all the social interaction you want anyway, but it still leaves the question of what you have done—you with your Ivy League degree— to help, even a little bit, solve the country's wrenching social problems that you either drive past or see on television.

The students from Washington High School were right: the worst thing about the verdict and its aftermath was that it offered negativity all around, offered everyone, black and white, a perfectly awful opportunity to sink deeper into their stereotypes, to confirm what they already thought—about the police, about the criminal justice system, about life in the ghetto—and to remark, once again, how sick and tired they were of all this.

"Let the poor live short and brutish lives," Shiva Naipaul wrote in 1980. Had he lived long enough, would he have altered that statement— a prevailing view, in his opinion—in any way? The unfortunate answer is no. He wouldn't have altered it in 1992, in the wake of the riots, and he wouldn't have altered it in 1994, in the wake of the Republican landslide in Congress, or in 1996 with welfare "reform" that will cast more than one million additional children into poverty. He knew about short attention spans and he knew how his "brown presence" could unhinge people. Most of all, he knew about self-interest, and he knew about mean-spiritedness, and he knew about venality.

The students who sat around that table, regardless of how naïve they might have been in their hopes for the future, were entitled to more than they were likely to get. When I asked Ronald what scenario he would create for himself if he could, this was what he said: "I'm not gonna let anything get in my way. I have many goals since I was young and I'm gonna try my best to achieve them. Just because Rodney King happened, I could sit back and think about it, but I can't do anything about it. . . . What makes you think they gonna listen to me? A lot of younger kids, they know a great deal about this and people just don't wanna listen to them. I don't know, why is that? Why do they wanna listen to the older folks but they don't wanna listen to us? We have a great deal of information about the things that are going on, but people just don't wanna listen to us."

What Ronald wanted to do, more than anything else, was "stop all these crimes. You can't go around killing people. You have to stop. You're just killing your own race and then this world is going to come to an end. To me, we are the last generation. . . . I don't think there's going to be any future, because the black race is going to kill theirself off the face of the earth, to tell you the truth about it."

But white America, a black girl named Aniedre said, had to admit that they were part of the problem. They were in a position to help "stop the mess," but to do that they had to stop doing things—"quick little escapes," she called them—like running ads for a Drug-Free America with a black kid pictured as the drug dealer. And they had to stop, once and for all, thinking of themselves as so much better than everyone else.

OUTSIDE, THE SUN WAS shining. It was spring, a splendid time of year almost anywhere you went, the time of year in which you could almost convince yourself that all was right with the world. But the country was not in splendid shape. Michael McGee was right. Violence, even the threat of it, was a pretty reliable way to capture people's attention, and always had been. But the difference between the Gulf War (which George Bush was pinning his reelection hopes on) and Los Angeles was that the country could galvanize itself (in an embarrassing display of patriotic zealotry) against the person and regime of Saddam Hussein, whereas there was no singular enemy in Los Angeles for everyone to agree on and be outraged against. As John Fitzgerald told me the evening before, "You could be opposed to the verdict, but were you opposed to the legal system that rendered the verdict or were you opposed to racism, period? Were you opposed to violence? There just seemed to be so many poorly defined things happening here, so difficult to respond to. And that's, I guess, why I really question whether or not there's going to be any really meaningful response. Was there clear racism involved on the jury, or was it institutionalized racism in that the jurists weren't handpicked to be white people, [but] the trial was moved to a county where there are very few African-Americans?" Where, he wanted to know, did you direct your energies in something like this? Aside from watching people clean up the streets with brooms, people who might not have had any contact with each other prior to this ("seems like a pretty horrible cost to bring that about"), he didn't trust that any kind of political solution would ultimately come.

"There'll be a lot of talk and a lot of screwing around as usual," he said. "Maybe a rechanneling of some money. But I sincerely doubt that much different will happen. . . . I mean, our attention span is pretty darn short." Not only did John find all the political finger-pointing distasteful— Bush blaming the riots on the Democrats and the failed policies of the sixties and Clinton countering that it was the twelve years under Reagan and Bush that were the underlying cause—but it only served to blur the fact that no one was exempt from blame.

In the case of Jesse Anderson, for instance, and his story about how he and his wife were attacked, John never doubted it (as he had doubted the black woman he encountered that night coming out of the movie). It *never* crossed his mind that Anderson might be lying. It didn't occur to him because "every single day" he would hear about "another murder, another murder, another murder, or somebody accused of it, and here was another one." When he found out that Anderson had killed his wife, he was angry— angry with Anderson for trying to dupe everybody, but even more angry with himself, that he had just accepted something that he should have at least questioned.

So what specifically was he going to do in response to what had happened in Los Angeles?

Well, for one thing, he had been talking with the kids he worked with about it, just as he had been talking with them all along about his involvement in the Beyond Racism project. And he was thinking that Los Angeles probably offered him a perfect vehicle to organize a neighborhood meeting to discuss all this.

But something was holding him back. He honestly wasn't sure he was ready to do it by himself. He felt he would need someone like Carvis to "balance it out racially." Some of his worst fears about Bay View had come a month earlier, when the *Milwaukee Journal* did an article about the area and how it had historically voted. John's reading of the article made him feel that he was living among racists, only confirming the worries he had when he first moved there from Sherman Park. No one he had spoken with so far agreed with the verdict, but he hadn't spoken with anyone in Bay View. That was one of the reasons he wanted to organize such a meeting— to reassure himself that his neighbors were as outraged by the verdict as he was.

"Are you going to do it?" I pressed him.

"I don't know," he said. "The thing that I've been stuck on is where to go from there once I've got people together. What would be the agenda?"

In his difficulty to move forward, to find out perhaps that people on either side of him thought the verdict in the Rodney King case was just fine, John Fitzgerald was still paralyzed by fear. It was different from the point of fear he had arrived at in Sherman Park, but it was fear nonetheless.

I didn't say this to him as we sat in his backyard, but he might have sensed what I was thinking because just before I left that night, he showed me a letter he had received from his father. Since Easter, he and his father had been talking about racism, and John had told him how he had come, reluctantly, to adopt the definition of it as prejudice plus power.

"I think an essential third ingredient may be fear," John read aloud from what his father wrote. "Whether the racism is expressed by the dominant majority race or by the dominated minority race, both fear and hate the other or the self. Conscious or unconscious is not essential.... Fear generates, magnifies hate, and hate in action is power, whether the action is by the majority or the minority. So chew on that a while...."

· · ·

THE MEETING JOHN THOUGHT about organizing for his neighborhood never took place, despite Carvis's willingness to help him with it. If Carvis was disappointed in John, he never said. (Carvis's wife became increasingly ill during the summer and passed away in late August.) Dealing with the quotidian can often be overwhelming, but it can just as often be used as an excuse for inaction, as a "reason" for insularity. For John Fitzgerald, as for many people, those two aspects usually and uneasily coexist. But when he was confronted with a situation, as he was with the woman from Oshkosh on the night of my talk, he sprang into action, didn't just sit there and allow her to leave without his saying something. Nor did he allow an incident that occurred with his son's best friend to pass without comment, without his attempting to take a stand.

John, Johnny, and Mike (who was getting ready to move away) were driving to an open house at Elm Creative Arts, Johnny's school on the North Side. "As we drive toward Elm," John wrote in his journal, "Johnny excitedly describes his familiarity with the route. He speaks to Mike as though Mike has never seen Milwaukee's downtown. I remind Johnny that Milwaukee is Mike's hometown, but in my mind I too question Mike's knowledge of the city beyond the Bay View neighborhood and I wonder at Johnny's sensitivity to Mike's isolation. . . . When we veer North on 43 Mike is lost. 'Where are we?' he wants to know. I reassure Mike that we are almost there and both boys become excited." But when they arrived at the school's parking lot, Mike's excitement turned to fear, and he began saying in a loud voice, "'Oh no. Oh no. It's all blacks! We don't have any of them at our school. I'm not doing this. Oh no.' The tension in Mike's voice is unmistakable and alarming. I glance in the rearview mirror to see that his entire body has stiffened. He looks scared. His legs are straight and rigid though he is sitting down. His eyes seem drawn to the window, but he doesn't seem to want to look. Johnny is good-naturedly teasing Mike. 'Come on, Mike, my best friend is black' . . . etc. I remember Mike saying, 'We have browns, but no blacks.' It sounds like they'll work this out, I think.

"But when I finally turn off the ignition Mike restates his decision. He will *not* go. Finally I turn in my seat to face Mike directly. I stare him in the eye and say, 'Mike, they are people. Lots of them are my friends.' Live dangerously, I advise him, know as many different people as you can. My words probably meant nothing, but my actions, combined with Johnny's, certainly sent an unmistakable message.

"As Johnny and I got out of the Tercel, Mike got out as well. He walked between us, a little behind. I remember noticing his posture and his resemblance to his older brothers. Hands in pockets, eyes downward. He still looked scared, but the same pose taken by a larger body might have conveyed strength and impenetrability.... Once in school Mike maintained his pose through two long hallways, but he loosened up enough to talk to some of Johnny's ex-teachers when introduced and soon he showed no nervousness at all. In a matter of twenty minutes or less Mike had moved from adamant refusal to engage in an event where blacks were present to running, eating, walking, and talking in the very midst of an undeniably integrated crowd. I take that as a sign of hope and as a reminder of the fears and obstacles we all face.

"What message has Mike received regarding people of color simply by attending a segregated grade school? What message will he receive now, moving from a segregated neighborhood to a segregated suburb—even further removed from contact with the people he has come to fear?"

FORTY-THREE

What, in hindsight, bears remembering about the summer of 1992 in America? That Congress, after a lot of wrangling, finally earmarked additional money for cities across the country to create more summer jobs—America's way of trying to control the steam in Los Angeles and everywhere else. That Ross Perot's address to the annual NAACP convention in Nashville was distinguished by his references to "you people"—references that created an ire he never seemed to fully comprehend but which led in part to his dropping out of the presidential race shortly afterward. That Bill Clinton toured the country by bus and increasingly avoided the "r word" as much as possible. That the Republican convention took Dan Quayle's earlier remarks about *Murphy Brown* and family values and went so far overboard (and toward the religious Right) that even they were embarrassed. That the Census Bureau's announcement that the gap between the median income of white households and black ones had narrowed slightly in the eighties was somewhat encouraging—as were the increases, proportionately speaking, of the number of blacks who had graduated from high school (from 31.4 percent in 1970 to 63.1 percent in 1990) and from college (from 8.4 percent in 1980 to 11.4 percent in 1990). Or that a federal grand jury had decided to indict the four acquitted police officers in the Rodney King incident on the grounds that they had violated King's civil rights—a tactic that was used on a number of occasions in the sixties when a verdict from a state or local court was thought to be a miscarriage of justice.

In Milwaukee, meanwhile, John Norquist was months into his second term and, as it turned out, was preparing to do battle with Howard Fuller—a battle that would, like the fall presidential campaign, scrupulously avoid mention of race, but would, everyone knew, largely be about it. Howard Fuller, with the approval of the school board, was going to be pushing a referendum that would be asking the citizens of Milwaukee to decide if they wanted new schools to be built and others to be renovated, if they wanted to see a public school system of smaller classes, of students learning under better conditions and with more resources, if they wanted the city schools to have more—more of what people had been fleeing Milwaukee to have in the suburbs. And if they wanted these things, they were going to have to say, by their vote, that they were willing to pay for them out of their property taxes. So here Fuller was, in only his second year on the job, showing the citizens, as he had in the school year gone past, that the things he talked about in his eloquent speeches were more than just talk, that he fully intended to oversee change in the Milwaukee Public Schools and he needed their help. His popularity rating in the metropolitan area was higher than that of either the governor or the mayor, but that alone wouldn't necessarily inspire people to part with more money—money, many were arguing, that probably wasn't going to solve MPS's many problems, problems that were too firmly entrenched for one man, no matter how popular or well intentioned, to erase.

The first sign that Mayor Norquist was against what Fuller was proposing came from his director of the Department of Administration, David Riemer. "If it passes, we'll have a massive tax increase," he told the *Milwaukee Journal*. "If it fails, the school system will be another year behind in dealing with their problems." But it wasn't until late October, less than a week before the school board finally yet reluctantly decided to put this before the voters in February, that the mayor himself weighed in with an alternative plan—a plan that was half the cost of Fuller's proposal and would avoid a referendum.

Fuller felt not only outraged, but that he had been lied to. He openly accused the mayor of pandering to the public, of submitting a plan that was full of "contradictions and inconsistencies," and of launching a "clear, unprecedented, and highly undesirable effort to take over responsibility for running the Milwaukee Public Schools." Norquist, for his part, said that "character assassinations are unwarranted and have no place in this discussion." He was disappointed that the school board didn't consider his alternative a viable one, he said, especially when "property-tax payers in this city cannot afford a huge tax increase." A line, it appeared, had been drawn in the sand, and it would now be up to Howard Fuller to make his argument, forcefully and clearly, to the voters, his argument that what he was asking for was more than just bricks and mortar—that it would all translate into a higher standard of education with tangible results.

While all this was going on, Michael McGee saw to it that he was not forgotten. In early October and again on the day before Bill Clinton was elected president of the United States (promising, among other things, "to end welfare as we know it"), McGee was doing part of what he had promised to do nearly three years earlier when he formed the Black Panther Militia—he and a group of others were rolling burning tires down city streets and along the freeway, making the Monday morning commute from Glendale a pleasant beginning to the week. He was charged with criminal disorderly conduct, but that didn't stop him, as he was released on bond, from assuring everyone that the tire burnings would continue. "What are they going to do, vote against me?" McGee said. "I'm an outlaw, and I'm going to show them what an outlaw does. I'm going to make your life miserable."

To my mind, he had become an increasingly sad figure. But he had not quite become the outlaw he claimed to be: he had become what so many ex-politicians were becoming once they left office—a radio talk-show host. Jerrel Jones had given him two hours on Saturday mornings, two hours in which to shower Milwaukee with *Verbs of Power* (as the show was called).

WHAT SPECIFICALLY WOULD THE Clinton presidency mean to the city of Milwaukee and to the country in terms of race relations? Having positioned himself as a New Democrat, a centrist, he had kept his distance from the subject of race (and from Jesse Jackson) as much as possible, had tried to blow kisses to everybody, to be whatever you wanted him to be. Aside from the fact that he garnered only 43 percent of the vote, therein lay, and would continue to lie, an even bigger problem: he was a chameleon, as much of one as my colleague had said race itself was. In the words of presidential historian Richard Reeves, the only thing people could count on when they went to sleep at night, in Milwaukee and everywhere else, was that when the morning came it would bring "another day, another Clinton." That sentiment was expressed well into his first term. At the beginning, though, there was so much hope, so much promise of change from the ways of the previous twelve years. And yet, even before the elation of the election had subsided, reality was setting in, the reality that even if Clinton wanted to use money as a way of attacking the myriad problems of the inner cities, the government coffers were empty, compliments of Reagan and Bush. Money, time, and willpower were, according to the *New York Times,* the three things that the new administration would need to wage this particular battle, and all three, it was soberly suggested, would be in short supply. There was much that needed to be done, not just in the cities, and yet Clinton was giving the impression (somewhat understandable in the heady wake of victory) that he wanted to attack all of it at once: the economy, the budget deficit, health care, welfare, gays in the military, and more. Whatever it was, he would take care of it—provided, that is, he reminded everyone, he could overcome political gridlock. The first member of the sixties generation had ascended to the White House, having talked (and talked) about John F. Kennedy and Franklin Roosevelt all along the way, and it was now time to see what he could do, to watch his hips (as Carvis Braxton would say), not his lips.

It was not that Clinton and George Bush hadn't shared common points of agreement as to what could help the inner cities. Both were in favor of enterprise zones and tenant-owned housing (though Bush didn't embrace these ideas—ideas that Jack Kemp had been harping on and that no one was listening to—until after Los Angeles exploded), and both were in agreement about the importance of work over welfare, of families staying together, and of giving parents as much choice as possible where their children went to school. But Clinton went further, much further, outlining how crucial it was, for both racial harmony and enlightened self-interest (a term that was now a permanent fixture in John Norquist's vocabulary), to continue to have an earned-income tax credit for full-time workers; community financial institutions that would provide capital for inner-city businesses; drug treatment on demand; a national service program as a way of earning a college scholarship; apprenticeship training; strict enforcement of child support; and increased community policing. He was praised, by *The New Republic,* for "displaying knowledge of the new scholarship on race" and for giving "powerful speeches" on the black underclass, and he was praised, by no less than the historian C. Vann Woodward, for being free of the "paternalistic and patronizing" traits that were often common in white guilt.

But there is a difference between being a masterful campaigner perpetually on the move (and, in Clinton's case, in being a remarkable phoenix, able to rise again and again from the ashes) and being someone who can hunker down and endure the day-to-day business of governing, of actually finding a way to achieve what he said he would.

On February 15, 1993, he appeared on national television to inform the American public—prepare them, might be more accurate—about part of what he was going to tell the Congress two nights later: that he would be seeking to raise taxes, not lower them, his campaign promise to do the latter notwithstanding. The ostensible reason, he said, was that the budget deficit was worse than he had been led to believe, that the numbers he had been given by the Bush Administration were not accurate.

FROM HOWARD FULLER'S HOME in Milwaukee there was silence. The timing couldn't have been worse. The referendum was being put before the voters the following day, and the president's dry run of an announcement was not likely to sway an undecided voter to vote yes. The debate over the referendum had become increasingly acerbic since November, and the money that was put toward defeating it far surpassed the money that MPS could legally expend in support of the measure. Bill Lawrence had broken the taboo and uttered out loud what nobody else was willing to—that it was about race—but that didn't tell the whole story. Even though the schools that were to be built and renovated were in the inner city, that didn't mean that every black person—whether he was a homeowner or not, a parent or not, someone who still had kids in school or whose kids were grown and gone—was automatically in favor of it.

In fact, the most vocal opponent turned out to be Polly Williams, the state representative who had been the driving force behind allowing public money to follow a finite number of children to private schools, a plan that the Bush Administration had made part of its America 2000 education initiative. Williams emerged as the only person, black or white, who was willing to debate the issues of the referendum with Howard Fuller, a debate that took place on the evening of February 7 and was broadcast on television. As it happened, it wasn't so much a debate as it was Williams shouting nonstop, shouting about how it was the schools themselves that needed to be changed, that teachers needed to learn how to reach black children, to *respect* black children, and that to ask the citizens to pour hard-earned money into a system that was broken, toward building and renovating new schools when there wasn't even any guarantee that the work was going to be done by black people, was just wrong, wrong, wrong, and that the superintendent, who had railed against MPS for so long, should know that better than anyone.

Frankly, it was astonishing that Fuller was able to maintain his composure for as long as he did. He had long ago learned how to argue, but this was more than anybody should have to endure. Williams was out of control. It's not that the points she was attempting to make weren't good ones, but she was turning the whole thing into an embarrassing debacle, into precisely the sort of incident that might lead a potential voter to conclude that if two black leaders couldn't agree between themselves that passage of this referendum was crucial to the future of Milwaukee, then how could he?

Early polling, done by Peter Hart and Associates, had indicated a favorable response to the referendum, and Fuller had won the backing of the business community, which would be responsible for about 45 percent of the tax increase. But by the third week of January, a poll by the *Milwaukee Sentinel* showed that only 37 percent of whites were likely to be in favor of it, as opposed to 78 percent of blacks. (On John Fitzgerald's street in Bay View, everywhere he looked there were VOTE NO signs in the front windows of houses.) As with much legislation, things kept getting added on, everyone had his hand out, and the school referendum was no exception. For a long time, there had been talk that the city needed a new building for Milwaukee Tech. Since Tech was on the South Side, the thinking went that adding this to the proposal might be just the thing to lure white voters in that part of town, a way of making them feel that all this money wasn't just going to help black kids in the inner city. Call it pragmatic, call it racially manipulative. It was politics, the timeless dance of trying to figure out what your constituents wanted or didn't want, of being in favor of something *only* if you got something in return, of citizens increasingly battling their own cynicism and indifference, trying to absorb and understand what was before them.

Tom Bell, the charismatic teacher from Victor Berger (which had been renamed and was now known as Martin Luther King Jr. Elementary), turned out not to be in favor of the measure. It wasn't just that he was a homeowner and didn't want to pay more in taxes. He had children in public school and he was not convinced that more pleasant surroundings or reduced busing or better resources would result in higher achievement for them or anyone else. His son even told him as much. He couldn't see how the referendum was more than bricks and mortar. He was supportive of everything that Howard Fuller was trying to do—his efforts to shift more money to elementary schools from middle and high schools, the beefing up of security, the push for higher standards and for greater accountability on the part of each school—but he could not in good conscience support this.

And neither could the citizens of Milwaukee. The referendum was defeated by about a 3–1 margin, and voter turnout, especially on the South and Northwest Sides, was defiantly heavy. In fact, the total number of votes cast was the most that had ever been cast in a February election. Howard Fuller had not been counting on that. That was one of the reasons February had been decided on; the lighter the turnout, the better chance the plan would have of passing. The day in question was cold but sunny—a perfect day for voting—and yet the number of people from the North Side who voted was relatively few. Whether, as can often happen, they had decided that the measure was going to lose so what's the point, or they were indifferent, or they didn't fully understand what was at stake, the fact remained: they had not turned out and John Fitzgerald's neighbors had.

ONE MONTH AFTER THE voters had spoken, Howard Fuller was, as usual, in his office on a Sunday afternoon. He had told me to yell up to his second-floor window when I arrived and he would come downstairs and let me in. Milwaukee might have become a big city with big-city problems, but it was still a small town.

As we walked up to his office, I couldn't help noticing how quiet the building was, eerily so, almost as if all the time and energy that Fuller and his colleagues had expended on the referendum had affected the building too, had worn it down. Fuller certainly looked that way, sitting at his desk, jazz playing in the background, picking at some food that his secretary had brought in for him; she, like his mother, constantly worried about his health and his habit of forgetting to eat.

Did he feel, I asked, that his job was both the most important thing he could be doing and the most impossible at the same time?

"It's important because of what it's all about in terms of the kids," he said. "It may be undoable because of all the issues that sort of converge: there are the money issues, there are the union issues, there's all the stuff that's happening to kids, there's just the dynamic of the system itself. There's the expectations of people, there's a growing lack of political support for public schools because of who's in public schools and who's not."

Because of who's in public schools and who's not was the way he had talked about race during the referendum battle without explicitly saying it, the way he had tried to be careful about not baldly fanning that particular flame.

While he insisted that the main reason the referendum was defeated was money—that people were "mad about taxes, period" and "we were the only ones out there where they had a chance to say no; they couldn't say no to the city, they couldn't say no to the county, Clinton gives a speech the night before saying I'm going to raise your taxes"—he conceded that it also turned on race. "But you're in a situation where, if you allow that to become the prominent issue, you lose automatically, because, unfortunately, African-American people don't have the numbers and they don't vote in significant numbers. Even in the African-American community there were splits on this. In part because of class and because a lot of black people have a lot of the same concerns about their property taxes. . . . But if I had to do it all over again, I'd do it again because I think the issues have to be raised. You can't *not* raise real issues. Because it hasn't been raised in twenty-two years is part of where we're at now."

Wouldn't this have been a good opportunity, I said, for someone like Michael McGee to have gotten behind the referendum, to have done something other than burn tires and roll them down freeways, to have helped do the kind of organizing that he and Fuller had done more than ten years earlier on behalf of Ernest Lacy's family?

"I think that would have helped," he said, "but we still would have lost." They had counted on winning with twenty-four thousand "yes" votes, wound up with thirty thousand, and still were defeated by a 3–1 margin.

As for the mayor and the position he took, it only confirmed for Fuller what he had sensed for a while—that the mayor no longer cared about public schools. "I think John is a straight political person. I think he looks at all of this stuff in cold-blooded ways."

I wasn't sure if Fuller really thought that or if he was still licking his wounds. When I pointed out that Norquist was someone who was liberal on social issues but fiscally conservative—another variation on being a New Democrat—Fuller didn't hesitate. "It's a fiscal conservatism that speaks to a certain political base. When you look at Milwaukee, that's the political base that wins. It's not an issue of leadership for what is right, it is an issue of leadership for what wins.

"The *Shepherd Express* asked me, 'Why would you put all of your popularity on the line for something like a referendum that's probably going to lose?' I guess I have the view, Jonathan, if you got any popularity, what good is it if you're not going to use it for something you think is right? What's its value? I don't think you should lead on the basis of what's popular."

But another element to his popularity was at work here, an element that was universal, that went beyond race and class, and was something he had had to contend with all his life. In the black community, be it in Milwaukee or elsewhere, the element of jealousy centered around "who's going to be the Head Negro," he said. It had most recently surfaced in the debate with Polly Williams, an encounter that hurt her (in his opinion), but had the even more harmful effect of showing two black leaders wrangling with each other in a manner that was more ugly than enlightening.

As for the job he was trying to do and whether he could last in it (the mortality rate for urban superintendents hardly ever exceeded two years), Fuller said that he had two or three basic problems, problems that were specific to him. The fact that he hadn't "come up through the ranks" was either a strength or a weakness, he said, depending on how you viewed it. While it meant that he had to rely on other people for specific advice, it also meant that he wasn't "married to a whole lot of stuff," that he was likely to ask questions that a lot of other people might not. His second "problem" was that he had not managed to keep "the kind of professional objectivity that you sort of need to survive in this job. I let too much stuff get to me. You can't let every incident report that comes across your desk . . . kids pulling knives or guns, fights, buses being shot at . . . every one of those incidents means something to me. It's not like a statistic. . . . I'm just concerned that people are starting to accept this stuff as the way it is." Three days earlier he had asked the mayor to set up a task force on juvenile violence. He didn't have any illusions that it would ultimately solve anything, but it was at least a way, he said, to keep the issue before the public, to "not just let it get woven into the 'urban lifestyle' or whatever it is."

His third and final "problem" had to do, he felt, with his own candor, candor that stemmed from the fact that he didn't see himself as a careerist, from his not wanting to be superintendent anywhere but Milwaukee. "I'm just interested in trying to figure out if we can come up with a way to better educate kids so that they'll have a chance in the twenty-first century. That's really all I want to do. And to figure out whether or not the public school system can be changed deep enough and fast enough to deal with the interests and the needs of the kids that we currently have"—not, as he had often said, the ones who used to be there, another veiled reference to the number of (mostly) white kids who had fled to the suburbs or to private schools.

His personal problems aside, two things had occurred recently that touched on race even more than the referendum had. One had to do with the renaming of Fulton Middle School, the second of the two African-American immersion schools to open in Milwaukee. The renaming of Victor Berger as Martin Luther King Jr. Elementary had gone smoothly the previous January, the decision having been arrived at by popular vote. Fulton turned out to be another matter. The choice was Malcolm X Academy, no doubt partly fueled by the past November's opening of Spike Lee's long-awaited movie. Certain members of the school board raised vehement objections, and they were not subtle about it: Malcolm X, in their opinion, was not a suitable role model, not someone to be admired. If they had seen the movie or even cared to find out more about him than they already knew—or thought they did—they would have realized that he deserved to have a school named after him. After all, so many people transparently donate huge amounts of money to have the same honor, and they are not always people of unassailable character. And what right did members of the school board have to interfere with the workings of democracy, to decide they wanted to change the rules of the game and start over just because they didn't agree with the outcome? (It was reminiscent of the enormous controversy that ensued after Maya Lin's design was chosen, in an anonymous competition, to be the design for the Vietnam Veterans Memorial.)

Finally, there was one last element here, an element deeply ironic and barely noted, and that involved Howard Fuller himself. Here was someone who had once said that Malcolm X had made him face up to his blackness more than anyone else, someone who had started a college in Malcolm's name; here was Howard Fuller, as superintendent of the Milwaukee Public Schools, being confronted with a sterling example of whites still trying to control things, no matter what the rules. Whether King was "safe" and Malcolm was not (in the eyes of white America) didn't matter. What mattered was that these schools were being attended by African-Americans, schools that were partly designed to help those attending them develop a stronger sense of self-esteem, and Dr. King and Malcolm X were figures clearly consistent with that intent. The good news was that the name "Malcolm X Academy" was allowed to stand, that democracy, ultimately, managed to prevail.

No sooner was that battle done with than another matter resolved itself, one involving how many black teachers would be allowed to teach at the immersion schools. Without waiting for the approval of the union, Fuller had allowed both schools to have a staff that was one-third African-American, which was roughly 10 percent more than the total number of blacks teaching within MPS. The teachers union argued that *no* school, immersion or not, should have more than the overall percentage of black faculty, and they filed a suit—a suit that had been decided a few days earlier in the union's favor. Fuller had done what he thought was right, what he thought would help give the schools the best chance of accomplishing their mission, but the union was powerful and the union won out.

As Fuller's second year was drawing to a close, though, there were things he felt positively about. He was moving the system along to being more a system of schools, schools whose principals and staff had greater latitude to make their own decisions, which they would be accountable for. He felt he was establishing a good relationship with the kids themselves. Third-grade reading scores had improved, partly because of more resources devoted to the elementary schools. The dropout rate had stabilized. The new disciplinary plan and safety policies had helped "somewhat."

Having said that, he also said that it wasn't clear how much longer he would be able to do the job. "The only way you can actually make a difference," he said, "is if you're able to stay for five, six, seven, or eight years." In the first couple of years, he said, "all you're going to hit is negatives," and he could see he was getting to the point where perhaps he had been in too many wars over the years.

"But you choose them," I reminded him.

"Right," he said, "I choose them . . . but what I'm saying is—"

"That's part of your makeup," I said. "You see a conflict or problem that a majority of people walk away from, you move toward it."

"Yeah, but it takes its toll. It's harder now to get up every day to go out there. The referendum was a physical and mental grind. The day after the referendum I was in a budget meeting for four hours. The day after that I was doing negotiations for five and a half hours. You know what I'm saying?"

I did know what he was saying. I had written a book about a man, a college president, who wound up disappearing of his own volition, partly because he had grown weary of the same grind Fuller was talking about, weary of "process and procedure, year after year." But I remembered a different Fuller, who, not long after he took the job, had said just the opposite—that he looked forward to getting up every day and fighting for the children of Milwaukee. So it was hard to gauge whether this was a temporary aberration, or whether he had serious doubts as to how much longer he could go on. He found it hard to accept that "you have a lot of people who work for this school district who don't like these kids. They work for it and are sort of pissed off at me because they probably blame me for some of the things that are happening. Some of it they ought to blame me for and I'm glad they do because I hope I am a part of changing some of the stuff."

Now that the referendum was over, I asked, did he plan to sit down with the mayor and find a way to move forward?

"I think the position dictates that I have to do that."

"What does he have to offer you?"

"Not a lot. I assume it's the perception that the mayor and the superintendent are working together. There are some things that John could help with, if he wanted to, that could bring some resources. But I just don't think that John has any commitment to public schools." As far as he was concerned, Fuller didn't see how a city—any city—could survive without a viable public school system. The vast majority of black kids were going to be in public schools and unless the complicated issues facing public schools were addressed, he didn't see how the long-term viability of Milwaukee could be.

He had recently gone to Germany to learn about that country's apprenticeship programs. Part of dealing with the kids who were currently in MPS was dealing with the fact that a large number would not be going on to college. One of the things being discussed in Milwaukee and elsewhere was a school-to-work program that would get them off the track of "general education that leads them to nowhere" and onto one that would be more tailored to the world of work and still be more academically oriented than the traditional vocational-technical program.

And yet, he said, there was still an element of Catch-22.

"To say you're going to prepare them for the world of work raises the question of Where's the work? That's the other side of the problem." It was one thing to have all these summer jobs, he said, but "America is not going to be saved" because of them. "That may keep kids from burning up stuff, or whatever, but it's an illusion. . . . The question is real jobs, ongoing, not just for kids, but for parents of the kids. I know that they [the Clinton Administration] know that. It's not like I'm sitting here with some great issue. I heard [Secretary of Labor Robert] Reich talk when I was out in Washington last week. I read his latest book and clearly he understands . . . but like all of us, once you get into these positions, then you start running into the reality of all the bullshit that you have to deal with. It becomes a real question: how much you can actually do, even though you have a vision of what ought to be done."

In Milwaukee, as in Washington, there was no "community consensus" as to the best way to move forward. "We're still in a lot of ways very factionalized," Fuller said. "Maybe all cities are that way, but I know we're seriously that way around issues of race." But even if there was unity, he said, he didn't know what specific strategy would ensure there would be jobs. "Ultimately, people that have capital have to be willing to invest it. I don't know if people are willing to do that."

On my way out to Howard's office that morning, I had driven past Steeltech, the minority-owned firm employing some one hundred (mainly inner-city) workers that was located along the Twenty-seventh Street corridor, one of the vacant-land areas that the city was trying to entice businesses to come in and develop. Steeltech's coming about had been slow and mired in difficulty, but it was there, a hopeful sign in itself.

When I asked Fuller about it, though, his response was less than enthusiastic. It wasn't that he didn't think Steeltech, or the Milwaukee Community Service Corps, or the efforts the city was making in Metcalfe Park weren't positive things to be embraced. It was just that you needed hundreds of things like this that were well managed and productive to make an impact. And yet at the same time he caught himself before he plunged into full-blown pessimism and cynicism. "If you approach this thing only at the macro level," he said, "then you'll throw up your hands. The kinds of programs that you're talking about are valuable and important, but when you look at the depth of the problem, you keep trying to figure out how much time do you have before we have another whole generation of people who are just not connected to anyplace."

FORTY-FOUR

John Fitzgerald was as disappointed by the defeat of the school referendum as anyone I talked with, his disappointment tempered by cynicism the night afterward, when President Clinton addressed the Congress. "As Clinton's new cabinet enters the House of Representatives," he wrote in his journal, "I can hear the emotion in Leslie's voice. She points out to Johnny that this cabinet includes women and people of color. This, I hear her telling Johnny, is an important moment in history." John's excitement about Clinton's election, though, was now marked by wariness, by the realization that Clinton's relentless effort to liken himself to JFK was a form of seduction for people like him, a seduction he would rather not participate in because, he wrote, "I want to defend myself from a hurt I remember.... My cynicism is laid bare ... and I want to nourish it. I want to hold on to it and feel protected. What tremendous risk there is in trusting again."

He was articulating something in a way I had never been able to, viewing the loss of national innocence that followed President Kennedy's assassination as a lovely relationship gone awry, making it difficult to find yourself that vulnerable once more.

But the issue of risk and trust for John Fitzgerald extended beyond the election of Bill Clinton. It lay at the core of why he had ventured into the Beyond Racism project in the first place and why he was having trouble doing just that—getting beyond racism. Even though he had formed his alliance with Carvis, even though he had talked about doing things in his neighborhood, he continued to live on some level as if racism didn't exist, choosing "*not* to deal with it," he wrote, continuing to "enjoy the status quo" instead. "To confront racism," he revealed in his journal, "I must threaten my own safety and status." The group he had gone through the training with had recently gotten together and L. G. Shanklin-Flowers had asked him what it had been like to be the oldest of ten and receive the kind of attention he must have received. "Privileged," had been his answer, supported, admired, referred to as "King." And what were the costs, she wondered, of being a "nice Catholic boy"? Not knowing himself, covering up, wearing masks, he told her.

"I'm a white adult male now," he wrote, "still 'nice' if not as Catholic and still hiding myself because to voice my feelings, resentments, anger would threaten my position—my status—my privilege. I'm aware of this at work—do I want to be perceived as *the* person who challenges norms— who reminds people *always* of their prejudices—who challenges each and every system?

"How about in my neighborhood? Do I want to pick up Racism like De [a cleaning woman at the hospital] picks up her dust rag everyday? Add it to my problems—atop all my other challenges—make it part of who I am. Man-Father-Son-Brother-Friend-challenger of racism-counselor-artist-boy-myself?"

Had he sounded consistently confident from the beginning about his ability to play a role in getting himself and others beyond racism, then this passage from his journal would have been surprising as well as disappointing—disappointing in that a mere year or so after he had embarked on this, he was having serious doubts about whether he could. But those doubts, in fact, had always been there; he was trying to overcome them, to be sure, but they were present nonetheless. I wasn't judging John, not really. But I also felt that if someone like John Fitzgerald came to the conclusion, rightly or wrongly, rationally or irrationally, that he couldn't carry his commitment forward, that his enjoyment of the status quo—regardless of guilt, the Catholic kind or any other—was finally more important to him than putting himself in a position to help, to *risk* bringing about change, then there was ample reason to despair that change would ever come, that the considerable chasm between blacks and whites would ever be bridged.

Was this something I raised with him, or even subtly suggested? The answer is no. Because his sensitivity and sense of responsibility was so finely honed already, it would have been a cruel thing to do, would have made him more frantic than he was anyway, trying, day in and day out, to make sense of his life. John Fitzgerald was the kind of person that Socrates would have had in mind when he said that "the unexamined life is not worth living."

WHEN JOHN AND CARVIS came to my room that March, it was the first time I had seen them together since the night of my talk at the university the previous May. Since his wife's death in August, Carvis had been balancing his work at the East Side Housing Action Coalition with his new responsibilities as a single parent. It was not easy and he was lonely, but he hadn't lost his sense of humor, revealing with a smile that there was no shortage of women who wanted to come over and cook him supper. (Actually, Carvis was a pretty good cook himself, as I discovered a week later when he had me over for catfish and an evening of March Madness, an evening in which I unintentionally rose in his estimation by bringing up the name of Tom Stith when our conversation turned to the past glory of St. Bonaventure basketball.) One of the things he had been doing at ESHAC was trying to get out a yes vote for the school referendum, but since many people who lived in that particular neighborhood were "conservative and older," with kids who were grown, "there wasn't that real gut closeness to the schools."

What bothered both Carvis and John was that their kids would come home and say they were against the referendum. Teachers at Johnny's school gave him the impression that a school like his might cease to exist if the measure were to pass, and Candace, Carvis's youngest, told him she had voted against it in a straw poll, which surprised him because they hadn't discussed it very much. John had found himself wondering if the result would have been different had a white superintendent brought the referendum, and Carvis sensed trouble in the way it was constantly referred to as "Howard's referendum," which only reinforced what he had told me when I first met him, his concern that it was dangerous to have too much invested in one individual, especially if that person were to suddenly shift direction and do something else. And yet, despite its resounding defeat, Carvis felt (as Fuller did) that bringing the referendum before the voters had been the right thing to do. "If this referendum was not raised," he said, "most folks" (and he included middle-class blacks in this category) "would have went on doing business as usual and wouldn't have been conscious of what was going on." He recalled, with some bitterness, the big education summit that had been held in Charlottesville in the fall of 1989, the one that proclaimed, in his words, "'Education gonna be number one agenda for the next decade.' Yep. Not public education. Isn't public education for poor folks that live in inner cities? Those that can get education send their kids to private schools or better schools."

Part of his bitterness had to do with feeling that the Milwaukee Public Schools hadn't taught his kids to learn—not to the extent that they should have. "You're working," he said, "doing these things to maintain yourself. You don't have the time and energy you'd like to have to make sure that they get a good education. Therefore you give it to the teachers and administration to make sure that they provide it. And they're not. I feel like I'm shortchanged, but right now it's the only system I have to work with. Can't afford to send them to private schools."

Neither could John, and neither of them really wanted to, but Johnny went to a magnet school, the kind of place where, Carvis said, "those who know how to use the system . . . get their kids in." John winced when Carvis said that, but he couldn't deny it. His wife had done just that, a matter of "Leslie learning the system and following up, and then a certain amount of luck with him just getting chosen somehow or another."

This subject could have been a source of tension between them, but they didn't allow it to be. Each of them spoke his mind and they moved on. John had done his best to be supportive of Carvis during his wife's illness and Carvis appreciated that. There was an ease to their relationship now that wasn't there before. They had found (finally) in Café Mélange a place where they could listen to music and where they both felt comfortable. They had gone to baseball games together and, a few nights earlier, to a Bucks game at the Bradley Center. John had come to Carvis's house after his wife died and he had gone to a birthday party for Carvis's brother, where he met family members who had come all the way from Buffalo ("Anything to get out of Buffalo," Carvis laughed), and Carvis was now kidding John that the "only thing you and I haven't had a chance to do is get drunk together."

John laughed for a second, but, all in all, he seemed rather gloomy. He had just heard Andrew Hacker (whose book *Two Nations* had come out in paperback) interviewed on National Public Radio, had heard him say that white America wasn't going to do anything about racism, that whites enjoyed "our privilege" far too much to do anything about it, and that "these feel-good groups that get together and have a good time meeting together and everything basically are hogwash. So I couldn't help but think about Beyond Racism and think, Is this really all just a waste of time?" John had recently decided to become a facilitator for the project and he had gone off for a weekend of training that he felt good about and then he heard the Hacker interview and "I had to admit that in the context of what Hacker was talking about, we hadn't done *anything* that was going to impact institutionalized racism. We didn't change any hiring practice in any local firm or anything like that. We'd just gotten together and talked out some stuff. Some people got some feelings out that were hard for them to express. I felt good. Then I heard this interview and I didn't feel so good about it anymore. Is this guy right, is this all just a waste of time? I thought about it since then and I haven't talked to Carvis about this yet, but I guess I've felt like, shit, I've spent all my working life working on things that are almost unchangeable" (by which he meant other people's drug and emotional problems and now racism).

Carvis listened to all of this without saying anything. Whether he recalled my bringing up Hacker's book during my talk at UWM (particularly the question Hacker had posed to his white students about what they would do if they suddenly discovered they were black), he didn't say. Nor did he say that he was disappointed in John for not actively trying to involve more white males in the process. But what he did say was not dissimilar to things he had said before, and it coincided, in its way and in its tone, with Hacker. "All the talk doesn't mean anything until you actually take the risk and interact with your neighbors. Black folks have to do it all the time. They lose friends, relationships, everything, trying to get folks involved." He leaned forward at that moment, looked directly at both of us, and said, weariness in his face, that he had arrived at a point, a point of feeling that unless white males either went through the process of trying to change things—"or even have the thought process that they need to do something"—then "no shit gonna happen."

As he said that, though, I also recalled the times he had said that blacks shouldn't be waiting around for whites to do anything, that the only way blacks could and should move forward was under their own steam. Like any relationship, any marriage, between two people—and this particular one between blacks and whites had been uneasy and strife-ridden for hundreds of years—the cooperation of both parties would be required to make it work, to achieve a delicate balance, to find a way that the interests and needs of both, including the need to be independent of each other, could be respected, equally. On the surface, it sounds like a reasonable thing to move toward, but reason has, alas, very little to do with it.

JOHN'S MOTHER HAD BEEN in Milwaukee recently and had decided to perform the role of devil's advocate, a role she had reprised numerous times over the years with her oldest son. She had come to celebrate her sixty-fifth birthday and John had been with members of his particular Beyond Racism group earlier in the day and he was talking with her about his thoughts, his doubts, and his fears of extending what he had learned to other people, of approaching them about a subject people would rather not talk about, a subject that was easier, far easier, to live in denial about than to face up to.

"She was playing some of those white people that you probably won't see in a Beyond Racism workshop," he said. "You know, 'What's in it for me?' Those questions are really hard to answer unless you're talking to somebody who's already struggling with it. . . . It's like, 'What the hell do I care? Why do I care if I ever meet anybody from that race? Why do I care if my kids ever hang out with them? What's my big loss? I've got millions of white people to hang out with, I don't live in those neighborhoods, I don't care to do that.'"

"How did you answer her?" I said.

He responded by recalling childhood, not just his necessarily, but the point at which (if you're white) you start "to be desensitized and trained into the role of keeping the system going," forgetting all the things you lose by doing that—"the friends that you could have had or that you did have but that you just didn't hang around with anymore, or relationships that you never even considered as possible even though the people were in your life." He also told her that the best he could do, he realized, was to "work with people that are interested . . . people like me who were already uncomfortable . . . who were aware of feeling afraid or isolated."

That, as it turned out, was the hidden reason Carvis had invited John to his brother's birthday party: he wanted him to meet blacks who were "solid on their feet," who could be "nurtured and organized to take an active role" both in Milwaukee and in the Beyond Racism project, to let John see what the next step, the one that John was having such a hard time taking, could be like. All his life, Carvis had been intent on trying to enable blacks to feel secure and comfortable enough with themselves that they could gain and have some sense of power and control. Unless that was accomplished first, he said, there was no point in even analyzing integration, or how race relations could be improved, or in talking about anything along those lines, for that matter.

Since I had spent a good bit of time talking with them months earlier about the Rodney King incident and its aftermath, I told them about an assignment I had given my writing class in the autumn, an assignment that posed the question "It's early September, four months have elapsed since the verdict in the Rodney King case; what has happened since that time?" I had asked them to write it, more or less, as a personal essay because I was curious to find out to what degree each of them had been affected by those events, to what degree each of them knew, or didn't know, what was being done to "rebuild L.A.," to what degree each of them was even still thinking about those events.

The best essay was written by a student who least needed the assignment, a student who was working at a shelter and was involved in many community projects. "Day after day," I told Carvis and John, "he would play basketball at this particular place, where he would be one of only two white kids on the court. After the verdict, he suddenly became aware of something that he hadn't been made aware of before—that he was white. They didn't want him playing with them anymore. That made him angry. He said, 'I'm the same kid who was here last week and the week before and the week before that and you were happy to have me play here, and now, basically I'm a white kid who can't jump.'" He found out what blacks had long experienced—that whatever individual qualities a person might have would be forgotten in the face of such a racially polarizing incident, that he would be lumped together and categorized as white, as an oppressor, as someone they didn't want around. Adam Cohen was smart enough to know that racism came from both directions, that it was often fueled more by emotion than by reason, but that wasn't of much consolation to him at that moment. Much as a person might like to believe that he is an exception, that what is true of other people is not necessarily true of him, that what can happen to other people won't necessarily happen to him, it is rarely the case. In instances like these, especially, the great maw of stereotype and generalization swallows everything and everyone in its path, and it does so indiscriminately.

The four acquitted police officers were about to come to trial again (in the civil suit), and Carvis wanted to know what, if anything, people in Virginia were saying about it. I told him that current talk was much more about the bombing at the World Trade Center, but I also told him that everyone seemed aware that if there was another acquittal, rioting could break out once more.

The new trial of the officers was about to take place at the same time as the trial of the four black youths who had pulled Reginald Denny out of his truck and viciously beaten him. Carvis's concern about that incident was that whites would feel *all* blacks agreed with that, that it was proper retribution for the verdict. "They were wrong," Carvis said. "Wrong is wrong. I mean, most normal average folks know they was wrong.... I don't know if that's the same perception outside the inner cities, thinking that all blacks think the same way and feel the same way. I hope not."

What the verdict in the King case only underlined for Carvis and John was the extent to which whites managed to accept things as they were and blacks to accept that nothing was going to change, at least not in any substantial way. "We're talking about something that people have denied for so long, not knowing that they're racist," Carvis said. Nonetheless, he had always made sure that even if his kids lived in a segregated neighborhood, they would go to places where whites were. It was, he said, a conscious decision he had made a long time before—just as he had decided to have a white man play New Orleans jazz at his wife's funeral.

He had mentioned this man to me previously, an Englishman named Norrie Cox, someone who believed, as Carvis did, in the necessity of preserving New Orleans jazz as a crucial part of black culture. Carvis knew that people might be unhappy about Cox's presence, but his feeling was that in order "to deal with this stuff, we have to do some unusual things and *not* do what's expected." But having Norrie Cox play jazz at the funeral, Carvis admitted, was probably not something he would have done had he not gone through the Beyond Racism process. Nobody, not one person, said anything to Carvis afterward, but instead of thinking that they were displeased, even angered, he chose to view their silence as affirmation that this was the way things *should* be.

TWO WEEKS EARLIER, THERE had been an anniversary of sorts: twenty-five years had passed since the release of the Kerner Commission's report. But there was little cause for celebration. The path that the report predicted America was on sadly turned out to be the path it had, by and large, taken— two societies, black and white, separate and unequal. The Los Angeles riots had reminded people of why the commission had been formed in the first place, reminded people that its warning had mainly gone unheeded. When four of the five living members of the original panel of eleven were contacted by the *Boston Globe,* they expressed the opinion that poverty, segregation, and lack of opportunity remained "as divisive and damning as ever."

A month later, in mid-April, two of the four officers in Los Angeles were found guilty and there was cheering at the church in South-Central where Jesse Jackson had gone to speak. But the cheering was more out of relief—delayed justice was certainly better than none—than out of any conviction that the problems South-Central (and communities like it) faced were going to be solved any time soon.

F O R T Y - F I V E

As I had found so often, something would happen, or someone would say something, that would bring me to a halt, would cause me to stand back from all that I was hearing and observing and thinking about and just stop. Such a moment occurred when Danny Tinnon, the co-facilitator of the Minority Male Opportunity and Responsibility program, suddenly began talking about how he measured success among the young men he worked with, about how it was more than the individual simply saying that he was willing to do whatever was necessary to improve himself and his community. What really convinced Tinnon that what he was doing was worthwhile was when a young man "can really, actually touch things in his environment—nature, trees—can see the blue sky, the moon, he can count the stars, he can see the different constellations and know the difference, and talk about it, can say, 'Hey, I'm one of those, talking about a star.'"

For Pamela Jefferson, Tinnon's partner, success was measured by the degree to which participants would open up about things that had bothered them for quite some time—things like being bused far from their neighborhood or holding up their hand and not being called upon ("psychological battery," one man called it) or being called stupid and ignorant, or being asked by the white principal of a 220 school in the suburbs to essentially tell state officials that everything was going fine and you were extremely happy when everything wasn't and you were anything but. She had one young man, about thirty, who had been on general assistance (GA) for eleven years and "no one had case-managed him. We began to say, 'Who loved you? When I look at you, I see myself.' We would give him hugs and just love him, and nurture him, and stroke him, and this guy began to shine, began to feel good about himself. He's still not really ready to get a job. There's still a long way to go. But I measure success in the fact that there's self-esteem and that they're beginning to feel good about themselves, their personal grooming, their self-growth, their culture. . . . They're going to the library . . . they're beginning to see how wonderful life really is and how much they have to offer. They're doing a lot of community work. We've been talking about community for a long time. About what has happened to our communities. And these guys are saying, 'I remember when this happened, I remember when this used to happen when I was a little boy.' Well, what happened, how did we lose that? So they're going back and they're recapturing that and they're passing it on to their families and they'll come back and they'll say, 'Mrs. Jefferson, we all sat down, we had dinner, we said the family grace just like my grandmother used to do it, we went to the movies.' Things that are so common to other people are so far from them." And it was because they seemed so common, so matter-of-fact, that the media, she complained, didn't seem as interested in them as they were in the next drive-by.

Having said all that, she understandably displayed little patience when the group got together the next day and began putting themselves down. She was sick and tired of hearing them do that, especially since they were avoiding what she called "the real issue" racism—"the hurt that most men won't talk about." There had been much talk about unity and how working to eliminate slavery had provided it, how segregation had, in a way, provided it, how the civil rights movement had provided it, how the abundance of low-skilled manufacturing jobs had provided it, how spiritual belief had provided it. But now "there's no more plural we, it's singular I," and everyone, it seemed, who had the means to move out of the inner city did (even if they weren't exactly welcomed in the neighborhoods where they moved), and families were breaking down and black men were more endangered than ever.

It was one thing to hear Pamela Jefferson tell me of someone who would raise his hand and be ignored in school and quite another to witness the pain in the face of a young man named Clarence as he recalled that happening to him as a child and wondering, along with the other black kids in the class, "What are we doing here? Aren't we as good as these white kids?" or recalling, when he was asked to read aloud, how no sooner did he begin than he was asked to speak up (regardless of how well he was reading) and to "spell that word on the board," whatever that word happened to be. "It made me question myself as far as reading in front of people. This angered me, because—and I'm putting this in a very blunt sentence— why would I want to be in an atmosphere where I constantly got shit on in my face?"

I didn't doubt what Clarence was telling me. I didn't doubt it because I had talked to enough other people who had recounted similar things, and because I saw enough nodding heads right in that room to convince me that Clarence's anger was shared by them. Did I think that Clarence—or anyone else, for that matter—was trying to present himself as a totally innocent victim of circumstance? No, I did not. But the accretion of all these experiences counted for something. When a teacher at a school blithely recites the beginning of the nursery rhyme that goes "Eenie, meenie, minie, mo, catch a nigger by the toe" and only receives the equivalent of a slap on the wrist, that is wrong. It sends a message, and those messages accumulate. That simply can't be tolerated. I shudder to think how many times I recited that rhyme when I was about six or seven—the same age Clarence was talking about—and nobody, not one person, told me not to. I guess that's part of what Kristie Jorgenson and Darlene Siebert meant when they talked about the socialization process. Well, it was in the late fifties when I first learned that pernicious rhyme and, I suppose, someone might argue it was unlikely that I would have been reprimanded for repeating it then. But the incident I'm referring to occurred in a suburb of Milwaukee, in 1993, and the teacher kept her job.

IT HAD BEEN A while since I had visited Tom Bell's classroom at Martin Luther King Jr. Elementary, and I went back to it now because I wanted to reassure myself that teachers like him were continuing to do what I had first seen them do in the fall of 1991—treat their students with the dignity and respect that Clarence and others said they had not been accorded. I wanted to find out how Princess Johnson and Shukuha Hoskins and Andrea Word were doing, as well as the boys I had gone to the wrestling match with—wanted to find out if the African-American immersion program was having its desired effects.

Bell himself was disappointed so far. He was disappointed that many of the people who had put themselves forward as mentors had either lost interest, had shifted their interest to Malcolm X Academy, or had become frustrated by the unwillingness of certain parents to allow a mentor relationship to truly develop with their children. He was disappointed that not all his students wore their navy-and-yellow uniforms (especially since they had helped to "keep down" the number of fights), and he was disappointed that parental involvement had not increased all that much.

But there were things he was pleased by too. The idea of his having the same group of kids for a three-year period provided both continuity and stability ("When I say I'm coming over, they know I'm coming. I say I'm calling, they know I'm calling"). The school now had a choir so excellent that the kids had been on TV and even gone as far as Chicago to perform. And yet, much as he might want to, he couldn't become each child's parent, nor could he prevent them—child and parent—from doing the things they did. He couldn't prevent Antonio from attacking a kid and "strong-arming" his tennis shoes—nor could he prevent Antonio and Tavares's mother from throwing away two bicycles that Bell had fixed up and given them, simply because they were moving and the bikes had flat tires and she didn't want to be bothered with repairing them. He couldn't prevent Danielle Jones's mother from keeping Danielle out of school just because Danielle decided she wanted to go shopping. He couldn't do much about the fact that nobody seemed to want Tremaine playing with their kids and that, as a result, he was likely to find a gang to play a different sort of game with.

Bell had been teaching long enough to know that he couldn't save everybody. So he just kept on, doing what seemed both natural and imperative to him, showing them articles in *Ebony* and *Jet* (articles that revealed that nearly every person who had become a success had become one because "somebody somewhere encouraged them some way"), continuing to go to after-school events with them "because the children can't get other people to watch them.

"You got to push them on," he said. "But we not doing that." Head Start and all-day kindergarten (which not every child was able to attend for lack of space) were fine, he pointed out, "but you still got that fourth-grade block. When the kids get to fourth grade, something happens. I don't know if you've followed that before."

I had. It was referred to as the fourth-grade "fade," and it had partly to do with peer pressure and partly to do with the fact that students didn't receive the same sort of nurturing that they had in Head Start and kindergarten. As far as Tom Bell was concerned, it had to do with the time and effort the upper grades required. Many of the parents were unable—for whatever reason—to help their kids with their work; at parents' night or when he made home visits, Bell would let them know that extra help was available and they had only to ask.

IN TOM BELL'S CLASSROOM the day after we talked at his house, I noticed something I either hadn't noticed before or that wasn't there: various mobiles hanging from the ceiling on thin pieces of string, tiny cutouts of white cardboard that revealed each person's dreams. Mr. Bell hoped for "unity within the black community," "success for all our children," "elimination of racism," "peace on Earth." Danielle Jones wanted "blacks and whites to live together." Ebony McFadden's dream was to "become a very good leader and become a great role model."

The children had been the toughest ones for me to talk with and observe because they were the ones who seemed the most defenseless and vulnerable, the ones who hadn't asked to be here, the ones whom our failure to reach closure on race, and all that attaches to it, affected most harshly. I had looked forward to seeing the children of Tom Bell's class again, but, quite honestly, I had dreaded it too, had dreaded the possibility of seeing faces and attitudes much harder and coarser than they had been nearly eighteen months before.

Princess Johnson had moved since I'd last seen her and now lived on a street where some white families did too, and just the day before, after a fresh snowfall, a white boy started throwing snowballs at her and she threw them back and he called her a nigger and she pushed his face down and he went upstairs and told his mother and she came outside. "She don't like people on her territory," Princess said. "She said that it was the last time I come on her territory 'cause she gonna call the police 'cause she called the police on this black man because he was trying to shovel her snow for free."

"He was just shoveling her snow for free and she called the police on him?" I asked.

"After he finished the snow, she called the police on him."

"Did she know he was out there shoveling?"

"Yeah. He told her husband that he was looking for work."

"He said he didn't want any money for it?"

"Yeah, he said I'll shovel your snow as long as you give me some food."

So the husband said they would give him a can of peas, but after he finished shoveling the woman wouldn't part with it, claiming that they needed it for themselves, and when he complained, she called the police.

The way Princess looked at it, if more blacks and whites went to school together, things like this just wouldn't happen.

Andrea had moved to St. Louis and back since I had last seen her, and she was the feisty star of the choir. She now lived way out in Silver Spring, but continued to come to King because of Mr. Bell.

Shukuha lived on First and Keefe, right near Marvin and Diane Howard and near the house that the Vice Lords operated out of ("a dope house," she called it, a house where "they be a whole bunch of TVs all up on the porch and stuff"). The Vice Lords had not tried to recruit her—at least not yet—but "they got my cousin. He in the gang. He up in Chicago. I remember one time we went up there for this Christmas vacation and my cousin and everybody in the family knew he steals. My aunt, she was up there from out of town and she left her purse up in the room. . . . First, we was watching him real, real good. Then we just left him alone. He went up in the room, took her purse. . . . She had over four hundred dollars."

She said all this so matter-of-factly it was frightening—said it in just the same way Princess related how her brother was in reform school and her sister's boyfriend had been shot just down the street from her house. The numbness and detachment that Kristie Jorgenson and her brother talked about had found its way into these children as well, but it was more profound. These children had seen too much and knew too much.

Nonetheless, they were all enthusiastic about a field trip they had taken to the Hyatt Regency, a trip in which they had fiercely recited "The Smart Creed," which Princess began to do now:

> I'm a small acorn, waiting to grow with the seeds of knowledge and experience into a mighty oak. Nothing will stop me because my superior thoughts will ignore society that shuts me out. I will pay no attention to doubts who lay over me since I know what I have the ability to become. Failure is just a word found in the dictionary. No one can make me a failure if I want to succeed. . . .
>
> I will use each day to the fullest to learn all I can, while I can, from anyone I can. . . . No one will love me if I don't love myself. No one will respect me if I don't respect myself. No one will believe in me if I don't believe in myself.

As soon as Princess finished and all three girls told me they had already seen *Malcolm X* three times and Andrea offered advice for both blacks and whites (blacks needed to learn more respect and whites needed to let go of their prejudice), Keithon Ausberry, one of the best students in the class, rushed up to me. I asked him what he had learned about black culture that he didn't know before, and he didn't hesitate. He didn't know that a black person was responsible for the gas mask, the ironing board, and the stop sign. He learned that Marcus Garvey "wanted us to go back to our African heritage and roots" and he now wanted to play the trumpet because Louis Armstrong had. But like Princess, Andrea, and Shukuha, he would prefer that his school be integrated. He also had a clear idea of what he wanted to do—go to college—and of what he would do everything in his power to prevent: allow any gang to "mess up my life."

So there they all were in Tom Bell's classroom, their hopes and dreams swirling ever so precariously above their heads.

FORTY-SIX

To be back in the company of Georgette Alexander was to be back in the embrace of sanity and clearheadedness, of humor and good nature and no cant, nowhere and nohow. She could be counted on to tell you what time it was, and she had stored up a lot of things to say since I had last seen her and Maron.

The good news was that Maron's decision to take that electronics class at the Urban League had led to a job at General Electric in Waukesha, a job he had held since October of 1991 and from which he brought home around three hundred dollars a week plus benefits. There had recently been talk of layoffs, but Maron had been laid off so many times in his life that he didn't panic when such talk arose, he expected it. The bad news was that his income and Georgette's was slightly too much for them to receive the earned-income tax credit that was created in the mid-seventies to help the working poor.

Everything is relative, though. There was more disturbing news to report and it had to do with Tennille.

Fourteen months earlier, in January of 1992, she had taken it upon herself to find her father's unloaded nine-millimeter pistol and carry it to Bay View High School one day in her bookbag. It seems she was trying to impress some boys with how tough she was, but it became much bigger than that and she was arrested and had to spend a night at the place where children were detained and, eventually, to attend two different alternative schools.

When I asked Georgette if Tennille were in a gang, she said no. Tennille and her friends, she said, were "just everyday girls. Their parents are struggling, so they feel the struggle. They're kind of rough because they have to be, but they're not out to fight anyone. They just want to look good, smell good, and talk to boys, basically."

Was Georgette more concerned about Tennille's getting pregnant now than she was two years before?

"I worry about her getting pregnant for her," she replied, consistent with what she had said earlier. "Me personally, she gets pregnant, that's her business. But for her, being that she's not the loving type, sitting and rocking a baby to sleep or read a book, I'm like, 'Please, for you personally, don't even try it.' It's just not in her makeup. Women are not born to be parents, it's a learned trait, and her, she don't want to learn. . . ."

Tennille would be home shortly, they said, and she could tell me her own self what had happened and why.

THE DEFEAT OF THE school referendum was depressing to the Alexanders because they felt so few people understood all the things that Howard Fuller was talking about, which were essentially many of the things they were talking about when I first met them. They never thought that new buildings in and of themselves were all that was required, and they were frustrated to realize that so many people seemed to think that that was all Fuller was asking for.

"He was not saying that MPS is perfect and by making buildings would make it even better," Maron said. "He was saying that would help, there would be more room, that would give them places to put the kids in kindergarten. He never said that he was finished with upgrading the school priorities or getting these kids to read. That costs money too, because you need better teachers. You gotta get people in there with the idea that they're to teach, not there just to get a paycheck. . . . That's all he was trying to do—make it even."

Georgette went beyond the defeat of the referendum, to the general state of the inner city. What she saw, more than anything else, was a vicious circle, one in which "for a minute you have something going on," in which "everything seems to be taken care of," but then, two weeks later, "it seems like it's right back where it started."

I asked her if she could be specific.

"We might see all of a sudden our streets appear to be fixed up. They get rid of all the potholes, depending on the election or whatever. Then, after everything is settled down, the dust settles down, that hole that they said they was gonna fix, it's still there. They dug the hole and they never filled it in. . . . You see the movement, you see someone starting to get things done, but it's never completed."

. . .

AS IT HAPPENED, I didn't see Tennille until a week later, but when I did, she didn't hesitate to tell me what had happened.

The day she was arrested was not the first time she had taken Maron's gun to school. She had taken it in one month earlier, had taken it in because her girlfriend Baisha was being picked on by members of the East Side Scooter Queens and she wanted to keep them from messing with her any further. Since she didn't know whether the gun was loaded or not, "didn't even know if it was on safety or not," she carried it "real gentle" and she showed it off to some boys in a remote hallway and some girls in the bathroom, and just having it, she said, gave her the feeling "that I was in a gang myself. . . . It was some kind of weird high. We thought we was tough, but then again we was still scared to be tough. It's the consequences of being tough. You could die from being tough."

"You're not ready to go yet, are you?" I asked.

"No," she said.

"You want to be around for a while?"

"Yeah," she said. "I mean, if I die, I guess I die, but I don't want to know that I'm dying. If I get shot walking down the street, I want to just die, immediately."

When she next brought the gun to school, it was January 22, 1992, the first day of exams, a day she recalled as warm, warm enough to stand outside the building, around ten, and talk to a boy she liked named Kwan. "We talked and we figured that we shouldn't talk anymore. Something weird about our relationship, where we used to talk to each other but then we stopped or something. Then he started liking a girl, Tangalaya. The East Side Scooter Queens didn't like Tangalaya. So they started spreading rumors around between me and Kwan that I had gave him some kind of disease or he gave me a disease or something where Tangalaya wouldn't like him no more. So, Tangalaya couldn't get her man. He came to me saying that I started it and I was trying to tell him that they started it. After a while, after about fifteen minutes of that, him blaming me, I got aggravated. I was like, 'Get outta my face.' My friend Lady, who was not my friend, was like, 'Get out of her face before she shoots you.' I was like, 'What'd you say that for?' She was like, 'No, no, he'll get scared.' He was like, 'You got a gun, you got a unit on you?' He told his friend that was sitting out in the car, 'Come here, dude, she's got a gun.' He was like, 'No, she don't.' Lady was like, 'Yes, she do.' He was like, 'Let me see it then.' She grabbed my bag off my arm and was like, 'See?' He was like, 'That's pretty, man, we should take it.' So she gave the bag back to me. He was pulling, I was pulling, back and forth. He was like, 'Let it go.' I was like, 'No.' He hit me in the eye. Well, he scratched me in my eye and I had a big sore. I couldn't see nothing. He was still pulling. Then I started getting leather burns from the strap and I was like, well, I gotta let it go. It dropped. He threw all my papers out and took it and ran."

Next thing she knew some East Side Scooter Queens came out of the building and "they was like, 'What's going on?' Lady told them what happened. 'She brought a gun to school, I think to shoot you all, and Kwan took it from her.' So they got mad that I was even thinking about shooting them. So they was trying to get me through the building, but a security guard grabbed me and pulled me in a door. They pulled me into the office and asked me what happened. I broke down and was like, 'I brought a gun to school and Kwan took it and the girls want to beat me up.' The police came, my daddy came, the police took me to a holding room."

It was a sad, pedestrian story, a story that has been told a thousand times in a thousand ways, a story whose only changing character, perhaps, has been the object of force wielded to settle the proverbial score. If at one time it was sticks and fists, it then became knives and guns. The same stuff went on in the suburbs, but, as Georgette reminded me, you simply didn't hear about it or read about it or see it on television nearly as much. Incidents of all kinds, whatever they might be, tended to disappear faster in affluent enclaves like River Hills. Incidents in the inner cities of America only reinforced the stereotypes people already held. It was another form of inequity, another way in which white privilege quietly exerted itself.

BEFORE TENNILLE WAS TRANSPORTED to the jail on State Street for booking, she sat in a concrete chair beside a concrete table and came to the conclusion that any hope she had of becoming a lawyer was probably over right then and there. As she was thinking this, a white police officer came into the holding room and made her an offer. She was fifteen and she was scared and his offer was this: He was just getting off work and he said that if she came home with him, he would see to it that the case was dropped and she would be free. "He was like, 'I'll help you out, I'll give you your shoes back because you look cold, but if you come to my house, you'll be warm.' I was like, 'No, that's okay, I'll stay here.' I was scared. I was like, he gonna come in here and he's gonna rape me."

At the county jail, things were no better. Another police officer told her and some other juveniles who were being booked that they were "'nothing but dirty, rotten criminals, you'll get treated like criminals, and you ain't gonna grow up to be nothing.' I was like, 'This is not what I need to hear.' He was like, 'This is your first time in jail, but you know you're going to be here again.' . . . I didn't know cops was like that. He was saying how he beat up this lady because she was disturbing the peace, she had her music up too loud, and she wouldn't turn it down. So he beat her up and he didn't get in trouble for it."

Things didn't improve for Tennille. At the detention center where she spent the night, she slept in a storage room next to a girl who had stabbed her mother's boyfriend and who kept banging and kicking the door until morning came.

When Tennille told me that Career Youth Development was one of the alternative schools she had gone to, I asked if she knew a girl named Shywonda.

"Is she dead?"

I said that she was, having learned about her from Anthony Adams. She had died in gang crossfire six months earlier.

"I knew her and I did not like her," Tennille said. Shywonda tried to convince everyone she was a Vice Lord when she wasn't. She claimed she was a dope dealer, Tennille said, but the beeper she carried was never turned on. "She was just carrying it, like I was carrying an empty gun. I knew I wasn't going to kill nobody, just like she knew she wasn't selling drugs. . . . She would constantly turn it on and off so it would beep, but she was doing it herself. Nobody was calling her."

Going to alternative school had its advantages and disadvantages, Tennille said. "If I'm trying to tell somebody I'm smart and intelligent, seeing that I was in alternative school does not help it. But if I'm trying to say, 'Don't bother me, I don't want you to charge me up and I don't want you to fight me,' then that'll help me 'cause they'll figure, 'She went to alternative school, she must be tough, we ain't gonna fight her.' So that helped me with other girls wanting to start fights with me. They was like, 'She went *there?* We ain't messing with her.'"

She had told me in April of 1991 that she was fourteen and she was nice, and she was now telling me with a laugh that she was sixteen and not quite as nice. She was still determined not to get pregnant (even though most of her friends who had one child when I first met her now had two), and she was still determined to go to college. But the thing I had feared when I talked with the kids in Tom Bell's class was evident on Tennille's face. She had lost her softness. Her sparkle was gone.

F O R T Y - S E V E N

The hat he was wearing said BERMUDA NO PROBLEM and he was looking forward to a dinner at the White House the next month for all the living presidents. But what was uppermost in his mind was the condition of a community that he felt had deteriorated badly in the two years since I had first come to his office on a freezing, rainy day, a community nearly the whole of which was crowded onto ten and a half square miles and that he referred to as the Plantation, a community, he was saying now, that needed nothing short of divine intervention to survive.

Jerrel Jones didn't keep me waiting in reception on this Saturday afternoon, as he had when I first came to see him and Michael McGee. In fact, he seemed almost pleased to see me, pleased to see that I had stuck around long enough to watch things change, even if that change had been for the worse.

No one could say he didn't do his part. Anyone who worked for him full-time was entitled to have all their children's educational expenses paid at any school or college of their choice for as long as they chose to attend. In lieu of medical benefits (he had the healthiest group of employees around, he laughed, "not a cold, not a nothing"), this was what he offered. The children also had to work at one of his businesses for at least a year after college. I was staggered when I learned of this. It was almost unimaginable that he would be willing to do that. His own children had all gone to college (one was still in high school but planning to go), and some of them had gone on to get advanced degrees. He knew what Howard Fuller knew: that education might not guarantee you anything, but you had to have it—especially since the economy of the country had changed so dramatically. Where he disagreed with Fuller was that he didn't see how getting kids "out of coat rooms and hallways and that kind of thing" was going to do very much. Without being willing to acknowledge that Fuller's referendum had tried to do a lot more than that, he said that the problem was the culture of the inner city itself, that you needed to take the child out of that environment entirely in order to educate him. "Isolate to educate" was the way he viewed it. He would take them to a remote area of two thousand acres and start all over. "There's something very therapeutic in horseshit, believe it or not," he said. "Getting stung by a bee. Very therapeutic. . . .

"See, these kids are sick. . . . I'm talking about these kids are warped. I could show you kids—ten, eleven years old right now that I could bring into this room—and there's no way in the world that I could convince you that those kids didn't have the minds of twenty-five- and thirty-year-old people. I can show you kids with no kid in them at all. I'm talking about *no kid in them at all*. . . . They're as adult as you and I. They've been exposed to anything you and I can get and more. They can tell you stories that make you stand on end." He was thinking of a thirteen-year-old who had just moved to Milwaukee from Chicago, a boy who had been a shooter for the El Rukns and had just gotten out of juvenile detention after four years. His mother had asked Jones to talk with him, "so I brought him into my office and I had a talk with him for about twenty minutes. In twenty minutes he had thoroughly convinced me that he was as grown as I was. I couldn't even relate to him as anything but a grown man. I got a kid that's sixteen. I've tried to allow my boy, although he's mature, I try to allow him to grow up every year at a time. Life is so short. Every year at a time. The football, the basketball, the girlfriends, the kind of shit like I did. These kids missed all of that. Some of these kids are totally responsible for themselves. And as far as school goes, there's nothing that they can teach these kids at school. These kids have made more money than you make. That's a fact. Can't offer them no job, these kids are making three, four, five hundred dollars a night. Some of them, probably fifteen hundred sometimes, two thousand a night. . . .

"Now how are you going to tell somebody that made that kind of money *anything?* You can't tell them *nothing*. And in order to deal drugs, you gotta be willing to take somebody's life. And if they haven't taken it, they're willing to. That's a whole other state you got to get to mentally. You know, they take soldiers and train them, through basic training camp and all that other shit, just to get them to a point where they're willing to kill somebody else. These are professional people that do this. These kids are now half that age, willing to kill somebody with no training. They think life is something to be lived in twenty years. Anything after twenty years they're not interested in. *Twenty years*. They will tell you right out . . . this is their whole mentality. They have no education, they can't hardly talk, none of them can read. Cannot read one word. How are you gonna make two thousand dollars a night and can't read? What can you do with somebody like that once that happens to them? You think you can send them back to learn to read and tell them to come up the highway and work for five, six bucks an hour? No, no, no. It don't work like that anymore. That's why they end up going to a bank, some of them, and start blowing away cashiers. Whatever they need to get the money. They'll take your car. They'll take you outta your car. That's what they did to Red, the guy I played chess with the other night. They walked right up, put a gun to his head, told him to get out of his car. Took his car. My brother, this guy made him take him home. They robbed his home, took his car and everything."

But the kids Jones was referring to didn't represent *all* kids in the inner city, and he knew that. The son of his regular chess partner was "Speech" from the music group Arrested Development. The singer Al Jarreau had come out of Milwaukee. So had Oprah Winfrey. Milton Coleman, a journalist with the *Washington Post*, had worked for Jones at one time. On a certain level—everything else notwithstanding—it was about making choices, moral ones. You might not have the same options as a kid in River Hills, and the obstacles might be considerably greater and harder to negotiate, but you could still make the right choice in terms of the direction you were going to go.

And yet there was still the paradox, as Jones mentioned when I first met him and which he brought up again now, the troublesome paradox of your achievements, no matter what they might be, being severely undercut and cheapened—dehumanized, really—by the fact that, deep down, you would always be viewed as a nigger. Beyond offering that opinion two years earlier, he hadn't been specific, but he was specific about it now. He and his wife had gone to a Wisconsin Press Association dinner in the northern part of the state in 1975, a year in which the *Courier* was supposed to win a number of awards and Jones had a good chance of being Publisher of the Year. He had, by his own admission, been acting "like a hot dog all day," but that didn't prepare him for what happened at the dinner that evening, a dinner attended by hundreds of people. Jones and his wife, who were sitting at a table with other blacks, ordered chicken (ever since he had been a member of the Nation of Islam, he hadn't eaten pork), and before he knew it, the head of the Pork Producers of Wisconsin picked up the microphone and wondered aloud what "those niggers" were doing eating chicken, as if they had personally offended him by doing so.

Jones didn't hesitate. He and his wife got up and walked out and went back to their room. People phoned them, knocked on their door, and eventually, the Joneses drove home. He reminded everyone he spoke with that it was just one man's comment, but in fact that one comment "took the gas out of me. I wasn't mad as much as I was disappointed, that whatever you do, you're still a nigger." He had won fifteen awards, missed Publisher of the Year by one vote, but it meant nothing to him. "I mean, at some point in your life that hits you. I don't care how much money you get, I don't care how much prestige you get, you still a nigger. Period. You get caught out here at night and one of them cops don't recognize you, you'll get your ass whipped just like Rodney King. Period. The size of your car don't make no difference, nothing make no difference. That's just a fact. And if you don't have to live with that fact, you can't really understand it. It's something you've got to live with. You can achieve all you want to achieve in life, but you can't never get past being a nigger. Not in this society. And it does something to you."

What worried Jerrel Jones about someone like Howard Fuller was his sense that his heart wasn't really in it anymore. "Howard realizes the hopelessness in what he's doing and he's on subconscious pilot. He's been on it for some time. Howard's going through the motions."

"Why do you say that?" I asked, surprised to hear Jones say this, but not persuaded that he wasn't just trying to be provocative.

Remember, Jones said, how Howard started off, intent on changing the world ("We all, I guess, were at a certain age"), founding his college in North Carolina as a way of liberating the whole black race. Then the focus of change became the United States and then, "about forty or fifty, we knock it down to just Milwaukee. And by the time you're sixty or seventy, you're not going to change a goddamned thing. You're lucky if you can change your mind. *Nothing* is going to change. I feel that Howard now realizes that."

It had to do with blacks ultimately having no power and, because of that, having little or no respect for themselves or each other, Jones said. "Howard can't respect anything that doesn't have power. That's where his disrespect for himself comes in, from his lack of power. He's always jumping from job to job, trying to find that in himself."

What he said about Fuller he applied to himself as well as to Michael McGee. "I think some of you dies when so many of your hopes die," he said. As much as anybody might think McGee was a black racist, he said, it wasn't the case—not for McGee or for any black person. "There's no black people who are racist," he insisted. "In order to be a racist, you have to have power.... It's that simple." White people want to give blacks the illusion they have power, he said, and as a result, "that's what most black people are suffering from. They have the illusion of power with no real power."

It had been two years since he had asked me to consider to whose benefit it was that the socioeconomic problems of America had not been solved, and he was zeroing in on this again. "Who runs America?" he demanded to know. "Let's cut all the bullshit out now. Who runs America? Do you think you run America, your vote? No. No. Your vote means doodly shit. And what you think means doodly shit." The question of who actually ran the country was so big, he said, that "you don't want to involve yourself in it because you really don't know. If you did, you'd be solid in your ideas and you could say, 'No, this couldn't happen because the people of the United States . . .'—you see what I mean? When you're vague, then it scares the shit out of me. Because if you ask that question around, you'll find that most people are very, very vague.

"Now, to answer the question 'Who runs America?' it's not so much who as *what* runs America. This is a capitalistic system. It's a materialistic system. We can boil down all of the fancy rhetoric and say it's the Golden Rule that runs America. He who has the gold rules."

Jerrel Jones had a certain amount of that gold and he did a certain amount of ruling; he had traveled all over the world and counted himself lucky to have lived the life that he had had so far. But to hear him tell it, America was still not his country and, as long as white people would not accept him unconditionally—without fear or prejudgment or discomfort— would not refrain from either talking or thinking about him as a nigger behind his back or to his face, it never would be.

MONTHS PASSED. DURING THAT time Milwaukee had a huge crisis with its water system (a crisis that resulted in more than a hundred deaths and which, some suggested, Michael McGee might have had something to do with, a suggestion McGee himself wouldn't rule out) and Bill Clinton had another crisis of his own—putting forward and then, two days after he had come to Milwaukee to essentially reassure everyone that he was putting the wheels back on his presidency, embarrassingly withdrawing the nomination of Lani Guinier as the head of the Justice Department's civil rights division, withdrawing it without even affording her, and the country, an opportunity to air her views before a congressional committee. He had run from race during his campaign and he was doing it once more.

I went to a conference in Richmond, Virginia, not long after that called "Healing the Heart of America," and I watched a grown woman from the South break down in tears as she openly apologized to blacks for all the indignities whites had visited upon them throughout the years; then, later that day, I heard a white city planner urge a roomful of people to be honest with themselves, to acknowledge that race played a part in *every* crucial decision a white person made, starting with where one chose to live and where one's children went to school.

When I went home that night, I held my infant daughter in my arms, the daughter to whom this book is dedicated. I spoke openly to Logan about my hopes for her future, my wish that she and the generation of which she is a part will prove Jerrel Jones wrong.

I RETURNED TO MILWAUKEE in the middle of August and Michael McGee was waiting for me, his appearance changed now by dreadlocks. He had no books in front of him, as he had when we first met, and even though he had been out of office for a year, he still had plenty to say—about what had come before and what lay ahead. As far as the election he had lost, he continued to insist that the votes had been diddled with, that some bags had mysteriously gone missing, and that he was convinced the mayor was ultimately behind this, the mayor whom he had helped elect in 1988 and who, he claimed, hadn't made good on a variety of promises. It was disappointing to hear him talk of sabotage—especially since there was no evidence to support this charge and because he had done so little in the way of campaigning. Redistricting had certainly hurt him, but had he exerted a little more effort, everyone seemed to agree, he would have won.

So what, beside his radio talk show, had he been doing?

He was vague about the current status of the Black Panther Militia but said that his 1995 deadline remained in place. He had been going to different cities, giving speeches, continuing to organize, throwing a punch at a white man on *Jerry Springer,* and forming a friendship with Tom Metzger, the head of the White Aryan Resistance, the leading white supremacist group in the country.

Bizarre as it might seem, their friendship was actually a matter of opposites attracting, of extremists finding common ground in their view that whites and blacks should live apart from each other. McGee initially met Metzger on *Jerry Springer* and wound up inviting him to be the keynote speaker at the Black Power Conference and Youth Summit (which was held three months earlier in Dallas, another city with its own black militia). Metzger came, and they had been in touch by phone ever since. In fact, McGee was planning to go to California and address Metzger's group. Theirs was a far different alliance from Carvis Braxton's and John Fitzgerald's, but it appeared to be serving a purpose that was satisfactory to them.

Outside the window of Jerrel Jones's office at that moment, right there on Teutonia Avenue, a young black man was getting arrested, his hands being pulled tight behind his back. This, Jerrel Jones emphasized, was what they saw each and every day. He made more than four hundred thousand dollars a year and this was what he saw; this was his view. In all likelihood, the young man was being hauled in for something to do with drugs, drug dealers being the number one employer in the community, and it prompted me to ask both Jones and McGee about Blondie, the notorious detective whom everyone seemed to know and no one wanted to speak of.

"Have you ever met this cop Blondie?" I asked McGee.

"No," he said.

"Do you know who he is?"

"No," he said again, but seemed so uncomfortable that I didn't believe him.

"His last name is Lewandowski," I said. "Does it ring a bell, Jerrel?"

"Yeah," Jones said.

"What do you know about him?"

"I've heard things," he said.

Like what?

Jones would not elaborate.

I pressed McGee again as to whether he'd heard of him.

"Mike knows Blondie," Jones said with a tense laugh. "He has *nothing* to say about Blondie."

"Are you afraid of Blondie?" I said, looking straight at McGee.

"I'm not," Jones answered instead.

I asked McGee why he said he didn't know him when he did.

McGee insisted he didn't know him.

Jones said he didn't know him either, but knew of him. He also said he was surprised, surprised that I knew these cops "as well as you know them"—but McGee said he wasn't. "He's one of these guys," McGee said, looking at Jones, rare smile on his face, "who has the ability to go to a place like Africa and hang around and follow the wildebeest. . . . I like that in him, that's good. We need all of this documented."

"Is Blondie some big secret?" I asked both of them.

"See," McGee said, "now he's going back to Blondie. Smooth. On that one, I'm leaving."

"Yeah, me too," Jones said, "I ain't got nothing to say either."

As IT HAPPENED, JONES stayed and kept talking. It was his office, his domain, his corner of the world, a world in which he could be conversing on the phone with Louis Farrakhan one moment and someone from the Republican National Committee the next. Meanwhile, the business with the young man outside the window was just about concluded. He was already in the police car and it was about to pull away. McGee and Jones (like Howard Fuller) had talked about another generation being lost, and this scene was tangible proof of it. This was what they wanted me to see and understand—that none of this would be going on (or at least not to the extent that it was) if it weren't for whites putting the drugs on the streets; for whites making it as easy for a kid to get an Uzi as it was for him to get a pack of bubble gum; for whites making money off the incarceration of blacks (incarceration being, along with recreation and information, America's biggest industries, in Jones's view); for whites making it so hard for blacks to either rent a place to live, get loans or insurance, buy houses, or even get a cab regardless of one's appearance; for whites papering the billboards of inner cities across America with ads for liquor and cigarettes. Jones had been to Germany, he had seen Auschwitz, and he wasn't surprised at all to learn that a disturbing number of people doubted the Holocaust had ever taken place; denial, he knew, was a far easier means of getting through each day. At the rate America was going, Jones believed, slavery would be perfected by the year 2000.

F O R T Y - E I G H T

Sitting in the basement of Howard Fuller's home, a photograph of him and the poet-playwright Amiri Baraka staring at us from across two decades, I could tell that Jerrel Jones had not been exaggerating. Fuller seemed even more depressed than he had in March and was even saying that he could understand how someone could arrive at the point of considering suicide. One month earlier, on the night he returned from a vacation in Jamaica, he wasn't sure that he would make it to the next day, so distressed was he by events that had taken place while he was gone and by the news that, hours after he got home, someone had randomly shot at his mother's apartment while she was out. (When the police arrived, the neighbor who called them was asked if the shots might have come from inside the apartment—a question that rankles Fuller to this day.)

One thing he had discovered since taking the superintendent's job was how much easier it was to wage a revolution than to actually preside over something as massive as the Milwaukee Public Schools. When you're an activist, operating from the outside, as he had throughout much of his life, you have "a particular ideological perspective," you're focused, you're centered on the task at hand. "Not that revolution is easy," he added, but you know what you're doing. When he was in Durham and was fighting for decent housing, he said, smiling, "I was younger and I knew everything. I was right and they were wrong." But when "you get into the system at this level, it's a very different situation. . . . You can no longer have the narrowest view because you got to now deal with a whole bunch of other issues and realities." When I suggested to him that both he and President Clinton were finding this out, he laughed. "When he starts to tackle all of these issues, man, I mean, you get hit with the reality of the resistance to fundamental change. You can talk all this stuff"—gays in the military, welfare reform, health care reform, the budget deficit, to name just a few of the things on Clinton's voluminous wish list as a candidate—"but when you get in there and you start trying to govern . . . it's like I've said to people,

'I'm not the czar, I'm the superintendent.' And he's not the czar, he's the president. And he's got to deal with all of these different interests as he's trying to negotiate significant change."

But there was something that Fuller had had to battle against that didn't really bear any similarity to Clinton's situation—the suggestion that he was nothing more than a puppet for the white establishment (so said various blacks in the community) because he had been making (or trying to make) changes that affected blacks more than they affected whites. The disciplinary plan that he put into effect and that a number of principals who had been transferred or demoted were black—these were just two issues for which Fuller had come under severe criticism. He had a policy of not publicly discussing the reasons behind personnel decisions, but he did share some of them off the record and, in each case, he had not acted hastily; in each case, there was a larger context for the decision. Still, the criticism hurt him personally. He was the superintendent for all the kids in the school system, a superintendent who happened to be black. To do the job he was hired to do, he had to get beyond the surface of race, to transcend it. If he couldn't do that, then he would be a puppet of the worst sort. Nonetheless, when he came back from vacation, that there was still a hue and cry over the removal of Bob Griffin as principal of Malcolm X Academy sent him into a tailspin, made him consider, seriously consider, how much longer he could go on. He had been, and would continue to be, passionately committed to his race throughout his life, but even as a "race man," he still had a job to do, a job he was rightly expected to carry out without fear or favor.

When Fuller first took the job two years earlier, he gave an interview in which he said he could now see the gray in things whereas before he always saw things in black and white. I reminded him of that comment, especially how it related to race, and his suggestion that we had to keep trying to build bridges despite the sense that most people didn't want to do that, that polarization and labels made it too easy for one to avoid the complexity of the matter.

Fuller said he had read a recent article in *U.S. News & World Report* about Rush Limbaugh, an article that showed "how you can take someone like him who appeals to probably the worst instincts in America" and elevate him into an icon because he keeps things simple, he reassures people there are "simple answers to all these questions," people "who are so frustrated by the country's seeming inability to grapple with these difficult issues that they want simple answers. In reality, those 'simple answers' are not answers, but they feed into people's thinking that 'Yeah, that's it.' . . . You got such a significant segment of the people out there now who are so anti-institution, anti-government, in part because of the arrogance of some of our institutions, the way that they function." There were all these things, Fuller said, that people *used* to be able to hold on to. "*This* job, *this* plan, and all of a sudden these jobs are gone, companies are cutting back ten thousand people. You just have this tremendous disruption in the American Dream. . . .

"So on the one hand I'm glad that I see gray in the sense that it means I'm looking at these problems deeper. But it is easier if you think it's black and white because you don't have to stop and worry about what's really happening because you know what's happening, *this* is what's happening, and you don't really listen to other people, you don't try to understand where they're coming from because you got your own viewpoint."

About the job he was trying to do, though, there were some things that were black and white: 80 percent of the kids in Milwaukee public schools received a free or reduced-price lunch; only 40 percent of the kids entering ninth grade eventually graduated; the third-grade reading scores had risen nine percentage points in his first year, but had dropped by the same amount in his second. As part of his reform efforts, all ninth-graders would now be required to take algebra. Efforts to put a school-to-work program into place for the following year were proceeding apace. Trying to build a constituency for the public schools was a lot harder than it was when he himself was in school and so many more of Milwaukee's home-owners sent their children to them. Still, it didn't help matters when some-one like Polly Williams came on television a week before the referendum and screamed and screamed. I had sensed that Polly Williams was one of the people he was referring to when he spoke of not really listening to others, so I asked him about her.

Williams had come to his house two weeks earlier and sat right where we were now and listened to Fuller tell her that, given the condition of the black community in Milwaukee, they didn't have "the luxury" to har-bor any kind of personal animosity. Just a few years earlier, she and he were trying to break up the school system by race, trying to do it without seri-ously changing the way schools were financed. He now realized that if they had been successful in that strategy, they actually would have made things worse; they would have wound up with a district "so damned impoverished" that nothing of substance could have been achieved anyway. "There's too much history of black folks who got these philosophical differences that get translated into personal animosities to the extent that you can't bring folks together to do anything in common." He wasn't suggesting that all blacks needed to think alike; he was merely saying that "when you're part of an oppressed community, you've got to be able to build some level of unity to get anything from the majority population."

What bothered him the most about that night on television—more than Williams's ranting—was that she was even there at all, instead of someone from the mayor's office or, better yet, the mayor himself. So in place of a useful debate, he found himself struggling to keep calm, to keep calm and keep raising issues, "because I didn't see how it would benefit to have two black people standing up there and hollering at each other. Nor was I going to be disrespectful, because I didn't think that would help us either."

Fuller hadn't eaten all day and wanted to order a pizza. Though he didn't eat much at any time, he was finicky about the things he ate, a piece of information conveyed to me by his youngest daughter, Kumba Miata, who was living at home for the summer, and who happened to come bounding down the steps at that moment. She and her father were close, but they had their disagreements, one of them being the name she should go by, Fuller preferring Kumba, she preferring Miata. I knew from talking with her that she worried about her father a great deal, worried that he worked too hard and cared too much and was going to burn out, and I knew from talking with her that it was not easy being his daughter, not easy that so much was expected of her. At least that was the way she viewed it. She had not heard us talking—she had been upstairs dishing with a girlfriend—and so would not have overheard him telling me about the night he contemplated suicide. He tried not to burden his children with the pressures he felt, but they knew; they knew that all their lives he had taken on one challenge after another, each usually bigger than the one before. Perhaps that explained why Miata, when I asked how her summer accounting job was going, said that it was going fine and, smiling, that it might not be the most exciting work, but she could at least count on making a living from it. "Which is more than you guys can say," she added.

In an evening that had me increasingly concerned about Fuller's well-being, it was a nice moment. After Miata went back upstairs, we talked, as we had often, about race and class, about how the two were so intertwined and got confused so readily in people's minds, and how imperative it was to always be vigilant about identifying one from the other. "Because of racism there are many issues we think are race things that are in fact class things," he said, "but they disproportionately affect people who are non-white because of racism. So the two merge. And a lot of times the solutions that we been coming up with that are race-based are not solutions because the fundamental part of the problem is in class, not race." Race-based solutions were not ultimately going to work, he stressed, as has William Julius Wilson. "The solution will be found more in a structural solution to inequity."

In Wilson's *The Declining Significance of Race*, published in 1978, the author took the position (as had Bayard Rustin, the chief organizer of the 1963 March on Washington) that the civil rights movement had essentially removed the barrier of racial discrimination and that what was needed was an apparatus that would bring the black poor into the workforce, a return to the days of the Works Progress Administration in a sense. Nearly twenty years later, Wilson would still be stressing the importance of doing this, of making sure that people had jobs. What those who have steady work perhaps forget sometimes is that, as Wilson writes, "regular employment provides the anchor for the spatial and temporal aspects of daily life," that it "determines where you are going to be and when you are going to be there," and that without it, life becomes "less coherent."

Even though Fuller said that integration (either residential or educational) was not *the* answer to the myriad problems facing those in the ghetto, he knew historically that "once something becomes mostly black and mostly poor . . . there's no power base from which to assure adequate resources."

So what about the notion of pooling resources, merging city and suburb together into one metropolitan area, all drawing from the same well? It was not a new idea, as the mayor had reminded me, but it had been given fresh currency by David Rusk (son of Dean Rusk, the former Secretary of State) in a book called *Cities Without Suburbs*, a book based on the premise that most cities could no longer be economically viable, could not exist as vibrant places unless this was done.

Fuller smiled when I brought this up; he smiled either because he saw me as a liberal who still hadn't been informed that the sixties were long gone, or because he thought I was baiting him. Regardless, the parallel between the fate of cities and the fate of the public schools within them was, to his mind, joined at the hip and starkly clear. "Realistically," he said, cutting his eyes at me, "white people out in the suburbs are not going to pay for and support stuff that's happening in the city. They want to take the resources for themselves and their families—*that's* why they went out there. And so you're sitting here with no real political power to affect the situation, and therefore the only answer is a 'metropolitan' answer. That's what people argue about schools. That you'll never be able to finance schools in the city of Milwaukee. The state legislature will never vote for it. So you sue and you hope you get remedy through the courts. . . .

"Even in the two years we've been talking," he said, gesturing outside, "you can see physical and community deterioration just in that two years. You know what I'm saying. It's not like you can go around here and all of a sudden you see big signs of hope and growth and development. What you see is continued deterioration. We've got a mayor that's calling television stations in to talk about violence on TV. . . . Talking to television stations about violence on television is almost absurd. The *issue* is what are we going to do about bringing jobs, what are we going to do about bringing development, what are we going to do about struggling over the values that kids have, what are we going to do about improving our institutions that service the framework?

"Those issues are so hard that what people do is they go after stuff that score big points with the public, but that don't mean shit because they're not addressing the fundamental issues that we're facing. That's the depressing part to me. And I think it does speak to the issue of political will. I don't think the question is, Do we have the wherewithal to deal with these problems? The question is, Do we have the political will? . . . I don't see anything that tells me that we do."

If one accepts Fuller's interpretation of the American Dream as one that says we're *all* going to be able to advance, then the dream is an illusion, a cruel joke at too many people's expense. It never was true, and is even less true today. A recent article pointed out that even though Milwaukee was America's seventeenth-largest city, it had the fifth-highest number of poverty tracts. "And those kids," he said, "are in our school district . . . trapped in a sea of poverty. When you talk about one out of every two black kids live in poverty in Milwaukee, that's a hell of a statement."

The Talented Tenth, he said, referring to Du Bois's term for the black elite, could do whatever they wanted, but that, he stressed, wasn't the issue (and in certain respects wasn't really true). The real issue—and this, he reiterated, was what really bothered him about Shelby Steele and all his talk about race fatigue and race-holding—continues to be "the people who have never left" the ghetto. If Fuller is correct, then those of us who don't reside there must come to terms with what has happened to them, what role we have played in what has happened to them, and, most important, we must come to some agreement about what has to be done.

FORTY-NINE

Why is it that so few of us who eat chicken ever stop and consider the process that has brought those chickens to our table? Why is it, David Webster wanted to know, that we feel so imperiously about those chickens?

It may sound like an absurd question to anyone other than an animal rights activist, but Webster was actually making an interesting point, a point about the way we often go about our lives unmindful of how our actions actually affect others.

To Webster, Mayor Norquist's chief of staff, the question of whether someone considered a chicken a living thing had much to do with racism, with the people who drove back and forth from the suburbs without giving much, if any, thought to the people living on either side of the freeway, the people living in the inner city. I told him that the reason I ate chicken was that I liked the taste of it, particularly fried chicken, preferably from Stroud's in Kansas City. I also told him that, quite honestly, when a chicken arrived on a plate in front of me, I didn't think of it as a (formerly) living thing, that I didn't think too much about it at all. "I can tell you point-blank," I said, "I don't fall into that camp."

"So basically you are to that chicken what the I-43 drivers are," he said. "What you have is almost this existential thought process of oppression that we need chickens to subsist, there would be too many of them if we didn't kill some of them off, it tastes good."

What was refreshing about Webster, who was white and had grown up poor, was his candor, his ability to provoke you to think about things. I could see why Fuller and Lawrence held such a high opinion of him. He was a former student of Fuller's at Marquette and had specialized in youth issues before taking the job as chief of staff.

In speaking of racism, he said that as a society, we were constantly going through "a continuum of movement" away from it, but he wasn't sure that "a racism-free existence" was possible. A "phase of conformity" (passage of an open housing ordinance, for example) might be followed by a "period of tolerance" (legally complying with whatever rules and regulations exist), he said, but too often that is the endpoint. "I think a lot of communities have gotten that far and they think they can rest on their laurels because we have open housing now. We've got whatever—anti-discrimination employment and so forth—so we are the be-all and end-all." What needed to happen, he said, was for people to value and use the laws as a way of enriching the quality of their lives, not just viewing them as things they were adhering to without any real commitment. At the same time, he said, one had to be careful not to confuse volition with discrimination—that, traditionally, one way that ethnic groups maintained their identity and a sense of security was by living close to each other.

But there was still the problem, I said, of the black community being isolated economically.

Once again, Webster surprised me.

"Right in that," he said, "is the essence of a racist fear. Because you're saying, 'You don't have ours, so you are pathological or deprived in some way.' I would argue that the suburbs are the deprived. Because they do not have the diversity in close proximity that the city has. The African-American community abuts the Latino community and the white community. . . .

"What value system establishes that the suburban lifestyle should be the goal of everyone?" he wanted to know. "I think American culture reinforces and plays right into the hands of racism and classism. For whatever reason—I don't know which is the chicken and which is the egg—we have established that moving yourself to homogeneity and isolation is a sign of being up-and-coming and achieving something," that wanting "woods on all sides of you on your own little lot where you can't see anybody or hear anybody else is to be aspired to," that not living "three feet away from the windows of someone who speaks a different language or looks differently than you do" is status. . . . "Why is it *that* way and not that you really have made it when you get to move into an integrated neighborhood? . . . I think if you can identify where *that* value system came from, you get much more into the roots of racism, rather than simply looking at pigmentation of skin and the pointing of fingers that's been going on for generations."

I agreed with what he was saying and told him that the majority of white people I had met appeared to find it easier to compartmentalize themselves than to explore the complexity of the situation, to explore their own feelings about the prickly matter of race. Found it easier to believe the issues had been resolved and that the whole business didn't particularly affect them anyway.

"I don't think in their heart of hearts they believe that," he said.

"Maybe," I said, "but a lot of people don't think about it."

"Sure," he shot back, "denial's a great thing. I think, though, if you could wire their brains and get one of their little cartoon bubbles to quietly say what they were really thinking, that much of that 'I don't want to talk about it' or 'It's settled' is sort of because they always see it dissolving into white folks keeping black folks down."

When I asked him, as I had asked Fuller, what he felt positive about in terms of the city and its relation to the black community, there were a number of things he pointed to (things, not surprisingly, to which the mayor had also alluded). The number of blacks that Mayor Norquist had hired since 1988 and his policy of holding everyone equally accountable for their performance. It was crucial that blacks not be viewed as "a protected class," he said, that they be expected to produce, and that if they didn't, they should be just as replaceable as the next person. The mayor, he said, was happy to say, to boast even (as he had done with me), that he had not only hired more blacks than any previous administration, he had fired more too.

The Milwaukee Community Service Corps, the Capital Access Program, the Milwaukee Guarantee—these were all things to be legitimately proud of, he said. But anyone expecting some huge Marshall-type plan to materialize, or anyone expecting the days of FDR and the re-creation of the Civilian Conservation Corps and the WPA to magically reappear, was sadly deluding himself. President Clinton (drawing on the advice of William Julius Wilson) was "toying with it on the fringes," Webster said, but it was too expensive and, frankly, the political and public will to do it didn't exist. "The difference was that back then you simply had the Depression throwing thousands of very skilled workers out of work. Which is very different than saying that you have thousands and thousands of individuals who are *unskilled*, in terms of market-honed—not that they don't have potential, but they aren't skilled."

When I told Webster that Howard Fuller didn't feel especially optimistic about anything that was going on in the city, including Steeltech and the Community Service Corps, his face tightened for a second, but he said he understood, understood "Howard sort of feeling like they're tsetse flies on the rump of some much larger beast, but I do believe to a certain extent that, inch by inch, you make some progress rather than standing around and bemoaning the cataclysmic situation. I think that we have come to a point in time where people are either comfortable and therefore un-motivated to disrupt their comfort to improve the lot of their brothers and sisters on the face of the earth, or they're so disenfranchised on the other end of the spectrum that they don't know how to use the power and tools that it will take to create systemic change.

"And then there are some of us in the middle who get up some morn-ings and feel like Howard and say, 'I can't think of anything that's work-ing or doing any good'—or you get up like Tony Perez [head of the MCSC] does and say, 'I've got sixty-five young lives that I can affect today and I may be dead tomorrow, so I might as well contribute while I'm here.' At day's end, the nuance of difference in terms of a world being better may not look much different from Howard's perspective or from Tony's per-spective, but chances are Tony's work during the day, rather than sit-ting around being depressed about it, has been taking a very minute step forward."

But putting Fuller's depression and Perez's determination aside, there was still a basic problem, Webster said. A human service system was in place that had gotten away from serving humans, that essentially just served the system's employees. As a result, Webster said, what you had was much cynicism and a fundamental belief that other initiatives—"another CCC or WPA or Marshall Plan or any other nifty idea that comes along"—would be "squandered, paid to the wrong people, and never have the outcome that you want to have."

That, in many respects, was how he felt about the public schools. Given all the work Webster had done with youth, one would have thought he had voted wholeheartedly for the referendum that Fuller had proposed. He had not. "For being who I am and what my background is and who my allegiances and long-term friendships are with," he said, "I voted against that referendum with a very clear conscience. It was a Band-Aid on a sys-temic problem, and we've been doing that for decades in this community. MPS's problem is not money and it's not buildings. I think Howard under-stands that and he has, in some cases, run himself into literally physical disability trying to change that. Human energy is finite. We sort of have this superhuman notion in our heads that with the cause being noble that people will find it somewhere to be able to slay the dragon no matter what.

I don't think that's the case. I think Howard has been a good link in the good fight, but I don't look for him to slay the dragon.

"I think that we have a system that is predicated on faulty curriculum given the needs and learning styles of kids in the 1990s. We have a physical structure, above and beyond a roof over their heads and no lead in the pipes, that is not at all parallel to the market that we're trying to prepare young people to work in. We have administrative structures and bargaining agreements that are antithetical to education."

At the same time, though, many people were working very hard on the school-to-work program that, if successful, would respond to some of what Webster was talking about. Still, programs like these required patience and money, two things that are often in short supply. (When Milwaukee's program officially began in the fall of 1994, it was one of the first of its type in the country.)

Talking about Fuller took Webster back to the time fourteen years earlier when he had been a graduate student of his at Marquette, taking a course called "Black Social Thought," a course that could be summarized, he said, by the catchy slogan that marked the Clinton campaign—"It's the economy, stupid!" What bothered Webster about the course was that he was one of only four whites in the class and knew more about black history than most of the black students did. The argument that Fuller was trying to make, Webster said, many of them simply did not understand. They didn't understand it, he added, because they "had basically latched on to that it's hatred and racism that are the issues. What Howard was trying to get people to see is if you focus only on that and you don't focus on the basic oppressive economic situations, and we don't ourselves use what limited resources we have now to multiply . . . then we are accomplices in this oppression."

But recalling that course also brought Michael McGee to mind for Webster. In his opinion, McGee had actually been an effective, formidable alderman when he was working within the system, raising all the crucial "Why are we so sure that it's right to be eating these chickens" questions. But once he decided to "play the hate card," Webster said, "he made himself much easier to deal with than if he stayed more incrementalist in his accomplishments, more genuine and truthful in trying to accomplish change." Once he formed the militia, it didn't "take much to convince the rest of the public that shooting white people on the freeway is not something you want around here. . . . I think even people of color were dumb-founded that he would basically stoop to the level of those that represent the same value system but from a different race or cultural perspective."

Having said that, Webster wasn't surprised in the least that McGee had apparently found an ally in Tom Metzger. In his view of the world, those on the edges are not beneficial to the dialogue; what is needed is a shared belief that life is valuable. In McGee's case, the militia might have been "plowed in new turf," but it just rekindled the belief, he said, that what McGee was after was "dominance, not equality."

Still, Webster found it difficult to deny that McGee's threats had possibly accelerated Milwaukee's plans for the inner city, but he was also bemused at how gullible the media could be, so quickly assuming, for instance, that a press conference in December of 1990 to announce a coordinated program for Metcalfe Park was in direct response to the *60 Minutes* piece about McGee and Milwaukee that aired the night before. (Ironically enough, the idea to target one section of the city had originated with Howard Fuller and had been presented to the mayor through a black member of his administration.) While it would take time to determine the long-term success of the program, setting it up in the first place was an attempt to counter what Webster saw as one of the major weaknesses of the Norquist Administration—having no comprehensive plan to attack housing, health, and employment problems in the inner city, which, as it happened, was essentially what McGee was asking for. Instead of the politics-as-usual "shotgun approach," as Webster called it, an approach that often led to overlap and working at cross-purposes, the administration basically said, "'We don't care where your funding comes from, what you call your department, who works where and when, but in this targeted area, this is the level of service we want, this is how we expect you to work together to get it done.'"

When I said that the mayor had complained about the same thing, Webster grimaced. He did so because he was of the opinion that one of the mayor's greatest problems was his inability to articulate his overall vision for the city. While he considered the mayor to be someone well read and brilliant, he felt strongly that those qualities didn't add up unless he were able to convey what he was thinking in a way that his administration could understand and act on. Leadership, as is usually the case in any organization, comes down from the top. To make sure that battles of turf don't take place, there needs to be some clear consensus or mandate of what everyone is working toward. Without that, you wind up with a degree of chaos, or people building little fiefdoms, or people working on pieces of a picture that nobody can say, with any certainty, what it's supposed to eventually look like. And so when money comes from Washington, or from the state, or from taxpayers, or from reserves, the lack of a unified plan often means that no significant change results.

As WEBSTER AND I left the restaurant, I noticed a copy of *Newsweek* that someone was apparently done with. The thirtieth anniversary of the 1963 March on Washington had occurred a few days earlier, and the cover story, not surprisingly, was about race, "The Struggle to Save the Black Family." On the surface, this appeared to be the kind of stuff that worried David Webster—articles that spoke of pathology rather than solutions, that resonated with a lot of angry finger-pointing and not much else. And yet that was only partly true of the articles contained within.

A survey of black adults revealed that 41 percent thought black families themselves were in the best position to improve their situation and only 14 percent thought government was. But as a report from the Joint Center for Political and Economic Studies put it, blacks alone could not, in point of fact, "create jobs on the scale needed; nor can we restore the economy to include more jobs of moderate skill and decent pay. . . . This is pre-eminently the work of government."

I walked down to Lake Michigan, magazine in hand, letting the debate over whether government should or should not assume this role proceed without me. I had walked along the lake many times before, but ever since Marvin Hannah and I had driven past it and he had told me there was no place for him there, I had found it difficult to go myself. But it was a beautiful day in early September and there was a breeze coming off the water and it was late afternoon; the combination of those three things has always been more than enough to turn me away, however briefly, from whatever else I might be doing.

On this day, though, it wasn't. I thought about Marvin anyway and I thought about Howard Fuller and I especially thought about Jerrel Jones and his insistence that a black person could never get past being viewed as black, no matter what he did. So what was I, as a white person, to do? Throw up my hands and concede that Jones was right? That a large number of whites will always look down on blacks? That integration (however one chooses to define it) has had a measure of success, but, by and large, it has failed, failed because we haven't been determined enough to make it work? That nothing can be done about the isolation and condition of our urban ghettos? Somehow I couldn't. Call it stubbornness, call it naïveté, call it eternal optimism, call it what you will.

And yet: it is almost impossible—is it not?—to listen, time and again, to Martin Luther King's stirring speech in late August of 1963 and not wince. When the official day to remember him rolls around every January, there is a hollowness to it, an aching sense of something unfulfilled. In the book he published one year before he was cut down in Memphis, he asked us, "Where do we go from here?" Good question.

Whites can either give up on the idea of racial harmony and just go on—living insular lives, content to say we tried, endlessly remarking on the gains and accomplishments of the black middle class and continuing to pay lip service to "valuing diversity"—or we can keep trying to find ways to change hearts and minds. If Orlando Patterson is right—that two white racists still exist for every black person in America—then this, it seems to me, is where the battle of race relations must continue to be waged, from the inside out. It may sound quaint and Emersonian, but if each person is willing to focus his energy on doing this, on searching deep inside and being courageous enough to confront and, if necessary, change what one finds there, then maybe, just maybe, we can regain a larger sense of collective purpose, a sense of just how important it is that this human dilemma be resolved for the generations to come.

But in order to get from the inside out, I thought to myself as I kept walking, seeing only a few black people as I headed up the shore, whites could no longer make their acceptance of blacks conditional on their being "more like us" or "acting white"; they could no longer fear that having blacks live in the same neighborhood would either bring disharmony or bring down the value of their property; they could no longer exploit, consciously or not, the advantages that come to them just because they are white. And blacks, for their part, must find a way beyond seeing themselves as victims in the instances where they are not, beyond seeing conspiracies where they don't exist, beyond seeing racism where it doesn't exist. They would have to keep in mind that they knew white people who were good and honorable and could be relied upon (just as whites had to keep that in mind about blacks), that staying away from polarization and stereotyping was an essential thing for both to do in taking the next step.

All this aside, though, blacks, as so many have said in this book, shouldn't be waiting around for a scenario like this to unfold. They have to do what they can where they can how they can. Those who have "made it" need to volunteer their time and energy; those who have not need to acquire skills and ward off the "forces of evil" as best they can. More and more churches (as Howard Fuller has suggested) have to open their doors wider and become learning centers as well as spiritual ones. Leaders of community-based organizations have to remember why they are there—to serve the needs of the community before their own.

The consequences of giving up the fight—especially the fight to improve the lives of those who have never left the ghetto—are more and more desultory accusations that lead us nowhere. For every alliance between a Carvis Braxton and a John Fitzgerald, there need to be thousands upon thousands more. The workplace, after all, is the one place where blacks and whites interact more than any other—more than where they live or where they pray or where they spend their leisure time. That's not to take anything away from a project like Beyond Racism; but Beyond Racism is totally voluntary, whereas two people being thrown together in a work environment is not. It's an opportunity. If nothing is made of it, though, then those two people might as well be living on different planets.

But *if* something is made of it, the terms *must* be equal. Each of us must be allowed to be who we are, and to be respected for who we are. As I left the lake and headed back to my room, a couple of questions, seemingly simple in nature, continued to gnaw at me. If daily life is trying enough, why, frankly, should blacks have to constantly watch their step? Why should they constantly be subjected to a different set of bells and whistles merely because they are black?

EPILOGUE

Bill Clinton went to Memphis in November of 1993 and spoke before the same congregation that Martin Luther King had the night before he was assassinated, the night he claimed to have seen the Promised Land but said that "I might not get there with you." In trying to imagine what Dr. King would say about the twenty five years that had passed since his death, the president delivered an emotional speech, a speech in which he claimed Dr. King would remind everyone that he had "fought for people to have the right to work, but not to have whole communities and people abandoned," that he had "fought to stop white people from being so filled with hate that they would wreak violence on black people," but not "for the right of black people to murder other black people with reckless abandon."

"The freedom to do that kind of thing," the president reiterated, "is not . . . what people gathered in this hallowed church for the night before he was assassinated in April of 1968. If you had told anybody who was here in that church on that night that we would abuse our freedom in that way, they would have found it hard to believe. And I tell you, it is our moral duty to turn it around. . . .

"We won't make all the work that has gone on here benefit just a few. We will do it together by the grace of God."

BUT IN *TIME* THE following month, Howard Fuller also spoke in terms of we—as in "Have we gone mad?" a question prompted by a list that he unsteadily held in his hands, "a list of all my kids who have died between 12/92 and 12/93." Fifteen of the kids on the list were under seventeen.

AS 1994 BEGAN, AN article by Nicholas Lemann in the *New York Times Magazine* argued that, historically, efforts to rebuild the ghetto didn't work, that the whole notion of "economic revitalization" had been tried under a variety of guises (from "urban renewal" in 1949 to "empowerment zones" in 1993), but all you needed to do was look around and you wouldn't find much private-sector activity in the inner cities of America. The irony of these efforts, Lemann pointed out, was that they "pass every test but one, the reality test. They are popular among all the key players in antipoverty policy; they sound good; they have bipartisan appeal; they are based on tax breaks rather than on spending and so are easier to pass. The only problem is that so far they haven't worked—which creates a larger problem.

"Think for a minute," he wrote, "about *why* most people believe that the Great Society was a failure. What's the evidence? It is the enduring physical and social deterioration of poor inner-city neighborhoods. The Government promised to turn these places around, and instead they got worse; *ipso facto,* Government can't do anything right." That, he said, was exactly "the button" the Bush Administration was trying to push when it singled out the Great Society as the real reason for the Los Angeles riots. "Attempts at economic revitalization," he wrote, "often take the place of other efforts that would do much more good (especially improving schools, housing and police protection), and they establish a public mission that can't be accomplished." Not only that, he wrote, but it must be remembered that poor neighborhoods have almost always been places in transition, places that people are constantly trying to move away from if they possibly can. "What is gained in the short run by making a promise that sounds more appealing—economic development—is far outweighed by what is lost in the long run when the dream doesn't come true." The overall task, as Lemann and others (including 55 percent of all African-Americans) see it, still remains: to include as many blacks as possible in the economic and social mainstream.

NEWT GINGRICH HAD HIS own form of dream, his own notion of what the voters wanted (or didn't want), and his dream came true in November of 1994 with the Republican landslide in Congress and his bold talk of a Contract with America, a contract that, he boasted, would break political gridlock and only take a hundred days to put in place, a contract that would make such drastic cuts in social programs that the actions of the Reagan and Bush administrations would seem downright beneficent by comparison. Mean-spiritedness was in vogue, cutting at the edges of this document, and neither the Clinton Administration nor Democrats in general had much in the way of a response. They were too stunned to mount one. Clinton had promised two years earlier to break the status quo and "end welfare as we know it." But aside from his waffling and having his primary focus elsewhere, he didn't anticipate the Draconian measures of Newt and his acolytes. Clinton had put the welfare ball out there, but since he hadn't protected it, it was hardly surprising that someone would come along and try to wrest it from him. Whether it was in Washington or on the meanest streets of Milwaukee, Darwin's rules still applied. If (depending on your point of view) one of the key mistakes of the War on Poverty was in by-passing the pork-laden "interests" of state and local officials, here, pre-sumably, was the sweetest retribution any governor could wish for: more autonomy, more say over how money would be spent, and far less inter-ference from Washington. The Reagan Revolution would, it appeared, finally manifest itself, carried out by a former college history professor with a brash, bull-in-a-china-shop style that was reminiscent of Lyndon John-son's. Washington was being put on notice. Either go along with us or get out of the way. It was a message not unlike that of Gary Hart's in his 1974 run for the Senate ("They had their turn. Now it's our turn"), but Gingrich had many more soldiers at the ready to carry it out, including the gover-nor of Wisconsin, Tommy Thompson, one of the leading proponents of state-controlled welfare programs.

AROUND THE SAME TIME that the Age of Newt was beginning, so was the Trial of the Century in Los Angeles. From the night of June 12, 1994, onward, the night that Nicole Brown Simpson and Ronald Goldman were brutally murdered, you couldn't turn anywhere, or so it seemed, without hearing or seeing the name and face of O. J. Simpson, a man who had run away from race, much in the way that Clarence Thomas had, and would have his own reasons for coming back to it, reasons that didn't include having those "chitlin flashbacks" that Polly Williams spoke of at that break-fast in Milwaukee. On the surface, it appeared that race had nothing to do with the matter—and there are people who will argue to this day that it didn't—but even before the prosecution introduced Detective Mark Fuhrman to the world at large, the notorious reputation of the Los Ange-les Police Department made it possible for the defense, led by Johnnie Cochran, to play the race card and claim that Simpson was being framed because he was black.

As everyone knows by now, the jury needed little time to officially deliberate: at a little past one o'clock, eastern time, on the first Tuesday of October in 1995, the clerk read the verdict and Simpson's shoulders relaxed. Though his smile said far more than the actual words "not guilty," that smile and tangible display of relief were far surpassed by reactions all across America, in barbershops and beauty salons, in taverns and in corporate suites, in nursing homes and day care centers, on college campuses and in elementary schools, reactions that made it forcefully and painfully clear how great the divide is between blacks and whites in this country. The glee and the shrieking—the letting off of steam—that all classes of black Americans displayed on October 3 (regardless of what many might have privately thought —or didn't want to believe) countered by the incredulous stupor of most white Americans was a moment that will not easily fade from memory.

Working on the subject of race for as long as I had made black America's reaction to the verdict easier to understand. It had far, far less to do with the case at hand than it had to with retribution and reparations and a distinct sense that this was one for *their* side. It had to do with all the lynchings, all the slights, all the put-downs, all the ways in which the system was set up against them in various ways. It had to do with Emmett Till, with the four little girls who were killed in Birmingham, with Yusuf Hawkins, with Rodney King, with anyone who had ever been stopped and given a hard time, often for no reason, in a white neighborhood. O. J. Simpson was the beneficiary of all this anger and frustration that had been submerged for so long. Simpson smiled and they shouted. Law students at Howard University went into a frenzy that no one who saw it on television is likely to forget. All of Shelby Steele's talk about race-holding and the importance of individual advancement seemed pretty inconsequential at that moment.

"Race is such a large decoy that it almost always causes us to get very important things wrong," wrote Stanley Crouch. "The Simpson case tested all of our contemporary democratic mythologies about good and evil, about race and fairness, about law enforcement and the criminal courts and justice. The Negroes who disturbed so many by celebrating, by cheering, and by dancing were responding to a dream of American possibility quite different from that assumed by the media."

In the same issue of *Esquire* in which Crouch was holding forth, Jimmy Breslin had this to say. "Before the Simpson verdict, people felt there was something wrong with anyone who talked too much about race. . . . Today, it's clear that race is the only interesting topic in the daily life of this country. The Simpson verdict just made it obvious that race has been uppermost in our minds all along." He was startled, he said, to hear President Clinton say how surprised he was at how wide the racial gulf was between blacks and whites after the verdict was announced. "What startled me," he wrote, "was how easily he can tell a cheap lie," referring to the time that Clinton had come to New York during the 1993 race for mayor and said that anybody who didn't vote for the black Democratic incumbent, David Dinkins, was a racist. That was as brazen—and ineffective—a use of the race card as could possibly be imagined.

THIRTEEN DAYS AFTER THE verdict, new images emerged, images of thousands and thousands of black men, spanning three generations, coming to Washington on a brilliant autumn day to take part in what was being called the Million Man March. Surrounded by controversy because it was conceived by Louis Farrakhan, it was intended to be an opportunity for black men to assert themselves, to show by their very presence that they were strong and capable and *responsible,* that they were concerned about their communities, that they were tired of being viewed as dangerous and less than human, that whatever past sins they had committed (either overtly or by omission) they had come to Washington to atone for. The sight of so many sons, fathers, and grandfathers (not to mention Howard Fuller, Michael McGee, and Jerrel Jones) gathered peacefully in one place was far more important than the question (which was debated and analyzed for weeks afterward) of whether a million of them actually were there.

On the same day that the march was taking place and everybody who was allowed to make a speech made one, at a time when the prospect of Colin Powell running for president (and winning) seemed very likely indeed, a time in which the number of all black men between the ages of twenty and twenty-nine who were "involved" in the criminal justice system had risen from one-fourth to one-third, a time in which the fractious issues of affirmative action and welfare reform threatened to become a flashpoint in the campaign of 1996, President Clinton left Washington and took to the hustings. In a speech delivered at the University of Texas, he told a primarily white audience that "in recent weeks, every one of us has been made aware of a simple truth: white Americans and black Americans often see the same world in drastically different ways, ways that go beyond and beneath the Simpson trial and its aftermath, which brought these perceptions so starkly into the open. The rift we see before us exists in spite of the remarkable progress black Americans have made in the last generation. . . .

"The reasons for this divide are many. Some are rooted in the awful history and stubborn persistence of racism. Some are rooted in the different ways we experience the threats of modern life to personal security, family values, and strong communities. Some are rooted in the fact that we still haven't learned to talk frankly, to listen carefully, and to work together across racial lines."

Clinton's path toward speaking out on race relations in Austin that day was, like the subject itself, a tortuous one. Given that he had been as surprised as anyone at the seeming extent of the racial divide in the wake of the Simpson verdict, he and his closest aides struggled for days (as is their wont) about how detailed he should be in terms of solutions, especially since the shelf was pretty bare in terms of what would satisfy both blacks and whites. So he opted to speak more generally and philosophically, warning blacks and whites that *each* needed to clean their houses of racism, evoking Lincoln's famous comment that "a house divided against itself cannot stand." There were far too many people today, he said, "on the left and the right, on the street corners and the radio waves, who seek to sow division for their own purposes. To them I say: No more. We must be one."

Two of the people he had in mind, neither of whom he mentioned by name, were Louis Farrakhan and Mark Fuhrman. In regard to the Nation of Islam leader, he said that "one million men do not make right one man's message of malice and division"; in reference to the Los Angeles detective whose racist sentiments had become imprinted in people's minds, he suggested that "the taped voice of one policeman should fill you with outrage."

Farrakhan and Fuhrman. McGee and Metzger. While there is nothing wrong with singling them out, these figures who appear to be on opposite ends of the pole but who share much in common (and who depend on each other so much), it is dangerous at the same time. It is dangerous because it suggests they are exceptions, when in fact they are spokesmen, audacious enough to give voice to what many people feel and think and yet, for a variety of reasons, will rarely say. So when a white person announces that nothing about Mark Fuhrman bears any relation to him, it is not true. Not only is it not true, but by denying any association, it makes it more difficult to acknowledge, and come to terms with, our own racism, to clean our house of it, as the president suggested.

By the time that Farrakhan rose, in the late afternoon, to give his rambling two-hour speech in Washington, he had already heard, thanks to modern technology, the president's remarks in Austin. He too chose to mention Lincoln, but focused on Lincoln's never truly being in favor of blacks "having equal status with the whites of this nation," on his position that if one group had to be superior, Lincoln "would rather the superior position be assigned to the white race." And then, moving from Lincoln to Clinton, he said that when the president spoke earlier about wanting "to heal the great divide," he didn't go far enough. "You did not dig deep enough at the malady that divides black and white, in order to effect a solution to the problem. And so today, we have to deal with the root so that, perhaps, a healing can take place."

Earlier, when Jesse Jackson spoke, he asked: "Why was the reaction to the O. J. verdict so different?" His answer: "Because there were wounds unhealed." And all these people, with all these unhealed wounds, had come to Washington, had come because "raw nerves of ancient longing for dignity" had been touched by this call to march.

LESS THAN ONE MONTH after the march, Colin Powell decided not to run for president, a decision that came, he said, from looking deep into his soul. What he presumably found there, among other things, was a concern, first voiced by a number of black friends during the summer, that despite everyone's hope that he could be the one to heal the nation's racial wounds if he became president, his color would undoubtedly become an issue and prevent him from doing so. The "incivility" of politics was the way the general delicately put it. His friends were more blunt: they said he was setting himself up to be made a fool of, that he would "ultimately be humiliated." Colin Powell may have bowed out with elegance, but he bowed out nonetheless.

AS I SIT AT my desk during the winter of 1996, snow piled up outside for as far as the eye can see, the Million Man March seems a distant specter, as does the fervor that surrounded Colin Powell. I recall a lunch I had with Milton Coleman, metro editor of the *Washington Post,* a week after the march, a lunch in which I asked him, a native of Milwaukee, what the long-term impact of the march would be, if any.

He honestly didn't know, he said. Speaking as a black American, as someone who by every measure had made it in the so-called mainstream and yet had endured more than his share of slings and arrows from both whites and blacks along the way, he couldn't say with any certainty whether it was "a temporary salve" or the beginning of something permanent.

To me, that was part of the problem. Unlike the March on Washington, this had taken place without any concrete connection to the nation's political agenda (unless you subscribed to the belief, as a goodly number of people did, that Newt Gingrich was the true organizer of the march). The 1963 march resulted in a civil rights act the following year; in 1995 there was halfhearted talk that maybe another Kerner Commission should be formed. The other part of the problem was that too many white Americans had viewed this day of atonement as something that had nothing to do with them, as yet one more convenient opportunity to say it's about time blacks stood up and took full responsibility for their own lives and the sorry conditions of many of their communities, as something they could watch from a safe distance (white office workers in Washington stayed home in droves) and feel the warm water of absolution wash over them. Who, after all, wouldn't welcome the idea of being let off the hook?

But being let off the hook must not be an option. Underlying all the visions and the political speeches and the personal agendas there are still facts, hard truths we need to grapple with, and solutions we need to agree on. *More than half of all black men between the ages of twenty-five and thirty-four either do not have jobs or don't make enough money to support a family of four above the poverty level. For every black man who goes to college, one hundred go to jail.* The color line that W.E.B. Du Bois spoke of at the beginning of the twentieth century is still there, defiant and seemingly immovable, as we approach the start of the twenty-first. We as a country have made much progress, but still the line remains, there to be reckoned with, a pox on all our houses. And so, in the end, it is up to us, *all* of us, to somehow find a way to cross over it, for good.

AFTERWORD

I n late March of 1996, nearly five years to the day since I had first arrived in Milwaukee, I returned on a bitterly cold Tuesday night. The temperature was eight degrees as my plane touched down at Mitchell International Airport and I headed toward my "second home" on Cass Street and the familiar confines of Room 252.

Bert Sweet had left word for me that she was tired and had gone to bed but would see me in the morning. And when morning came, there was a lot she wanted to tell me, especially about how her niece had finally married the young man she had been seeing for eight years and that the wedding was lovely, lovely in every respect but one. In all that time, Bert's brother and his wife were never able to give their daughter the blessing she wanted. They came to the wedding but barely said a word and, with the exception of a money order for two thousand dollars that they gave the couple as a gift, have had little contact with them since.

Though no one asked her opinion, Bert offered it to her sister-in-law anyway. "This is not a throwaway world, Betty," she said, having lost her own daughter to cancer two years earlier. "We can't throw people out of our lives."

ONE WEEK BEFORE MY return, John Norquist had been reelected to his third term as mayor, and most of the talk centered around the way the vote had split heavily along racial lines. His opponent was the popular Richard Artison, former sheriff of Milwaukee County. But Artison hardly campaigned and it was difficult to determine whether the black votes he garnered were because he was black or because they represented disapproval with the mayor and his efforts toward the inner city. Asked by the local paper what, if anything, the results said about the state of race relations, the mayor curtly replied, "We need to join together and build a stronger Milwaukee." That aside, black voter turnout had been light, despite the intensive efforts that were made to register people, efforts that had been primarily inspired by the Million Man March.

Outside Milwaukee, John Norquist's profile continued to rise (two days after the election the *Wall Street Journal*'s editorial page wrote about him for the second time) and there was speculation that he would run for governor in 1998.

THE NATIONAL PROFILE OF Wisconsin's governor, Tommy Thompson, continued to rise too. For months he was on the short list of vice presidents whom Bob Dole might choose, and his welfare plan, Wisconsin Works, won legislative approval and took effect in 1997. "The days of something for nothing are over," the governor said upon signing the bill. "The welfare check is history."

HOWARD FULLER RESIGNED AS superintendent of the Milwaukee Public Schools in the spring of 1995, not long after a school board election that would, in his opinion, have made it even more difficult for him to do his job. One week prior to his emotional resignation—to his indignantly saying that he was not and had never been "in the hip pocket of the 'downtown business interests,'" that he was not prepared to die "by a thousand cuts," not going to wind up becoming "a bureaucrat protecting the status quo"—an article in *Business Week* praised the reforms he had begun to institute and which were already showing some progress, reforms, the magazine predicted, that would "outlive his tenure." Deciding that he would be more effective working for educational reform from outside the system, he currently serves as a consultant for a number of foundations and as Distinguished Professor of Education at Marquette University, where he began the Institute for the Transformation of Learning. In the fall of 1995, he married Deborah McGriff, former superintendent of the Detroit Public Schools and vice president of the Edison Project.

As for the Million Man March and what import he felt it had had, he said, without hesitation, that it had been one of the most positive and uplifting experiences of his life. "It was a model," he said softly, "of what it could be like."

. . .

MICHAEL MCGEE WAS SO energized by the march that he considered running for Congress in the fall of 1996. While those plans never materialized, he continues to be a radio talk-show host on WNOV. As for the 1995 deadline he imposed on Milwaukee when he formed the Black Panther Militia, it came and went without incident, though he spent fifteen days in jail for his role in overturning a police car (in protest of a black youth's being shot by a white officer who mistook a cassette for a gun). He temporarily lost his home to the government (though Jerrel Jones and others bought it back for him), and in May of 1996 he was implicated in a series of small fires at a Korean-owned beauty supply store on the North Side, a place where, he claimed repeatedly on his radio show, blacks were constantly harassed and where they shouldn't be spending their money anyway.

TOM DONEGAN FINALLY MOVED out of Sherman Park but still lives in the city.

MARVIN HANNAH MOVED AS well and resides in Mequon.

MARON ALEXANDER STILL WORKS for General Electric and Georgette now works as a cook at Sacred Heart School of Theology, where she earns more money than she did at Marquette and has benefits and vacation time as well. They moved too, to a three-bedroom duplex a little farther out, around Forty-ninth and Hampton, and even though Tennille is now at college, at the University of Wisconsin—Parkside in Kenosha, they still worry about her.

Maron and his friends considered going to the Million Man March, but then decided against it. In his view, the march was about the same principles that he tried to live by every day.

TOM BROPHY RETIRED FROM public service without seeing a grand-scale Marshall Plan put in place for Milwaukee.

. . .

CARVIS BRAXTON REMARRIED, IN a large African ceremony, in the summer of 1995 and now lives in Sherman Park. He is the chief community organizer for Harambee (the position that Tommie Williams once held). Not only do he and John Fitzgerald continue to see each other, but his daughter Candace and Johnny Fitzgerald attended the same middle school, where Johnny became the first white student ever to join the Brothers of Kwanzaa. Johnny also, for a short period of time, was part of a music group called the Interracials, a group that eventually fell apart because they didn't practice enough.

L. G. SHANKLIN-FLOWERS BEGAN her own consulting business and she and her husband reunited in December of 1995. Though she now had the money to move away from Thirty-fifth and Cherry, "to go upscale," as she says, she decided not to, decided that figuring out a way to "reclaim this neighborhood" was what she was meant to do. About her daughter, Davita, who turned nine in 1996, she couldn't be more pleased. "She's a powerful young person," L. G. said, "who *expects* the world to do right by her." Davita, she said, was very conscious of being both African-American and European-American, and she didn't let any comments that kids might make affect her in any way.

But that didn't mean that nothing bothered her. They had recently flown somewhere and experienced such bad weather that Davita asked her mother if they were going to die. "No," L. G. said to her, "we have great work to do. It's not our time to go."

What she said to me, when I asked about the future, was that "despite the tough times, I am very hopeful. The Million Man March was a wonderful, powerful statement, all those black men saying, 'We're fine, and we're going to survive, and we've got some work to do.' . . . Those of us who are clear are going to do well. I'm not giving up on my future. I'm going to be part of the group that figures it out."

What, specifically, was "it"? I asked her.

"How we heal ourselves and our country of the vestiges of an oppressive system that is not working for *anybody,*" she said bluntly, letting that last word hang suspended in air before quoting some Scripture to me:

All creation stood on tiptoe to see
the children of God come into their own.

As I drove around Milwaukee, I kept that image in my mind, fascinated by the way that religious passages had insinuated themselves into the story from the beginning, from when I had first gone to Montgomery and written about the Civil Rights Memorial for *Time* magazine. Whether it was that fascination that took me to Cross Lutheran Church on Palm Sunday of 1996 I cannot say. All I knew was that the church had been closed for more than a year—the result of an electrical fire, not an act of arson—and was reopening that very day.

But when I got there, I learned—and saw—so much more. I saw an integrated congregation in an inner-city neighborhood, a congregation so overcome with joy that its doors were open again that they marched all the way around the block holding stalks of palm in their hands. They were led by their pastor, Reverend Joseph Ellwanger, who was white and had been active in Selma during the civil rights movement. The gathering of people that Palm Sunday in Milwaukee—of black and white together, singing and locking arms and swaying from side to side, of people passing by me and extending a hand and looking straight into my eyes when they said, "Peace be with you"—naturally took me back to that Sunday in Montgomery more than six years earlier.

While the picture of harmony was still misleading, it was a moment to savor and hold on to nonetheless.

NEARLY FIVE MONTHS LATER, a moment of a different sort occurred at the White House. On August 22, 1996, President Bill Clinton, sitting behind a placard that promised "A New Beginning," signed legislation that ended welfare. But where the jobs are for all the people who will now be required to find work—not to mention the money needed to train many of them—remains unclear.

As does the outcome of a year-long race initiative the president announced in June of 1997. In an effort to secure the legacy of his time in office, President Clinton asked the country to begin a "great and unprecedented conversation about race," a conversation that would take place in town meetings around the nation. But, he warned, "if we do nothing more than talk, it will be interesting but it won't be enough. If we do nothing more than propose disconnected acts of policy it would be helpful but it won't be enough. But if ten years from now people can look back and see that this year's honest dialogue and concerted action helped to lift the burdens of race from our children's future we will have given a precious gift to America."

ACKNOWLEDGMENTS

NOTES

SELECTED BIBLIOGRAPHY

INDEX

ACKNOWLEDGMENTS

My long journey through the minefield of race in America began in Montgomery, Alabama, in the spring of 1989. I had gone there to do a piece about Maya Lin and the Civil Rights Memorial, which was to be placed in front of the Southern Poverty Law Center (SPLC) and dedicated that autumn. At the time, I couldn't possibly have known that working on that article would become the jumping-off point for this book. As with my first two books, I started with a few questions; those questions—and the responses I received—led to more questions. A writer learns so much from other people when he embarks on a project like this, and it wouldn't be proper not to acknowledge those debts.

In Montgomery, Morris Dees, Richard Cohen, and Sara Bullard of the SPLC opened their doors to me, and Morris introduced me to Red's Little Schoolhouse, in Dublin, Alabama, for which I will always be grateful. In Selma, Alice West sat me in a chair and talked and talked, especially about how odd it was that my first name was the same as Jonathan Daniels's (the seminarian killed during the civil rights movement whom she always viewed as a member of her family) and that my last was the same as that of the man who shot him, Tom Coleman. Alice's daughter, Rachel West Nelson, and her childhood friend, Sheyann Webb Christburg (whom Martin Luther King Jr. called "my littlest freedom fighters") took me to a restaurant in Selma, where, just as they predicted, we were stared at all night long. In Birmingham, Chris McNair, in talking of Denise, gave me an inkling of what it would be like to lose a child. The folks who work at the jewel of a public library there are among the most knowledgeable and helpful group I have ever come across in one place.

In Milwaukee, the friendship of Chuck and Pat Schuster sustained me, even though I didn't see them nearly as much as I would have liked. Janet and Andy Fitch were able (and, at times, contentious) researchers. Harry Kemp, who lived next door to me at the Plaza and happened to be the chief photographer for Milwaukee's three black newspapers, always tried to make sure I was getting things straight (or more accurately, see-ing things his way). Jeff Bentoff, press secretary to Mayor John Norquist (and a former journalist), was especially helpful in arranging time with the mayor. To everyone else who opened their doors and their lives to me, a simple thanks is inadequate.

In Charlottesville, Andrea Shen was a marvelous help, as was Peter Ronayne, John Galinsky, Mary Hall, and Bryson Clevenger. Amy Lemley went over the manuscript with care and asked all the tough questions. The constancy of Tan Lin's friendship helped me through difficult times. My other friends—particularly Ann Beattie, Maryanne Vollers, Bill Campbell, Mary and David Kalergis, Rita Dove, and Gabe and Karen Silverman—were a steady source of support. The very existence of my daughter, to whom this book is dedicated, was a guarantee that I would never give up.

In New York, my agent, Owen Laster, waited and waited for me to complete this book and then proved, once again, to be a class act. The people at Atlantic Monthly Press welcomed this book and proceeded to shower it with old-fashioned care. To Morgan Entrekin, Anton Mueller, Lissa Smith, Judy Hottensen, Kirsten Giebutowski, Charles Woods, Eric Price, and (my former landlady) Joan Bingham, many thanks.

Thanks also to E. Ethelbert Miller and Robert Norrell for their will-ingness to read the book in manuscript and offer their candid impressions of it.

I have known Tobi Zion Effron since I was ten years old. She elevates the word "friend" to a new plane.

A final note. During the process of revising this book, I met someone named Cooper. For the record, she has a first name (Camille), but "Cooper" is how I affectionately refer to her. Not long after we met, the odyssey of this book took a strange and anxious turn. A period of time followed in which I was tested in every way. Cooper understood, better than I, what was going on. That she always had faith, that she was convinced what was happening was happening for a reason, are a testament in part of who she is. For that, and for showing me her half of the sky, I give thanks.

J.C.
June 3, 1997

NOTES

The primary source material for this book comes from the countless hours of interviews I conducted with hundreds of people, many of whose names do not appear here but without whom my task would have been considerably harder. As often as possible, I have identified my sources within the text itself; for the instances where I felt to do so would interrupt the flow of the narrative, I list those additional sources below.

In addition to the interviews, nearly all of which were tape-recorded, and my own presence at many of the events I describe, I drew on a vast array of other sources: letters; books; diaries; journals; newspaper and magazine articles; photographs; police reports; appointment calendars; telephone logs; depositions; school yearbooks; and other memoranda and documents.

PROLOGUE

vii "MALIGNANCY": From interview with Henry Cisneros, former Secretary of Housing and Urban Development, in "Housing Secretary Carves Out Role As a Lonely Clarion Against Racism," *New York Times,* July 8, 1993.

"GREAT ACHILLES' HEEL": Ibid.

"BETTER ANGELS OF OUR NATURE": From President Abraham Lincoln's 1861 Inaugural Address. The entire sentence reads: "The mystic chords of memory, stretching from every battlefield and patriot grave, to every living hearth and hearthstone, all over the broad land, will yet swell the chorus of the Union, when again touched, as surely they will be, by the better angels of our nature." See *A Treasury of the World's Greatest Speeches* (Simon and Schuster, 1954, 1965), pp. 510–12.

viii AS LONG AS ROUGHLY THREE-FIFTHS OF WHITES: From "Ethnic Images," a December 1990 survey conducted by the National Opinion Research Center.

JESSICA BRADFORD: "Getting Ready to Die Young," *Washington Post,* November 1, 1993.

EPIGRAPH

ix Robert Kennedy quoted Aeschlyus in a 1968 speech he gave in Indianapolis upon learning of the death of Martin Luther King Jr. I couldn't find the translation Kennedy used, but here are two others: *of Zeus who put men on the way to wisdom/*

by making it a valid law/that by suffering they shall learn./There drips before the heart instead of sleep/pain that reminds them of their wounds;/and against their will comes dis-cretion (from *The Oresteia,* translated by Hugh Lloyd Jones, University of California Press, 1993) and *Zeus the Guide, who made man turn/ Thoughtward, Zeus, who did ordain/Man by suffering shall Learn./So the heart of him, again/Aching with remembered pain,/Bleeds and sleepeth not, until/Wisdom comes against his will./'Tis the gift of One by strife/Lifted to the throne of Life* (from *The Complete Plays of Aeschylus,* translated by Gilbert Murray, George Allen & Unwin, 1952).

James (Son) Thomas was a singer and guitarist who played traditional Mississippi Delta blues. See *New York Times* obituary, July 12, 1993.

CHAPTER 1

3 EMMETT TILL PHOTOGRAPHS: These appeared in *Jet* on September 22, 1955.

MEDGAR EVERS: Byron De La Beckwith, the killer of the civil rights activist, was convicted in February 1994, more than thirty years after the murder.

FOUR TIMES MORE BLACK FAMILIES WITH INCOMES ABOVE $50,000: *New Yorker,* April 29–May 6, 1996, p. 10.

4 HOWARD BEACH and BENSONHURST: Howard Beach is a section of Queens, New York, where a young black male (Michael Stewart) was struck and killed by a car after being chased onto a highway by whites in 1986. Bensonhurst is a predominantly white section of Brooklyn, New York, where a young black male (Yusuf Hawkins) was killed by a group of whites in August of 1989.

"WELFARE QUEENS": During the 1976 presidential campaign, Ronald Reagan, in making a point about the abuses of welfare, referred to a woman from Chicago who "has 80 names, 30 addresses, 12 Social Security cards. . . ." As it turned out, Reagan's claim about Linda Taylor (whom he never mentioned by name) was not entirely accurate. See *New York Times,* February 15, 1976, p. 51.

5 "MOVING TOWARD TWO SOCIETIES": See *Report of the National Advisory Commission on Civil Disorders* (Dutton, 1968).

CHAPTER 2

6 THE BUCKS: The Milwaukee Bucks won the 1971 professional basketball championship.

ANTHONY TROLLOPE: "Milwaukee is a pleasant town, a very pleasant town," Trollope wrote. "How many of my readers can boast that they know anything of Milwaukee, or even have heard of it?" Trollope, *North America* (Lippincott, 1862), pp. 130–36.

"HEARTLAND OF THE HEARTLAND": "A Hard Right Turn," *Newsweek,* June 14, 1993.

PROCTER & GAMBLE: Interview with Jerrel Jones and employee of Procter & Gamble, who asked not to be identified.

ONE OF THE MOST SEGREGATED METROPOLITAN AREAS: "Milwaukee Area Found to Be Most Segregated," *Milwaukee Sentinel,* May 14, 1992. The article cites a U.S. Census Bureau Report by Roderick J. Harrison and Daniel H. Weinberg.

"HYPERSEGREGATED": Douglas S. Massey and Nancy A. Denton, "Hypersegregation in U.S. Metropolitan Areas: Black and Hispanic Segregation Along Five Dimensions," *Demography* 26 (1989), pp. 378–79.

ONE OF THE HIGHEST RATES OF BLACK-TO-WHITE UNEMPLOYMENT: See *Statistical Record of Black America,* which reprints a table from a Bureau of Labor Statistics profile ("Unemployment Rates: Selected SMSA's, 1990") that shows the rate at 5.533 to 1. At times, the rate has been as high as 6 to 1 ("Making Minority Hires a Priority," *Milwaukee Journal Sentinel,* September 25, 1995.

ONE OF THE HIGHEST RATES OF BLACK TEENAGE PREGNANCY: "New Report Ranks City Fifth for Births to Black Teenagers," *Milwaukee Journal,* February 20, 1991. *State of America's Children 1991* (Children's Defense Fund).

ONE OF THE HIGHEST TURNDOWN RATES FOR MINORITY LOAN APPLICATIONS: "Blacks Denied S&L Loans Twice as Often as Whites," *Atlanta Journal-Constitution,* January 22, 1989. The article found that blacks were rejected nearly four times more than whites in the Milwaukee metropolitan area. A task force was formed as a result of this article. Even though the task force pointed out that the high acceptance rate of mortgages applied for by whites was the main reason for the wide disparity, a report issued by the city of Milwaukee in 1994 revealed that Milwaukee was still at the top of the list among the 50 cities studied.

ONE OF THE LOWEST PERCENTAGES OF BLACK OWNER-OCCUPIED HOUSING: According to Census figures for 1990, only 29.7 percent of blacks in Milwaukee lived in their own homes, whereas 43 percent did nationwide. Also see R.L. McNeely and Melvin Kinlow, *Milwaukee Today: A Racial Gap Study,* published in 1987 by the Milwaukee Urban League.

ONE OF THE HIGHEST PERCENTAGES OF BLACKS LIVING BELOW THE POVERTY LINE: According to Census figures for 1990, 42 percent of blacks in Milwaukee were living below the poverty level—$12,700 for a family of four—a percentage only exceeded by blacks in Miami. Nationwide, the percentage was slightly less than a third. *Rocky Mountain News,* October 30, 1994.

MCGEE'S THREAT AND PROPOSAL: Black Panther Militia manifesto. "McGee Plans Panther Militia," *Milwaukee Journal,* March 1, 1990.

7   JEFFERSON'S CONTRADICTIONS ON RACE: "UNFORTUNATE DIFFERENCE OF COLOUR" ("This unfortunate difference of colour, and perhaps of faculty, is a powerful obstacle to the emancipation of these people"); "DISPOSITION TO THEFT" ("That disposition to theft, with which they have been branded, must be ascribed to their situation . . ."); "DISAGREEABLE ODOUR" ("They secrete less by the kidneys, and more by the glands of their skin, which gives them a very strong and disagreeable odour"); "MORE ARDENT AFTER THEIR FEMALE" ("They are more ardent after their female: but love seems with them to be more an eager desire than a tender delicate mixture of sentiment and sensation"); "AS BRAVE, AND MORE ADVENTURESOME" ("They are at least as brave, and more adventuresome. But this may perhaps proceed from a want of forethought, which prevents their seeing a danger 'til it be present"); "MORE GENERALLY GIFTED THAN WHITES" ("In music they are more generally gifted than whites with accurate ears for tune and time. . . . Whether they will be equal to the composition of a more extensive run of melody, or of

complicated harmony, is yet to be proved"). *Notes on the State of Virginia* (Lilly and Wait, 1832; originally published in 1787), pp. 145–49.

8 "I AM THE MAN . . .": Quotation from Walt Whitman's "Song of Myself," line 827 (edited by Edwin Haviland Miller, "Walt Whitman's 'Song of Myself': A Mosaic of Interpretations," University of Iowa Press, 1989, p. 27).

9 *MILWAUKEE JOURNAL*'s SERIES ON RACE: The *Journal*'s series ("Race: The Rawest Nerve") began on April 7, 1991 and ran, on and off, for the next year.
"RACE PROBLEM": Interview with Michael McGee; "Race: The Rawest Nerve," *Milwaukee Journal*, April 7, 1991.

10 NEARLY A THIRD OF BLACKS IN U.S. LIVE IN POVERTY: U.S. Bureau of the Census, from *Health, United States,* 1995. In 1990, the percentage was 31.9; in 1991, 32.7; 1992, 33.4; 1993, 33.1; 1994, 30.6.
MCGEE BACKGROUND: Interviews with McGee and John Norquist. *Milwaukee Magazine,* November 1989. "Midwest Alderman With a Militia Threatens to 'Disrupt White Life,'" *Washington Post,* July 18, 1990.

11 "HAPPENS FIVE AND SIX . . .": Actually, if one divides the number of black homicide victims by 365, the daily average is more than thirty. In 1990, there were 12,144 black homicide victims; in 1991, 12,958; in 1992, 12,318. These figures come from *Vital Statistics of the United States* (U.S. National Center for Health Statistics).
"FOR ALL OF THE TURMOIL . . .": Black Panther Militia manifesto.

12 "TO DEMAND SOME DIGNITY": Shiva Naipaul, *Journey to Nowhere* (Simon and Schuster, 1981), p. 282.
BREIER'S NOT TALKING TO BLACKS: Interviews with Tommie Williams and Arthur Jones, the newly appointed chief (as of 1996) of the Milwaukee Police Department. "THE KKK IN BLUE": *Milwaukee Magazine,* November 1989.

14 CHIPPEWAS AND COMPLAINTS ABOUT THEIR SPEARFISHING: Five years after Jerrel Jones and the newspapers first brought this to my attention, the controversy continued. Having caught an average of between 21,000 and 31,000 walleye since 1990, the six Chippewa tribes announced they wanted to spear 54,000 walleye in 1996—an announcement that met with the threat of an injunction by Governor Tommy Thompson. "Tribe Gives Notice to Start Spearing . . . ," *Milwaukee Journal Sentinel,* April 11, 1996.

CHAPTER 3

15 ALDERMANIC DISTRICT 10 (as of 1991): City of Milwaukee's Engineer's Office (2.67 square miles). 1990 Census (36,816 people).
MILWAUKEE URBAN LEAGUE STUDY: *Milwaukee Today: A Racial Gap Study.*

16 LOSS OF 60,000 MANUFACTURING JOBS: "How Milwaukee Boomed But Left Its Blacks Behind," *New York Times,* March 19, 1991. While the *Times* piece cites the Milwaukee Economic Development Corporation as its source, other sources, for the period 1979–1989, place the loss around 43,000 (Sammis B. White, *Journal of Urban Affairs,* 1995, Vol. 17, number 1; State Association of Commerce).
SUBURBAN VOTE IN 1992 ELECTION: "Women Won on the Merits," *New York Times,* November 7, 1992,

17 ONLY 9,000 OF THE 60,000 JOBS WERE RESTORED: "How Milwaukee Boomed . . . ," *New York Times,* March 19, 1991.

UNEMPLOYMENT RATE FOR BLACKS AND WHITES IN MILWAUKEE: Ibid (citing the Bureau of Labor Statistics).

BLACKS ON PUBLIC ASSISTANCE IN MILWAUKEE: Speech by Howard Fuller in 1988, when he was director of Health and Human Services for Milwaukee County.

QUOTATION FROM ROBERT MILBOURNE: "How Milwaukee Boomed But Left Its Blacks Behind," *New York Times,* March 19, 1991.

1942 HEARINGS IN CHICAGO: Joe William Trotter Jr., *Black Milwaukee: The Making of an Industrial Proletariat, 1915–45* (University of Illinois Press, 1988) pp. 166–69.

22 MILWAUKEE PUBLIC SCHOOLS DEMOGRAPHICS: Milwaukee Public Schools.

THOSE WHO SAID MONEY WAS NOT THE ISSUE: Interview with Howard Fuller, who cited Eric Hanushek (*Making Schools Work*) as one of the leading proponents of this idea.

CHAPTER 4

24 "WE SUBMIT . . .": William H. Grier and Price M. Cobbs, *Black Rage,* (Basic Books, 1968).

MORE BLACKS IN PRISON THAN COLLEGE: Marc Mauer, "Young Black Men and the Criminal Justice System: A Growing National Problem" (The Sentencing Project, February 1990).

25 MCGEE IN WAITING ROOM: *Milwaukee Magazine,* November 1989.

26 GREAT SOCIETY PROGRAMS: Nicholas Lemann, *The Promised Land: The Great Black Migration and How It Changed America* (Alfred A. Knopf, 1991).

27 "OF SUBSTANCE, OF FLESH . . .": Ralph Ellison, *Invisible Man* (Vintage Books, 1952).

ARTHUR SCHLESINGER JR. ON MULTICULTURALISM: Arthur Schlesinger Jr., *The Disuniting of America: Reflections on a Multicultural Society* (W.W. Norton, 1992). "Whose America?" *Time,* July 8, 1991.

CHAPTER 5

30 WHITE PRIVILEGE: Peggy McIntosh, "White Privilege: Unpacking the Invisible Knapsack," *Peace and Freedom,* July/August 1989.

31 NEARLY 80 PERCENT . . . : Orlando Patterson, "The Paradox of Integration," *The New Republic,* November 6, 1995.

32 "NONE OF US IS FREE . . .": Martin Luther King Jr. said this often, but the first expression of this sentiment may have come from Herbert Spencer, the British social theorist, who wrote, in *Social Statics* (1851), that "No one can be perfectly free till all are free. . . ."

CHAPTER 6

35 COVER STORIES ON RACE: *Atlantic* (May 1991); *Newsweek* (May 6, 1991); *U.S. News & World Report* (July 22, 1991); *Business Week* (July 8, 1991).

BUSH ADMINISTRATION FIGHTING NEW CIVIL RIGHTS BILL: "End of the Non-Quota Issue," *New York Times,* April 24, 1991.

THE TREATMENT BLACKS RECEIVE IN STORES: "When Blacks Shop, Bias Often Accompanies Sale," *New York Times,* April 30, 1991.

ILLINOIS SCHOOL TO HAVE SEPARATE PROMS: "Separate Senior Proms Reveal an Unspanned Racial Divide," *New York Times,* May 5, 1991.

GEORGIA SCHOOL TO HAVE SEPARATE VALEDICTORIANS: "Judge Says 2 Should Share Honor," *New York Times,* June 7, 1991.

MORE BLACKS IN COLLEGE THAN EVER BEFORE: "A Crisis of Shattered Dreams," *Newsweek,* May 6, 1991.

36 "TIRED OF BEING CALLED GUILTY": Ibid.

"RACE FATIGUE": Shelby Steele, *The Content of Our Character: A New Vision of Race in America* (St. Martin's Press, 1990), p. 23.

"RACE DOES NOT DETERMINE . . .": Ibid.

"A DEEP WEARINESS . . .": Ibid.

"INTEGRATION SHOCK": Ibid.

"BLACKS STILL SUFFER . . .": Ibid.

"GATHERING PLACE BY THE RIVERS": "This is Manawaukee-Seepe—the great council place of many tribes, the gathering place by the rivers" (the Milwaukee, Menomonee, and Kinnickinnic). H. Russell Austin, *The Milwaukee Story* (*Milwaukee Journal,* 1946), p. 11.

GROPPI MARCHES: "Black Milwaukee Has History Full of Struggle, Turmoil," *Milwaukee Journal,* April 10, 1991. The Milwaukee Public Library has some wonderful documents related to Groppi and the marches.

37 THE OPEN (OR FAIR) HOUSING ACT (1968): While this act prohibited discrimination on the basis of race in 80 percent of all rental and sale housing, it was difficult to enforce, partly because of small budgets and partly because of weak penalties.

"LACKEY" AND "HYPOCRITE": Interview with Michael McGee. "Midwest Alderman With a Militia Threatens to 'Disrupt White Life,'" *Washington Post,* July 18, 1990.

MOLOTOV COCKTAIL: Interview with Howard Fuller.

38 BACKGROUND OF HOWARD FULLER: Interviews with Fuller, Juanita Smith (his mother). "Who Is Howard Fuller and What Does He Want?" *Milwaukee Magazine,* July 1988.

41 "POWER CONCEDES NOTHING . . .": Frederick Douglass speech on August 4, 1857.

42 FULLER AND MCGEE SNIPING: "Midwest Alderman With a Militia Threatens to 'Disrupt White Life,'" *Washington Post,* July 18, 1990.

44 IF ALL THE EXISTING JOB OPENINGS . . . : "Expected to Work, But No Jobs" (1991 report from the Social Development Commission). By 1995, the "job gap" had increased to 53,198.

JOB PROGRAMS FOR YOUTH: The Private Industry Council's combined summer programs placed 4,109 youths in jobs in the summer of 1991, an increase of 11 percent from 1990. "Teen Job Program Sees Big Jump," *Milwaukee Journal,* September 6, 1991.

"THE TROUBLE WITH CONFRONTING RACISM": "Suburbs Lag to Integration, Norquist Says," *Milwaukee Journal,* May 15, 1991.

CHAPTER 7

49 GREATER MILWAUKEE COMMITTEE FORMING INNER CITY TASK FORCE: "Task Force Confident of Solutions . . . ," *Milwaukee Journal,* December 17, 1990.

RESEARCH ON TAVERNS AND LIQUOR OUTLETS: Walter C. Farrell Jr. and Bobbi Marsells, "Outlet Densities in Black Communities: A 1985 Case Study of Milwaukee, Wisconsin." "Pratt Proposes Cut in Liquor Licenses," *Milwaukee Journal,* January 20, 1992.

50 "THE DEVASTATING SOCIAL . . .": "A Quarter-Century of Slipping Backward," *Los Angeles Times,* August 10, 1990.

51 BLACK PANTHERS AND GENOCIDE: Hugh Pearson, *The Shadow of the Panther: Huey Newton and the Price of Black Power in America* (Addison-Wesley, 1994). Naipaul, *Journey to Nowhere,* pp. 288–89.

BLACK FEMALE SUSPENDED: "Culture Clashes With Corporations," *Milwaukee Journal,* April 11, 1990.

54 SHELBY STEELE AND AFFIRMATIVE ACTION: Steele, *The Content of Our Character,* pp. 111–27.

55 UNDERCOUNT OF 1990 CENSUS: "Poor Americans, Still Discounted," *New York Times,* July 19, 1991.

CHAPTER 8

58 PHOTOS OF HOMICIDE VICTIMS: "Homicide's Tragic, Costly Toll Will Live On For Years," *Milwaukee Journal,* January 3, 1991.

60 ALUMINUM BRINGING 50 CENTS A POUND: Actually, several recycling shops in Milwaukee said the price was closer to $.45 in 1991. By 1996, the price had dropped another ten cents.

CHAPTER 9

61 AMERICA'S NEW MURDER CAPITALS: "Big Crimes, Small Cities," *Newsweek,* June 10, 1991.

"WE DON'T DESERVE . . . ": "Murder Makes Milwaukee Famous?" *Milwaukee Journal,* June 5, 1991.

62 DEFENDANTS WERE CHILDREN: "Today's Young Offenders More Prone to Violence," *Milwaukee Journal,* June 2, 1991.

CHILDREN'S DEFENSE FUND STUDY: "More Children Thrust into Poverty in '80s," *Milwaukee Journal,* June 3, 1991.

31 PERCENT OF BLACKS IN POVERTY IN U.S., 42 PERCENT IN MILWAUKEE: According to 1990 Census figures and a University of Pittsburgh study of the 1990 Census.

MILWAUKEE MOST SEGREGATED BY INCOME: According to Urban Institute study, reported in "Urban Poor Found Most Isolated Here," *Milwaukee Journal,* May 6, 1994.

62 "ONLY IN PART ABOUT CIVIL RIGHTS": Elizabeth Drew, "Letter from Washington," *New Yorker,* June 17, 1991.

REAGAN AND BUSH MOVING COUNTRY BACKWARD: "Our Racial Problems Are Very Patient," *Washington Post,* August 21, 1990.

"NOT ABOVE EXPLOITING RACIAL TENSIONS . . .": Elizabeth Drew, *New Yorker,* June 17, 1991.

64 "30 PERCENT OF THE POPULATION . . .": The 30 percent is correct, but the 90 percent is not; it is closer to 50 percent. According to the Milwaukee Police Department's figures, of the 57,632 arrests in 1990, 36,440 of the individuals were nonwhites. Given that blacks make up 83 percent of Milwaukee's nonwhite population, the percentage of blacks committing crimes would be around 50 percent.

PERCENTAGE OF WHITES, AGES 15 TO 19, HAVING BABIES . . . : Andrew Hacker, *Two Nations: Black and White, Separate, Hostile, Unequal* (Scribner, 1992), p. 82.

65 THREE-FIFTHS OF ALL AFDC MOTHERS . . . : According to a Congressional Budget Office Report (Federal Document Clearing House, Inc., GAO/HEHS-94–112, 1994).

CHAPTER 10

68 THREE TIMES AS MANY INTERRACIAL COUPLES: According to Census data and Current Population Survey data, there were 310,000 interracial couples in 1970 and 964,000 in 1990.

69 "PEOPLE WHO ARE NOT RACIST . . .": "You Can't Join Their Clubs," *Newsweek,* June 10, 1991.

INCIDENT ON LONG ISLAND: "3 Arrested in Beating of Black," *New York Times,* June 6, 1991.

73 ROBERT MOSES: Robert Caro, *The Power Broker: Robert Moses and the Fall of New York* (Vintage Books, 1975), pp. 318–19.

CHAPTER 11

78 MPS TEXTBOOKS: As it turns out, Holt was incorrect. At the time we talked, in June of 1991, textbooks were being used that contained information about blacks and black leadership during the Civil War and afterward. As for information about black inventors, according to Karen Salzbrenner at MPS, there was some.

"WITH ALL DELIBERATE SPEED": One year after the *Brown* decision, the Supreme Court declined to order an immediate end to school segregation. It instructed the lower courts to issue decrees that the admitting of the plaintiff children to schools should proceed "on a racially nondiscriminatory basis with all deliberate speed. . . ."

79 HIGH RATES OF HYPERTENSION AND HEART DISEASE: According to U.S. Center for National Health Statistics, there were 267.9 black males who died of heart disease (per 100,000 residents in 1993) as compared with 190.3 white males; 165.3 black females who died as compared with 99.2 white females. As for hypertension, during the years 1988–91, 37.4 percent of black males (ages 20–74) suffered from it as compared with 25.1 percent of white males; 31 percent of white females as compared with 18.3 percent of white females.

CHAPTER 12

83 THIRTEEN-YEAR-OLD BOY WITH UZI: Interview with June Perry, director of New Concepts.

CHAPTER 13

85 BUSH'S APPROVAL RATING: "The President's Petulance," *New York Times,* June 12, 1991.

"THEY'RE TRYING TO MAKE . . .": "Fiery Speech from Harkin Rouses Faithful," *Milwaukee Journal,* June 16, 1991.

86 "I GET SICK AND TIRED . . .": "His Turn: Bush Returns Fire in Visit Here," *Milwaukee Journal,* June 18, 1991.

"ONE THING WE WON'T DO . . .": "Called Complacent, N.A.A.C.P. Looks to Future," *New York Times,* June 10, 1991.

"A LITTLE COMPLACENT": Ibid.

87 IMPORTANCE OF RACE TO AMERICA'S FUTURE: "Race: The Rawest Nerve," *Milwaukee Journal,* April 7, 1991.

INCIDENT IN MEXIA, TEXAS: Information drawn from author's interviews and reports in *Dallas Times-Herald* and *New York Times.*

88 "WITH ALL THE VIOLENCE . . .": *Milwaukee Sentinel,* June 14, 1991.

GREG STANFORD COLUMN: "City Hall Needs Help in Improving Life in the Inner City," *Milwaukee Journal,* May 29, 1991.

89 INFORMATION ON THE CONSTITUTION AND RECONSTRUCTION: Interview with James Cameron. Richard Kluger, *Simple Justice* (Vintage, 1977) and Lerone Bennett Jr., *Before the Mayflower* (Penguin, 1993, 6th edition).

90 DEMAND FOR REPARATIONS CONTINUES: "Blacks Press the Case for Reparations for Slavery," *New York Times,* July 21, 1994.

93 "YOU ARE ALWAYS BLACK FIRST": "What Color is Black?" *Newsweek,* February 13, 1995.

94 "INCOGNEGROES" AND "AFROPEANS": "Don't Blame Me!" *New York,* June 3, 1991.

MARTIN LUTHER KING JR. AS "DE LAWD": J. Anthony Lukas, *Common Ground: A Turbulent Decade in the Lives of Three American Families* (Alfred A. Knopf, 1985), p. 11.

CHAPTER 14

98 94 PERCENT OF ALL BLACKS KILLED . . . : "A Week in the Death of America," *Newsweek,* August 15, 1994.

99 DANIEL PATRICK MOYNIHAN: Lemann, *The Promised Land.*

SHELBY STEELE: Steele, *The Content of Our Character,* pp. 21–37.

CORNEL WEST: West, *Race Matters* (Beacon Press, 1993).

CHAPTER 15

102 "REAL REFORM TAKES TIME": "Sophomore Superintendent," *Milwaukee Journal,* August 23, 1992.

"THE MANAGER OF MISERY": "Manager of Misery: Brophy Ready for Role," *Milwaukee Journal,* June 19, 1991.

104 BACKGROUND OF HOWARD FULLER: Interviews with Fuller and Juanita Smith (his mother). "Who is Howard Fuller and What Does He Want?", *Milwaukee Magazine,* July 1988.

108 MORE OF THE GRAVY AND LESS OF THE JERKY: Interview with Rev. LeHavre Buck, June 1991.

"HOWARD IS OUR JESUS": *Milwaukee Magazine,* July 1988.

CHAPTER 16

109 THURGOOD MARSHALL RESIGNATION: "Marshall Retires from High Court; Blow to Liberals," *New York Times,* June 28, 1991.

"DESEGREGATION IS NOT . . .": "A Slave's Great-Grandson Who Used Law to Lead the Rights Revolution," *New York Times,* June 28, 1991.

110 "YOU NOT ONLY GOT MY . . .": Kluger, *Simple Justice,* p.177.

"WHEN MY SUCCESSOR IS QUALIFIED": "My Dear Mr. President," *New York Times,* June 28, 1991.

"MILWAUKEE HAS BEEN IDENTIFIED . . .": "US Task Force May Target Local Drug Dealing, Gangs," *Milwaukee Sentinel,* June 28, 1991.

112 "FACE UP TO MY BLACKNESS . . .": "Who is Howard Fuller and What Does He Want?", *Milwaukee Magazine,* July 1988.

113 SHELBY STEELE AND INDIVIDUAL RESPONSIBILITY: Steele, *The Content of Our Character,* pp. 29–35.

CHAPTER 17

114 PRESIDENT BUSH CLAIMING CLARENCE THOMAS TO BE MOST QUALIFIED: Various articles in *New York Times,* July 2, 1991.

"AN EXCUSE FOR DOING WRONG . . .": Ibid.

"I EMPHASIZE BLACK SELF-HELP . . .": Clarence Thomas, *Wall Street Journal,* February 20, 1987.

115 "THE REAL ISSUE . . .": Thomas, *Los Angeles Times,* November 15, 1985.

BACKGROUND OF CLARENCE THOMAS: Various articles in *New York Times,* July 2, 1991. "Visible Man," *New York,* July 29, 1991.

116 CIVIL RIGHTS LEADERS BITCH, MOAN, AND WHINE: "EEOC Chairman Blasts Black Leaders," *Washington Post,* October 25, 1984.

117 PAY PHONES BEING BLOCKED FROM RECEIVING INCOMING CALLS: "Ma Bell Hangs Up On Dealers," *Los Angeles Times,* May 30, 1990.

SPUR POSSE: Joan Didion, "Letter from California," *New Yorker,* July 26, 1993.

118 FIRE AND POLICE COMMISSION REPORT: "Complaints of Brutality Get Nowhere," *Milwaukee Journal,* July 7, 1991.

119 BLACK LAW PARTNER: According to Carl Ashley, there were only five black attorneys who were partners in Milwaukee law firms in 1996.

CHAPTER 18

122 LEWIS MUMFORD PREDICTION: From a section called "Urban Devastation" in Mumford, *The City in History: Its Origins, Its Transformations, and Its Prospects* (Harbinger, 1961).

"IRON RING": George J. Lankevich, ed. *Milwaukee: A Chronological & Documentary History, 1673–1977* (Oceana Publications, 1977), p. 71.

125 COMMISSION APPOINTED IN 1934: Ibid., p. 67.

CHAPTER 19

134 HARAMBEE'S PROPOSAL: This resulted in the Neighborhood Family Initiative, which is funded by the Ford Foundation and which extends beyond the issues Williams is talking about.

139 MARTIN LUTHER KING'S DISCUSSIONS WITH ELIJAH MUHAMMAD: King met with the Nation of Islam leader in Chicago in February 1966, and they both agreed to form a "common front" to deal with the city's racial problems. See James A. Colaiaco, *Martin Luther King, Jr.: Apostle of Militant Nonviolence* (St. Martin's Press, 1988).

140 MARCUS GARVEY AND CONSPIRACY: "In analyzing questions and issues that confront a race I want to point out to you a treacherous bit of conspiracy to defeat the aspirations, the aims and the hopes of this struggling race of ours. A world conspiracy is launched to again enslave this race probably for another century or for eternity. . . ." From *Marcus Garvey and the Universal Negro Improvement Association Papers: Volume III, September 1920–August 1921,* edited by Robert A. Hill (University of California Press, 1984), p. 582.

141 ANGELA DAVIS ON GENOCIDE: "Only a united front—led in the first place by the national libertarian movements and the working people—can decisively counter . . . the increasingly fascistic and genocidal posture of the ruling clique." From preface (co-written with Bettina Aptheker) to James Baldwin's *If They Come in the Morning* (Okpaku Publishing, 1971), p. 8.

HUEY P. NEWTON ON GENOCIDE: "Considering how we must live, it is not hard to accept the concept of revolutionary suicide. In this we are different from white radicals. They are not faced with genocide." From *Revolutionary Suicide* (Harcourt Brace Jovanovich, 1973), p. 6.

$25,000 A YEAR FOR REFORM SCHOOL: McGee is actually understating the case. It costs $45,000 a year to send a youth to Ethan Allen (in Wales, Wisconsin). "Corps Runs on Public, Private Funds," *Milwaukee Journal,* October 3, 1991.

THINGS MCGEE HAD TRIED TO ACHIEVE: Here, McGee is distorting. He is referring to the Phoenix Redevelopment Project, which received federal money and whose workmanship came under attack. No one I spoke with—including Alderman Marvin Pratt—has any recollection of McGee's group home proposal.

CHAPTER 20

147 INCIDENT WITH KONERAK SINTHASOMPHONE: "Police Probe Later Calls about Konerak," *Milwaukee Journal,* Sept. 9, 1991. "Fleeing in Terror," *Milwaukee Journal,* July 26, 1991.

148 "IF SOME OF THE BLACK LEADERS . . .": Interview with Marvin Hannah, August 1991.

149 THREE-QUARTERS OF BLOCK-GRANT MONEY: The mayor was overstating this; it was closer to 60 percent. By 1996, the amount had dropped to 50 percent.

151 FULLER'S COMMENTS ABOUT KIDS: "Superintendents Find Common Ground on Aims," *Milwaukee Journal,* July 23, 1991.

152 30 PERCENT OF MILWAUKEE HIGH SCHOOL GRADUATES WHO DIDN'T PLAN ON FURTHERING THEIR EDUCATION: Based on MPS exit surveys of students who were neither going on to college or to vocational school.

CHAPTER 22

162　CERTAIN 60S PROGRAMS WOULD HAVE WORKED BETTER WITH MORE FUNDING: Lemann, *The Promised Land*.

FULLER'S STEPFATHER BEING TERMINATED: "Who is Howard Fuller and What Does He Want?", *Milwaukee Magazine*, July 1988.

164　FULLER ON 1964 CIVIL RIGHTS ACT: Fuller's view that the bill was "*not* that big a deal" was echoed by Nicholas Katzenbach, the former Attorney General who was responsible for implementing the law during the Johnson Administration. Katzenbach called it "a drop in a very large bucket. . . . It did nothing, nothing for the great mass of African-American citizens in this country." "Civil Rights Act Failed, Movement Veterans Say," *New York Times*, November 6, 1994.

166　"COMPENSATORY GRANDIOSITY": Steele, *The Content of Our Character*, p. 62.

"THERE ARE IMAGES OF IT EVERYWHERE . . .": Ibid.

CHAPTER 23

169　"INSTEAD OF VIEWING AMERICA'S INNER CITIES . . .": "The Ghetto's Hidden Wealth," *Fortune*, July 29, 1991.

JAMES CAMERON'S NEAR LYNCHING: Interview with Cameron. "Man's Museum of Memories Relieves the Terror for Blacks," *New York Times*, July 10, 1995.

THE PENNY ROCK: As with many stories, this one has many versions. From interviews with Howard Fuller, Reuben Harpole, and Fred Olson, a professor emeritus of history at the University of Wisconsin—Milwaukee, who initially recommended that the rock be moved. Since the rock was dedicated to Increase Lapham (whom Harpole calls "the father of meteorology"), Olson thought it made sense to have it in front of Lapham Hall.

170　MAN PERSUADING THE CITY NOT TO PLANT FLOWERS: Reuben Harpole was referring to Richard Perrin, Milwaukee's first official in charge of historic preservation. Perrin's widow, while acknowledging the story, said it was "absolutely untrue" and suggested that Mayor Henry Maier might have been responsible. "Henry Maier wasn't one for the blacks," she said. "He may have done this and pointed the finger at Dick." As to her husband's reaction to the accusation, she said: "He never said a thing, but it devastated him."

GOVERNOR KNOWLES'S MONEY TO CITY: "State Board OKs 6 Core Programs," *Milwaukee Journal*, June 12, 1968.

EFFORTS TO INTEGRATE SUBURBAN SCHOOLS: These efforts were made through a group called MUSIC—Milwaukee United for School Integration Committee.

171　SHERMAN BOOTH'S EFFORTS TO HELP JOSHUA GLOVER ESCAPE: At his trial on federal charges of aiding and abetting Glover's escape, Booth said: "I rejoice that in the first attempt of the slave hunters to convert our jail into a slave pen and our citizens into slave catchers they have been significantly foiled. . . ." Booth was freed and the Fugitive Slave Act declared unconstitutional. "The Negro in Wisconsin," *Milwaukee Sentinel*, February 13 and 14, 1967. Milwaukee County Historical Society.

CENTRAL CITY INITIATIVE: The initiative is still in place and the budget has gradually increased since 1991. The key to making it work remains the willingness of suburban employers to hire workers from the inner city and the ability of those workers to get to those jobs. Interview with Corey Hoze, director of Governor Tommy Thompson's Milwaukee office.

CHAPTER 24

177 TELLING ONESELF STORIES IN ORDER TO LIVE: Joan Didion, *The White Album* (Simon and Schuster, 1979), p. 11.

178 BLACK CHILDREN STILL PREFERRING WHITE DOLLS: In a 1987 study conducted by Michael Barnes, Sharon McNichol, and Darlene Powell-Hopson and presented to the American Psychology Association, about two-thirds of black children chose a white doll. The children then heard the psychologists compliment those children who had chosen black dolls. When the experiment was conducted again, two-thirds of both black and white children chose black dolls. Nonetheless, the media, the psychologists complained, misinterpreted the results of their study, suggesting that the black children who selected white dolls did not possess feelings of self-hatred; rather, their preference for white dolls reflected our culture's standards of beauty that hold up whiteness as an ideal, which of course is a huge problem in itself. The psychologists also pointed out that until roughly the age of seven, racial identification does not generally occur. "Black Child's Self-View Is Still Low, Study Finds," *New York Times,* August 31, 1987. "Psychologist Says Media Misread Studies," *St. Petersburg Times,* September 21, 1987.

179 ARTHUR ASHE ON RACE: "Ashe Legacy: Strong Talk From Heart," *New York Times,* June 8, 1993.

CHAPTER 25

181 "MECHANIZATION ON THE FARM . . .": I.F. Stone, *In a Time of Torment* (Random House, 1967), p. 158.

"THE TRUTH . . .": Naipaul, *Journey to Nowhere,* p. 291.

182 ABOLISH WELFARE: Charles Murray, *Losing Ground: American Social Policy, 1950–80* (Basic Books, 1984).

BLACKS AND IQ: Charles Murray and Richard Herrnstein, *The Bell Curve: Intelligence and Class Structure in American Life* (Free Press, 1994).

183 SOME 80 PERCENT OF WHITES KILLED BY OTHER WHITES . . . : "A Week in the Death of America," *Newsweek,* August 15, 1994.

185 GUNNAR MYRDAL AND UNDERCLASS: Rising unemployment in the United States, Myrdal speculated in his 1962 book *Challenge to Affluence,* might "trap an 'underclass' of unemployed and, gradually, unemployable and underemployed persons and families at the bottom of a society." He then pointed out, in a footnote, that "the word 'under-class' does not seem to be used in English." But it wasn't until twenty years later, with the 1982 publication of Ken Auletta's *The Underclass,* that the term began to be used widely. See Lemann, *The Promised Land,* pp. 281ff.

LORD ACTON'S OBSERVATIONS: *Acton in America: The American Journal of Sir John Acton, 1853* (edited by S.W. Jackman, Patmos Press, 1979).

TOCQUEVILLE'S OBSERVATIONS: Alexis de Tocqueville, *Democracy in America* (Vintage Books, 1956).

186 ABIGAIL ADAMS LETTER TO JOHN ADAMS: J. Anthony Lukas, *Common Ground*, p. 54.

CHAPTER 26

187 "I'VE DECIDED TO STICK WITH LOVE . . .": It appears that Queen Hyler "added" the part about sticking with love, because the actual quote, which comes from a Christmas sermon that Dr. King delivered at Ebenezer Baptist in Atlanta, is as follows: "I've seen too much hate to want to hate, myself, and I've seen hate on the faces of too many sheriffs, too many white citizens' councilors, and too many Klansmen of the South to want to hate, myself; and every time I see it, I say to myself, hate is too great a burden to bear." See Martin Luther King Jr., *The Trumpet of Conscience* (Harper and Row, 1968), p. 74.

"WE MUST LIVE TOGETHER . . .": From a speech by King in St. Louis on March 22, 1964.

JFK'S QUOTE: The actual comment, made during a televised address to the nation on June 11, 1963 (the day that Governor George Wallace tried to prevent the integration of the University of Alabama), was this: "If an American, because his skin is dark, cannot eat lunch in a restaurant open to the public, if he cannot send his children to the best public schools available, if he cannot vote for the public officials who represent him . . . then who among us would be content to have the color of his skin changed? Who among us would then be content with the counsels of patience and delay?" See Richard Reeves, *President Kennedy: Profile of Power* (Simon and Schuster, 1993), p. 522.

188 ANDREW HACKER'S STUDENTS: Hacker, *Two Nations,* p. 32.

"CULTURE OF COMPLAINT": Robert Hughes, *Culture of Complaint: The Fraying of America* (Oxford University Press, 1993).

CHAPTER 27

191 ONLY 40% OF FRESHMEN GRADUATE FROM HIGH SCHOOL IN MILWAUKEE PUBLIC SCHOOLS: According to Gary Peterson, a research specialist with Milwaukee Public Schools, over a four-year period about 40 percent of MPS students have graduated, 40 percent have dropped out, 16 percent have transferred out of the district, and 4 percent are still enrolled in school. "Milwaukee Schools' Males: The Lost Classmates," *Milwaukee Journal Sentinel,* June 10, 1996.

25,000 CHILDREN COULD NOT ATTEND NEIGHBORHOOD SCHOOL: Karen Salzbrenner, Milwaukee Public Schools.

72% OF MILWAUKEEANS . . . : Drawn from the Hyco Report.

192 100,000 DISCIPLINARY INCIDENTS IN '90–'91 SCHOOL YEAR: Milwaukee Public Schools.

CHAPTER 28

196 "REALLY WHITE BREAD AND BUTTER" AND "SOMEONE TOUGH": Interviews with Gretchen Schuldt and Leonard Sykes of the *Milwaukee Journal Sentinel.*

202 THREE BLACK FAMILIES IN WEST ALLIS: Actually, there were more than fifty, according to the 1990 Census.

CHAPTER 29

209 WELFARE PAYMENTS IN MILWAUKEE COUNTY WORTH LESS IN 1991 THAN IN 1987: Interview with Thomas Brophy, director of Health and Human Services for Milwaukee County.

CHAPTER 31

219 BLACK UNEMPLOYMENT IN MILWAUKEE SIX TIMES THAT OF WHITES: See note in Chapter 2.

HIGHEST PROPORTION OF TEEN PREGNANCY OF ANY CITY IN COUNTRY: See note in Chapter 2.

BLACK INFANT MORTALITY RATE OF 18 PER 100,000: According to *The Health of America's Children* (based on information from the National Center for Health Statistics and calculated by the Children's Defense Fund).

HIGHEST RATE OF TURNDOWNS FOR BLACKS SEEKING BUSINESS LOANS AND MORTGAGES: See note in Chapter 2.

220 TESTIMONY OF WALTER FARRELL AND LAWRENCE MEAD: This testimony was offered on July 25, 1991. The other people testifying were Rebecca Blank of Northwestern University and Pat Ruggles of the Urban Institute.

222 NBC NEWS BROADCAST: The segment aired on *Exposé* in August of 1991.

AFROCENTRISM IN *TIME* AND *NEWSWEEK*: The cover story in *Time* ("Who Are We?") appeared on July 8, 1991, and in *Newsweek* on September 23, 1991.

LEONARD JEFFRIES'S COMMENTS ABOUT JEWS IN HOLLYWOOD: On July 20, 1991, Professor Jeffries said, in a speech in Albany, New York, that there was a conspiracy to denigrate blacks in movies "planned, plotted and programmed out of Hollywood" by people with names like "Greenberg and Weisberg. . . ." See "CUNY Professor Criticizes Jews," *New York Times*, August 6, 1991.

228 "A SEPARATE HISTORY FOR AND BY BLACK PEOPLE" AND "INTELLECTUAL APARTHEID": "African Dreams," *Newsweek*, September 23, 1991.

CHAPTER 32

234 POST-TRAUMATIC STRESS DISORDER: " 'Cultural Psychosis' Defense Attempts to Blame Society," *Milwaukee Journal*, December 6, 1991.

235 CORNEL WEST ON BLACK SEXUALITY: West, *Race Matters*, p. 83.

"MORE ARDENT AFTER THEIR FEMALE": See note in Chapter 2 on Jefferson's contradictions on race.

CHAPTER 33

245 "SLAVERY AND SEGREGATION . . .": The actual quote is "All segregation statutes are unjust because segregation distorts the soul and damages the personality."

This is contained in King's "Letter From Birmingham Jail" (1963). See *I Have a Dream* (edited by James Melvin Washington, HarperCollins San Francisco, 1992).

246 ONE BLACK IN BONNERS FERRY, IDAHO: 1990 Census.

CHAPTER 34

250 MCGEE'S THREAT TO DISRUPT CONVENTION BUSINESS: "Convention Planners Undeterred By Threats," *Milwaukee Journal*, August 30, 1991.

OPERATION CORPORATE STORM: "McGee Vows to Disrupt Life in North Shore," *Milwaukee Journal*, November 14, 1991.

MCGEE'S PLAN TO CHALLENGE NORQUIST: "McGee Plans to Enter Race Against Norquist," *Milwaukee Journal*, November 20, 1991.

MCGEE'S SON TO CHALLENGE NORQUIST: "Son is Mayoral Candidate," *Milwaukee Sentinel*, November 28, 1991.

"TO GET THE COLORED PEOPLE OFF HIS BACK": "Community Reaction to Firings is Mixed," *Milwaukee Journal*, September 7, 1991.

RUMORS OF WHITE KILL DAY: "Fuller Ousts Principal at Marshall," *Milwaukee Sentinel*, October 19, 1991.

NORQUIST TALK AT HAMILTON: "Mayor Faces Grilling at Hamilton High," *Milwaukee Journal*, October 24, 1991.

251 WISCONSIN'S CHILD-SUPPORT LAW: In 1987 Wisconsin became the first state to implement an "immediate withholding" law to ensure that parents with custody of children are paid on a regular basis.

MEDIA COVERAGE: Challenging the Business Community; Goals 2000 Report; Money for Milwaukee Community Service Corps; Vacant Lots Available; Money from HUD; Money Committed for Housing; Community-Based Policing: all these topics were covered in the *Milwaukee Journal* and *Milwaukee Sentinel* during October and November of 1991.

252 "HIT-OR-MISS STRATEGIES . . .": "Hit-or-Miss Strategies Barely Make a Dent," *Milwaukee Journal*, October 13, 1991.

"WHERE DO THE ANSWERS LIE?": "Where do the Answers Lie?" *Milwaukee Journal*, October 20, 1991.

CHAPTER 35

253 "YOU ALL ARE GOING TO BE WHITE TODAY": "Officials Pledge Drive to Counter Bias Attack," *New York Times*, January 8, 1992.

"LEAN AND ANGRY": "Black or White," *Newsweek*, December 30, 1991.

BUSH'S SIGNING 1991 CIVIL RIGHTS ACT: "Reaffirming Commitment, Bush Signs Rights Bill," *New York Times*, November 22, 1991.

"WHITES DON'T RESPECT BLACKS": "The People's 1991 . . . ," *Milwaukee Journal*, December 29, 1991.

255 "INVISIBLE LANDSCAPE": Interview with Pamela Jefferson.

258 STORY OF EDMUND PERRY: Robert Sam Anson, *Best Intentions: The Education and Killing of Edmund Perry* (Random House, 1987).

263 FEDERAL VIOLENCE INITIATIVE; Robert Wright, "The Biology of Violence," *New Yorker*, pp. 68–77.

264 MCGEE HOLDING SHOTGUN: "McGee Vows to Launch Revolution in '92 If He Loses in 10th District; Says Riot Call is Meant as Warning," *Milwaukee Journal*, January 15, 1992.

265 RUMORS OF WHITE KILL DAY: "School Confrontations Leave Students 'Scared, Confused'," *Milwaukee Sentinel*, January 18, 1992.

266 BLACK PANTHERS DOING THUGLIKE THINGS: Hugh Pearson, *The Shadow of the Panther*. Shiva Naipaul, *Journey to Nowhere*.

SPEECH OF REVEREND LEON SULLIVAN: "Three Crisis Points in America and in the World."

268 $25,000 A YEAR TO HOUSE KID AT ETHAN ALLEN: As cited in notes to Chapter 19, the cost was actually $45,000 a year.

CHAPTER 37

280 MILWAUKEE'S INVESTMENT IN STEELTECH: Department of City Development.

CHAPTER 38

287 PERCENTAGE OF BLACKS IN EAST ST. LOUIS, ILLINOIS: 1990 Census.

292 FORMER TEACHER FROM SOUTH DIVISION: Interview with Cynthia Ellwood.

294 FREDERICK DOUGLASS PASSAGE: Lerone Bennett Jr., *Before the Mayflower*, p. 217.

CHAPTER 39

295 "NINETY PERCENT OF THE PEOPLE . . .": Lawrence is overstating the case. According to *The State of the Black Population in the United States 1993–1994*, 71.7 percent of black full-time workers made less than $30,000 (as compared to 81.6 percent of all blacks, 15 years and older), and 54.2 percent of white full-time workers made less than $30,000 (as compared to 69 percent of all whites).

"THE AVERAGE WAGE IN MILWAUKEE . . .": What Lawrence is referring to is the average wage of manufacturing jobs. Jobs in the service economy paid, on average, slightly more than half that amount.

296 RON EDMONDS QUOTATION: What Ron Edmonds, widely acknowledged as the founder of the effective-schools movement, actually said was that "We can, whenever and wherever we choose, successfully teach all children whose schooling is of interest to us. We already know more than we need in order to do this. Whether we do it must finally depend on how we feel about the fact that we haven't so far." See Constance Clayton, "We *Can* Educate All Our Children," *The Nation*, July 24/31, 1989.

WAUWATOSA VOTING DOWN TWO REFERENDUMS: This occurred in 1991 and again in 1992.

CHAPTER 40

301 BUSH ADMINISTRATION BLAMING RIOTS ON POLICIES OF '60S: "White House Links Riots to Welfare," *New York Times*, May 5, 1992.

303 STUDENTS DISCUSSING RIOTS IN CLASSES: "Los Angeles Riots Stir Students in Connecticut," *New York Times,* May 6, 1992.

CHAPTER 41
308 MEETINGS WITH CHIEF ARREOLA: Interview with Tommie Williams.
   CONTROLLING THE STEAM: Tom Wolfe, *Bonfire of the Vanities* (Farrar, Straus and Giroux, 1987).

CHAPTER 42
322 ANDREW HACKER: Hacker, *Two Nations,* p.32.
323 "EMOTIONAL INTELLIGENCE": From review in *New York Times* (September 7, 1995) of Daniel Goleman's *Emotional Intelligence* (Bantam, 1995): "Emotional intelligence, the capacity to empathize, judge, relate . . . are crucial for someone to be truly integrated and successful."
   "LET THE POOR LIVE SHORT AND BRUTISH LIVES": Naipaul, *Journey to Nowhere.*
326 VOTING IN BAY VIEW: "Bay View Bellwether Fernwood Precinct . . . ," *Milwaukee Journal,* April 3, 1992.

CHAPTER 43
329 CONGRESS EARMARKING MONEY: "Riots and Reading Lips," *New York Times,* October 10, 1992.
330 FULLER'S POPULARITY RATING: "Fuller's Popularity High in Survey," *Milwaukee Journal,* May 28, 1992.
   "IF IT PASSES . . .": "Norquist Aide Raps School Building Plan," *Milwaukee Journal,* October 1, 1992.
   QUOTATIONS FROM FULLER: "MPS Vote Set; Fuller Rips Mayor . . . ," *Milwaukee Sentinel,* November 5, 1992.
   QUOTATIONS FROM NORQUIST: Ibid.
331 MCGEE'S ACTIONS: "McGee Burns Tires in Street, Warning of Blockade this Year," *Milwaukee Sentinel,* October 7, 1992.
   "ANOTHER DAY, ANOTHER CLINTON": "The 'Why Me?' President," *New York Observer,* April 24, 1995.
332 MONEY, TIME, AND WILLPOWER: "The Transition: How to Lift the Poor," *New York Times,* November 10, 1992.
   POINTS OF AGREEMENT BETWEEN BUSH AND CLINTON: *U.S. News & World Report,* May 18, 1992.
   QUOTATION FROM C. VANN WOODWARD: Woodward, "The Bubbas," *New Republic,* February 1, 1993.
333 CLINTON'S FEB. 15, 1993 SPEECH TO NATION: "Clinton Tells Middle Class It Now Faces A Tax Increase . . . ," *New York Times,* February 16, 1993.
   BILL LAWRENCE COMMENTS: "Poll Shows Most Blacks Back Plan . . . ," *Milwaukee Sentinel,* January 23, 1993.
334 EARLY POLLING SHOWED SUPPORT: "46% Support $366 Million Plan for MPS . . . ," *Milwaukee Sentinel,* December 7, 1992.

FULLER WINNING SUPPORT OF BUSINESS COMMUNITY: "A Powerful Ally for School Plan," *Milwaukee Journal,* December 24, 1992.

POLL IN LATE JANUARY: "Poll Shows Most Blacks Back Plan . . . ," *Milwaukee Sentinel,* January 23, 1993.

MILWAUKEE TECH ON REFERENDUM: Interview with Bill Lawrence.

335 TOTAL NUMBER OF VOTES CAST: The turnout for the referendum was nearly seven times higher than for previous February elections. "Stream of Voters Doomed Schools' Building Plan," *Milwaukee Journal,* February 17, 1993.

341 ROBERT REICH BOOK: *The Work of Nations: Preparing Ourselves for 21st Century Capitalism* (Alfred A. Knopf, 1991).

CHAPTER 44

344 SOCRATES QUOTE: From *The Apology* in Plato's *Five Dialogues* (translated by G.M.A. Grube, Hackett Publishing, 1981), p. 41.

351 "AS DIVISIVE AND DAMNING AS EVER": "Panelists Who Studied '60s Riots See Little Progress on Underlying Ills," *Boston Globe,* May 6, 1992.

VERDICT IN RODNEY KING CIVIL TRIAL: "2 Guilty, 2 Acquitted . . . ," *Dallas Morning News,* April 18, 1993.

CHAPTER 45

354 TEACHER AND NURSERY RHYME: "Racism Abounds . . . ," *Milwaukee Sentinel,* January 13, 1993. "Teacher's Rebuke for Slur . . . ," *Milwaukee Journal,* January 23, 1993.

355 FOURTH-GRADE "FADE": "Moving Ahead on Head Start," *New York Times,* April 18, 1993.

358 BLACK INVENTIONS: "Up from the Slave Ships: Museum Tells the Story," *New York Times,* April 12, 1997.

CHAPTER 46

359 EARNED-INCOME TAX CREDIT: "Clinton Defends Income Tax Credit Against G.O.P. Cut," *New York Times,* September 19, 1995.

363 DEATH OF SHYWONDA: "Man, 19, Charged in Slaying of 15-Year-Old Girl," *Milwaukee Journal,* August 28, 1992.

CHAPTER 47

369 WATER CRISIS IN MILWAUKEE: Cryptosporidium, found in the city's water supply, caused more than 100 deaths and 403,000 people to become ill, according to the Department of Public Works. Interview with Michael McGee.

CHAPTER 48

374 RANDOM SHOTS AT FULLER'S MOTHER'S APARTMENT: "Fuller Says Racism is Unchanged," *Milwaukee Sentinel,* July 21, 1993; "Shot Inquiry Defended by Arreola," *Sentinel,* July 22, 1993.

375 FULLER INTERVIEW: *Wisconsin* magazine, August 25, 1991.

378 "REGULAR EMPLOYMENT . . .": "Dr. Wilson's Neighborhood," *New Yorker,* April 29–May 6, 1996.

CHAPTER 49

387 NEWSWEEK ARTICLE: "Endangered Family," August 30, 1993.

388 KING BOOK: *Where Do We Go From Here: Chaos or Community?* (Harper and Row, 1967).
TWO WHITE RACISTS: Orlando Patterson, *The New Republic,* November 6, 1995.

EPILOGUE

393 CLINTON IN MEMPHIS: "Clinton Delivers Emotional Appeal on Stopping Crime," *New York Times,* November 14, 1993.
QUOTATION FROM FULLER: "Have We Gone Mad?" *Time,* December 20, 1993.
LEMANN ARTICLE: "The Myth of Community Development," *New York Times Magazine,* January 9, 1994.

395 HART'S SLOGAN: David S. Broder, *Changing of the Guard: Power and Leadership in America* (Simon and Schuster, 1980), p. 475.

396 "RACE IS SUCH A LARGE DECOY . . .": Stanley Crouch, "The Bad News, the Good News. O.J. Simpson Verdict. Two Opposing Views," *Esquire,* December 1995.
"BEFORE THE SIMPSON . . .": Jimmy Breslin, *Esquire,* December 1995.

397 BLACK MEN IN CRIMINAL JUSTICE SYSTEM: "More Blacks in Their 20's Have Trouble With the Law," *New York Times,* October 5, 1995.
CLINTON'S SPEECH AT TEXAS: "Clinton, in Solemn Speech, Chides Racists of All Colors," *New York Times,* October 17, 1995.

398 "A HOUSE DIVIDED AGAINST ITSELF . . .": This is from a speech Lincoln made on June 16, 1958, in Springfield, Illinois. The speech continues: "I believe this government cannot endure permanently half slave and half free. I do not expect the Union to be dissolved—I do not expect the house to fall—but I do expect it will cease to be divided. . . ." Lois J. Einhorn, ed., *Abraham Lincoln the Orator* (Greenwood Press, 1992), p. 135.

399 FARRAKHAN'S COMMENTS AT MILLION MAN MARCH: "The March on Washington: Excerpts from Farrakhan Talk," *New York Times,* October 17, 1995. Minister Farrakhan's comments regarding Lincoln come from Lincoln's speech in Charleston, Illinois, on September 18, 1858. "I will say then that I am not, nor ever have been, in favor of bringing about in any way the social and political equality of the white and black races. . . . I as much as any other man am in favor of having the superior position assigned to the white race."
JESSE JACKSON COMMENTS: "The March on Washington: Excerpts from Jackson's Address to Washington March," *New York Times,* October 17, 1995.
POWELL'S DECISION NOT TO RUN: "The Final Order," *New York Times,* November 12, 1995.

400 WHITE OFFICE WORKERS STAYING HOME FROM WORK: "And Now What?", *Newsweek,* October 30, 1995.
STATISTICS ON BLACK MEN: *New Yorker,* April 29–May 6, 1996, p. 106, p. 131.
DU BOIS ON THE COLOR LINE: ". . . the problem of the Twentieth Century is the problem of the color line," W.E.B. Du Bois wrote in "The Forethought" to *The Souls of Black Folk* in 1903.

AFTERWORD

404 NORQUIST IN *WALL STREET JOURNAL:* "A Genuine New Democrat," March 21, 1996.
FULLER'S COMMENTS: "Resignation Statement Tells of Political Stalemate," *Milwaukee Journal Sentinel,* April 19, 1995.

BUSINESS WEEK ARTICLE: "Milwaukee's Lesson Plan," April 17, 1995.

405 MCGEE AND BEAUTY-SUPPLY STORE: "McGee's Latest Campaign Has Predictable Tactics," *Milwaukee Journal Sentinel,* May 5, 1996.

407 QUOTATION FROM SCRIPTURE: The translation that I found (by J.B. Philips) is from Romans 8: 19–21 and reads as follows: *The whole creation is on tiptoe to see the wonderful sight of the sons of God coming into their own.*

ARTICLE ON CIVIL RIGHTS MEMORIAL: "First She Looks Inward," *Time,* November 6, 1989.

QUOTATIONS FROM CLINTON ON RACE INITIATIVE: "Defending Affirmative Action, Clinton Urges Debate on Race," *New York Times,* June 15, 1997.

SELECTED
BIBLIOGRAPHY

In addition to the books and articles already cited in the Notes, I would like to cite the following as helpful to me during the years I worked on this book.

Allport, Gordon. *The Nature of Prejudice*. Addison-Wesley, 1979 (25th anniversary edition).

Billingsley, Andrew. *Climbing Jacob's Ladder: The Enduring Legacy of African-American Families*. Simon and Schuster, 1992.

Branch, Taylor. *Parting the Waters: America in the King Years 1954-63.* Simon and Schuster, 1988.

Brown, Claude. *Manchild in the Promised Land*. Macmillan, 1965.

Bullard, Sara. *Free At Last: A History of the Civil Rights Movement and Those Who Died in the Struggle*. Oxford University Press, 1993.

D'Souza, Dinesh. *The End of Racism*. Free Press, 1995.

Early, Gerald, ed. *Lure and Loathing: Essays on Race, Identity, and the Ambivalence of Assimilation*. Allen Lane, 1993.

Edsall, Thomas Byrne and Mary D. *Chain Reaction: The Impact of Race, Rights, and Taxes on American Politics*. W.W. Norton, 1991.

Franklin, John Hope. *The Color Line: Legacy for the Twenty-First Century*. University of Missouri Press, 1993.

Garrow, David J. *Bearing the Cross: Martin Luther King, Jr. and the Southern Leadership Conference*. Vintage Books, 1988.

Hagedorn, John, with Perry Macon. *People and Folks: Gangs, Crime and the Underclass in a Rustbelt City*. Lake View Press, 1988.

Harrington, Walt. *Crossings: A White Man's Journey into Black America*. HarperCollins, 1993.

Jacobs, Jane. *The Death and Life of Great American Cities*. Vintage, 1961.

Kotlowitz, Alex. *There Are No Children Here: The Story of Two Boys Growing Up in the Other America*. Doubleday, 1991.

Kozol, Jonathan. *Savage Inequalties: Children in America's Schools*. Crown, 1991.

Kunstler, James Howard. *The Geography of Nowhere: The Rise and Decline of America's Man-Made Landscape*. Simon and Schuster, 1993.

Maier, Henry W. *Challenge to the Cities: An Approach to a Theory of Urban Leadership*. Random House, 1966.

————. *The Mayor Who Made Milwaukee Famous: An Autobiography*. Madison Books, 1993.

Malcolm X. *The Autobiography of Malcolm X*. Grove Press, 1966.

Massey, Douglas S., and Denton, Nancy A. *American Apartheid: Segregation and the Making of the Underclass*. Harvard University Press, 1993.

McFeely, William S. *Frederick Douglass*. W.W. Norton, 1991.

Naipaul, V.S. *A Turn in the South*. Vintage Books, 1990.

Price, Richard. *Clockers*. Houghton Mifflin, 1992.

Rusk, David. *Cities Without Suburbs*. Woodrow Wilson Center Press, 1993.

Schell, Jonathan. *History in Sherman Park: An American Family and the Reagan-Mondale Election*. Alfred A. Knopf, 1987.

Still, Bayrd. *Milwaukee: The History of a City*. State Historical Society of Wisconsin, 1948.

Wells, Robert W. *This is Milwaukee*. Renaissance Books, 1970.

Willhelm, Sidney M. *Who Needs the Negro?* Schenkman Publishing, 1970.

Williams, Juan. *Eyes on the Prize: America's Civil Rights Years, 1954–65*. Viking, 1987.

INDEX

ABOUT THE AUTHOR

JONATHAN COLEMAN was born in 1951 in Allentown, Pennsylvania. A graduate of the University of Virginia, he is a former senior editor in book publishing and a former journalist with CBS News. His first book, *At Mother's Request,* was hailed as "a masterwork of reporting" (*Washington Post Book World*) and became a bestseller. His second, *Exit the Rainmaker,* was called "a fascinating, symbolic statement of the American psyche" (*Los Angeles Times Book Review*) and also became a bestseller. He has contributed to *Time* and the *New York Times Book Review,* among other publications, and has lectured at universities around the country.

Mr. Coleman lives in Charlottesville, where he taught writing at the University of Virginia from 1986 to 1993.